THE ECONOMIC CONSTITUTION

The Economic Constitution

TONY PROSSER

OXFORD
UNIVERSITY PRESS

OXFORD
UNIVERSITY PRESS

Great Clarendon Street, Oxford, OX2 6DP,
United Kingdom

Oxford University Press is a department of the University of Oxford.
It furthers the University's objective of excellence in research, scholarship,
and education by publishing worldwide. Oxford is a registered trade mark of
Oxford University Press in the UK and in certain other countries

First Edition published in 2014
Impression: 1

Published in the United States of America by Oxford University Press
198 Madison Avenue, New York, NY 10016, United States of America

British Library Cataloguing in Publication Data
Data available

Library of Congress Control Number: 2013952794

ISBN 978–0–19–964453–7

Printed in Great Britain by
CPI Group (UK) Ltd, Croydon, CR0 4YY

Preface

In this book I have attempted to perform two tasks. The first is to provide coverage of areas of the constitution which have been neglected in the major public law texts and in other forms of academic study; those which are concerned with economic management. This should fill a major gap; issues such as the allocation of public funds and monetary policy are too important to be overlooked, especially in the current times of financial crises. Direct economic management by government has also been relatively neglected in the regulation literature, and I hope that some of the lessons derived from that literature can be applied successfully to it. An inspiration is Sabino Cassese's book *La Nuova Costituzione Economica*, now in its fifth edition and widely available in Italy. There is no UK equivalent, and casting light on the workings of the economic constitution will, I hope, in itself justify the publication of this book.

The second task is a more critical one. In Chapter 1 I set out various meanings of the term 'economic constitution'; these are drawn from legal and social theory and European Union (EU) law and politics rather than from the UK itself, but nevertheless are of value for suggesting possible ways of understanding our own constitutional arrangements. They also raise the question of the relationship between an economic constitution and democratic politics; does such a constitution operate as a straitjacket on governments, restricting political choices and so casting economic policy from a single mould? I return to this point in my conclusion, where I begin to develop the concept of a plural constitution, plural in both its ideological bases and in its arrangements for institutional scrutiny. This has both advantages in openness and disadvantages in lack of coordination. This book is thus both normative and critical.

Choosing to address both these tasks imposes limitations on the full achievement of each. Thus the coverage of areas of economic management cannot be fully comprehensive, though I hope that I have managed to treat the most important areas and so to give a more general feel for the way in which the economy is managed in the UK. In view of the substantial coverage elsewhere, I have omitted substantive competition law (despite its importance in the origins of the idea of an economic constitution) and sectoral regulation of the utilities; there is only brief coverage of the role of local government. A particular problem has been to achieve a balance between long-standing practices and those introduced as responses to the economic crises of recent years; much has changed since 2008. I hope that the balance I have found is a reasonable one which is up-to-date yet not too reliant on passing political and institutional fads.

The more normative approach is given in outline, especially in Chapters 1 and 10 but also as a base for the discussion of the substantive areas which I cover. Given the constraints of a general account of this kind, there has not been room for either full theoretical development of the constitutional and regulatory approach I take, nor for detailed comparative accounts of other economic constitutions; I hope to remedy both these gaps through future work.

I am grateful for intellectual and personal support without which, of course, this book could not have been written. The idea originated when I worked in the Centre for Socio-Legal Studies at the University of Sheffield, a uniquely stimulating environment for work of this kind, and was developed further at the University of Glasgow where I picked up a viewpoint which was both Scottish and more European. The University of Bristol has supported me not just intellectually but through its generous policy of research leave.

Once more, my greatest thanks go to Charlotte, Amelia, and Laurie for their tolerance and support.

The law is stated as at 1 October 2013.

Tony Prosser

Table of Contents

Table of Cases

AUSTRALIA

EUROPEAN COURT OF HUMAN RIGHTS

EUROPEAN COURT OF JUSTICE

GERMANY

UNITED KINGDOM

Table of European Legislation

DIRECTIVES

DECISIONS

Table of Statutes

Abbreviations

AME	Annually Managed Expenditure
ARROW	Advanced Risk-Responsive Operating Framework
BEAPFF	Bank of England Asset Purchase Facility Fund Limited
BIS	Department for Business, Innovation and Skills
BRE	Better Regulation Executive (within BIS)
CSR	Comprehensive Spending Review
DE&S	Defence Equipment and Support
DEL	Departmental Spending Limits
DMO	Debt Management Office
EBA	European Banking Authority
ECB	European Central Bank
ECJ	European Court of Justice
ECOFIN	Economic and Financial Affairs Council
EIOPA	European Insurance and Occupational Pensions Authority
EMIR	European Market Infrastructure Regulation
ESCB	European System of Central Banks
ESFS	European System of Financial Supervision
ESMA	European Securities and Markets Authority
EU	European Union
FCA	Financial Conduct Authority
FPC	Financial Policy Committee (of the Bank of England)
FSA	Financial Services Authority
FSB	Financial Stability Board
GAAP	generally accepted accounting practice
GATS	General Agreement on Trade and Services
GATT	General Agreement on Tariffs and Trade
GPA	Agreement on Government Procurement
HBOS	Halifax Bank of Scotland
HMRC	HM Revenue & Customs
IASB	International Accounting Standards Board
IFRS	International Financial Reporting Standards Board
IMF	International Monetary Fund
LEC	local enterprise company

LEP	local enterprise partnership
MPC	Monetary Policy Committee (of the Bank of England)
NAO	National Audit Office
NAPNOC	no acceptable price, no contract
NGO	non-governmental organization
NS&I	National Savings & Investments
OECD	Organisation for Economic Co-operation and Development
OGC	Office of Government Commerce (of the Cabinet Office)
PAC	Public Accounts Committee
PEX	Public Expenditure Committee
PFI	Private Finance Initiative
PRA	Prudential Regulation Authority
PSA	public service agreements
RAB	resource accounting and budgeting
RBS	Royal Bank of Scotland
SMEs	small and medium-sized enterprises
SR	Spending Review
TEU	Treaty on European Union
TFEU	Treaty on the Functioning of the European Union
TSB	(Lloyds) Trustee Savings Bank
TSC	Treasury Select Committee
UKFI	UK Financial Investments Limited
WTO	World Trade Organization

1

Economic Constitutions

The interdependence of the market and the state can never have been as obvious as in the years since the financial crisis of 2008. The previous 30 years had been the years of deregulation, of reliance on the dispersed wisdom of unfettered markets, and of the 'rolling back' of the state. Yet when markets proved unable to provide not merely social justice but also economic stability and solvency, it was the state that was called to the rescue. This was followed by the sovereign debt and banking crises in the eurozone, emphasizing fiscal constraints on governments and the need for cooperation between states to prevent financial collapse.

Of course, any idea that the state could withdraw from the economy had already been proved illusory. This was apparent, for example, in the growth of the concept of regulation as both an academic discipline and a concern of practical politics. Regulation was necessary not just to limit the operation of markets, to protect human rights, and to guarantee the provision of basic services, but also to make markets work, as was evident from the vastly increasing importance of competition law and policy and of the regulation of financial services.[1] Yet this concern with regulation tended to underestimate the extent to which markets and the core state were intertwined; regulation was classically portrayed as the work of independent agencies at 'arm's length' from government, setting out a framework within which market transactions could freely operate. The events of recent years have shown that governments have been called on to intervene in ways which are far deeper, and far more costly, than merely setting a framework of regulation.[2] Moreover, the range of techniques used is much wider than the use of conventional regulatory instruments. For example, in the UK, management of public expenditure has become the central plank in the Government's

[1] For the extraordinary rise of competition law in this context, see S. Wilks, 'Competition Policy' in D. Coen and W. Grant (eds), *The Oxford Handbook of Business and Government* (Oxford: Oxford University Press, 2010), 730–56.

[2] See e.g. J. Braithwaite, *Regulatory Capitalism: How it Works, Ideas for Making it Work Better* (Cheltenham: Edward Elgar, 2008), esp. ch. 1.

economic policy from 2010, and elsewhere it is fundamental in responding to the sovereign debt crisis.

This book will portray a wide range of different techniques and institutions which the UK Government has used as part of economic management. It will concentrate on those techniques used directly by government rather than through the establishment of separate agencies such as the competition authorities or the utility regulators, though there will be consideration of financial services regulation carried out in part through independent agencies given its systemic effects and its close relations with government economic policy.

However, to refer to 'government' is itself to oversimplify. Policy is in fact devised and implemented through a network of different bodies, including government departments but also trans-national organizations (notably the European Union (EU) and the World Trade Organization (WTO)) and an array of institutions which are not core government departments but are closely linked to them. One objective of this book will be to map and document these complex networks, examining their coherence and their abilities to communicate and to cooperate, both of which were seriously challenged during the financial crisis.

The second objective will be to assess the legitimacy and accountability of these complex arrangements as they work in practice. Traditionally the major areas of government economic activity, taxation and spending, were in the UK constitutionally required to be accountable to Parliament. Given the complexity of the modern arrangements for economic management, and the limited capacities of Parliament itself, this has proved to be impracticable. Instead, other means for accountability have arisen, some involving Parliament, but others operating outside it. This book will examine these and assess to what extent constitutional requirements of accountability are being met in diverse new ways.

These two central objectives will be addressed through an introductory account of the major institutions and a more detailed analysis and critique of their operation in a number of key areas of economic management. These are taxation and borrowing; public expenditure; monetary policy; regulation of financial services (including of the banks); government shareholdings and industrial policy; and public procurement. It is hoped that these will be sufficient to assemble a reasonably comprehensive, though inevitably not exhaustive, account of the way in which the modern UK government manages the economy. Before describing the different forms of intervention and institutional arrangements in greater detail, it will be necessary to say a little about the two concepts central to the book; those of economic management and the concept of an economic constitution. The first of these will broaden the field of study, taking it beyond traditional accounts of constitutional law and of regulation, whilst the second will give it focus by suggesting the key analytical themes and normative principles to be employed.

Government and economic management

Economic management and regulation

The definition of regulation used by academic writers (at least in the sociological literature) has considerably broadened in recent years, moving from 'command and control' regulation to include self-regulation, co-regulation, private regulation, and now regulatory capitalism. It has lost its former emphasis on the use of rules and on work of regulatory agencies distanced from central government; nor is regulation assumed to involve a hierarchical relationship in which a regulator imposes outcomes on those regulated. Thus 'regulation means influencing the flow of events. Conceived in this broad way, regulation means much the same thing as governance . . . '.[3] There would thus seem to be good reason to treat a wide range of government techniques of economic management as types of regulation. Some of the arrangements studied here clearly fall within existing regulatory studies, for example regulation of financial services.

However, in general the regulatory literature has not included direct economic management by central government in its coverage of regulation, particularly the use of financial resources. There are exceptions; thus in a long programme of work Daintith has emphasized the importance not just of 'imperium', referring to the use of command by government, but of 'dominium', the use of its wealth.[4] This has led him to analyze the employment of a wide variety of different policy instruments, including the deployment of governmental resources, in examining state-economy relations.[5] He has also examined in detail the process for public expenditure allocation in the UK.[6]

[3] C. Parker and J. Braithwaite, 'Regulation', in P. Cane and M. Tushnet (eds), *Oxford Handbook of Legal Studies* (Oxford: Oxford University Press, 2003), 119–45, 119. See also C. Scott, 'Reflexive Governance, Regulation and Meta-Regulation: Control or Learning?' in O. de Schutter and J. Lenoble (eds), *Reflexive Governance: Redefining the Public Interest in a Pluralistic World* (Oxford: Hart Publishing, 2010), 43–63, 47.

[4] See esp. T.C. Daintith, 'Legal Analysis of Economic Policy' (1982) 9 *Journal of Law and Society* 191–224, esp. 211–16.

[5] T.C. Daintith, 'Regulation' in International Association of Legal Science, *International Encyclopedia of Comparative Law* (Dordrecht: Martinus Nijhoff Publishers, 1997), vol. XVII, ch. 10, paras 10-24, 10-92–10-142, 10-184.

[6] T. Daintith and A. Page, *The Executive in the Constitution: Structure, Autonomy and Internal Control* (Oxford: Oxford University Press, 1999), esp. chs 4–6.

Similarly, a recent study of social housing has emphasized the importance of the allocation of money in regulation; here 'money has become one of the most ubiquitous mechanisms of governing'.[7] Yet examination of the allocation of money has not become central to regulatory studies.

This may be because public finance is seen as essentially a technical matter; yet, as we shall see throughout this book, the use of financial resources and other techniques of economic management, such as public procurement, are intimately linked to policy goals. It may be for the opposite reason; that these matters are at the heart of government policy and so gain legitimacy through a combination of electoral mandate and ministerial responsibility. However, electoral mandates do not in any explicit sense cover the complex and often arcane processes to be described here, and many key choices are not subject to any effective form of ministerial responsibility. Some decisions, such as the allocation of public spending, may be seen as outside the scope of regulation proper as they do not involve relations between a public regulator and regulated private actors. However, regulatory literature has moved away from requiring such a hierarchical relationship and many of the most important types of regulation concern the delivery of public services such as health and education. Indeed, '[o]ne of the defining features of regulatory capitalism is that parts of states are set up with independent capacities to regulate other parts of the state'.[8] In this connection, it is clear that the unity of the state (the Crown in a UK context) is merely a legal fiction; '[t]he fact is that the United Kingdom executive is more plural than unitary'.[9] Thus it is warranted to consider as examples of regulation the relations between different parts of the state, both institutional and in terms of the allocation of resources between them.

Techniques of government economic management

Treating economic management as a type of regulation makes it clear that a wide range of different techniques and instruments is used by government to achieve economic goals. As noted earlier, a seminal distinction was made by Daintith in distinguishing between 'dominium' and 'imperium'. He explained the distinction as follows:

[7] M. McDermont, *Governing, Independence and Expertise: The Business of Housing Associations* (Oxford: Hart Publishing, 2010), 108.

[8] Braithwaite, *Regulatory Capitalism* (n 2) 25.

[9] Daintith and Page, *The Executive in the Constitution* (n 6) 6.

> I . . . use *imperium* as a generic term to describe those instruments of policy which involve the deployment of force by government (recalling here that force usually means the *threat* of force); *dominium* on the other hand describes those policy instruments which involve the deployment of wealth by government.

He also refers to respect and the provision of information as other resources which governments can deploy.[10]

Dealing first with 'imperium', the core means of state intervention has traditionally been seen as through 'command and control' regulation. This is, however, a surprisingly difficult concept to deploy and examples of pure 'command and control' are rare; more commonly, the term is used as a politically charged metaphor for bad or inflexible regulation. 'Command and control' regulation assumes that a public authority, gaining its legitimacy from the political process, issues orders to companies or individuals requiring them to meet goals laid down in public policy. The implication is that these orders are obeyed, often unwillingly, but obeyed nevertheless. This concept has however been subjected to a barrage of criticism in recent years. One reason for this has been a burgeoning literature on the difficulties facing regulators and government in gaining knowledge and understanding of systems they are regulating, and that law is a blunt tool for intervening in other systems.[11] A second reason is that even where regulation ostensibly takes the form of command and control, the reality has been shown to involve negotiation between regulators and those they regulate, both through consultation when rules are made and through selective enforcement in which rules are implemented not as binding orders but as the basis for negotiation to achieve reasonable results.[12] There are thus few examples of command and control in this book; even in the levying of taxes which might seem to be non-negotiable demands from the authorities, we shall find that there may be considerable room for negotiation of tax liability in practice; this has become a highly controversial topic.

Economic management is also carried out through rules which are used not to compel a definite outcome but to set out structures and determine procedures within which various actors are to operate, and examination of these will be central to this book. Examples would be the EU and the WTO rules in relation to the award of public contracts, which do not pre-determine

[10] Daintith 'Legal Analysis of Economic Policy' (n 4) 215–16 (emphasis retained); see also Daintith 'Regulation' (n 5) paras 10-62–10-67.

[11] This is to be found as a central theme in the literature inspired by the concept of autopoiesis; see e.g. G. Teubner, *Law as an Autopoietic System* (Oxford: Blackwell, 1993).

[12] One example from a large literature is K. Hawkins, *Law as Last Resort: Prosecution Decision-Making in a Regulatory Agency* (Oxford: Oxford University Press, 2002).

outcomes but seek to improve the transparency of the process; opening up budgetary and fiscal policy through the role of the independent Office for Budget Responsibility provides another example. One important regulatory technique is that of proceduralization, and this may avoid problems of command and control regulation through not seeking directly to intervene but to facilitate agreement between others, both public and private. This links to an important trend in regulatory studies; emphasis on the development of self-regulation and co-regulation as alternatives to more traditional techniques. Such a trend might seem to be promising in relation to the complex areas to be examined in this book, and indeed in financial services so-called 'self-regulation' (in fact highly complex forms of co-regulation) had an important role to play, especially before the financial crisis. However, what is more apparent is the use of self- and co-regulation within government itself; even the role of the Treasury in relation to spending policy has been characterized in this way, and more recent examples of executive self-regulation include the Spending Review process and the regulatory reform initiatives. Moreover the use of procurement, for example through the Private Finance Initiative, can be seen as a means of delegating responsibilities to the private sector, as can some of the arrangements for implementing an attenuated industrial policy through partnerships with the private sector. In other cases there is a combination of state action and the use of markets, for example in the role of the Bank of England in monetary policy both through setting interest rates and through operations in the money markets.

Some techniques used for economic management thus correspond in part to the most common instruments traditionally used for other types of regulation; others, however, display major differences. Much more important is the deployment of wealth as a means of government influence; Daintith's concept of 'dominium'. This is most evident within government itself through the use of the Spending Review as a means not just of allocating resources but of changing the direction of policy and engaging in public sector reform, as will be seen in Chapter 5. As regards relations with those outside government, an area of wealth deployment which has unexpectedly revived since 2008 has been the use of government shareholdings. Once used as a means of public ownership of key (or, more often, failing) industries, purchase of shares in the banks has been a major part of the Government's strategy for dealing with the financial crisis, in the UK as elsewhere.[13] The massive shareholdings are intended to be temporary, but the timing of

[13] See J. Black, 'The Credit Crisis and the Constitution' in D. Oliver, T. Prosser, and R. Rawlings (eds), *The Regulatory State: Constitutional Implications* (Oxford: Oxford University Press, 2010), 92–128.

disposal of the largest holding in Royal Bank of Scotland is uncertain and in the meantime they illustrate a further means of government economic management. Another example of the use of wealth by government is in the area of procurement. This is partly structured by EU and WTO rules requiring transparency and a more formal process, but some areas of contracting remain outside these, and the ability to use contracting to implement such policies as equal treatment has been controversial. A particularly fraught issue, which will be examined in detail in Chapter 9, is that of defence procurement where the competing goals of industrial policy, ensuring security of supply of defence goods and services, and value for money have not been successfully integrated and this failure has produced a pathological failure to deliver any of them. A further area which combines public regulation with the use of governmental resources is that of monetary policy, to be considered in Chapter 6.[14]

Throughout this book, then, economic management will be treated as one form of regulation which, because of the role of the executive, raises particularly strong constitutional concerns. However, to adopt a broad concept of regulation risks losing focus; if regulation is wide enough to include almost all areas of social control, further analytical tools are needed to identify those areas of regulation which raise major questions of constitutional importance. Moreover, what principles can we have for assessing what constitutes good regulation, either in a substantive sense (does it work or produce fair results) or in a procedural one (is it responsive to its environment and affected interests)? How can constitutional principles help us in such a normative task?

Economic constitutions

Different conceptions of the economic constitution

This is where the concept of the economic constitution becomes important, both as an analytical device to provide clearer focus, and as a source of normative principles of how regulation should seek to achieve constitutional legitimacy. Thinking in terms of an economic constitution has one particularly valuable result; that the descriptive and the normative are both relevant to analysis of economic management. Thus constitutions are at one level mapping documents; they set out the key state institutions, their interrelations, and their

[14] For the role of monetary policy in this context, see Daintith, 'Regulation' (n 5) paras 10–109–10–113.

relationship with civil society. They also permit effective governance and the coordinated development and implementation of public policy. Constitutions are also, however, essentially normative documents; they set out the key principles of how we can expect government to conduct itself in its organization and relations with others (including its own agencies). In particular, the idea of a constitution strives towards a certain ideal of coherence in the organization of public power. Thus one concern in this book will be the extent to which the various arrangements for economic management form a coherent whole, and in particular with the extent to which they permit effective communication within different parts of government, with market actors and with others who may be affected by decisions.[15]

The term 'economic constitution' is an unusual one in the UK, and may be used in several different senses. The first is a largely descriptive one, referring to the key constitutional principles and institutional arrangements which may be relevant to management of the economy. In many countries with a written constitution key provisions relating, for example, to taxation, expenditure, and property rights will be obvious candidates for inclusion, but the scope of the relevant principles will go far beyond these to include other law, both 'hard' and 'soft', and the institutional arrangements through which the rules operate.[16] Moreover, inevitably there will be a major international dimension to such study due to membership of international organizations, notably the EU and the WTO.[17] One purpose of this work will be to undertake such an analysis for the UK; as we shall see, despite the lack of a written constitutional base it is by no means impossible to extract principles from law and practices, and the constitutional rules are extensive and highly varied in form and coherence. In the absence of detailed coverage elsewhere, providing even a descriptive account of the economic constitution should be valuable in itself.

A second, more normative, use of the concept of an 'economic constitution' is particularly associated with the German 'ordoliberalism' of the post-Second World War period, a movement which was to have considerable influence over the development of competition law in what is now the EU. David Gerber has summarized their position well:

> the ordoliberals added a 'constitutional dimension' to their analysis of economic problems. A community's political constitution and its choices in using law to

[15] See J. Habermas, *Between Facts and Norms* (Cambridge: Polity Press, 1996), 168–93, 427–46.

[16] For a notable application of this approach, see Sabino Cassese's masterly work on Italy; *La Nuova Costituzione Economica*, 5th edn (Rome; Editori Laterza, 2012).

[17] See G. Anderson, 'Beyond "Constitutionalism Beyond the State"' (2012) 39 *Journal of Law and Society* 359–83.

> implement that constitution, they said, must ultimately establish the characteristics of its economic system. Economic systems did not just 'happen'; they were 'formed' through political and legal decision-making. These fundamental choices determined a nation's 'economic constitution'...[18]

Central to this approach is thus the belief that economic life is constituted, not simply by transactions in the market-place, but by key political choices. The outcome of these choices took the form of an economic constitution with both a substantive and a procedural role, and the economic constitution provided both a source for key governmental decisions and a constraint on them. Thus it served to translate economic philosophy into law through providing the basic principles of economic conduct and so the underlying standards for competition law. It also required that government in undertaking economic management should act only to implement the general norms derived from the economic constitution, rather than using discretionary powers. 'Law would provide basic principles of economic conduct, and government officials would not have discretion to intervene in the economy except for the purpose of enforcing those principles.'[19] The basic principles in the economic constitution would be both 'constitutive' (fundamental norms such as the stability of the currency and private property) and 'regulative', to implement the more fundamental norms, notably through competition law.[20] Thus, for the ordoliberals, the major constitutional questions included the balance between the private, market realm and that of the state, something needing explicit consideration in countries such as Germany with a more developed state tradition than the UK.[21] They also addressed the institutional design of state bodies involved in economic management. Thus they advocated, rather than decision-making by the executive, an independent cartel office supervised by the judiciary to ensure compliance with the economic constitution. Notably, they accepted that implementation of the constitutional principles would require a strong, not a weak, state but one constrained by the legal process.[22]

[18] D. Gerber, *Law and Competition in Twentieth Century Europe: Protecting Prometheus* (Oxford: Clarendon Press, 1998), 245. For a more detailed account, see Gerber, 'Constitutionalizing the Economy: German Neo-liberalism, Competition Law and the "New" Europe' (1994) 42 *American Journal of Comparative Law* 25–84, esp. 44–9, 75–7 and on the relationship between ordoliberalism and the EU, see J. Drexl, 'La constitution économique européenne—l'actualité du modèle ordolibéral' (2011) XXV *Revue Internationale de Droit Economique* 419–54, esp. 423–36.

[19] Gerber, *Law and Competition in Twentieth Century Europe* (n 18) 247.

[20] Gerber, *Law and Competition in Twentieth Century Europe* (n 18) 248–9.

[21] See Wilks, 'Competition Policy' (n 1) 739.

[22] Gerber, *Law and Competition in Twentieth Century Europe* (n 18) 249–50; Drexl, 'La constitution économique européenne—l'actualité du modèle ordolibéral' (n 18) 433–4.

Explicitly normative work on the economic constitution has, of course, a long pedigree. A famous example, drawing on some of the same roots as those of the ordoliberal school though with major differences of substance, is that of Hayek on 'The Constitution of Liberty' setting out conditions in which a constitutional structure would permit markets to operate freely and so contribute both to individual freedom and decentralized learning achieved through the marketplace.[23] Within economics, a normative approach of this kind can also be found in the work of James Buchanan on the best constitutional design for the organization of governmental or collective action; as he put it in his lecture on receiving the Nobel prize in economics: 'I urged economists to look at the "constitution of economic policy", to examine the rules, the constraints within which political agents act.... my purpose was ultimately normative rather than antiseptically scientific.'[24] In both cases, however, the normative concern was very different from that in this book; they reflected principles of constitutional design on a priori grounds to protect liberty or reflect the rational choices of individuals. This gives us our third version of an economic constitution; a deliberately designed set of principles to promote a particular value or set of social values in the process of economic management.

A fourth version of the economic constitution has emerged more recently in the form of the 'new constitutionalism', and can be seen as a mirror-image of the preceding one. It draws on neo-Marxist and neo-Gramscian traditions, and suggests that the normative concerns of protecting private investors have been achieved all too successfully through the development of constitutional rules, mainly at trans-national level, which have the effect of entrenching the position of private capital. Within political studies, Gill has argued that:

> [i]n sum, new constitutionalism is a subtle attempt to legitimate neo-liberal globalisation. It mandates a particular set of state policies geared to maintaining business confidence through the delivery of a consistent climate for investment and thus for the accumulation of capital. It relies on a combination of political and economic discipline and ideas concerning efficiency, welfare and democracy. It stresses the rule of law. Thus we are witnessing an expansion of state activity to provide greater legal and other protections for business, and efforts to stabilise the investment climate worldwide.[25]

[23] F.A. Hayek, *The Constitution of Liberty* (London: Routledge and Kegan Paul, 1960), esp. ch. 12.

[24] J.M. Buchanan, 'The Constitution of Economic Policy' (1987) 77 *The American Economic Review* 243–50, 243. See also J.M. Buchanan and G. Tullock *The Calculus of Consent: Logical Foundations of Constitutional Democracy* (Ann Arbor: University of Michigan Press, 1962), esp. ch. 6.

[25] S. Gill, 'New Constitutionalism, Democratisation and Global Political Economy' in R. Wilkinson (ed.), *The Global Governance Reader* (London: Routledge, 2005), 174–86, 184, and see Anderson, 'Beyond "Constitutionalism Beyond the State"' (n 17) 367–9.

The normative concern here is a critical one; rather than celebrating the idea of constitutionalism as a protection for individual freedoms, it is seen as an illegitimate constraint on collective democratic choice through its 'objective of removing contingency from politics'.[26] A similar argument has been made in the context of UK constitutional law by Nicol, who maintains that a certain type of politics, termed 'neo-liberalism', has acquired entrenched constitutional status as a result of developments in the WTO, the EU, and through the European Convention on Human Rights. Entrenched neo-liberalism has severely limited the opportunities of national governments to choose substantive economic policies, in contrast to the relatively neutral traditional British constitution based on absolute parliamentary sovereignty.[27] This raises important questions, to be considered later in this book, about the extent to which the economic constitution retains flexibility, and the extent to which recent international developments really reflect a unitary and coherent neo-liberal vision. The responses to the 2008 economic crisis and to the later sovereign debt and banking crises promise to be particularly revealing on these questions.

The European economic constitution

The more common employment of the term 'economic constitution' in Continental European jurisdictions rather than in the UK has resulted in its use in the context of the EU.[28] It may refer to the general basis and orientation of EU economic law. For example, Joerges has discussed the EU economic constitution as originally ordoliberal, and as particularly appropriate for its project of integration through its decoupling of the social dimension from competition, the former being a task for Member States. However, he suggests that little is now left of this economic constitution because of its replacement by the incorporation of other goals including monetary union and new forms of social regulation: '[t]he Maastricht Treaty was the end of the "economic constitution".'[29]

[26] Anderson, 'Beyond "Constitutionalism Beyond the State"' (n 17) 367.

[27] D. Nicol, *The Constitutional Protection of Capitalism* (Oxford: Hart Publishing, 2010). See also Wilks, 'Competition Policy' (n 1) 752.

[28] For a particular useful set of analyses of the meanings of the economic constitution in the context of the European Union, see the essays in the special issue on 'La Constitution Economique Europèene Revisiteé' (2011) XXV(4) *Revue Internationale de Droit Economique* 411–599. For an overview, see W. Sauter, 'The Economic Constitution of the European Union' (1998) 4 *Columbia Journal of European Law* 27–68.

[29] C. Joerges, 'What is Left of the European Economic Constitution? A Melancholic Euology' (2005) 30 *European Law Review* 461–89, 474.

Others have concentrated more closely on the work of the European Court of Justice, and have adopted a more nuanced and pluralistic vision of the economic constitution. Thus Maduro, in his analysis of interpretation of what is now article 34 TFEU on free movement of goods, begins by analyzing the different approaches taken by the court to this article as part of a process of constitutional development, and then describes three different models of the economic constitution which can be drawn from it.[30] These are positive integration by the EU institutions, negative integration leaving it to the market to select the most appropriate rules, and a decentralized model with a greater role for the Member States.[31] The second model is in large part drawn from the work of the ordoliberals, but Maduro is particularly critical of it as misreading the political values of the Treaty, which include not only economic freedom and efficiency but also social and redistributive values.[32] He prefers a more discursive constitutional model which ensures that there is no under-representation in national political processes of the interests of nationals of other Member States.[33]

Cruz has undertaken analysis of the competition and free movement principles of EU law from a similar perspective, though he prefers to use the term 'economic constitutional law'.[34] This is also a broader concept than that of the ordoliberals; in contrast to their work

> an approach based on the concept of economic constitutional law would use constitutional methods of interpretation, in particular inferences from the structure of the constitution as a whole, taking into account non-economic values and not lightly assuming a default rule of general economic liberty in case of a gap.[35]

This would permit the development of other constitutional themes including 'private economic power, the guarantee and reach of the social state and social rights, and the globalisation of markets and politics'.[36] He also advocates a more discursive and democratically legitimate basis for economic constitutional law.[37]

What is clear from these accounts is that one cannot point to a single European economic constitution. There are in fact different and competing

[30] M. Poiares Maduro, *We the Court: The European Court of Justice and the European Economic Constitution* (Oxford: Hart Publishing, 1998).

[31] Maduro, *We the Court* (n 30) ch. 4.

[32] Maduro, *We the Court* (n 30) 126–31, 159–64.

[33] Maduro, *We the Court* (n 30) 166–75.

[34] J. Baquero Cruz, *Between Competition and Free Movement: The Economic Constitutional Law of the European Community* (Oxford: Hart Publishing, 2002).

[35] Cruz, *Between Competition and Free Movement* (n 34) 28.

[36] Cruz, *Between Competition and Free Movement* (n 34) 31.

[37] See his discussion of the state action doctrine (n 34) 155–61.

constitutional visions; other writers have pointed to an emerging environmental constitution based on sustainable development and an emerging constitution of citizenship; indeed, it has been argued that the EU has shifted over time between an economic constitution and juridical, political, social, and security constitutions.[38] This in itself suggests that the new constitutionalist claim of a single economic constitution entrenching neo-liberalism is a serious over-simplification, without undermining the utility of a more plural concept of the economic constitution. However, the sovereign debt crisis has resulted in a further version of the economic constitution for the eurozone in the form of the rules included as the fiscal pact in the Treaty on Stability, Coordination and Governance, which include major constraints on the ability of the national governments covered to run deficits; these had already been prefigured in the ineffective Stability and Growth Pact adopted in 1997.[39] This new form of economic constitution raises major questions of the relationship between economic principle and national democracy central to the 'new constitutionalist' project, and will be considered more fully in Chapter 3 and in my concluding chapter.

Clearly, there are huge differences between the European economic constitution and that of the UK, not least in the absence of a central institution like the European Court of Justice responsible for determining matters of constitutional principle. The sources of such principle are, as we shall see, many and highly varied. My concern in this book is, however, closer to those of Maduro and Cruz than that of the ordoliberals, the Hayekian, or 'new constitutionalist' traditions in that it is concerned mainly with institutional questions and process values. Of course, economic management raises important questions of substantive justice, including distributional justice. Indeed, this is one of the major lessons of the financial crisis since 2008 and of government attempts to deal with it, and of the more recent sovereign debt crisis. I have also argued elsewhere that regulation involves both procedural values of deliberation and substantive values of efficiency, consumer choice, human rights, and social solidarity.[40] However, a prerequisite for such substantive values to be considered in decision-making is that there are

[38] M. Pallemaerts, 'La Constitution Economique Européene et le "Développement Durable de l'Europe"' (2011) XXV *Revue Internationale de Droit Economique* 511–41; L. Azoulai, 'Constitution Economique et Citoyenneté de l'Union Européene' (2011) XXV *Revue Internationale de Droit Economique* 543–57; K. Tuori. 'La Constitution Economique Parmi les Constitutions Européenes' (2011) XXV *Revue Internationale de Droit Economique* 559–99; Sauter, 'The Economic Constitution of the European Union' (n 28) 57–68.

[39] See Joerges, 'What is Left of the European Economic Constitution?' (n 29) 476–8.

[40] T. Prosser, *The Regulatory Enterprise: Government, Regulation and Legitimacy* (Oxford: Oxford University Press, 2010), 11–19.

open and transparent processes available through which they can be incorporated, and this book will be centrally concerned with institutional and process values as part of the economic constitution. Thus in addition to mapping the arrangements for economic management I shall examine the extent to which they fulfil constitutional expectations of transparency and accountability.[41] Before describing my normative approach in greater detail, more needs to be said about the first, and more descriptive, type of constitutional analysis.

The institutional map

My first task will thus be to develop an institutional map of economic governance, bearing in mind Moran's warning that:

> the appealing metaphor of a map of government is misleading, because it wrongly implies that there exists one scale of measurement which will allow us to gauge how far an agency is from the centre. The contrary is true; there exist numerous indicators and they can all give different readings.[42]

Although economic management clearly falls within the broad concept of regulation used here, we have seen that the techniques used are rather different from those covered in most regulatory studies. The same is true of the institutions, with a greater role for core central government, although as we shall see there is also considerable use made of arm's length bodies and of networks of different types of organization. In studying the institutions, it is important to note that informal rules will often be much more important than the more formal ones, and indeed informal rules of the executive itself may set out major constitutional principles. This point was well made by Daintith and Page:

> [t]o attempt this book would be pointless without the belief that norms generated within the executive might properly form part of the constitution.... we see no reason... [to deny] the adjective 'constitutional' both to norms that are not wholly immune to modification by parliamentary legislation and to norms which may not be susceptible to third-party (especially judicial) enforcement.[43]

[41] For an influential earlier attempt to do so, see I. Harden and N. Lewis, *The Noble Lie: The British Constitution and the Rule of Law* (London: Hutchinson, 1986), esp. 92–100, 129–36.

[42] M. Moran, 'Monetary Policy and the Machinery of Government' (1981) 59 *Public Administration* 47–61, 47.

[43] Daintith and Page, *The Executive in the Constitution* (n 6) 18–19; Cassese, *La Nuova Costituzione Economica* (n 16) ch. 1.

In this book I shall discuss some formal norms of 'hard law', for example the Bank of England Act and the EU procurement rules, though even in these cases the interest will lie not only in the formal substance of the rules but in the operation of the institutions and procedures which they set up. I shall also discuss a wide range of less formal norms comprising the 'soft law' of economic management, including, for example, the now extensive norms relating to government contracting.

The range of institutions examined will also be a catholic one. As noted earlier, Daintith and Page stress that, despite the formal legal concept of the unified Crown, the UK executive is actually highly pluralistic, and much discussion in this book will be concerned with the interrelations between the different elements comprising it.[44] In the following chapter I shall describe the key institutions which make up the executive, including the Treasury and the Cabinet Office at the centre, and then say something about government departments and their executive agencies. This does not, however, exhaust the range of bodies involved. Although the UK Coalition Government attempted to cut the number of 'quangos' or arm's length bodies, this did little to restrict institutional proliferation and, for example, the Bank of England's Monetary Policy Committee, UK Financial Investments Ltd, which manages state shareholdings, the Office for Budget Responsibility, and the new bodies regulating financial services are all important actors in the process of economic management. The institutional pattern is thus a complex one, and it must not be forgotten that all this occurs within an international context in which the institutions of the EU and of the WTO assume enormous importance. The EU itself has also been associated with a growing number of agencies and networks performing regulatory functions, most notably in the area of financial regulation, and these will be considered in Chapters 3 and 7.

One outcome of this complexity is particularly noteworthy. As I have argued in relation to other regulatory institutions, it is not enough to study each in isolation.[45] Especially when considering questions of accountability, rather than one institution of government subject to democratic accountability, we have a complex of different bodies subject to multiple and varied accountabilities. This is evoked by the celebrated image of the 'hollowing-out' of the state.[46] Thus 'to call one institution to account for how it has operated is to disregard key features of the differentiated polity. Policy is the

[44] Daintith and Page, *The Executive in the Constitution* (n 6) 6–9, 380–98.

[45] Prosser, *The Regulatory Enterprise* (n 40) 6–8.

[46] R. Rhodes, *Understanding Governance: Policy Networks, Governance, Reflexivity and Accountability* (Buckingham: Open University Press, 1997), esp 17–19, 53–5 and ch. 5.

responsibility of no one institution but emerges from the interaction of several'.[47] Although the implication from the 'hollowing-out' metaphor that the role of the core state has declined is a highly controversial one, it is not necessary to accept this proposition to emphasize the importance of networks beyond the core state.[48] As a result it is not simply individual institutions themselves which need to be studied but the relations between them; these will often be complex. Networks are thus central to descriptive analysis of the economic constitution, and it is also necessary to consider the extent to which these are managed in a transparent way and in a way which facilitates internal and external communication. Moreover, networks may themselves contribute to the pursuit of accountability, especially (but not only) in the context of multilevel governance.[49] I shall assess the roles of both Parliament and the courts in holding accountable the institutions described here; in some cases these roles have been of fundamental constitutional importance. However, in practice less formal arrangements may be of considerably greater practical importance in the constitution as it now operates, especially arrangements developed by government itself.

The normative approach

I stressed early on in this chapter that I shall be adopting a normative approach to economic management on constitutional grounds rather than simply describing the nature of the arrangements which are in operation. This will differ from some other accounts of executive and economic management. For example, Daintith and Page deny that such a normative constitutional enterprise is possible:

> we do not think that this task can be attempted through the identification of constitutional principles and values. Such principles and values are, of necessity, normative in nature. How can one say whether a given principle or value forms part of our *positive* constitution?[50]

As I mentioned earlier, other writers such as Hayek and Buchanan have used the concept of the economic constitution in an explicitly normative way, but

[47] R. Rhodes, *Beyond Westminster and Whitehall* (London: Unwin Hyman, 1988), 404.

[48] For a particularly good discussion of the large literature on this point, see Braithwaite, *Regulatory Capitalism* (n 2) ch. 1.

[49] See C. Harlow and R. Rawlings, 'Promoting Accountability in Multilevel Governance: A Network Approach' (2007) 13 *European Law Journal* 542–62; C. Scott, 'Accountability in the Regulatory State' (2000) 27 *Journal of Law and Society* 38–60.

[50] Daintith and Page, *The Executive in the Constitution* (n 6) 19–20 (emphasis retained).

on a very different basis from my own approach. Thus Hayek's concern was with the necessary constitutional conditions to secure economic liberty; Buchanan's with establishing the constitutional rules which would be chosen by rational individuals in order to mirror their preferences most accurately. For them, the function of the economic constitution is to apply substantive extra-constitutional norms.

Such concerns have found expression in substantive constitutional rules limiting aspects of economic management, most famously in requirements that budgets be balanced. This is now required, for example, by a 2009 amendment to the German Federal Constitution which will limit the scope for running a deficit after 2016 (subject to exceptions for natural disasters or exceptional emergencies outside state control).[51] Similar provisions applying to members of the eurozone are contained in the Treaty on Coordination, Stability and Governance as a response to the sovereign debt crisis. Indeed, attempts were made to develop such forms of budgetary self-restraint in the UK, initially through soft law but then through statute in the form of the Fiscal Responsibility Act 2010 requiring a halving of public borrowing by 2014. The requirement was of limited effect (the then Chancellor noted that '[t]he Act was eventually introduced in early 2010 to almost universal derision. Legislation is no substitute for sound judgement'[52]) and has now been replaced by the Budget Responsibility and National Audit Act 2011, requiring the Chancellor to develop a Charter for Budget Responsibility containing the objectives and mandate for fiscal policy.

Restrictions on borrowing will be discussed in detail in Chapters 4 and 5 in the context of finance and expenditure, and the requirements in relation to the eurozone will be considered in Chapter 3. However, this book will not primarily be concerned with substantive constitutional constraints on policy of this kind, which of course raise serious issues about the democratic legitimacy of the constitutionalization and internationalization of a particular (and contested) approach to economic policy. These questions will be considered in my conclusion. Instead, my concerns in the substantive chapters are mainly with institutional and process values; with legitimacy, deliberation, and accountability. This includes the extent to which the arrangements described in this book have an inner coherence. A constitution is in part a means of establishing such coherence between different parts of the state, and a degree of coherence is necessary for successful coordination and

[51] The Constitution of the Federal Republic of Germany (Grundgesetz), arts 109–15.

[52] A Darling, *Back from the Brink: 1,000 Days at Number 11* (London: Atlantic Books, 2011), 268.

communication. This is not incompatible with a plurality of constitutional objectives and institutions.

A background assumption is that there has always been a constitutional expectation that government economic management has been subject to outside scrutiny and accountability.[53] Traditionally, this was through Parliament's scrutiny of government taxation and expenditure; indeed the existence of such scrutiny was a major achievement of the seventeenth-century settlement after the civil war and of the 'Glorious Revolution'. The expectation was partly due to the effect of taxation on individual property rights, but also reflected the principle that the use of public funds needed proper explanation and justification. However, two major changes made this scrutiny ineffective. First, the scope of government economic management vastly increased and was not limited to the areas which fell within the formal scrutiny of Parliament; it included the management of monetary policy, borrowing funds from the markets, and regulation of private economic activity. Secondly, as is well documented elsewhere, with the growth of party dominance of the House of Commons (where powers of scrutiny of economic policy almost exclusively lay), Parliament became increasingly ineffective as an independent power in examining the executive, especially in relation to proposed spending. As it was vividly put in a report by the Hansard Society:

> [i]n the view of many commentators, Parliament's influence over government proposals for taxation and expenditure, and priorities within that expenditure, is virtually non-existent. The essential relationship between Parliament and government is that the latter proposes and the former simply agrees. To draw an analogy, the government decides the value of the cheque, to whom it should be paid and when, and Parliament simply signs it.[54]

Other events showed clearly the weaknesses of some traditional constitutional assumptions; for example, one response to the 2008 economic crisis was action which violated existing domestic constitutional norms, including the use of exceptionally wide Henry VIII clauses, retrospective legislation, and permanent powers for the Treasury to override statute.[55]

This decline in constitutional scrutiny by Parliament did not change the expectation of accountability for economic management, but created a void in formal means for securing it. Instead, as we shall see throughout the book,

[53] This argument is made strongly in Harden and Lewis, *The Noble Lie* (n 41) esp. 92–100, 129–36.

[54] A. Brazier and V. Ram, *The Fiscal Maze: Parliament, Government and Public Money* (London: Hansard Society, 2006), para. 2.4.

[55] Banking (Special Provisions) Act 2008; Banking Act 2009 discussed in detail by Julia Black in 'The Credit Crisis and the Constitution' (n 13) 118–19.

a variety of different institutions was to contribute in different ways to accountability; institutions as diverse as the Monetary Policy Committee of the Bank of England, the Office for Budget Responsibility, the regulatory reform institutions, and international bodies such as the EU institutions in the case of public procurement and state aids. Moreover, even though Parliament's advance powers of control of spending and use of financial resources were virtually non-existent, through the work of the National Audit Office, the Public Accounts Committee, and other select committees it did develop an important role in *ex post facto* scrutiny of expenditure to secure value for money. Even the courts, which had traditionally not examined economic management closely except in relation to some aspects of taxation, began to take an interest.[56]

One aim of this book will be to assess how the network of institutions for scrutiny and accountability has succeeded in fulfilling the need for constitutional legitimacy and scrutiny which Parliament cannot meet. It will do so in part by using lessons derived from studies of more conventional areas of regulation. The starting point for this will be to look at the institutions' transparency, openness, and reflexivity, by which is meant their ability to engage in a process of mutual learning; reflexive learning 'involves the establishment of institutions and processes which facilitate the actors within a domain for learning not only about policy options, but also about their own interests and preferences'.[57] Essential presuppositions for such a reflexive approach are transparency and provision of information about government proposals and actions; a willingness to receive and consider outside information and arguments; the giving of reasoned justifications for decisions; and the provision of opportunities for debate and deliberation. All these were associated with the ideal of parliamentary scrutiny, if not the practice; how have they been developed in the new institutional arrangements? They are also themes familiar from regulatory developments elsewhere, both in the theoretical literature and in the actual arrangements by which regulators take decisions.[58]

56 See e.g. *R v Secretary of State for Foreign and Commonwealth Affairs, ex parte World Development Movement Ltd* [1995] 1 WLR 386.

57 C. Scott, quoted in J. Lenoble and M. Maesschalck, 'Reviewing the Theory of Public Interest: The Quest for a Reflexive and Learning-based Approach to Governance', in de Schutter and Lenoble, *Reflexive Governance* (n 3) 3–21, 6.

58 For the theoretical developments, see J. Black, 'Proceduralising Regulation' (2000) 20 *Oxford Journal of Legal Studies* 597–614 and (2001) 21 *Oxford Journal of Legal Studies* 33–58 and the essays in de Schutter and Lenoble, *Reflexive Governance* (n 3). For practical developments see T. Prosser, *Law and the Regulators* (Oxford: Oxford University Press, 1997) and Prosser, *The Regulatory Enterprise* (n 40).

In particular, two normative themes will be developed in this work. The first has already been mentioned. It is the question of the coherence and openness of relations between the different institutions, and networks, which engage in economic management by or on behalf of government. It has already been noted that there is no single unitary executive responsible for economic management but rather a plethora of different bodies, both within and outside core government. This obviously creates the risk of contradiction, confusion, and blockages in communication between them; this was precisely what happened with the breakdown of the tripartite relationship between the Treasury, the Bank of England, and the Financial Services Authority in the 2008 financial crisis. By contrast, it is possible for regulatory institutions to develop a mutually supportive allocation of responsibilities; one example would be that of the decisions of the German Federal Constitutional Court making the availability of parliamentary scrutiny of revenue and expenditure central to the constitutionality of guarantees for Greece and increased liabilities to the European Stability Mechanism.[59] As we shall see, there have been attempts by UK governments to exert greater central control, most recently through the Spending Review process; moreover, informal networks have grown up to facilitate communication. The book will map the arrangements and attempt to assess their success in creating a clear formal or informal allocation of responsibilities, transparency, and opportunities for effective communication between different parts of the system. In doing so, the role of 'soft' rules such as memoranda of understanding and codes of practice will be of considerable importance.

The second normative theme will be to examine each institution and to assess arrangements for transparency, deliberation, and accountability. These may apply between different institutions, or may be internal to individual institutions. For example the centre has imposed extended requirements as a result of the regulatory reform initiatives located in the Better Regulation Executive in the Department for Business, Innovation and Skills.[60] Other requirements may be imposed by law; for example, the requirement for publication of minutes by the Bank of England's Monetary Policy Committee. Arrangements for transparency and accountability developed by institutions themselves, and an assessment of the extent to which these are accessible to stakeholders and others outside government, are also important. This theme will reinforce the insights of Daintith and Page who emphasize that

[59] Decision of 7 September 2011, BVerfG, 2 BvR 987/10 vom 7.9.2011, paras 104–7, 121–9, 141: Decision of 12 September 2012, BVerf G, 2BvR 13/90 vom 12.9.2012, paras 194–6.

[60] For fuller discussion of 'Better Regulation', see S. Weatherill (ed.), *Better Regulation* (Oxford: Hart Publishing, 2007) and Prosser, *The Regulatory Enterprise* (n 40) ch. 10.

'[e]xecutive self-restraint constitutes one of the essential underpinnings of democracy and of the rule of law'.[61] Of course, a full examination of the workings of internal arrangements would require extensive empirical research outside the scope of this book, but it is hoped that here there can be some analysis of such internal forms of accountability.

This book will also assess the external accountability of the institutions described here to Parliament, to the courts, and to other forms of administrative justice.[62] It has already been suggested that Parliament's formal role in authorizing public spending is now ineffective; however it has built up scrutiny involving the National Audit Office, the Public Accounts Committee, and other select committees which perform an important role in assessing the value for money of expenditure which has already been made. There will also be an assessment of the extent to which parliamentary scrutiny extends to other forms of economic management, for example monetary policy. As regards the courts, they have traditionally played only a limited role in the areas to be described here, except in the case of taxation which is seen as impinging directly on the property rights of citizens. However, they do have the tools for more extensive scrutiny and this is developing further in the area of procurement.

I shall return to these themes in the concluding chapter. In brief, it will suggest that we have a highly plural constitution, both in terms of the institutional map and arrangements for securing accountability. Pluralism has virtues, in particular through permitting the testing of decisions by a range of different bodies and providing opportunities for mutual learning. However, it may lead to incoherence, as vividly demonstrated with the collapse of communication between the three leading authorities in the 2008 financial crisis. Legal, political, and administrative forms of scrutiny are vital to hold together the different parts of the constitution through different forms of deliberative process; it is on their coherence and interrelations that constitutional attention now needs to be focused.

[61] Daintith and Page *The Executive in the Constitution* (n 6) 380.

[62] For the interdependence of internal and external controls, see Daintith and Page, *The Executive in the Constitution* (n 6) 3, 107.

2

A Map of the Institutions

In this chapter I provide a map of the key domestic institutions responsible for economic management in the UK; discussion of international institutions will follow in Chapter 3. Two points need to be made at the outset. First, the map is extremely complex. This is partly due to the lack of a coherent constitutional scheme for the allocation of powers in the UK system, and also due to a preference for the use of various types of arm's length body to carry out public functions. Despite the claims by successive governments that they will cull 'quangos' (a highly misleading characterization of such institutions), there is no sign of any substantial move away from their use in this field. Indeed, the financial crisis of 2008 led to the creation of a number of important new arm's length bodies. A further result of this complexity is that it will be important to examine not just the institutions themselves but their interrelations, whether bilateral or as part of networks; the 'tripartite' relationship between the key institutions broke down during the financial crisis and has been restructured in an attempt to avoid this recurring in the future.

A second important point is that as a result of the sheer number of institutions, a single chapter can provide merely an introduction to them. Discussion in more detail will be left to the later chapters examining particular aspects of economic management; thus we shall learn more about the Treasury when examining public expenditure, and about the Bank of England through an account of monetary policy. The final section of this chapter will provide a brief introduction to institutional means for scrutiny and accountability, in particular through Parliament and the courts. This will also provide only basic information with fuller discussion and analysis reserved for later.

The major institutions of economic governance

HM Treasury

Even the most superficial acquaintance with UK economic management suggests that the Treasury is its core institution. Indeed, popular and political opinion often suggests that it is a looming and restrictive presence dominating the heart of government like Dickens's 'Circumlocution Office'.[1] The reality is much more nuanced, but the role of the Treasury is nevertheless fundamental. It acts as the Government's finance ministry and, as well as having an important role in raising revenue, disburses funds to spending departments. It is also the economics ministry aiming to promote sustainable economic growth. A major function of the Treasury is to secure economic stability, a role which placed it at the heart of the response to the financial crisis and which raises major questions about its relationship with the Bank of England.

The Treasury has a long history, dating from around the time of the Norman Conquest; it acquired authority over spending departments in the seventeenth century. It only became responsible for broader economic management of the economy in the 1940s owing to the 'accident' of the minister of economic affairs inheriting the Treasury after the resignation of the Chancellor.[2] This responsibility was briefly lost in the 1960s to a Department for Economic Affairs, but the latter was disbanded in 1969 and responsibility for economic planning and management returned to the Treasury. The Treasury finally lost responsibility for civil service staffing and pay matters when these functions were transferred to the Prime Minister as Minister for the Civil Service in 1995.

The latter year was the date of publication of the most detailed and fully researched account of the Treasury role in relation to public expenditure.[3] This work emphasized the importance of the interaction of the Treasury with other institutions through the role of 'the Whitehall policy network' and of the 'negotiated discretion' characteristic of the actual operation of expenditure control. Thus

> [t]he central argument of this book is that the Treasury failed to achieve both the short-term and medium-term objectives for public spending set by successive governments through the years 1976–93. It failed also to achieve its historic mission to restrain the growth of public spending. We argue that the causes of

[1] 'The Circumlocution Office was (as everybody knows without being told) the most important Department under government. No public business of any kind could possibly be done at any time, without the acquiescence of the Circumlocution Office. Its finger was in the largest public pie, and in the smallest public tart.... Whatever was required to be done, the Circumlocution Office was beforehand with all the public departments in the art of perceiving—HOW NOT TO DO IT.' C. Dickens, *Little Dorrit* (Harmondsworth: Penguin, 1998, originally published 1857), 119.

[2] See C. Thain, 'Treasury Rules OK? The Further Evolution of a British Institution' (2004) 6 *British Journal of Politics and International Relations* 121–8, 122.

[3] C. Thain and M. Wright, *The Treasury and Whitehall: The Planning and Control of Public Expenditure, 1976–1993* (Oxford: Clarendon Press, 1995).

> that failure inhere in the constitutional and practical limitations to the exercise of Treasury control. In other than exceptional and temporary circumstances, such as acute economic or financial crisis, the Treasury cannot dictate to departments nor impose its will upon them. Their relationships are interdependent; their room for discretionary manoeuvre mutually constrained. The paradigm of the politics of public spending at the heart of British central government is negotiated discretion.[4]

Similarly, a more recent account suggested that 'although the Treasury has always possessed important powers of control over departments, it has never strayed far from an approach which treats the primary responsibility for financial as well as policy decisions as belonging to spending departments'.[5]

Much has changed since 1995, and some changes have increased the influence of the Treasury. Setting aside developments in Treasury internal organization, it assumed a high political profile during the Blair Governments of 1997–2007 owing to the 'emergence of Gordon Brown as the most powerful chancellor since Cripps'.[6] Not only did this ensure the presence of the Treasury at the very heart of policy-making, it was accompanied by major reforms to create a more rational system of expenditure control through the Comprehensive Spending Review. As we shall see in Chapter 5, this is not wholly a Treasury-driven system, but nevertheless inevitably increases the central Treasury role in determining the spending framework.[7] That role increased further after the election of the Coalition Government in 2010, whose Spending Review imposed substantial cuts across government and was central to the Coalition's policy vision; again this will be fully discussed in Chapter 5. That chapter will also examine the introduction of resource accounting and budgeting for government departments, a reform likely to make more effective Treasury monitoring of the use of financial resources.

Under the Labour Governments, detailed objectives and targets for government departments in the form of public service agreements (PSAs) linked to the Spending Review had been developed; these were monitored by the Treasury which could also take action if they were not met.[8] In the words of the Treasury Select Committee, '[t]he new Spending Review and PSA

[4] Thain and Wright, *The Treasury and Whitehall* (n 3) 5–6.

[5] T. Daintith and A. Page, *The Executive in the Constitution: Structure, Autonomy, and Internal Control* (Oxford: Oxford University Press, 1999).

[6] Thain, 'Treasury Rules OK?' (n 2) 122; for fuller discussion based on new empirical work, see P. Fawcett, 'Metagovernance and the Treasury's Evolving Role within the British Core Executive, 1997–2007' (2010) at: <http://www.researchgate.net/publication/228538229_Metagovernance_and_the_Treasury's_Evolving_Role_within_the_British_Core_Executive_1997-2007?ev=sim_pub>.

[7] Fawcett, 'Metagovernance and the Treasury's Evolving Role' (n 6) 8–9.

[8] See O. James, 'The UK Executive's Use of Public Service Agreements as a Tool of Governance' (2004) 82 *Public Administration* 397–419.

process . . . are powerful new tools by which the Treasury can exert influence over the management of departments' resources. These developments have occurred gradually, without explicit parliamentary debate or assent'.[9] The PSA system has however been abandoned by the Coalition Government in favour of Departmental Business Plans and this may reduce opportunities for Treasury involvement in policy delivery. The Treasury also acquired a rather surprising role in social policy through its role as lead department for delivering the Labour Governments' objective of halving the number of children in poverty by 2010–11 and eradicating child poverty by 2020. This was only one example of Treasury involvement in issues of policy-making and delivery; another example was the creation of the Enterprise and Growth Unit within it in 1997 as a form of 'mini think-tank' on important areas of economic activity within the responsibilities of spending departments.[10] The Treasury Select Committee commented in 2001 that:

> *[w]e are concerned that the Treasury as an institution has recently begun to exert too much influence over policy areas which are properly the business of other departments and that this is not necessarily in the best interests of the Treasury or the Government as a whole.*[11]

However, under the 2010 Coalition Government the Treasury has lost its social policy role which is likely to make it more focused on its core tasks of expenditure control and allocation, though it also retains responsibility for tax policy, the promotion of growth including infrastructure policy, and the framework for financial services regulation.

Against the increased role of the Treasury through the Spending Review must be set one important loss of responsibility; that for monetary policy and in particular the setting of interest rates, which passed to the Monetary Policy Committee of the Bank of England almost immediately after the election of the Labour Government in 1997, formalized in the Bank of England Act 1998. This will be examined in detail in Chapter 6, but at this stage it should merely be stated that, although the granting of this power to an independent body is clearly a major administrative, and indeed constitutional, development, it has not taken the Treasury completely out of the picture. Its role remains important in the setting of objectives and determining the remit of the Monetary Policy Committee; once more the emphasis must be on the interrelationship between institutions rather than assuming their autonomy.

[9] Treasury Committee, *HM Treasury* (HC 2000–01, 73), para. 40.

[10] Fawcett, 'Metagovernance and the Treasury's Evolving Role' (n 6) 11–12.

[11] Treasury Committee *HM Treasury* (n 9), para. 21 (emphasis retained). See also Treasury Committee, *Administration and Expenditure of the Chancellor's Departments 2006–2007* (HC 2006–07, 57), para. 48.

The role of the Treasury has also been affected by the growth of other institutions filling what was historically a void at the centre of government, notably the Cabinet Office, to which the Office of Government Commerce was transferred from the Treasury by the Coalition. Finally, the picture painted by the then Chancellor during the financial crisis is far from that of an all-powerful Treasury able to bend other institutions to its will.[12] This is a point to which I shall return later in discussing the weaknesses of the tripartite system intended to coordinate the work of the Treasury, the Bank of England, and the then Financial Services Authority.

The current objectives of the Treasury are set out in its Business Plan, and reflect both the breadth of its different areas of activity and the priorities of the Coalition.[13] Thus the Treasury has three structural reform priorities; to '[r]educe the structural deficit in a fair and responsible way', to '[s]ecure an economy that is more resilient, and more balanced between public and private sectors', and to '[r]eform the regulatory framework for the financial sector to avoid future financial crises'. More details are set out in its Structural Reform Plan included in the business plan, including lists of detailed actions and sub-actions and monthly reports on implementation. Progress in delivering priorities is also described in more detail in the new-style annual report of the Treasury.[14] The objectives are a more focused list than previously, no longer including intervention in substantive areas of policy such as the elimination of child poverty, though they include economic objectives, including working with other departments to implement the cross-Government Growth Review.

The Treasury is part of the Treasury Group; this also includes other bodies to be considered later. It is of course headed by the Chancellor and the other ministers; these are currently the Chief Secretary to the Treasury (whose responsibilities include the Spending Review), the Financial Secretary to the Treasury (responsible for financial services and bank support), the Exchequer Secretary to the Treasury (responsible for tax matters), the Economic Secretary to the Treasury, and the Commercial Secretary to the Treasury. The most senior committee is the Treasury Board chaired by the Chancellor and comprised of equal numbers of ministers, non-executive, and executive board members. It met formally only once during 2011–12 but delegates to supporting committees; this lack of meetings was criticized by the Public Accounts Committee as limiting its ability to steer the Treasury, and the

[12] A. Darling, *Back from the Brink: 1,000 Days at Number 11* (London: Atlantic Books, 2011).

[13] HM Treasury, *Business Plan 2012–2015* (2012), at: <https://www.gov.uk/government/publications/hm-treasury-business-plan-2012-to-2015>.

[14] HM Treasury, *Annual Report and Accounts 2012–13* (HC 2012–13, 34).

Committee also accused the Treasury of neglecting its role of finance ministry.[15] Management is in the hands of an Executive Management Board and 16 director-led groups covering, for example, economics, financial stability, and public spending. Though the Treasury has a major role in tax policy, the administration of that policy and the collection of taxes is the responsibility of HM Revenue & Customs, to be considered separately later.

The Treasury, the financial crisis, and the Constitution

The financial crisis of 2008 also increased the visibility and centrality of the Treasury, though the response to the crisis also involved the Bank of England and the Financial Services Authority, forming with the Treasury the tripartite system. Given that this response will appear frequently in these pages, it is worth noting its scale:

> In the UK, between September 2007 and February 2010, the government nationalized, in whole or in part, four banks, arranged for the transfer of assets of two building societies and two subsidiaries of Icelandic banks; injected £37bn into Royal Bank of Scotland (RBS) and Lloyds Group through recapitalization, and in November 2009 agreed to purchase a further £39bn in shares (mainly in RBS); extended over £280m in liquidity support; created £200bn of new money through "quantitative easing" to support banks by buying their UK gilts, leading to the Bank of England owning 20 per cent of the gilt market; agreed to guarantee up to £250bn of wholesale borrowing by banks and to underwrite £281bn of RBS's assets. It provided approximately £40bn of loans and other funding to Bradford & Bingley and the Financial Services Compensation Scheme. At December 2009 its net cash outlay for lending to banks and purchase of shares stood at £117bn.[16]

New schemes included the Special Liquidity Scheme to improve liquidity and increase market confidence; the Credit Guarantee Scheme to guarantee bank borrowing on the wholesale markets; the Asset Protection Scheme to protect against future credit losses on certain assets, and quantitative easing to purchase government bonds from the banks and improve liquidity in credit markets.[17]

It has been suggested that the constitution, especially when EU constraints such as state aid law are taken into account, is inflexible and restricts

[15] Public Accounts Committee, *HM Treasury: Annual Reports and Accounts 2011–12* (HC 2012–13, 659) 5.

[16] J. Black, 'The Credit Crisis and the Constitution' in D. Oliver, T. Prosser, and R. Rawlings (eds), *The Regulatory State: Constitutional Implications* (Oxford: Oxford University Press, 2010), 92–128, 92 (footnote omitted).

[17] Black, 'The Credit Crisis and the Constitution' (n 16) 98–104.

the opportunities for government to implement public goals and policies in an interventionist fashion.[18] Yet, faced with crisis, the constitution showed a remarkable flexibility; indeed major principles of accountability were set aside with ease. It also revealed a marked lack of coordination when the tripartite system failed in conditions of stress.

One example of the remarkable flexibility of the constitution in the crisis was ability to make secret emergency loans to the banks; RBS, Lloyds, and HBOS received loans from the Bank of England of up to £60bn in exchange for collateral but backed by an £18bn indemnity from the Treasury.[19] It was not reported to Parliament but only discovered through a later National Audit Office report. This breached a convention set out in Treasury guidance that indemnities should be notified to the Public Accounts Committee and the Treasury Select Committee, or their Chairs where confidentiality was required. The Public Accounts Committee was highly critical, concluding that '*[t]here can be no excuse for flouting Parliamentary procedure*' and that the failure to notify it was unacceptable. In future, as a minimum in very exceptional circumstances, the Chair of the Committee should be given a full oral briefing in the presence of the Comptroller and Auditor-General.[20] The Treasury Committee was less critical; whilst finding that there had been a breach of the Treasury's own well-established guidance, it understood the need for secrecy and proposed that in future there should be an oral briefing in such circumstances to reduce the risk of leaks.[21] Black may well be correct to comment that, in the circumstances, 'the PAC adopted a highly formalistic approach, whilst the TSC had a more contextualized understanding of the circumstances in which the decision was taken'.[22] However, this saga shows how easily normal convention could be dropped in time of crisis.

A second example concerns the legislation to take the major banks into public ownership. The first was the Banking (Special Provisions) Act 2008, which lapsed after a year. The second was the permanent Banking Act 2009. As Black has documented, it contains Henry VIII clauses permitting the amendment of primary legislation by ministerial order; for example, section 74 permits the Treasury to make regulations relating to the fiscal treatment of the exercise of a stabilization power; these may modify or disapply an enactment, and may have retrospective effect for up to three months. Even

[18] For a detailed statement of this theme, see D. Nicol, *The Constitutional Protection of Capitalism* (Oxford: Hart Publishing, 2010).

[19] For fuller discussion, see Black, 'The Credit Crisis and the Constitution' (n 16) 103, 120–1.

[20] Public Accounts Committee, *Maintaining Financial Stability Across the UK Banking System* (HC 2009–10, 190), para. 9 (emphasis retained).

[21] Treasury Committee, *Reporting Contingent Financial Liabilities to Parliament* (HC 2009–10, 181).

[22] Black, 'The Credit Crisis and the Constitution' (n 16) 121.

more strikingly, section 75 gives the Treasury a general power to amend the law (both statute and common law) to enable the powers conferred by the Act to be used effectively, and this may have retrospective effect where the Treasury considers it to be necessary or desirable. The retrospective effect was heavily criticized by the House of Lords Select Committee on the Constitution, but nevertheless became law.[23] Once more, constitutional concerns have not prevented the assumption of the broadest discretionary powers by Government in conditions of the crisis. As we shall see later, there were serious problems in the Treasury's relationship with the other key institution of the Bank of England, and the Treasury's own review of its response to the financial crisis found that it was stretched and could have been better prepared.[24]

The Bank of England

The second of the major governing institutions of the UK economy is the Bank of England, itself of course closely linked to the Treasury. It also has a long history, being founded as a private bank in 1694 and nationalized by the Bank of England Act 1946, with important changes in its duties and governance under the Bank of England Act 1998, the Banking Act 2009, and the Financial Services Act 2012. Its major tasks are the setting of interest rates (carried out by the Monetary Policy Committee and examined in detail in Chapter 6), issuing banknotes, and maintaining the stability of the banking system, including providing liquidity to depositing banks and acting as lender of last resort. Obviously, the Bank was one of the key actors in the attempts to resolve the financial crisis during 2008–09. It acquired major new responsibilities relating to the maintenance of financial stability and prudential regulation in the reforms of financial regulation after the financial crisis.

The Bank's core purposes are to achieve monetary stability, as defined by the Government's inflation target, and to protect and enhance financial stability. Governance arrangements were changed by the Banking Act 2009, reducing in size the Bank's Court of Directors (which is responsible for managing its affairs apart from monetary policy) and further reform is made by the Financial Services Act 2012, so that the Court comprises the Governor, three deputy governors, and not more than nine non-executive

[23] House of Lords Select Committee on the Constitution, *Banking Act 2009: Supplementary Report on Retrospective Legislation* (HL 2008–09, 97). For discussion, see Black, 'The Credit Crisis and the Constitution' (n 16) 118–19.

[24] HM Treasury, *Review of HM Treasury's Management Response to the Financial Crisis* (2012).

directors.[25] The Bank of England also has 12 regional agencies around the UK, whose primary task is to assess economic conditions affecting businesses in their area.

The role of the Bank's Monetary Policy Committee (MPC) in setting interest rates and in other aspects of monetary policy is in many ways institutionally distinct from the rest of its work. This will be discussed in detail in Chapter 6 but it will be useful to give a brief outline of the institutional arrangements here. The MPC was established by the Bank of England Act 1998; the Treasury's power (never used) to give directions to the Bank was specifically disapplied from the area of monetary policy.[26] The objectives of the Bank in relation to monetary policy were specified as 'to maintain price stability' and, subject to this, to support the economic policy of the Government, including objectives for growth and employment. The Treasury was given the power to specify what price stability is to be taken to consist of and what the economic policy of the Government is to be; in practice these are stated in an annual remit from the Chancellor.[27] The Act requires the MPC to publish the minutes of its monthly meetings within six weeks; in practice they are published on the Wednesday of the second week after the meeting.[28] Should the actual rate of inflation differ by more than one percentage point from the target set out in the MPC's remit, the Governor must write an open letter to the Chancellor explaining why this has occurred and what action will be taken to deal with it. The arrangements for transparency in the setting of monetary policy are thus substantial and impressive. The Treasury has a reserve power to issue directions on monetary policy subject to parliamentary approval, and so in effect to override the Committee, if satisfied that they are required in the public interest and 'by extreme economic circumstances'.[29] Given the effect on the markets, it is highly unlikely that this power will ever be used. The decisions of the MPC are implemented by the Bank's operations in the sterling money markets.

A further responsibility of the MPC has been to manage the process of quantitative easing. This aims to compensate for the very low level of the Bank rate by helping to increase the availability of corporate credit through asset purchases for monetary policy purposes. It provides a way in which the MPC can inject money into the economy through purchasing securities using central bank money. The scale of purchases has been huge; in 2011–12

[25] Banking Act 2009, ss 238–47; Financial Services Act 2012, s 2.

[26] Bank of England Act 1998, ss 10, 13.

[27] Bank of England Act 1998, ss 11–12; HM Treasury, *Remit for the Monetary Policy Committee* (2013) at: <https://www.gov.uk/government/uploads/system/uploads/attachment_data/file/221566/chx_letter_to_boe_monetary_policy_framework_200313.pdf>.

[28] Bank of England Act 1998, s 15.

[29] Bank of England Act 1998, s 19.

quantitative easing purchases reached a total of £375bn. The transactions are undertaken by a subsidiary company of the Bank: the Bank of England Asset Purchase Facility Fund Limited (BEAPFF).

Turning now to its responsibilities for financial stability, the Bank was centrally involved in the response to the financial crisis, in particular through its role as lender of last resort. In April 2008, after lending £25bn to UK banks, it introduced the Special Liquidity Scheme to improve liquidity and increase confidence in the markets by lending gilts to them in exchange for collateral, and this was extended to £208bn by the autumn.[30] It also provided the emergency loans to banks with a government indemnity mentioned earlier. Under the Banking Act 2009 a special resolution scheme was created to manage failing banks with a central role for the Bank alongside the Treasury and the then Financial Services Authority.[31]

The crisis resulted in a succession of reforms which substantially increase the Bank's role in financial supervision. The 2009 Act imposed a new financial stability duty on the Bank to contribute to protecting and enhancing the stability of the UK financial systems, and required it to set up a Financial Stability Committee of the Court for this purpose; the 2012 Act amends the duty and replaces the Committee with a new Financial Policy Committee much closer in form to the Monetary Policy Committee; for example, it includes independent members and is obliged to publish a record of its meetings. The Committee will be subject to recommendations from the Treasury to which it must respond.[32] The Committee is responsible for contributing to the achievement of a financial stability strategy drafted by the Bank's Court, and for monitoring and reporting on the stability of the UK financial system; it may issue directions to other regulatory bodies for financial services. It must publish a Financial Stability Report at least annually. A new Prudential Regulation Authority is also established under the 2012 Act as a Bank subsidiary, giving the Bank a major role in financial services regulation.[33] It takes over much of the work previously carried out by the Financial Services Authority relating to the authorization and supervision of those providing financial services, and has as its general objective to promote the safety and soundness of those whom it authorizes. This is a substantial organizational change, adding 1,300 new staff to the Bank's previous total of 1,800, and will be described in more detail in the analysis

[30] Black, 'The Credit Crisis and the Constitution' (n 16) 101–2.

[31] Black, 'The Credit Crisis and the Constitution' (n 16) 117–18; Banking Act 2009, pt 1.

[32] Financial Services Act 2012, ss 2, 4 adding new ss 9A–9ZA to the Financial Services and Markets Act 2000.

[33] Financial Services Act 2012, s 6, adding new ss 2A–2P to the Financial Services and Markets Act 2000.

of financial services regulation in Chapter 7. The Bank also administers the Funding for Lending scheme to encourage bank lending to households and small businesses; this will be discussed in Chapter 8.

This substantial increase in the Bank's responsibilities has created major questions of accountability. Governance was an issue in the Bank's rather belated reviews of its performance in the crisis, which were published in late 2012; that into the Bank's framework for providing liquidity to the banking system was critical of the position of the Governor and the highly centralized decision-making structure, and of a tendency for less senior staff to 'filter' recommendations to secure their acceptability to more senior staff.[34] The Bank is, of course, not a government department headed by a minister responsible to Parliament, nor is it a regulatory agency subject to the transparency requirements now generally applied to such bodies. For example, the Freedom of Information Act does not apply to the Bank in relation to monetary policy or the support of financial institutions to maintain stability.[35] The issue was put succinctly by the former Chancellor: '[t]he Bank is an autocratic institution, run by its Governor. It always has been. To invest so much power in one man or woman runs counter to any modern idea of corporate governance. The court of the Bank of England, to whom the Governor is in theory answerable, is an anachronism'.[36] The Treasury Select Committee made the same point in more detail in a critical report on the Bank's governance and accountability.[37] The Committee recommended that the Court be transformed into a smaller supervisory board with greater expertise in prudential policy and a majority of external members; its minutes should be published and it should conduct published reviews of the Bank's action. Lines of responsibility between the Chancellor, the Treasury, and the Bank in times of financial difficulty should also be clarified and the Governor should be appointed for a shorter term, with the Committee having a statutory veto. In its response to the Committee, the Court of the Bank proposed merely an internal Oversight Committee as a sub-committee of the Court. It would have the power to commission external reviews, but would not be able to 'second-guess' or take sides on the substance of decisions, and was considered wholly inadequate by the Treasury Committee.[38]

[34] Bank of England, *Review of the Bank of England's Framework for Providing Liquidity to the Banking System* (2012).

[35] Freedom of Information Act 2000, sch. 1, pt VI, para. 1.

[36] Darling, *Back from the Brink* (n 12) 319.

[37] Treasury Committee, *Accountability of the Bank of England* (HC 2010–12, 874).

[38] Treasury Committee, *Accountability of the Bank of England: Response from the Court of the Bank to the Twenty-first Report from the Committee* (HC 2010–12, 1769), paras 18–19.

The Financial Services Act 2012 partly meets these criticisms. The Court has been recast with a majority of non-executive directors and will be required to publish its minutes, as will the Financial Policy Committee. The term of the appointment of the Governor has been reduced to eight years, though there is no requirement for parliamentary approval of the appointment. A new Oversight Committee of Court must be established, comprised of the non-executive directors to keep under review the Bank's performance in relation to meeting its objectives and its strategy as well as reviewing procedures.[39] It remains to be seen how successful these changes will be in the general context of the reform of financial services regulation; what is certain is that the Bank has acquired major new responsibilities without fundamental reform to its structure. The role of the Governor remains the key; and this also emphasizes the importance of the Chancellor's power of appointment. The choice of Governor appointed in 2012 was very much a personal one by the Chancellor.[40]

The Financial Services Authority and the Financial Conduct Authority

The third of the major actors in the financial crisis, the Financial Services Authority (FSA), need be covered only briefly here because it has been replaced as part of the Coalition's reforms of financial services regulation. It was established under the Financial Services and Markets Act 2000 to replace a complex system involving use of self-regulation. The FSA was a company limited by guarantee under the Companies Act; it was, however, subject to extensive statutory regulation through the Act setting objectives and principles and specifying procedures.[41] Its relationship with the Treasury and Bank of England was set out in a tripartite agreement, to be discussed later.

The FSA itself has now been abolished in the reforms to financial regulation implemented by the Financial Services Act 2012. These will be discussed in detail in Chapter 7, but, as mentioned, macro-prudential regulation passes to the Financial Policy Committee of the Bank of England, and prudential regulation of individual firms to the Prudential Regulation Authority. Consumer protection and markets regulation are given to a third body, the

39 Financial Services Act 2012, s 3 and sch. 1.

40 C. Giles, 'Appointment Seals Treasury Supremacy over BoE', *The Financial Times*, 28 November 2012.

41 For a brief summary, see T. Prosser, 'The Powers and Accountability of Agencies and Regulators' in D. Feldman (ed.), *English Public Law*, 2nd edn (Oxford: Oxford University Press, 2009), 241–80, 269–71.

Financial Conduct Authority, which adopts the existing legal corporate identity of the FSA but with powers amended (not entirely replaced) under the new Act. Its strategic objective is to ensure that the markets it regulates operate well, and it must have regard to operational objectives of consumer protection, integrity, and competition.[42] As we shall see in Chapter 7, it will be expected to take a different approach from that of its predecessor, which was discredited by its failure to anticipate the financial crisis and to regulate accordingly.

Institutional interrelations and the tripartite system

At the time of the financial crisis, even the most important and sensitive responsibilities in relation to financial management were spread amongst three different bodies. Coordination was to take place through the tripartite agreement, a memorandum of understanding between the Treasury, the Bank of England, and the Financial Services Authority agreed in 1997 and revised in 2002 and 2006.[43] Institutional collaboration was to take place through the Standing Committee on Financial Stability chaired by the Treasury and with representation of each of the three institutions, and through cross-board membership.

It is now agreed that the tripartite system failed dismally during the financial crisis. The point was made succinctly once more by the then Chancellor, Alistair Darling: '[t]he whole system depended on the chairman of the FSA, the Governor of the Bank and the Chancellor seeing things in exactly the same way. The problem was that, in September 2007, we simply did not see things in the same way'.[44] The Treasury Select Committee made the same point at greater length:

> *Whatever the final outcome of any institutional arrangements it is absolutely imperative that responsibilities are clear. The biggest failings of the Tripartite's handling of Northern Rock were that it was not clear who was in charge, and, because the Tripartite took a minimalist view of their respective responsibilities, necessary actions fell between three stools. We are not confident that this issue has yet been adequately resolved. Where before no-one had a formal responsibility for financial stability, now many do—the Bank of England, the FSA, the Treasury, the Council for Financial*

[42] Financial Services Act 2012, s 6, adding a new s 1B to the Financial Services and Markets Act 2000.

[43] HM Treasury, the Bank of England and the Financial Services Authority, *Memorandum of Understanding Between HM Treasury, the Bank of England and the Financial Services Authority* (2006) at: <http://www.bankofengland.co.uk/financialstability/mou.pdf>. See also Black, 'The Credit Crisis and the Constitution' (n 16) 97–8.

[44] Darling, *Back from the Brink* (n 12) 21.

Stability and the Bank's Financial Stability Committee. Where responsibility lies for strategic decisions and executive action was, and remains, a muddle.[45]

In an attempt to resolve this, the Financial Services Bill, the last of the Labour Government's legislative interventions in this area, originally contained provision for the creation of a statutory Council on Financial Stability to coordinate the strategies of the Bank of England and the FSA; however, these provisions were lost in the 'wash-up' at the end of the Parliament when the parties negotiate provisions in outstanding bills which can be saved. The Financial Services Act 2010 set a new financial stability objective for the FSA; a similar objective had already been set for the Bank of England by the Banking Act 2009.[46]

However, more radical changes were introduced by the Coalition Government with a greater concentration of powers in the Bank of England. This still leaves the potential for problems of coordination, both between the new regulatory bodies themselves and especially between the Treasury and the Bank. The attempted solutions are complex and will be dealt with in detail in Chapter 7. In brief, there is a new duty on the Bank to notify the Treasury of a possible need for public funds, for example to provide financial assistance to a bank, and for a power of direction by the Treasury to the Bank requiring the latter to exercise its powers relating to assistance for banks. This may be beneficial in concentrating decisions relating to public funds in political hands. A memorandum of understanding has been agreed between the Treasury and the Bank (and the Prudential Regulation Authority) on crisis management. The Treasury has the power to specify matters relevant to its economic policy and to issue recommendations to the Financial Policy Committee, providing some of the advantages of the Treasury remit which has worked well for the Monetary Policy Committee, and there are further requirements for consultation and for a meeting (with a published record) between the Governor and the Chancellor after each Financial Stability Report is published by the Committee. There is also some cross-membership of the new institutions. These requirements for cooperation appear substantial, but all will depend on how they work out on the ground, and this is difficult to predict. It is precisely in circumstances of crisis that rules of both soft and hard law are likely to be replaced by conflictual personalized relations, as we saw in the 2008 financial crisis. For the moment, it need just be said that, whatever the effectiveness and accountability of individual

[45] Treasury Committee, *Banking Crisis: Regulation and Supervision* (HC 2008–09, 767), para. 114 (emphasis retained).

[46] Financial Services Act 2010, s 1; Banking Act 2009, s 238.

institutions, judging from past experience, it is their interrelations which are likely to provide the greatest headaches in any future crisis.

The centre of government: the Cabinet Office

The traditional weakness of the centre of UK government has been partially remedied by the growth of the role of the Cabinet Office, one of its functions being to provide support to the Prime Minister and Deputy Prime Minister.[47] The Cabinet Office only became a separate part of government machinery in 1968, becoming responsible for organizing and managing the civil service; providing an organizational and administrative base for inquiries and analysis of specific issues; and an institutional base for a number of 'sinecure' ministers.[48] It has been subject to several phases of reform since, including the establishment of an Office of Public Service (now the Efficiency and Reform Group) within it. Its responsibilities now include constitutional reform and government efficiency. One example is the presence within the Cabinet Office of the Major Projects Authority, with a remit of developing the Government's portfolio of major projects, reviewing their progress, and offering assistance where there is cause for concern.[49] The role of the Authority is thus an important example of executive self-regulation.

A further important change was the transfer in June 2010 from the Treasury to the Cabinet Office of the Office of Government Commerce (OGC) and the public sector procurement agency, Buying Solutions. The OGC is responsible for providing policy standards and guidance on best practice in procurement, projects and estate management, and monitors departments' performance against these standards; as we shall see in Chapter 9, in the absence of a developed domestic law of public procurement, the guidance on procurement is of considerable importance. The OGC now forms part of the Cabinet Office Efficiency and Reform Group, which also contains the Public Sector Transparency Board to support the Government's transparency agenda.

The Cabinet Office is thus responsible for making government more efficient and reforming the way in which public services are provided. Set alongside the presence of the Prime Minister's Office, this means that there is now an alternative source of central government authority in addition to that of the Treasury, and this is of importance both for service provision and

[47] For an account of the history, see House of Commons Library, Research Paper 05/92, *The Centre of Government—No 10, the Cabinet Office and HM Treasury* (2005), 37–48.

[48] *The Centre of Government—No 10, the Cabinet Office and HM Treasury* (n 47) 38.

[49] See HM Government, *Major Projects Authority*, at: <https://www.gov.uk/government/policy-teams/major-projects-authority>.

procurement. What the Cabinet Office does not provide, though, is a resource for effective strategic planning, and this is a major gap in governance arrangements to which I shall return in my concluding chapter.[50]

The changes to the Cabinet Office have been more important than changes in the Cabinet itself. Thus in October 2008 during the financial crisis a National Economic Council was set up as a Cabinet Committee chaired by the Prime Minister. Although welcomed as having the capacity to inject greater collective Cabinet involvement into economic policy, in reality it was unwieldy and, in the words of the then Chancellor, '[a]t the end of the day, the Treasury can always say no—no economic council or Cabinet committee can change that. I put up with it'.[51] After the change of Government, it was replaced by an Economic Affairs Committee chaired by the Chancellor.

The Department for Business, Innovation and Skills

Turning now to spending departments, several will be considered in this book, including, for example, the Ministry of Defence given the importance, and serious problems, of defence procurement. However, the most important of these for our purposes is the Department for Business, Innovation and Skills (BIS). This has responsibility for a wide range of different business sectors and policy areas. It is here that many of the remaining elements of industrial policy are to be found. Policy areas include support for clusters of interconnected companies and suppliers and economic development. As we shall see in Chapter 8, this worked through regional offices and the Regional Development Agencies, but these are now replaced by Local Enterprise Partnerships, non-statutory joint local authority-business bodies. BIS is also responsible for consumer protection and consumer law. Issues of overlap between its policy responsibilities and those of the Treasury have arisen in the past; according to one nameless official, its predecessor Department of Trade and Industry was 'sort of pretty comprehensively second-guessed' by the Treasury.[52] This may still prove to be a problem, given that the Treasury rather than BIS is responsible for leading on the Government's economic growth agenda.

BIS also has responsibility for the regulatory reform agenda in government, having taken this over from the Cabinet Office in 2007; it is coordinated by

[50] Public Administration Committee, *Strategic Thinking in Government; Without National Strategy, Can Viable Government Strategy Emerge?* (HC 2010–12, 1625).

[51] C. Thain, 'A Very Peculiar British crisis?: Institutions, Ideas and Policy Responses to the Credit Crunch' (2009) 4 *British Politics* 434–49, 445; Darling, *Back from the Brink* (n 12) 194–5.

[52] Quoted in Fawcett, 'Metagovernance and the Treasury's Evolving Role within the British Core Executive, 1997–2007' (n 6) 11.

the Better Regulation Executive (BRE) within BIS. The agenda has a long history, and its aims have included removing or simplifying existing regulations; reducing the overall volume of new regulation by introducing regulation only as a last resort; improving the quality of remaining new regulation; and moving to less onerous and less bureaucratic enforcement regimes where inspections are targeted and risk-based. Principles of good regulation were also developed.[53] The Coalition Government introduced the use of a one-in, two-out system by which new regulatory costs will have to be accompanied by larger reductions; various other changes have also been made to strengthen the role of the BRE.[54] The process of examining new regulations through the use of impact analysis was also strengthened by the Coalition, to provide scrutiny of all new regulatory proposals, including those intended for consultation. The BRE is assisted in its work by an external Regulatory Policy Committee, which comments on the quality of analysis supporting policy decisions on new regulations and on whether benefits justify costs; it also reviews the performance of regulators. The regulatory reform agenda has had a substantial (and not always popular) effect on both departments and arm's length regulators.

Arm's length bodies

We now move into the areas of extended government or the 'hollowed-out' state.[55] There is no need to discuss the extensive literature in this area, but merely to point out that there is an extraordinary number of different bodies engaged in economic management, with radically different degrees of independence from with government. I shall begin by describing examples in which a degree of independence is central to the legitimacy of the institutions: competition policy, the Office for Budget Responsibility, the UK Statistics Authority, and Her Majesty's Revenue & Customs. I shall then examine other institutions more closely linked to core government. I shall not cover the utility regulators, which, although important in sectoral economic management, have been subject to detailed coverage elsewhere.[56] The reader

[53] For a more detailed account, see T. Prosser, *The Regulatory Enterprise* (Oxford: Oxford University Press, 2010), ch. 10.

[54] For current policies, see BIS, *Reducing the Impact of Regulation on Business* (2012) at: <https://www.gov.uk/government/policies/reducing-the-impact-of-regulation-on-business>. A draft Deregulation Bill was issued in 2013 with the aim of taking the deregulation process further.

[55] See e.g. R. Rhodes, *Understanding Governance: Policy Networks, Governance, Reflexivity and Accountability* (Buckingham: Open University Press, 1997).

[56] T. Prosser, *Law and the Regulators* (Oxford: Oxford University Press, 1997); *The Regulatory Enterprise* (n 53) ch. 9.

should be warned that the style of this chapter will now become somewhat staccato given the sheer number of relevant bodies and difficulties in classifying them in a way which gives clear unifying themes.

Competition institutions

Competition law and policy can act both as a policy instrument for government and as a constraint on its ability to implement its policies. Since 1998 there has been a fundamental change in the structure and working of UK competition law from a public interest approach largely implemented by ministers to a competition-based approach implemented by independent authorities. Importantly, competition law does not apply only to the private sector but, subject to a number of complex exemptions, may apply to public bodies. Further reform has now created a new single-tier Competition and Markets Authority replacing the Office of Fair Trading and the Competition Commission.[57]

The independence of the competition authorities from government does, however, have its limits. As part of the 2008 bank rescue, Lloyds and HBOS agreed to merge; this had strong Government support and, as Black has noted, there were rumours that the merger was prompted by direct intervention from the Prime Minister.[58] This would normally have required a lengthy examination by the competition authorities which could have blocked the merger on competition grounds. Instead, the Enterprise Act 2002 was rapidly amended by order to add the stability of the UK financial system to the short list of 'public interest grounds' permitting the Secretary of State to intervene and consider these alongside competition issues.[59] On this basis, the merger was swiftly approved.

Office for Budget Responsibility

An innovation made by the incoming Coalition Government was to establish an Office for Budget Responsibility. The Office is responsible for making independent assessments of public finances and the economy. These include preparing and publishing the official five-year forecasts for the economy that accompany each budget and Autumn Statement; assessing whether the Government is on course to meet its fiscal targets; scrutinizing and reporting

[57] Enterprise and Regulatory Reform Act 2013, pt 3.

[58] Black, 'The Credit Crisis and the Constitution' (n 16) 102.

[59] The Enterprise Act 2002 (Specification of Additional Section 58 Consideration) Order 2008, SI 2008/2645.

on the Treasury's assessment of the amount that particular tax and spending measures will raise or cost; and analyzing and reporting on the health of the public sector balance sheet and the long-term sustainability of public finances. There were initial criticisms of a perceived lack of independence of the interim Office established shortly after the 2010 election, due partly to its location within the Treasury and staffing by Treasury civil servants, and partly to suggestions that it had provided advance data to assist the Government against opposition criticisms of potential public sector job losses. However, the Treasury Select Committee praised its contribution to transparency, and the Chair appointed to it was agreed to be highly independent.[60] The Office was given a statutory basis by the Budget Responsibility and National Audit Act 2011, which establishes it as a body corporate acting on behalf of the Crown.[61] Very unusually, appointments are subject not simply to scrutiny but to veto by the Treasury Select Committee.[62] The role of the new Office is of enormous importance both as a source of information and as a means of independent comment on the public finances; as we shall see in Chapter 5, it has not hesitated to be critical of government claims in relation to fiscal policy.

The UK Statistics Authority and the Office for National Statistics

One other set of institutions needs to be mentioned in this context in view of their importance in securing transparency of national accounts; the UK Statistics Authority and the Office for National Statistics. After a serious decline of trust in UK national statistics, the Statistics and Registration Service Act 2009 provided for the establishment of the Authority as a non-ministerial department at arm's length from government, with its own independent board. It is responsible for overseeing the Office for National Statistics, its executive arm (replacing earlier oversight by the Treasury), and for independent scrutiny of all UK official statistics. It also has the duty to develop a code of practice on the quality and integrity of official statistics, and gives them formal accreditation as 'national statistics'.[63] Decisions relating to national statistics have had on occasions an important effect on government financial policy and its room for manoeuvre; for example in February 2008 the Office announced that the borrowings of the failed bank Northern Rock

[60] Treasury Committee, *Office for Budget Responsibility* (HC 2010–11, 385), para. 8; *Appointment of Robert Chote as Chair of the Office for Budget Responsibility* (2010–11, HC 476).

[61] Budget Responsibility and National Audit Act 2011, s 3 and sch. 1.

[62] Budget Responsibility and National Audit Act 2011, sch. 1 para. 1.

[63] Statistics and Registration Service Act 2009, ss 10–19.

were to appear on government accounts. The total effect was to raise public sector debt by no less than £102.3 billion, or 7.2 per cent of GDP, thereby making untenable the Treasury's policy that net debt should be below 40 per cent of national income. It has published a detailed analysis of the classification of public sector interventions as a result of the financial crisis, covering both classification in relation to public sector borrowing and debt of entities using public finances, and the recording of the interventions themselves.[64] The Office also provides extensive information on the public finances, including monthly data on public sector net borrowing and net debt. Its decisions have not always been uncontroversial; for example, a decision to treat interest from quantitative easing as public sector revenue was criticized because it was made by its Public Sector Finances Advisory Group, which includes government officials.[65]

HM Revenue & Customs

General tax policy is the responsibility of the Treasury, and the responsible minister is the Exchequer Secretary. Its implementation through dealing with the affairs of individual taxpayers is undertaken independently by HM Revenue & Customs (HMRC). HMRC is responsible for administering the major forms of taxation, including income tax, VAT, and National Insurance and is responsible for the payment of tax credits and child benefit, along with enforcing the National Minimum Wage and administering the collection of student loans. It was formed under the Commissioners for Revenue and Customs Act 2005 from the two distinct departments of the Inland Revenue and Customs and Excise.[66] HRMC is a non-ministerial government department with Commissioners appointed by the Crown and acting on its behalf; in 2008 a new governance structure was introduced with a non-executive Chairman and Board and Chief Executive and Executive Committee. The Act contains powers for the Treasury to issue 'directions of a general nature' to the Commissioners, with which they must comply.[67] This replaces a variety of differently worded provisions in earlier legislation, but does not permit the Treasury to intervene in decisions on the affairs of

[64] Office for National Statistics, *Public Sector Interventions in the Financial Crisis—Statistical Classification Decisions* (2009).

[65] C. Giles, 'Britain's Official Statistics are no Longer to be Trusted', *The Financial Times*, 28 February 2013.

[66] For the background to the merger, see HM Treasury, *Financing Britain's Future—Review of the Revenue Departments* (Cm 6164, 2004) and Treasury Committee, *The Merger of Customs & Excise and the Inland Revenue* (HC 2003–04, 556).

[67] Commissioners for Revenue and Customs Act 2005, s 11.

individual taxpayers. The Treasury publishes a remit for HMRC annually, and a business plan is published, as is an annual report on how the remit has been met.

As we shall see in Chapter 4, there are serious problems in the institutional arrangements. Thus the relationship with the Treasury on tax policy has been seriously criticized for lack of coordination. The former Chancellor was also critical of an arrangement by which he was accountable in Parliament for administrative errors relating to a catastrophic loss of data of which he was not fully informed.[68] As we shall see in Chapter 4, there have also been serious criticisms by the Treasury Select Committee of weaknesses of service delivery by HRMC, notably extremely low staff morale and poor service standards. The Public Accounts Committee has heavily criticized HMRC's arrangements for settlements and collection of taxes from multinational companies.

Executive agencies and related bodies

We now enter into an area of considerable complexity involving the 'extended executive'. Even in relation to the Chancellor's departments (which form only a small proportion of the bodies to be examined here) the Treasury Committee noted well before the crisis that relationships with the central Treasury were unclear and requested clarification; clarity has, if anything, decreased, as we shall see.[69] This reflects a much broader literature relating to the formation of 'Next Steps' agencies and similar bodies, which has highlighted problems both of accountability and of coordination with the core executive, as revealed in major difficulties involving the prison service and the UK Border Agency.[70] In particular, the use of framework documents was originally envisaged as a means of clearly delimiting responsibilities of the department and of the agency, but has not done so comprehensively or consistently, nor has a distinction between 'policy' and 'operational' matters worked as a means of allocating responsibility. In 2002, a review by the Treasury and the Prime Minister's Office of Public Services Reform identified as the main problem with agency performance that some agencies had become disconnected from their parent departments. Among other issues, it

[68] Darling, *Back from the Brink* (n 12) 49–53.

[69] Treasury Committee, *HM Treasury* (n 9) para. 51.

[70] For a summary, see P. Craig, *Administrative Law*, 7th edn (London: Sweet and Maxwell, 2012), 86–91, 104–6; A. Barker, 'Political Responsibility for UK Prison Security—Ministers Escape Again' (1998) 76 *Public Administration* 1–23; Home Affairs Committee, *UK Border Controls* (HC 2010–12, 1647).

noted substantial deficiencies in framework documents, which often had not been updated to reflect major changes since they had first been drafted.[71] The Cabinet Office later issued a guide for departments on the creation of agencies, emphasizing the importance of framework documents and listing in detail the information that they should all include, as well as suggesting other improvements in clarifying relations and accountability.[72] Nevertheless, problems have continued. I shall now briefly describe the role of each body, and, once more, further information, including that relating to difficulties in coordination, will be given in later chapters.

The UK Debt Management Office

The first of the Treasury executive agencies is the UK Debt Management Office. It is

> the executive agency of the Treasury specializing in the provision of policy advice on and the delivery of the government's financing needs. It acts as a key gateway for government to the wholesale financial markets and performs these functions primarily to support the Treasury's objective of maintaining sound public finances.[73]

Relations with the Treasury are set out in a published framework document, and an annual remit is provided to the Office by the Treasury specifying the annual total of gilts to be auctioned and related matters.[74] The Office played an important role in the government response to the financial crisis; it was made responsible for administering the Credit Guarantee Scheme introduced in October 2008 guaranteeing bank borrowing, and the Asset Guarantee Scheme introduced in April 2009, guaranteeing the securitization of mortgages.[75] It had to sell government gilts on an unprecedented scale; its remit for 2009–10 was for the sale of £220bn of gilts, more than the total of sales in its first seven years from 1998.[76] This use of the Office has been praised as showing an imaginative, swift response to the financial crisis.[77]

[71] HM Treasury and the Prime Minister's Office of Public Services Reform, *Better Government Services: Executive Agencies in the 21st Century* (2002).

[72] Cabinet Office, *Executive Agencies: A Guide for Departments* (2006).

[73] HM Treasury, *Annual Report and Accounts 2008–09* (HC 2008–09, 611).

[74] United Kingdom Debt Management Office, *Executive Agency Framework Document* (2005) at: <http://www.dmo.gov.uk/documentview.aspx?docname=publications/corpgovernance/fwork040405.pdf &page=>.

[75] Black, 'The Credit Crunch and the Constitution' (n 16) 112.

[76] Treasury Committee, *Administration and Expenditure of the Chancellor's Departments, 2008–09* (HC 2009–10, 156), para. 22.

[77] Thain, 'A Very Peculiar British Crisis?' (n 51) 442.

National Savings & Investments

National Savings & Investments (NS& I) is also an executive agency of the Treasury, but has a long history as the Post Office Savings Bank, founded in 1861. It also forms part of the government's debt management arrangements and, according to its mission statement,

> [o]ur overall aim is to help reduce the cost to the taxpayer of government borrowing now and in the future. With this in mind, our single, long-term strategic objective is to provide the Government with cost-effective retail finance compared with raising funds on the wholesale market.[78]

It also has a framework document setting out relations with the Treasury.[79]

As a result of the financial crisis, the agency attracted a record amount of new business as a potentially more secure form of savings than then offered by commercial institutions. This created a dilemma due to the potential conflict between providing a good deal for its customers and supporting government macro-economic policy; indeed, it could appear too attractive to customers when the Government was attempting to re-inject confidence into the commercial banking system. The solution agreed between the agency and the Treasury was that it should cease all discretionary marketing of its services but remain open for business; it also reduced its interest rates. The Treasury Committee noted that the events showed that 'at the bottom line, the NS& I is there for the Government rather than customers', quoting the evidence of the Exchequer Secretary that '[t]he sole aim of the NS& I is to reduce cost to the taxpayer of Government borrowing now and in the future, and they do that through the sale of savings and investment products to the retail market'.[80] Two points may be taken from this; the first is that of the ubiquity of the effects of the financial crisis, the second that an executive agency is not merely a means of service delivery to customers but may play an important role in the implementation of economic policy. Since the crisis NS& I has expanded to offer business-to-business services.

The Asset Protection Agency

This was a further executive agency, owing its existence to the financial crisis. It was established in December 2009 to manage £281bn of Royal Bank of

[78] Treasury Committee, *Administration and Expenditure of the Chancellor's Departments, 2008–09* (n 76) para. 77.

[79] *NS& I Framework Document* (2009) at: <http://www.nsandi.com/files/asset/pdf/framework_document.pdf>.

[80] Treasury Committee, *Administration and Expenditure of the Chancellor's Departments, 2008–09* (n 76) para. 79.

Scotland assets which are supported by Asset Protection Scheme, effectively underwriting them on behalf of the taxpayer.[81] With the exit of Royal Bank of Scotland from the scheme, the Agency was closed at the end of October 2012.

UK Financial Investments Ltd

In addition to these executive agencies of the Treasury, there are several other bodies acting at arm's length. Government shareholdings are managed by the Shareholder Executive, sponsored by BIS and to be discussed shortly. However, special arrangements in the form of UK Financial Investments Ltd (UKFI) were made for bank investments acquired during the financial crisis. Its operations will be discussed in more detail in Chapter 8, but a little needs to be said here about the institution itself.

UKFI takes the form of a wholly-owned Government company. It manages the Government shareholdings in the Royal Bank of Scotland Group, Lloyd's Banking Group (the 'Market Investments'), and the Government's 100 per cent shareholdings in Northern Rock (Asset Management) and Bradford & Bingley, having successfully managed the sale of Northern Rock in 2011. It acts in a commercial way rather than using the holdings as a means of implementing public policy.

Relations with the Treasury are set out in a framework document which sets out a single overarching objective of developing a strategy for the disposal of investments in an orderly and active way, maximizing value for the taxpayer, financial stability, and competition. It is also emphasized that UKFI will manage investments on a commercial basis and will not intervene in the day-to-day management decisions of the companies. Principles are set out for relations with the Treasury; the latter appoints the Chairman of the Board of UKFI and two government directors, and authorizes other board appointments. The Treasury also determines UKFI's high-level objectives and budget and monitors compliance with its business plan; its consent is required for some key decisions. Finally the Treasury may give UKFI general or specific directions; the Board must comply with such directions or resign.[82] The framework document is supplemented by an investment mandate which sets out in more detail UKFI decision-making responsibilities and the extent to which Treasury approval is needed.[83] Despite its importance,

81 Black, 'The Credit Crisis and the Constitution' (n 16) 109.

82 UK Financial Investments Ltd, *UKFI Shareholder Relationship Framework Document* (2010) at: <http://www.ukfi.co.uk/releases/UKFI_FD_180110v2.pdf>.

83 UK Financial Investments Ltd, *UKFI Investment Mandate* (2010) at: <http://www.ukfi.co.uk/releases/UKFI_IM_20101001.pdf>.

UKFI is a small body, with only 12 staff. It has created a single holding company, UK Asset Resolution Ltd for its investments in Northern Rock (Asset Management) and Bradford & Bingley.

It is already clear that relations between the Treasury and UKFI are of some complexity. Particular tensions are likely to be imposed by the contrast between their private law relationship through the Treasury's role as shareholder, and its public policy responsibilities; the Treasury Select Committee in 2010 concluded that

> *[i]t appears to us that the relationship between the Treasury and UKFI remains a work in progress, and we recommend that the Government considers whether the formal terms of the relationship need some redefinition in the light of experience. It is important that the lines of demarcation are clear, and reflect the realities on the ground, not least to ensure that other shareholders are properly protected.*[84]

The same applies to UKFI's relationship with the investee companies. This issue will be examined in detail in Chapter 8.

The Royal Mint

The Royal Mint dates back centuries, but has operated as a trading fund since 1975, thus operating on commercial lines, and in 1990 became an executive agency of the Treasury. After some delays, on 31 December 2009 the Mint's assets were vested in The Royal Mint Limited, a company limited by guarantee and wholly owned by the Treasury and a subsidiary of the trading fund. The aim of this change of status was to allow the Mint to take advantage of wider commercial opportunities, including the introduction of private capital, acquisitions, and joint ventures. It is required to comply with financial objectives set by the Treasury and with other ministerial targets. It is now a target for possible privatization.

Infrastructure UK

Infrastructure UK is the successor to Partnerships UK, which played a major role in relation to the Private Finance Initiative and other forms of public/private partnership. The latter itself took the form of a public/private partnership, but Infrastructure UK is a unit within the Treasury on a smaller scale than its predecessor. Its remit is to develop a cost-cutting approach to investment in infrastructure and to support the delivery of major infrastructure projects

[84] Treasury Committee, *Administration and Expenditure of the Chancellor's Departments, 2008–09* (n 76) para. 21 (emphasis retained).

where there is capital investment from the public sector. The role and mandate of Infrastructure UK is strengthened as a result of the 2012 review of public private partnerships, to be discussed in Chapter 9.

The Shareholder Executive

Extended government is not of course limited to those bodies linked to the Treasury; BIS also has a network of related bodies in the form of nine executive agencies (including Companies House and the Insolvency Service) and no fewer than 62 partner organizations. The bodies responsible for better regulation were mentioned earlier; one other needs discussion here. The Shareholder Executive is an executive agency of the department. Its work is to manage the government's capabilities and performance as a shareholder through its portfolio of 19 businesses, ranging from the Royal Mail to the UK Hydrographic Office. It also offers corporate finance advice to a range of departmental clients across government. Such advice was important in the early stages of the financial crisis, although the shareholdings in the publicly-owned banks are administered by UKFI, as just noted.[85] In 2012 the Shareholder Executive also took responsibility for setting up the new Green Investment Bank.

Devolved Government

In addition to coverage of the UK institutions involved in economic management, brief mention must be made of the devolved government institutions in Scotland, Wales, and Northern Ireland.[86] These are relevant both in terms of their relationships with the UK Government and their own powers of economic management, some of which date back to before devolution.

The Scottish Government and Parliament have the most fully developed powers in this area. Public spending is financed through the 'Barnett Formula', by which a proportionate share of any increase or decrease in comparable English spending processes is applied to Scotland.[87] The Formula, and the fact that it is not needs based, have been subject to considerable

[85] Black, 'The Credit Crisis and the Constitution' (n 16) 105.

[86] For background, see A. McHarg, 'Devolution and the Regulatory State: Constraints and Opportunities' in D. Oliver, T. Prosser, and R. Rawlings, *The Regulatory State: Constitutional Implications* (Oxford: Oxford University Press, 2010), 67–91.

[87] For detailed description, see the Scottish Parliament Information Centre, Research Note RM 00/31 *The Barnett Formula* (2000).

criticism, though there are no immediate plans for its abolition.[88] The Scottish Parliament also has limited powers to vary income tax, but these have never been used. However, its financial powers have been increased by the Scotland Act 2012, which provides for the Scottish Parliament to set a rate of income tax for Scotland and to take over stamp duty, land tax and landfill tax. The Act also gives the Scottish Government further borrowing powers, subject to Treasury approval.[89] The Scottish Government undertakes a Spending Review, involving participation by the public and committees of the Scottish Parliament; this will be considered in more detail in Chapter 5.

Devolved government in Scotland also has major responsibilities for economic management. Thus it has ministers for Finance, Employment and Sustainable Growth, and for Enterprise, Energy and Tourism, supported by Finance and Enterprise Directorates. It also has a Council of Economic Advisors and a National Economic Forum. Importantly, its well-established development agencies, Scottish Enterprise and Highlands and Islands Enterprise, have been retained, unlike the equivalent English bodies, and these will be covered in Chapter 8. There is also a Scottish Futures Trust responsible for delivering public/private infrastructure projects and a Scottish Investment Bank.

Devolution to Wales has been in many respects more limited than that to Scotland, but it has many similar features to those just described. The Government of Wales Act 2006 was of particular importance, separating the executive and legislative arms of the National Assembly for Wales and providing for the establishment of the Welsh Government. It currently has no direct tax-levying powers, and payments are made into the Welsh Consolidated Fund by the UK Secretary of State; the Welsh Government currently has only extremely restricted borrowing powers. The UK Government now intends to devolve land fill tax and stamp duty tax in Wales, to give the Welsh Government borrowing powers for investment and to organize a referendum on whether income tax should be partially devolved. There is an annual budget process and expenditures must be supported by an annual budget resolution of the Assembly. A number of the Welsh Assembly Government's functions relate to economic management, for example infrastructure, inward investment, and business.

The case of Northern Ireland is similar in that the Assembly has no direct tax-raising powers; once more the Northern Ireland Executive is allocated funds by UK central government and undertakes a budget process to allocate

[88] See House of Lords Select Committee on the Barnett Formula, *The Barnett Formula* (HL 2008–09, 139).

[89] Scotland Act 2012, ss 23–33.

those funds; this takes the form of spending plans for three years ahead and annually. The Executive has a Department of Finance and Personnel which undertakes this exercise; it also has Departments for Enterprise, Trade and Investment and for Regional Development.

Local government

This book will not cover local government comprehensively or in detail. There are two reasons for this. The first is that it concentrates on national institutions and policy, and to cover, for example, local authority procurement or its complex financial relations with central government in detail would detract from this focus. Secondly, local government and the constitution is a matter which is covered more fully in the existing literature than the other areas covered in this book, and including them would provide unnecessary duplication.[90] However, one area needs some fuller coverage as closely bound up with central government initiatives; that of local authority support for economic development, and this will be considered in Chapter 8. Of considerable importance in this context is the gradual widening of local authority powers to engage in and support business and industrial activities, culminating in the Localism Act 2011 giving local authorities a general power of competence 'to do anything that individuals generally may do'.[91] Several major cities have also been granted extra powers to borrow for infrastructure investment and to manage some budgets. However, wider legal powers for government have been accompanied by major restrictions in central government funding for them and by the 'Big Society' theme of further outsourcing of service provision through tendering, leaving the future role of local authorities in the field of economic development uncertain. The Heseltine Review of strategy for growth has recommended a major devolution of powers of industrial support from central to local level, and the Government has accepted this recommendation. However, as we shall see in Chapter 8, funding is to be administered by Local Enterprise Partnerships rather than directly by local authorities themselves.

[90] For an introduction, see I. Leigh, 'The Changing Nature of Local and Regional Democracy' in J. Jowell and D. Oliver (eds), *The Changing Constitution*, 7th edn (Oxford: Oxford University Press, 2011), 237–59 and, for more detailed treatment, M. Loughlin, *Legality and Locality: The Role of Law in Central-Local Government Relations* (Oxford: Clarendon Press, 1996) and S.H. Bailey, 'The Structure, Powers, and Accountability of Local Government' in D. Feldman (ed.), *English Public Law*, 2nd edn (Oxford: Oxford University Press, 2009), 199–240.

[91] Localism Act 2011, s 1(1).

Scrutiny and accountability: an institutional introduction

Having outlined the complex pattern of institutions involved in processes of UK economic management, it is now necessary to say a little about those institutions which hold them accountable. Once more, this is only the briefest of introductions with more detail available in the case studies included in later chapters; coverage of the important role of the EU institutions will also be postponed until Chapter 3.

Internal scrutiny

It is well-documented that internal means of scrutiny and accountability within government are of the greatest importance in the UK, involving both the Treasury and spending departments themselves. To quote the authoritative study by Daintith and Page,

> it is in the sphere of the control of action and of the exercise of legally-recognized power that the basic structure of the United Kingdom executive has produced its most important constitutional results. The picture that emerges . . . is of a system of internal control which has been shaped by the plural structure of the executive branch, but which is in the course of significant change, largely but not solely as a result of the public service reforms pursued by successive governments over the last twenty years.[92]

As they emphasize, in the past such internal control was based on a recognition of considerable departmental autonomy; in particular, unlike in France or Italy, responsibility for compliance was placed on departments themselves rather than being the tasks of Treasury representatives in the spending departments.[93] This worked in tandem with the arrangements for parliamentary audit.

The quotation from Daintith and Page acknowledges, however, that the decentralization is subject to considerable change, and this has continued in more recent years. In particular, two developments have potential for injecting greater coherence into processes for internal scrutiny. The first is that of the Spending Review process. Not only does this attempt to assess spending needs in a more far-reaching and unified way, it is associated with reforms in the public sector seeking greater efficiency. This was particularly striking where the Review was linked to PSAs setting objectives and targets for

[92] Daintith and Page *The Executive in the Constitution* (n 5) 380–1.
[93] Daintith and Page *The Executive in the Constitution* (n 5) 382.

departments; these have now been replaced by departmental business plans which also permit assessment of performance, as does the introduction of resource accounting. More will be said on developments linked to the Spending Review in Chapter 5. Secondly, the regulatory reform agenda has also provided a means of internal assessment of performance in several ways. These include the development of principles of good regulation and the requirement of regulatory impact analysis; this emphasis on better regulation has existed alongside the stress on less regulation also characteristic of regulatory reform, although with the more recent move to a 'one-in, two-out' approach the latter has become more dominant.[94] In some cases regulatory reform has produced statutory references to principles of good regulation, for example, in the case of the new financial services regulators to be discussed in Chapter 7.[95]

Audit and parliamentary scrutiny

As we shall see in Chapters 4 and 5, Parliament, or more precisely the House of Commons, has, as a matter of constitutional principle, major powers in relation to the raising of taxation and the spending of public funds; the development of these powers was indeed a central reason for the UK's last civil war in the seventeenth century. For the moment it should merely be noted that, especially in relation to expenditure, Parliament's powers of advance scrutiny are minimal, and what is of far greater importance is its power of scrutiny of spending *ex post facto* and the drawing of future lessons from it.

The most important institution for parliamentary scrutiny is the National Audit Office (NAO), which is headed by the Comptroller and Auditor-General, an officer of Parliament; it is wholly independent of government. The Auditor-General is required to examine and certify the accounts of government departments and many other public bodies; rights of access to non-departmental bodies have been considerably extended in recent years. Even more importantly for the purposes of this work, the NAO is empowered to undertake value for money examinations of departments and other public bodies; these assess the 'economy, efficiency and effectiveness' of the use of resources.[96] The NAO has also had an important role in the regulatory reform initiatives, for example through examination of impact

[94] For a summary see Prosser, *The Regulatory Enterprise* (n 53) ch. 10; see also the Enterprise and Regulatory Reform Act 2013.

[95] Financial Services Act 2012, s 6, adding a new s 3B to the Financial Services and Markets Act 2000.

[96] National Audit Act 1983, s 6; see J. McEldowney, 'Public Expenditure and the Control of Public Finance' in J. Jowell and D. Oliver, *The Changing Constitution*, 7th edn (Oxford: Oxford University Press, 2011), 334–64, 359–6.

assessment processes and reviews of the extent to which regulatory bodies have met the criteria set out in the Hampton Report on reducing administrative burdens.[97] In 2010 the NAO published 151 reports, in 2011 124, and in 2012 131, including examinations of the Asset Protection Scheme, bank support, the Private Finance Initiative, and Ministry of Defence major projects. As we shall see in later chapters, the reports will be of great importance for the subjects examined in detail in this book. There are also similar arrangements for audit in Scotland, Wales, and Northern Ireland.[98] For example, Audit Scotland and the Auditor-General for Scotland have similar powers to those of the National Audit Office and Comptroller and Auditor-General.[99]

Selected reports from the NAO are considered by the Committee of Public Accounts (PAC), the oldest and most prestigious of the parliamentary select committees; it examines both whether expenditure has been properly occurred and its value for money, producing about 50 reports per year. These are debated twice a year by the House of Commons, and provide both an important source of information and guidance for the future. Together with the NAO, the Committee is the nearest we have to a Cour des Comptes characteristic of Continental jurisdictions and responsible for financial and good governance audit of government.

We shall see frequently in later chapters that other select committees of Parliament have also played a central role in scrutiny of decisions relating to economic management. Of particular importance are the departmental select committees responsible for examining the 'expenditure, administration and policy' of government departments and their associated public bodies, the latter term permitting examination of non-departmental public bodies appointed by ministers. The Treasury Committee in particular will be frequently referred to in this book, having conducted examinations of the Spending Review process, the response to the banking crisis, reform of financial services regulation, and many other important areas of economic management.[100] In 2002 a Scrutiny Unit was established to provide the

[97] See E. Humpherson, 'Auditing Regulatory Reform' in D. Oliver, T. Prosser, and R. Rawlings, *The Regulatory State: Constitutional Implications* (Oxford: Oxford University Press, 2010), 267–82.

[98] For a summary, see A. Brazier and V. Ram, *The Fiscal Maze: Parliament, Government and Public Money* (London: Hansard Society, 2006), ch. 7; the Public Audit (Wales) Act 2013 has strengthened the arrangements there, creating a Wales Audit Office.

[99] See T. Mullen and T. Prosser, 'Financing and Auditing Scottish Government: The Public Finance and Accountability (Scotland) Act 2000' (2001) 7 *European Public Law* 157–64.

[100] See e.g. Treasury Committee, *Spending Review 2010* (HC 2010–12, 544); *Banking Crisis: Dealing with the Failure of the UK Banks* (HC 2008–09, 416); *Financial Regulation: a Preliminary Consideration of the Government's Proposals* (HC 2010–11, 430).

committees with specialist support analogous to that provided on a much larger scale to the PAC by the NAO. One particular area of importance in the Unit's work is that of financial scrutiny, and this fills a major gap due to lack of specialist expertise. The select committees have also increasingly sought to play a more forward-looking role through examining draft legislation and reporting on persons appointed to major public positions, including membership of the Monetary Policy Committee. The reports on appointments do not carry with them any right of veto, although a precedent is created by the Budget Responsibility and National Audit Act 2011, which gives the Treasury Committee such a veto over the appointment of the Chairman and some members of the Office for Budget Responsibility.

The courts and administrative justice

The area of economic management by central government is one in which the courts have traditionally been reluctant to intervene by judicial review, and this has been especially so in relation to decisions involving discretionary resource allocation.[101] Thus 'the levels of public expenditure and the incidence and distribution of taxation are matters for Parliament'.[102] This stands in marked contrast to their attitude to local government expenditure where they have been at times highly interventionist, developing the concept of a fiduciary duty towards those funding expenditure and interpreting the concept of ultra vires strictly.[103] The courts also took a much stricter approach to the imposition of taxation (as distinct from the formulation of general tax policy), where the direct impact on traditional property rights has provided a much clearer point of entry for judicial control of government.[104] There have been recent signs that they are now in principle prepared to take a role in other fields of economic management whilst still showing considerable deference to public authorities on matters of economic policy and detailed management.[105] This has partly been due to the general growth of a more

[101] R. Rawlings, 'Changed Conditions, Old Truths: Judicial Review in a Regulatory Laboratory' in D. Oliver, T. Prosser, and R. Rawlings, *The Regulatory State: Constitutional Implications* (Oxford: Oxford University Press, 2010), 283–305; J.A. King, 'The Justiciability of Resource Allocation' (2007) 70(2) *Modern Law Review* 197–224.

[102] *Nottinghamshire County Council v Secretary of State for the Environment* [1986] AC 240, per Lord Scarman at 250.

[103] See e.g. *Bromley London Borough Council v Greater London Council* [1983] AC 768, *Hazell v Hammersmith London Borough Council* [1992] 2 AC 1; *Credit Suisse v Allerdale Borough Council* [1997] QB 306.

[104] See e.g. *Bowles v Bank of England* [1913] 1 Ch 57; *AG v Wilts United Dairies Ltd* (1921) 37 TLR 884; *Congreve v Home Office* [1976] QB 629.

[105] See Rawlings, 'Changed Conditions, Old Truths' (n 101) esp. 282–3, 299.

searching form of judicial review, strongly facilitated by the Human Rights Act 1998, but also due to their growing confidence in handling material far removed from the traditional subject-matter of judicial review.

A few turning points are worth mentioning. One of considerable importance was the case of *Datafin* in which the Court of Appeal held that decisions of the Takeover Panel were subject to judicial review despite the lack of any statutory basis for the Panel's decisions; what was important was that it was performing a public duty, its decisions affected the rights of citizens, and were underpinned by the statutory powers of government.[106] The court did, however, emphasize that on substance it would be slow to intervene. Of similar importance was the decision in the 'Pergau Dam' case.[107] Apart from confirming a much enlarged concept of standing permitting challenges to be brought by interested pressure groups, the court was prepared to hold unlawful the use of a power to promote economic development to finance a project which was fundamentally economically unsound. One general problem limiting the scope of review was that the courts treated powers of intervention labelled contractual as essentially private matters and so outside the scope of judicial review.[108] This restriction also now seems to have loosened, perhaps influenced by the growing role of the High Court in procurement matters as a result of the remedies sought there under the EU public contracts rules (see Chapter 9).[109]

Apart from the role of judicial review, the arrangements for statutory appeals from regulatory bodies to the courts are messy and incoherent; some appeals lie to the courts, some to tribunals, and the scope of the appeals varies widely.[110] There are, however, some signs of greater coherence developing, permitting a greater degree of intervention by the appellate authorities. The most important is the right of appeal to the Competition Appeal Tribunal from decisions of the competition authorities and some decisions of economic regulators. In many cases this appeal is on the merits; in others it is limited to grounds similar to those for judicial review, but the Tribunal has taken a generous approach to its powers.[111] In a number of cases, the

[106] *R v Panel on Takeovers and Mergers, ex parte Datafin plc* [1987] QB 815.

[107] *R v Secretary of State for Foreign and Commonwealth Affairs, ex parte the World Development Movement Ltd* [1995] 1 WLR 386; for detailed analysis, see I. Harden, F. White, and K. Hollingsworth, 'Value for Money and Administrative Law' [1996] *Public Law* 661–81.

[108] See *R v Lord Chancellor, ex parte Hibbit and Saunders* [1993] COD 326.

[109] For willingness to intervene on a matter characterized as the procurement of services through contract, see *R (the Law Society) v Legal Services Commission* [2010] EWHC 2550 (Admin).

[110] See T. Prosser, 'The Place of Appeals in Regulation: Continuity and Change' in P. Vass (ed.), *Regulatory Review 2004/5* (Centre for the Study of Regulated Industries, 2005), 195–212.

[111] See *Office of Fair Trading v IBA Health Ltd* [2004] EWCA Civ 142, [2004] 4 All ER 1103; Rawlings, 'Changed Conditions, Old Truths' (n 101) 302–3.

Tribunal has had to consider in detail complex matters involving economic analysis.[112]

In addition to the development of the Competition Appeal Tribunal, the general tribunal system was subject to rationalization under the Tribunals, Courts and Enforcement Act 2007, establishing new First-tier and Upper Tribunals.[113] The First-tier Tribunal includes a Tax Chamber (tax decisions have always attracted developed rights of appeal for those assessed) and a General Regulatory Chamber. The latter handles a variety of different matters, for example appeals against civil penalties imposed by regulators under the Regulatory Enforcement and Sanctions Act 2008, and may in future provide the basis for a unified regulatory appeals system.

Finally, a number of ombudsmen handle grievances in the areas to be discussed in this book. Apart from the general work of the Parliamentary Ombudsman, the Financial Services Ombudsman has played a major role, receiving over two million complaints and inquiries and resolving over 200,000 formal disputes in 2012–13. In some individual areas to be discussed in this book, we shall also see examples of other forms of dispute resolution machinery, for example the work of the Adjudicator's Office in tax.

Conclusion

It should now be obvious that there is a bewildering range of different bodies engaged in economic management. This may not in itself be a bad thing; as we shall see when we discuss the restrictions on the use of agencies by the European Commission in Chapter 3, over-restrictive constitutional norms may seriously hinder the opportunity to react effectively to changing governance requirements. Moreover,

> the formal and operational autonomy of the bodies within the extended executive has the potential to operate as an internal system of checks and balances that operates not as a system of post hoc accountability structures but as a system of co-decision-making and polycentric regulation. There are significant interdependencies between them, but each has a different remit, and as such each had and has different and potentially conflicting interests that it sought to pursue, and continues to pursue.[114]

[112] For a rehearing involving such detailed economic analysis, see *Albion Water Ltd v Water Services Regulation Authority* [2006] CAT 23.

[113] For discussion, see Rawlings, 'Changed Conditions, Old Truths' (n 101) 287.

[114] Black, 'The Credit Crisis and the Constitution' (n 16) 113.

This may come with a cost, particularly in times of crisis; that of policy and administrative incoherence and conflict. At the top of Government this was shown by the collapse of the tripartite system during the financial crisis, and the role of personalized politics in blocking communication, notably between the Chancellor and the Bank of England.[115] The new arrangements for coordination in financial services regulation are also highly complex and have yet to be tested. In relation to the other bodies examined here, there have been some attempts to develop structured arrangements for coordination and communication in response to earlier criticisms of relations between departments and their agencies, for example through the better use of framework documents and memoranda of understanding, but the coverage of these is often patchy. What is very evident is that the economic constitution in the sense of the allocation of powers is not one of governing principle, but rather a highly complex empirical reality. Its operation can thus only be properly examined in the particular contexts covered in the later chapters.

The danger is thus one of conflict of policies and administration rather than mutual learning, and of the absence of any effective overview of the system. This is emphasized by the lack of fit between the different institutions and the arrangements for scrutiny and accountability. Both the Spending Review process and the regulatory reform agenda have potential for increasing institutional coordination and internal scrutiny, but, as we shall see, this has yet to be fully realized. The problem is less serious owing to the wide range of bodies subject to select committee scrutiny and the less formalistic approach by the courts to the scope of their judicial review jurisdiction in recent years. However, scrutiny itself is also a fragmented area, with little scope for collaboration between the courts and Parliament in developing complementary means for holding government accountable. This is to be contrasted, for example, with the decisions of the German Federal Constitutional Court, mentioned in Chapter 1, requiring financial scrutiny of expenditure by the Bundestag's Budget Committee. The Court used constitutional norms to require a form of prior parliamentary scrutiny which is lacking in the UK, as we shall see. Nor in the UK are there the 'accountability networks' identified by Harlow and Rawlings as emerging in EU governance.[116]

[115] See Thain, 'A Very Peculiar British Crisis?' (n 51) 448 and in general Darling, *Back from the Brink* (n 12).

[116] C. Harlow and R. Rawlings, 'Promoting Accountability in Multilevel Governance: A Network Approach' (2007) 13 *European Law Journal* 542–62.

It was suggested in Chapter 1 that a function of a constitution is to provide some degree of coherence in the organization of public power. An overview of the institutions for economic management and their scrutiny suggests that this is very much lacking in the UK, and that this has given rise to problems, as shown vividly in the response to the economic crisis. The international context adds several further layers of complexity to those already described.

3

The International Context

It should be unnecessary to state that the international context is of fundamental importance, shaping outcomes in many of the most important areas of economic management; much of the UK's economic constitution can be found in international sources. More precisely, the international context may act both as a constraint and a resource for national governments. Many important measures will require international agreement (once more illustrated in the response to the financial crisis and especially in relation to the sovereign debt crisis); other international obligations will limit the scope for national action, for example through restrictions on the provision of state aid. At the outset it should be noted, however, that, despite the existence of these constraints, considerable space remains for flexibility and national discretion. Moreover, the international context can also provide a resource for the UK Government. International negotiations may provide the basis of a deeper anchoring of policies than would be permitted under purely national arrangements, and may be of considerable assistance to governments seeking to engage in economic liberalization.[1] Particularly important examples illustrating this will be competition law, state aid, and public procurement. The dual nature of the international context has been illustrated vividly in the sovereign debt crisis, where it acts both as a constraint on the ability of national governments to tax and spend (and, in the eurozone, has the potential to form a new substantive economic constitution) and as a resource for governments seeking to impose fiscal discipline.

Of course, the international context does not consist solely of *legal* constraints on government. The role of international financial markets is central to determining the scope for policy development and the extent of public provision in national economies. This has been most evident in the case of the serious problems of some eurozone economies, particularly Greece, but has also been clear in the UK in controlling public expenditure and the timing of deficit reduction. Of course, there is nothing new in this; financial markets

[1] See D. Nicol, *The Constitutional Protection of Capitalism* (Oxford: Hart Publishing, 2010).

have long had such a major effect on national policies, notably in limiting the options of Labour Governments in the 1960s and 1970s. However, recent crises and the size of public debt have brought their role into sharp relief. This theme, including the role of credit rating agencies, will be more fully examined in Chapters 4 and 5, which will examine public borrowing and public expenditure control in the UK, but the role of the markets is also of massive importance internationally.

The European Union

In discussing the international context of the UK economic constitution, it is obvious that our starting point must be the law and policies of the EU. There is irony in this given the failure of the attempt to create a more explicitly constitutional basis for the EU via the Constitutional Treaty produced in 2003 by the Constitutional Convention, but subsequently rejected by referenda in France and the Netherlands. Nevertheless, the existing regimes for the single market and in other areas do clearly create a form of constitution for economic life:

> [t]he economic constitutional order that results from the Treaty of Rome may also be a good example of... [the] category of constitutions with an economic bite. According to the interpretation given by the European Court of Justice, economic integration and the constitutional provisions in pursuance thereof (competition and free movement) constitute effective limits on the conduct of governments, legislature and private actors.[2]

The form and nature of the European economic constitution have been much debated, but one important point needs to be made here. Although its commitment to competition and market freedoms is clear, there is still considerable scope for different, contested versions of the constitution, for example as to the extent to which competition law can be balanced against the provision of universal public services.[3] There are also differences based on divergent national traditions of the role of the market. The point was illustrated in the European Council meeting of June 2007 designed to rescue

[2] J. Baquero Cruz, *Between Competition and Free Movement: The Economic Constitutional Law of the European Community* (Oxford: Hart Publishing, 2002), 33. See also the essays in the special issue on 'La Constitution Economique Europèene Revisitée' (2011) XXV(4) *Revue Internationale de Droit Economique* 411–599.

[3] See T. Prosser, *The Limits of Competition Law: Markets and Public Services* (Oxford: Oxford University Press, 2005), chs 6–8; K. Tuori, 'La Constitution Economique Parmi les Constitutions Européenes' (2011) XXV *Revue Internationale de Droit Economique* 559–99.

parts of the draft Constitutional Treaty. The French President achieved what was perceived as the major coup of removing the draft Treaty's inclusion of free and undistorted competition as an objective of the Union. This was partly the result of a perception that the draft was too 'Anglo-Saxon' and threatened public services based on citizenship; it was greeted with outrage in the UK and by some competition lawyers. However, both market-based principles and those of solidarity have long appeared in EU law and the balance between them has always been contested and potentially politically incendiary. The Treaty on European Union (TEU), after setting out social values including human rights and solidarity, now refers to 'a highly competitive social market economy, aiming at full employment and social progress' and to the combating of social exclusion and discrimination and promotion of economic, social, and territorial cohesion.[4] Free competition is now referred to in article 119 of the Treaty on the Functioning of the European Union (TFEU) as a means of achieving the purposes set out in the TEU. Moreover, the important article stating that the Treaty in no way prejudices national rules relating to property ownership remains; however, as we shall see competition and state aid rules impose constraints on the operation of public enterprises. The fiscal pact attempting to resolve the sovereign debt crisis comes much closer than previous initiatives to imposing a particular model of economic management on eurozone Member States.

Enforcement and accountability

EU law is given a particular constitutional status in Member States through the doctrines of direct effect and supremacy, developed early on by the European Court of Justice (ECJ). These do not need full discussion here, but in essence directly effective rights under EU law may be invoked in the domestic courts of Member States and those courts have a duty to apply them.[5] EU law also prevails over any incompatible law in the Member States.[6] Moreover, all national law must be interpreted in accordance with EU law.[7] In combination, these principles offer far more effective opportunities for enforcement than those of other international regimes, and mean that EU law pervades national law much more directly and extensively than

[4] Arts 2–3; see also the Treaty on the Functioning of the European Union, arts 8–14, 119, 318.

[5] The leading case is Case 26/62 *van Gend en Loos* [1963] ECR 1.

[6] The principle was established in Case 6/64 *Costa v ENEL* [1964] ECR 585. For the UK position, see *R v Secretary of State for Transport, ex parte Factortame (No 2)* [1991] AC 603.

[7] Case C-106/89 *Marleasing* [1990] ECR I-4135.

does any other form of international law. Many areas of regulation are in essence governed by EU rather than domestic law.

EU law also of course has its own enforcement mechanisms against Member States. The central role in enforcement is that of the European Commission, which may ultimately take action before the ECJ against a Member State; other Member States may also bring an action before the Court.[8] Enforcement by the Commission has been of particular importance in the competition law field, although this is now shared with national competition authorities and courts as a result of decentralization in 2004.[9] It should also be added that in some circumstances Member States may be directly liable for damages for failure properly to implement EU law.[10] Thus the arrangements for coordination of EU law and the actions of Member States are far more developed than in the case of other international bodies.

There are serious problems of accountability in EU governance.[11] In particular, the parliamentary forms of accountability so central, at least in theory, to the UK Constitution are largely absent.[12] By contrast, judicial review by the General Court and the ECJ is highly developed and has played a particularly strong role in relation to competition law, where resort to review is frequent and the Court has been prepared to adopt demanding standards in examining decisions of the Commission.[13] As with national systems, audit is also of importance; rather than being carried out through parliamentary bodies as in the UK, it is the task of the European Court of Auditors which examines the legality and regularity of EU income and expenditure and attempts to ensure that there has been sound financial management; this may include value for money audit.[14] Finally, in some circumstances there may be liability in damages by EU institutions for a sufficiently serious breach of duty.[15]

Taken together, these various elements in the general constitutional law of the EU will have a major effect in relation to management of the economy. The economic freedoms, notably freedom of movement of goods and services, are of particular importance, as is the central role of the internal market.

[8] TFEU, arts 258–60; for discussion, see C. Harlow, *Accountability in the European Union* (Oxford: Oxford University Press, 2002), 71–4.

[9] Council Regulation 1/2003 implementing Arts 81 and 82 [2003] OJ L1/1; see A. Jones and B. Sufrin, *EU Competition Law*, 4th edn (Oxford: Oxford University Press, 2011), Ch. 14.

[10] See Cases 6/90 and 9/90 *Francovich and Bonifaci v Italy* [1991] ECR I-5357.

[11] For general discussion, see Harlow, *Accountability in the European Union* (n 8).

[12] See Harlow, *Accountability in the European Union* (n 8) Ch. 4.

[13] See Jones and Sufrin, *EU Competition Law* (n 9) 1131–52.

[14] TFEU, arts 285–7; Harlow, *Accountability in the European Union* (n 8) ch 5.

[15] TFEU, art. 340.

These will not, however, be discussed in detail here as they have been subject to extensive analysis elsewhere.[16] Instead I shall here concentrate on some particular areas of especial relevance to the processes of economic management discussed in this book. I shall begin with discussion of areas of fiscal and monetary policy, where the direct impact of EU policy is relatively limited in the UK; the domestic position will be covered in detail in Chapters 4–6. As we shall see, although the new fiscal pact in the Treaty on Stability, Coordination and Governance and monetary union do not apply directly to the UK, they do have important national implications, both because of economic interdependence within the single market and because they are linked to other mechanisms which are applicable.

Taxation, borrowing, and the sovereign debt crisis

The role of the EU has been fundamental to many areas involving taxes through the basic requirement of the common market for the withdrawal of tariff barriers, now contained in article 28 TFEU. There is, however, no fully harmonized tax regime, and in relation to direct taxation there is no prospect of one, although Member States must not discriminate on the basis of nationality in relation to tax matters and must respect the basic Treaty principles on free movement of workers, of services and of capital, and freedom of establishment. In the case of indirect taxation, article 113 TFEU provides for harmonization as necessary for the internal market and to avoid distortion of competition, and extensive secondary legislation has been issued to secure it. This includes setting minimum rates for VAT, although the very wide derogations to these provisions prevent a coherent system of rates from being established across the EU. There is also extensive provision for mutual assistance and administrative cooperation between Member States in the fields of both direct and indirect taxes, and most recently in relation to tax evasion.

Turning to borrowing and public expenditure, the Stability and Growth Pact was adopted in 1997, together with an excessive deficit procedure.[17] The Pact was based around a reference value for the existence of an excessive deficit of 3 per cent of gross domestic product and a debt-to-GDP ratio of 60 per cent. Scrutiny of national fiscal performance is undertaken by the

[16] For fuller discussion, see e.g. Maduro, *We the Court: The European Court of Justice and the European Economic Constitution* (Oxford: Hart Publishing, 1998); Cruz, *Between Competition and Free Movement* (n2), and C. Barnard and J. Scott (eds), *The Law of the Single European Market: Unpacking the Premises* (Oxford: Hart Publishing, 2002).

[17] See TFEU, art. 126 and Protocol (No 12) TFEU on the Excessive Deficit Procedure and Council Regulation 1467/97 on speeding up and clarifying the implementation of the excessive deficit procedure OJ [1997] L209/6.

Commission, and the ECOFIN Council can determine that an excessive deficit exists in a Member State. If it does so, it may issue recommendations to the Member State; if these are not complied with, the Council may impose penalties or fines and invite the European Investment Bank to reconsider its policies towards the Member State. No sanctions may be issued in relation to the UK because of its opt-out from full monetary union, although it will still 'endeavour to avoid an excessive government deficit' and the Commission scrutinizes its performance and may issue a report to the Council.[18] The Stability and Growth Pact proved, however, extraordinarily ineffective, mainly because it had been breached in 2003 by Germany and France which had successfully resisted the imposition of any sanctions. By 2012 all the eurozone countries had been made subject to the excessive deficit procedure with the exception of Luxembourg, Finland, and Estonia, and it had been initiated for the UK with a report by the Commission in 2008.

The sovereign debt crisis resulted in major reform.[19] One response was the establishment of the European Financial Stabilisation Mechanism and European Financial Stability Facility for the provision of loans to Member States in difficulty based on article 122(2) TFEU, which applies where a Member State is seriously threatened with severe difficulties caused by exceptional occurrences beyond its control. A permanent European Stability Mechanism to provide temporary stability support to Member States in the eurozone, subject to strict conditionality, was agreed by a Treaty signed by the eurozone members in 2012, and its legality was upheld by the ECJ.[20] The Stability and Growth Pact was strengthened through the so-called 'six pack' of legislative measures adopted at the end of 2011, and a 'European Semester' involves greater reflexion of EU priorities in national fiscal frameworks through review by the Commission.[21] However, the system still contains considerable flexibility, and in 2013 the deadlines for correcting the excessive deficit were extended for six states, including France and Spain.

For the eurozone, the most important constitutional reform is the fiscal pact implemented in the Treaty on Stability, Coordination and Governance.[22] At

[18] Protocol (No 15) TFEU on certain provisions relating to the United Kingdom of Great Britain and Northern Ireland, arts 4–5.

[19] For an excellent account, see the House of Lords European Union Committee, *The Euro Area Crisis* (HL 2010–12, 260).

[20] Treaty Establishing the European Stability Mechanism, T/ESM 2012/en1, and see TFEU, art. 136 as amended; Case C-370/12 *Thomas Pringle v Government of Ireland*.

[21] Regulation 1175/2011 amending Council Regulation EC No 1455/97 on the strengthening of the surveillance of budgetary positions and the surveillance and coordination of economic policies [2011] OJ L306/12.

[22] Treaty on Stability, Coordination and Governance in the Economic and Monetary Union (2012). For the background and analysis, see House of Lords European Union Committee, *The*

the Summit in December 2011 the UK refused to accept Treaty amendments without concessions on other policies, notably the regulation of financial services, and so a new intergovernmental treaty was drafted between 25 Member States, excluding the UK and the Czech Republic; this was signed in March 2012. The provisions of the Treaty, which applies to eurozone members and other Member States which join the Euro or agree to be bound, appear extraordinarily far-reaching. The Treaty sets out a fiscal compact, which will require Member States covered by the Treaty to achieve a balanced budget with a structural deficit which must not exceed 0.5 per cent of GDP. There must also be an automatic correction mechanism should a state deviate from a country-specific medium-term objective for achieving this. These rules must take effect in national law 'through provisions of binding force and permanent character, preferably constitutional, or otherwise guaranteed to be fully respected and adhered to throughout the national budget processes'.[23] This requirement is to be enforced by the European Court of Justice.[24] There is, however, an exception to the fiscal rules in the case of an unusual event outside the control of the Member State or periods of severe economic downturn, so long as this does not endanger fiscal stability in the medium term. The Treaty also provides that, where the ratio of debt to GDP exceeds 60 per cent, it must be reduced by an average of one-twentieth per year. Further provisions deal with enhanced policy coordination between the Member States subject to the Treaty, including discussion *ex ante* with the Commission of all major economic policy reforms.

This could be seen as the ultimate attempt to create an economic constitution limiting political action and choices; indeed, even the *Financial Times* has criticized it as 'a legalistic hammer to club down politics wherever it rears its unpredictable head'.[25] However, the Treaty falls short in some ways from a full constitutional balanced budget requirement.[26] Thus, as mentioned earlier, the key provision which requires implementation in national law is subject to a qualification in some economic circumstances. Moreover, a qualified majority of eurozone members may overrule Commission proposals based on breach of the deficit criterion, and this may permit larger countries

Euro Area Crisis (n 19), Ch. 5 and P. Craig, 'The Stability, Coordination and Governance Treaty: Principle, Politics and Pragmatism' (2012) 37 *European Law Review* 231–48.

[23] Treaty on Stability, Coordination and Governance in the Economic and Monetary Union, art. 3(2).

[24] Treaty on Stability, Coordination and Governance in the Economic and Monetary Union, art. 8.

[25] 'Law meets politics', Leader, *The Financial Times*, 7 March 2012.

[26] See Craig, 'The Stability, Coordination and Governance Treaty' (n 22), 235–9.

in effect to agree to opt out, as they did from the Stability and Growth Pact.[27] Secondly, there is a difference between adopting a balanced budget rule as a matter of general constitutional principle, and strengthening the rules of the eurozone, which Member States entered voluntarily and has since proved to have been subject to fundamental flaws. There is of course no question of extending the new Treaty to countries not in the eurozone; the role of the Stability and Growth Pact will be examined further in the context of public borrowing in Chapter 4.

Monetary policy and the European Central Bank

The area of monetary policy is another in which the EU role is of major importance, even while the UK remains outside the eurozone and so sets its own interest rates through a process to be described in Chapter 6.[28]

The mandate of the European System of Central Banks (the ESCB, which comprises the European Central Bank and the national banks of the EU Member States) is set out in article 127 TFEU. It is to maintain price stability through the control of inflation; note that this does not include the maintenance of financial stability, which is not considered by the Bank to be part of its core mandate.[29] Subject to this, the ESCB is to support the general economic policies of the EU. Article 130 of the Treaty prohibits the European Central Bank (ECB) and national central banks from taking instructions from Union institutions or the governments of Member States. The UK has an opt-out from these provisions, although, as we shall see in Chapter 6, the current legal position of the Bank of England has some major similarities to them. The ECB has a Governing Council comprising its Executive Board and governors of the national central banks of eurozone members; its tasks include the definition and implementation of monetary policy for the eurozone, the conduct of foreign exchange operations and the management of the foreign reserves of eurozone members, and the operation of payment systems. The major decisions are taken by the Governing Council. There have been serious criticisms of the lack of accountability of the ECB, especially because, unlike the Monetary Policy Committee of the Bank of England, it had strongly resisted pressures to publish minutes of the meetings in which it

[27] Treaty on Stability, Coordination and Governance in the Economic and Monetary Union, art. 7.

[28] For an excellent discussion of the background, see T. Daintith, 'Between Domestic Democracy and an Alien Rule of Law? Some Thoughts on the "Independence" of the Bank of England' [1995] *Public Law* 118–32.

[29] House of Lords European Union Committee, *The Euro Area Crisis* (n 19) para. 55.

takes monetary policy decisions, though in 2013 this resistance was weakening with plans for greater transparency being drawn up, and tentative moves were made towards pre-commitment to lower interest rates for an extended period.[30] In the absence of published minutes, the ECB claims to be accountable through the organization of a monthly press conference to explain decisions on monetary policy, and through the publication of a monthly bulletin and annual reports. The Bank can also be held accountable by the European Parliament through reporting and through quarterly hearings before the Parliament's Committee on Monetary Affairs.[31] It is subject to judicial review before the European courts.[32]

Apart from monetary policy, and despite its narrow mandate, the ECB and the ESCB have other major responsibilities in the field of economic management. Thus the ECB publishes a Financial Stability Review twice a year setting out potential sources of risk and stability for the eurozone. The Bank also played an important role in rescues during the sovereign debt crisis through the European Financial Stability Facility, for example through suspending the minimum threshold for the use of Greek bonds as collateral, thereby giving the Greek Government access to further finance. Importantly, it has provided massive loans to European banks to enhance liquidity; by March 2012 banks had been loaned no less than 1 trillion Euro for three years at only 1 per cent interest. These loans proved successful in relieving pressure on the banks and financial markets. The Bank also announced that, if necessary, it would undertake unlimited 'outright monetary transactions' to buy government bonds in order to reduce borrowing costs, an announcement that had a substantial effect in easing market conditions for the countries experiencing a sovereign debt crisis, and which is subject to controversial constitutional challenge in Germany.

EU competition law

EU competition law is of enormous importance and is highly developed; indeed, its principles now form the basis for national systems throughout the capitalist world (including the UK). Indeed, it can be seen as the central ordoliberal-inspired core of the EU economic constitution.[33] Competition

[30] See Harlow, *Accountability in the European Union* (n 8) 47–52.

[31] For a summary of the position, see 'The Accountability of the ECB', *ECB Monthly Bulletin* (November 2002), 45–57.

[32] TFEU, art. 263.

[33] See J. Drexl, 'La constitution économique européenne—l'actualité du modèle ordolibéral' (2011) XXV *Revue Internationale de Droit Economique* 419–54.

law might at first sight appear of limited relevance to a book examining *state* management of the economy given that it is applied to *undertakings* engaged in economic activity. These may be public or private, but the main thrust of the law is concerned with the operation of markets rather than state action, and the competition rules cannot be applied directly to measures adopted by Member States. However, the rules may have important indirect implications for state intervention, and are applied to undertakings (public or private) which have been entrusted with the performance of public functions.[34]

As regards the application of the rules to the state, the EU does not have a simple equivalent to the US 'State action doctrine' establishing an immunity for the States from competition law, and it may in some circumstances be applied to public action.[35] There are a number of ways in which this application may be required. First, and of least importance, is what is now article 37 TFEU, requiring adjustment of state monopolies to avoid discrimination between nationals of Member States; it has rarely been used and is now in practice supplanted by other articles. Secondly, there is a general duty on Member States under article 4(3) TEU to 'facilitate the achievement of the Union's tasks and refrain from any measure which could jeopardise the attainment of the Union's objectives'. Finally, there is the application of the competition rules through article 106(1). This article is addressed to Member States, and prohibits them, in the case of public undertakings and undertakings to which they grant special or exclusive rights, from enacting or maintaining in force any measure contrary to the competition rules. These rules prohibit anti-competitive agreements between undertakings and concerted practices (article 101 TFEU), and abuse of a dominant position by an undertaking (article 102 TFEU). The overall effect is that a Member State will be prohibited from requiring or favouring agreements or concerted practices which infringe article 101, from delegating decisions to private operators which affect the private sphere and are anti-competitive, and from placing an undertaking in a position of economic strength enabling it to behave to an appreciable extent independently of its competitors, customers, and consumers.[36] These categories are not closed, but there has been no wholesale application of the competition rules to states themselves, only to state action which reinforces or supports private behaviour.[37]

[34] For a detailed summary of this area, see Jones and Sufrin, *EU Competition Law* (n 9) Ch. 8.

[35] Cruz, *Between Competition and Free Movement* (n 2) 127–8.

[36] Cruz, *Between Competition and Free Movement* (n 2) 154; for a judicial summary, see Case 153/93 *Delta Schiffahrts-Und Speditionsgesellschaft* [1994] ECR I-2157, para. 14.

[37] Maduro, *We the Court* (n 16) 75.

A related issue is that of the application of the competition rules not to the core state but to undertakings, public or private, which are entrusted with the provision of a public service.[38] It is important to distinguish two questions which are often confused; the scope of application of the competition rules and their possible qualification. The rules apply to undertakings engaged in economic activity. This excludes a number of important activities, notably those which are part of the 'intrinsic prerogatives of the state' and not provided for remuneration, and activities such as social security systems organized on a basis of social solidarity.[39] An example of this doctrine can also be seen in the case of *FENIN*, in which it was held that purchasing supplies for a solidarity-based organization (a national health service) was not covered by the competition rules.[40] The decisions have important implications for the management of public services; should a Member State decide that they are best provided on a non-market, solidarity-based system, the competition rules will not be applicable. However, if the state introduces market competition to a system, it will then have to play by the competition rules.

Even if these rules are applicable, there is an important qualification contained in TFEU article 106(2). This states that

> [u]ndertakings entrusted with the operation of services of general economic interest... shall be subject to the rules contained in this Treaty, in particular to the rules on competition, insofar as the application of such rules does not obstruct the performance, in law or in fact, of the particular tasks assigned to them. The development of trade must not be affected to such an extent as would be contrary to the interests of the Union.

The effect of this provision has been controversial, with extensive case law from the EU courts interpreting it.[41] In brief, it is for the Member State to determine what constitutes a service of general economic interest and to determine the mission of the service provider, which must be clearly defined. This is subject to a test of 'manifest error' applied by the Commission and the courts. In applying the test of whether full application of the rules of competition law would obstruct the performance of the tasks assigned to the undertaking, the test is one of proportionality. The Commission and the courts will ask whether an exception is necessary for the undertaking to perform its task. In early cases the courts took a highly restrictive approach to this question, holding that, for an exception to the competition rules to be

[38] The position is discussed in detail in Prosser, *The Limits of Competition Law* (n 3) Ch. 6.

[39] See Case 263/86 *Humbel* [1988] ECR 5365; Cases C-159/91 and 160/91 *Poucet and Pistre* [1993] ECR I-637.

[40] Case C-205/03 *FENIN* [2006] ECR I-6295.

[41] For fuller discussion, see Prosser, *The Limits of Competition Law* (n 3) 132–41.

justified, it must otherwise be impossible for the undertaking to perform its public interest mission.[42] However, in more recent cases a more relaxed approach has been taken, asking not whether the exception is indispensable, but whether without it the undertaking would not be able to perform its mission in economically acceptable conditions; in particular, the court will not ask whether alternative means of performing the mission exist which are more compatible with free competition.[43] This approach was bolstered by the introduction under the Treaty of Amsterdam of what now forms part of article 14 TFEU, requiring Member States and the Commission to take care that services of general interest 'operate on the basis of principles and conditions, particularly economic and financial conditions, which enable them to fulfil their missions'. As a result, Member States do appear to have considerable flexibility in requiring undertakings, public or private, to undertake public service tasks, though this is subject to the crucially important rules on state aid discussed in the next subsection.

The European Commission also has an important jurisdiction over mergers, now based on a test of whether the merger would significantly impede effective competition in the common market or a significant part of it.[44] This is subject to the merger satisfying a test of whether it has a 'Community dimension', in which case it will fall exclusively for scrutiny by the Commission; if it does not, the national authorities will assess it. On this basis, the Government-sponsored merger between Lloyds TSB and HBOS, referred to in the previous chapter, escaped Commission scrutiny as the bulk of the undertakings' turnover was in a single Member State. Member States also possess powers to intervene to protect 'legitimate interests' not protected under the Merger Regulation itself; these are stated to be public security, plurality of the media, and prudential rules.[45] The provision was used, for example, to permit review by the domestic authorities on the basis of media plurality of the proposed takeover of BSkyB by News International, alongside the competition assessment undertaken by the Commission.

Finally, there are important provisions in EU law concerned with the provision of services, which can only be discussed briefly here. They are now the subject of articles 56–62 TFEU, providing for freedom to provide services within the Union. Importantly, article 51, which applies to freedom of establishment, is also expressed to apply to the provision of services. This

[42] See e.g. Case C-18/88 *RTT* [1991] ECR I-5941, para. 22.

[43] See Case C-320/91 *Paul Corbeau* [1993] ECR I-2533; Case T-289/03 *BUPA and others v Commission* [2008] ECR II-81, para. 270.

[44] Council Regulation 139/2004 on the control of concentrations between undertakings [2004] OJ L24/1; for detailed discussion, see Jones and Sufrin, *EU Competition Law* (n 9) Ch. 12.

[45] Regulation 139/2004, art. 21(4).

states that '[t]he provisions of this Chapter shall not apply, so far as any given Member State is concerned, to activities which in that State are connected, even occasionally, with the exercise of official authority'.[46] This has normally arisen in cases concerned with the provision of professional services, but it clearly has scope for application in relation to the techniques of economic management described in this book. It should also be noted that the EU Services Directive, which liberalizes the supply of services in important respects, does not apply to financial services nor to public services such as healthcare and social services.[47]

State aid law

The next subject is one which is of crucial importance for many of the areas discussed in this book; that of state aid. Its importance was vividly illustrated in relation to the rescue of the banks during the financial crisis; in the words of Julia Black, 'it is the Commission, rather than the UK Parliament, which is the body outside the UK executive which has had the greatest involvement in determining how UK taxpayers' money will be spend'.[48]

The basic law on state aid is now contained in articles 107 and 108 TFEU. Article 107 prohibits state aid which distorts or threatens to distort competition. Article 107 then sets out a number of exceptions to this general rule, for example to promote regional development or to remedy a serious disturbance in the economy of a Member State, both of which are discretionary exceptions for which the Commission determines whether the aid is compatible with the internal market. Article 108 provides for the supervision of state aid by the Commission, imposing a duty on Member States to notify it of any plans to grant or to alter aid. In the case of public enterprises, the system is reinforced by a Directive requiring transparency in their financial relations with government, and that separate accounts are kept for services of general economic interest and for commercial activities.[49]

Much of state aid law has been controversial, for example in relation to the funding of public service obligations and the degree to which various forms of

[46] For discussion, see M. Krajewski, 'Public Services and Trade Liberalization: Mapping the Legal Framework' (2003) 6 *Journal of International Economic Law* 341–67.

[47] Directive 2006/123 on services in the internal market [2003] OJ L376/36.

[48] J. Black, 'The Credit Crisis and the Constitution' in D. Oliver, T. Prosser, and R. Rawlings (eds), *The Regulatory State: Constitutional Implications* (Oxford: Oxford University Press, 2010), 92–128, 93.

[49] Directive 2006/111/EC on the transparency of financial relations between Member States and public undertakings [2006] OJ L318/17.

funding can be granted to enterprises in difficulty; examples will be considered in Chapter 8.[50] Unsurprisingly, the role of state aid law was of major importance in shaping the response of national governments to the financial crisis. The Commission was faced with considerable pressure from Member States to relax the rules; according to the Commissioner responsible for competition,

> [t]his scenario, we believed, would be the first step towards repeating a Great Depression. To avoid this fate we set out to argue the case for continued application of not only state aid control but all competition rules. We promoted this as a way to maintain a level playing field in the EU and avoid large scale movements of funds between Member States by investors in search of the highest level of protection. In other words, we wanted to stop a subsidy war.[51]

In the event the Commission issued a number of measures based on its powers relating to remedying a serious disturbance in the economy of a Member State, and these will be considered in detail in Chapter 8.[52] The overall position has been summarized by Black; initially the Commission had almost no choice but to approve rescue aid, and in practice approval came some time after action had been implemented. However, after the immediate crisis, 'the Commission did not simply act as a rubber stamp'. In particular, support for the Royal Bank of Scotland (amounting to a state recapitalization of £20 billion) was subject to 'long, detailed and hard-fought negotiations' and the Commissioner noted that, should the bank not deliver on its balance sheet reduction targets, the Commission could intervene once more and require further divestments.[53]

Public procurement

This important and complex area need be covered only briefly as it forms the core of the discussion in Chapter 9. Procurement is an area where, in English common law, there was only very limited protection for disappointed tenderers and where the constraints on the powers of central government were minimal; this would apply even if contracts were being used for regulatory

[50] For discussion, see Prosser, *The Limits of Competition Law* (n 3) 141–51; Nicol, *The Constitutional Protection of Capitalism* (n 1) 117–24.

[51] Commissioner Neelie Kroes, 'Competition Policy and the Crisis—the Commission's Approach to Banking and Beyond' (2010) 10 *Competition Policy Newsletter* 3–6, 3.

[52] TFEU, art. 107(3)(b).

[53] Black, 'The Credit Crisis and the Constitution' (n 48) 123. See also Commission Press Release IP/09/1915 (2009) *State aid: Commission Approves Impaired Asset Relief Measure and Restructuring plan of Royal Bank of Scotland.*

purposes.[54] It was mentioned in the previous chapter that judicial review may now be available in relation to the exercise of contractual powers, but far more important for tendering procedures are the requirements of the EU procurement regime, which may also have implications for the substantive conditions on which contracts are awarded.

First, general Treaty provisions impose a basic regime for procurement. Thus the basic principle of non-discrimination applies and there must be a sufficient degree of advertising to enable the market to be opened up to competition and the impartiality of the procurement process to be reviewed.[55] These requirements have been further elaborated through a Communication from the Commission on the subject.[56] Much more far-reaching provisions are contained in two Directives setting out procedures for procurement and the criteria on the basis of which contracts are to be awarded.[57] They are implemented in national law by regulations.[58] The provisions apply to tendering processes above a certain threshold, and require advertising in the EU Official Journal. Four procurement procedures are set out; the open procedure under which all those interested may respond to a tender; the restricted procedure under which a selection is made of those who respond and only those selected are invited to tender; the competitive dialogue procedure under which a dialogue is entered into with potential bidders, and the negotiated procedure under which the purchaser may select one or more potential bidders with whom to negotiate the terms of the contract. The award of the contract may be made on the basis of the 'lowest price' or the 'most economically advantageous tender'; the latter is normally used to secure value for money. It is important to note that these full requirements do not apply to some important categories of contract where only the general Treaty obligations will apply; one example is that of the procurement of health and social services.[59]

[54] See T. Daintith, 'Regulation by Contract: The New Prerogative' [1979] 32 *Current Legal Problems* 41–64.

[55] Case C-324/98 *Teleaustria v Telekom Austria* [2000] ECR I-10745.

[56] Commission Interpretative Communication on the Community law applicable to contract awards not or not fully subject to the requirements of the Public Procurement Directives [2006] OJ C197/2.

[57] Directive 2004/18/EC on the coordination of procedures for the award of public works contracts, public supply contracts and public service contracts [2004] OJ L134/114; Directive 2004/17/EC coordinating the procurement procedures of entities operating in the water, energy, transport and postal services sectors [2004] OJ L134/1.

[58] The Public Contracts Regulations 2006, SI 2006/7; the Utilities Contracts Regulations, SI 2006/6.

[59] For fuller discussion, see N. Boeger and T. Prosser, 'United Kingdom' in M. Krajewski, U. Neergaard, and J. van de Gronden (eds), *The Changing Legal Framework for Services of General Interest in Europe: Between Competition and Solidarity* (The Hague: T.M.C. Asser Press, 2009), 357–82.

The Directives and Regulations also set out special enforcement procedures providing remedies for disappointed suppliers and contractors in the High Court. Remedies include suspension of an incomplete contract and ineffectiveness or cancellation of the contract for serious breaches; the Court may also award damages, and a standstill period is required between the decision on the award of the contract and its signature to allow for the provision of information on which a challenge can be based.[60]

Although not all contracts are covered, the EU procurement regime is thus highly developed. As we shall see in Chapter 9, there has been controversy about the extent to which this represents the most effective way of encouraging responsive procurement and about when non-market considerations may be used in the process, for example to support employment and to improve environmental standards. Reform is now imminent to increase the flexibility of the procurement rules.

EU regulation

Apart from the effect of general competition law, both liberalization and regulation have a major EU dimension. One important area of liberalization in recent years has been that of the utilities sectors of electronic communications, energy, and postal services. Here regulation is for national independent regulatory authorities with a growing degree of coordination at EU level. The scope of a direct EU regulatory capacity has been controversial, both because of hostility from Member States and of limitations imposed by the Court of Justice in the *Meroni* decision. The European Court of Justice held that delegation by the EU institutions to other bodies was only permissible in the case of clearly defined executive powers, not in the case of powers involving the exercise of a wide margin of discretion.[61] In contrast to the extreme flexibility of the UK arrangements discussed in the previous chapter, the case seriously restricted the establishment of regulatory authorities with independent powers to take binding decisions at the EU level, although the recent establishment of a new body for regulatory coordination in the energy sector with some powers of binding decision does suggest a greater willingness to move towards some degree of centralized EU regulation.[62]

[60] See Directive 2007/66/EC on improving the effectiveness of review procedures concerning the award of public contracts [2007] OJ L335/31, and the Public Contracts (Amendment) Regulations 2009, SI 2009/2992.

[61] Case 9/56 *Meroni v High Authority* [1958] ECR 133.

[62] See S. Lavrijessen and L. Hancher, 'Networks on Track: From European Regulatory Networks to European Regulatory "Network" Agencies' (2009) 36 *Legal Issues of European Integration* 23–55.

Other sectors are subject to extensive regulation at EU level, including the setting of the basic normative principles; a major example is that of food standards, where the European Food Safety Authority has responsibility for scientific decisions and risk analysis.

One area in which the effect of the *Meroni* decision was far-reaching was that of the regulation of financial services, where the pre-crisis institutions for regulation were weak and had no power to issue binding rules or to impose binding decisions on authorities in Member States. They have now been replaced by a European System of Financial Supervision, which has a complex division of responsibilities with the Commission to avoid falling foul of *Meroni*: this will be discussed in detail in Chapter 7. In 2012 it was agreed that banking supervision in the eurozone should be strengthened by passing prudential supervision to the European Central Bank, in cooperation with other regulatory bodies. This relies on powers to confer tasks on the Bank already provided by articles 127(6) and 132 TFEU, thereby avoiding the *Meroni* problem.[63] I shall return to this theme in Chapter 7: for the moment, it is enough to note the contrast between the extreme flexibility of the UK domestic position on the use of agencies and the highly inflexible EU constitutional approach, which reflects the position in some of the other Member States where there are constitutional restrictions on delegation of powers to agencies.[64]

The World Trade Organization and GATS

Although World Trade Organization (WTO) law is neither directly effective nor supreme over other legal sources, there is debate about the extent to which it represents an economic constitution.[65] One view is that WTO law uses both techniques and substantive principles characteristic of constitutionalism, for example the distinction between constitutional and other rules, protection of freedom and non-discrimination, and protection of a separation of powers.[66] By contrast, Deborah Cass prefers the term 'trading

[63] European Commission, *Proposal for a Council Regulation Conferring Specific Tasks on the European Central Bank*, COM(2012) 511 final.

[64] For a comparative account, see R. Caranta, M. Andenas, and D. Fairgrieve (eds), *Independent Administrative Authorities* (London: British Institute of International and Comparative Law, 2004), esp. chs 2 (France) and 3 (Germany).

[65] See e.g. the essays in C. Joerges and E. Petersmann (eds), *Constitutionalism, Multilevel Trade Governance and International Economic Law* (Oxford: Hart Publishing, 2011).

[66] E. Petersmann, 'Multilevel Trade Governance in the WTO Requires Multilevel Constitutionalism' in Joerges and Petersmann, *Constitutionalism, Multilevel Trade Governance and International Economic Law* (n 65) 5–57, esp. 32–5.

democracy' rather than 'constitutionalization' because of the unbalanced implications of a normative constitution associated with free trade prevailing over other values, and the lack of some essential characteristics of a constitution, such as a new *grundnorm* and provision of effective processes of deliberation and communication.[67] These conditions for a constitution are more formalist and demanding than those set out in the first chapter of this book, and, though there may be room for debate about the extent to which the WTO system itself is constitutionalized, there is no doubt that it forms part of the UK's economic constitution.[68]

The WTO itself was established in 1995 to provide 'the common institutional framework for the conduct of trade relations among its members' in relation to trade agreements between them. It replaced the General Agreement on Tariffs and Trade (GATT) established in 1947, retaining its most important principle, the 'most favoured nation' rule, requiring members to extend to all countries the most favourable trading treatment granted to any. Of particular importance was the adoption of a new system for dispute resolution, through the use of panels and an Appellate Body. Their decisions have a much greater degree of binding force on member states than previously; whereas under GATT the system took the form of conciliation requiring consensus, in the WTO system consensus is necessary to reject rather than to accept a finding.[69] The system is also important in establishing a system of case law laying down principles for the position of future disputes. As a result, it has been claimed that:

> [t]he constitutional reality is that, on behalf of almost the entire world, the Panels and Appellate Body determine the permissible balance between the interests of the free market on the one hand and competing policies on the other. This role, inherent in the logic of the WTO text, has made the WTO not a mere 'specialist' trade treaty but rather an instrument for world governance.[70]

The other major development was the conclusion of the General Agreement on Trade and Services (GATS) in 1995. GATS may appear voluntary, in that it is up to states party to the agreement (and to the EU negotiating on their behalf) to negotiate those sectors to be included in liberalization under it, and to determine the degree of liberalization through choosing the mode of

[67] D. Cass, *The Constitutionalization of the World Trade Organization: Legitimacy, Democracy and Community in the International Trading System* (Oxford: Oxford University Press, 2005), esp. 32–8, 132, 143–4, 22–4.

[68] See also Nicol, *The Constitutional Protection of Capitalism* (n 1) 47–81.

[69] See D. Palmeter and P.C. Movroidis, *Dispute Settlement in the World Trade Organization*, 2nd edn (Cambridge: Cambridge University Press, 2004), 85.

[70] Nicol, *The Constitutional Protection of Capitalism* (n 1) 67.

liberalization under the Agreement. However, once liberalization has been agreed, it is extremely difficult to reverse. Particularly important and controversial issues are the extent to which commitments under GATS impose limits on government management of the economy, and the central role of its dispute resolution arrangements and their lack of openness and accountability.[71]

The provisions of GATS relating to governmental activities and public services are extremely unclear and badly drafted. Thus article 1:3 GATS defines as services within the scope of the Agreement those in any sector except services 'supplied in the exercise of governmental authority'; the latter is further defined as 'any service which is supplied neither on a commercial basis, nor in competition with one or more service suppliers'. The Preamble to GATS also includes the words '[r]ecognising the rights of Members to regulate, and to introduce new regulations, on the supply of services within their territories in order to meet national policy objectives, such as universal service, affordable prices, etc'. This suggests a similar position to that which applies on defining an undertaking to which EU competition law applies; GATS will not apply to regulatory decisions taken under state prerogatives, but should the state decide to supply a service under competitive conditions rather than on the basis of social solidarity, rules about market opening may then apply.

Special provision is made for financial services in an Annex to GATS; here services supplied in the exercise of governmental authority are activities by a central bank or monetary authority or by any other public entity in pursuit of monetary or exchange rate policies; statutory social security, or 'other activities conducted by a public entity for the account or with the guarantee or using the financial resources of the Government.'[72] When these subjects are opened to competition, however, they may fall under GATS. This exemption explains the relatively low profile of GATS (compared to the EU) in relation to the response to the financial crisis. It also provides considerable scope for the use of financial incentives and subsidies to modify market outcomes.[73]

In the now stalled Doha round of negotiations, considerable concern was expressed by supporters of public services as to the effects of GATS on their

[71] On the first matter, see M. Krajewski, 'Public Services and Trade Liberalization: Mapping the Legal Framework' (2003) 6(2) *Journal of International Economic Law* 341–67; on the second, P. Eeckhout, 'The Scales of Trade—Reflections on the Growth and Functions of the WTO Adjudicative Branch' (2010) 13(1) *Journal of International Economic Law* 3–26.

[72] Annex on Financial Services, art. 1(b); see Krajewski, 'Public Services and Trade Liberalization' (n 71) 355.

[73] R. Adlung, 'Public Services and the GATS' (2006) 9(2) *Journal of International Economic Law* 455–85, 482–3.

role and operation.[74] On the other hand, according to the UK Government, '[t]he EC has said in its requests that it is not seeking the dismantling of public services or state-owned companies. . . . Privatisation is not in itself an objective of the GATS, and cannot be forced on any government through the GATS process'.[75] Thus the EU, which negotiates on behalf of Member States, had in the earlier round placed a horizontal limitation on the application of GATS in relation to public utilities, permitting them to be subject to public monopolies or to exclusive rights granted to private operators. It proposed the retention of this exception in the Doha round, although there were requests from other countries to lift it. No commitments were made by the EU in health or education; in telecommunications and postal services, market opening was expressed to be subject to the retention of universal service safeguards.

Further difficulties are introduced by article VI:4 of GATS setting out a work programme which appears to apply to all sectors, not just those in which members have made explicit commitments. It commits members to 'disciplines' on domestic regulation, including licensing requirements, which

> shall aim to ensure that such requirements are, inter alia:
>
> a) based on objective and transparent criteria, such as competence and the ability to supply the service;
>
> b) not more burdensome than necessary to ensure the quality of the service;
>
> c) in the case of licensing procedures, not in themselves a restriction on the supply of the service.

Once more, the UK Government was optimistic, claiming that there was no intention to prevent members from regulating to implement domestic policy objectives.[76] Others do not agree; according to the World Development Movement, on the question of whether regulations are 'burdensome' or 'necessary' '[s]uch judgments are inherently political and should not be left to a small body of trade lawyers in Geneva'.[77]

It is obvious from the vagueness of many of the provisions just discussed that decisions and case law of the dispute panels and the Appellate Body will be of the greatest importance. Indeed, these institutions perform a major function in developing the law and are not limited to undertaking narrow

[74] For a detailed statement of the objections, see esp. World Development Movement, *Serving (Up) the Nation* (London: World Development Movement, 2002).

[75] Department of Trade and Industry, *Liberalising Trade in Services: A New Consultation on the World Trade Organisation GATS Negotiations* (2002), para. 2.10.

[76] DTI, *Liberalising Trade in Services: A New Consultation* (n 75) para. 5.15.

[77] World Development Movement, *Serving (Up) the Nation* (n 74) 16.

economic analysis.[78] They have been subject to considerable criticism for lack of transparency, because of the limited scope for participation of interested parties in hearings and the confidentiality of documents.[79] Important proposals were made in the Sutherland Report on WTO institutional reform, notably for public hearings, though it offered only limited support for the greater use of amicus briefs to permit third party influence, a subject which had earlier proved highly controversial.[80] Public hearings have been agreed by individual panels and the Appellate Body on a discretionary basis with the agreement of the parties, and in a limited number of cases amicus briefs have been accepted, for example to facilitate input by non-governmental organizations (NGOs).[81]

Finally, mention should be made of the position in relation to government procurement, to be considered in greater detail in Chapter 9. Article XIII GATS excludes procurement by government agencies of services purchased for governmental purposes from the application of the principles of market access and national treatment. However, there is also a 1995 WTO Agreement on Government Procurement; amendments, for example to expand the range of government bodies covered, were adopted in 2011.[82] The agreement, like GATS, is dependent on commitments by members to coverage of particular areas of services, and its scope is by no means complete; as in the case of the EU, there has been controversy about the extent to which it prevents the promotion of secondary policy objectives such as environmental protection and human rights.[83]

It is thus clear that the role of the WTO and GATS has been much more limited than that of the EU in relation to the economic management discussed in this book; however, there is considerable scope for future developments of greater importance, and predictions are difficult to make given the unfinished negotiations in the Doha round and the vagueness of key provisions in GATS. It can safely be said, however, that serious criticisms of the WTO for lack of transparency and the lack of accessibility to

[78] See Eeckhout, 'The Scales of Trade' (n 71).

[79] See M. Piewitt, 'Participatory Governance in the WTO: How Inclusive Is Global Civil Society?' (2010) 44 *Journal of World Trade* 467–88.

[80] WTO, *The Future of the WTO: Report by the Consultative Board to the Director General Supachai Panitchapkdui* (WTO, 2004), paras 260–2.

[81] See L. Ehring, 'Public Access to Dispute Settlement Hearings in the World Trade Organisation' (2008) 11 *Journal of International Economic Law* 1021–34.

[82] For discussion, see A. Reich, 'Legislative Comment: the New Text of the Agreement on Government Procurement: an Analysis and Assessment' (2009) 12(4) *Journal of International Economic Law*, 989–1022.

[83] Reich, 'Legislative Comment' (n 82) 1011–13.

non-member bodies such as NGOs are frequent and convincing.[84] Moreover, given the difficulty in gaining agreement between members, any process of reform of substance or of institutional arrangements is extraordinarily difficult and drawn-out.

The Council of Europe and the European Convention on Human Rights

Since the passing of the Human Rights Act 1998, making the European Convention on Human Rights enforceable in UK courts, the Convention has come to dominate much of the UK's public law. In economic management the civil and political rights protected by the Convention are less likely to be affected than in other fields, but there are some provisions in the Convention which are of importance. The first is article1 of Protocol 1 to the Convention. This provides that:

> Every natural or legal person is entitled to the peaceful enjoyment of his possessions. No one shall be deprived of his possessions except in the public interest and subject to the conditions provided for by law and by the general principles of international law.
>
> The preceding provisions shall not, however, in any way impair the right of a State to enforce such laws as it deems necessary to control the use of property in accordance with the general interest or to secure the payment of taxes or other contributions or penalties.

Both the European Court of Human Rights and domestic courts have interpreted this provision as giving a considerable degree of leeway to states in their conduct of economic management, subject to a balancing test between the demands of the general interest of the community and the requirements for the protection of individual rights.[85] For example, in *James v UK*, a challenge to leasehold enfranchisement, the European Court of Human Rights accepted that national authorities are better placed than the court to assess the public interest, and the political context was highly relevant in determining an acceptable standard for the assessment of compensation.[86] Similarly, in *Lithgow v UK*, a challenge to the terms of nationalization failed because they fell within the state's 'wide margin of appreciation'; the Court

[84] See e.g. R.B. Stewart and M. Ratton Sanchez Badin, 'The World Trade Organization and Global Administrative Law' in Joerges and Petersmann, *Constitutionalism, Multilevel Trade Governance and International Economic Law* (n 65) 457–93.

[85] For discussion, see Nicol, *The Constitutional Protection of Capitalism* (n 1) 128–51.

[86] (1986) 8 EHRR 123, paras 48, 54.

'will respect the legislature's judgment in this connection unless that judgment was manifestly without reasonable foundation'.[87]

This issue arose directly out of the measures taken by the Government as a response to the financial crisis in the case of *R (SRM Global Master Fund LP) v Treasury Commissioners*.[88] The terms on which Northern Rock had been acquired by the Government were challenged by shareholders in it (two hedge funds which had acquired shares during the crisis, and a number of small investors). The basic question was whether the value of the compensation terms should reflect the value of government financial support; without this the shares would have to be treated as in effect valueless. The Court of Appeal held that the Strasbourg case law established basic principles that a balance between the public interest and private rights should be struck; that this would be assessed using a proportionality test and that there should be a margin of appreciation for the state. The latter might require compensation of less than full market value to reflect political and social goals.[89] In particular, in the context of macro-economic policy, the margin of appreciation must be a wide one and the court would only interfere if the state's judgment as to what was in the public interest was manifestly without reasonable foundation.[90] The European Court of Human Rights held that the claim was manifestly ill-founded and so inadmissible on grounds very similar to those of the Court of Appeal.[91] By contrast, in a decision concerning not a governmental economic decision but an error of law by a regulatory body which had deprived a company of a financial benefit to which it was entitled, the Court of Appeal was prepared to award damages based on an infringement of article 1 of the Protocol.[92]

The second relevant provision of the Convention is article 6, providing a right to a hearing before an independent tribunal in the determination of civil rights and obligations. This article has had a major influence in the design of regulatory institutions, notably in the area of financial services, though some doubt remains as to its scope. In the Northern Rock case it was held that the availability of judicial review was adequate to satisfy this procedural requirement.[93]

[87] (1986) 8 EHRR 329, para. 122. [88] [2009] EWCA 788. [89] Para. 56.

[90] Para. 75. See also *International Transport Roth GmbH v Secretary of State for the Home Department* [2002] EWCA Civ 158, [2003] QB 728, para. 87.

[91] *Grainger v UK*, European Court of Human Rights application 34940/10, 10 July 2012.

[92] *The Gas and Electricity Markets Authority v Infinis plc* [2013] EWCA Civ 70.

[93] *R (SRM Global Master Fund LP) v Treasury Commissioners* (n 88) para. 84. See also *Tsfayo v UK* (2009) 48 EHRR 18; *R (Alconbury Developments) v Secretary of State for the Environment, Transport and the Regions* [2001] UKHL 23, [2003] 2 AC 295; *Ali v Birmingham City Council* [2010] UKSC 8, [2010] 2 AC 39.

The work of the Council of Europe is not limited, of course, to the European Convention on Human Rights. Other important measures include the European Social Charter, but this has weaker enforcement mechanisms and has not been made enforceable in domestic law. The Council has also had a major role in other areas of standard-setting and monitoring, including those of regional and local democracy and good governance, for example through the European Charter of Local Self-Government.

The Organisation for Economic Co-operation and Development

Reference should also be made to the Organisation for Economic Co-Operation and Development (the OECD). This is different from the international organizations discussed earlier in that it has no power to make decisions which are binding on member states. However, its influence has been extensive. First, it provides a means for developing the basis for agreements to be entered into by states themselves. For example, substantial efforts have been made to limit international tax evasion and to ensure cooperation in tax matters, leading to the signing of over 300 bilateral agreements on exchange of information for tax purposes. The OECD itself has issued a Model Tax Convention and Transfer Pricing Guidelines for multinational enterprises; the latter are incorporated into UK law as an aid to interpretation.[94] It is undertaking further work on tackling multinational tax avoidance. The OECD has also issued a statement of Best Practices for Budget Transparency.

Secondly, the OECD has had a major influence on the process of regulatory reform. It makes detailed recommendations for such reform, and undertakes monitoring of individual countries. The recommendations have undergone an interesting evolution. In the earlier work, the stress was very much on the need for deregulation; for example, a recommendation was to '[r]eform economic regulations in all sectors to stimulate competition, and eliminate them except where clear evidence demonstrates that they are the best ways to serve broad public interests'.[95] In later work the emphasis has been on the interdependence of regulation and liberalization, and on the importance of improving regulatory governance rather than simply adopting deregulation.[96] Most recently, the OECD has recommended the adoption of

[94] Taxation (International and Other Provisions) Act 2010, s 164.

[95] *The OECD Report on Regulatory Reform: Synthesis* (Paris: OECD, 1997) 33.

[96] See e.g. *OECD Guiding Principles for Regulatory Quality and Performance* (Paris: OECD, 2005).

an explicit whole-of-government policy for regulatory quality, including consideration of economic, social, and environmental benefits and distributional effects.[97] Better regulation is no longer equated with fewer regulations.

The World Bank and the International Monetary Fund

Finally, brief reference should be made to the role of the World Bank Group and the International Monetary Fund (IMF).[98] Of course, neither organization makes binding law for states; however, they both have an important role in assessing economic conditions and the need for reform in economic management, and in responses to economic crisis. For example, the World Bank 'Doing Business' reports assess the regulatory environment in different states, and rank them in terms of the ease of doing business there. In addition, conditions on loans for structural adjustment will provide for the implementation of a policy programme agreed between the country and the IMF, and this will be tied to liberalization and other economic reforms. A particular concern has been the use of these powers in relation to developing countries; however, they have also been used in response to the sovereign debt crisis, and the IMF has made loans with conditions requiring structural reform to Greece, Ireland, and Portugal in joint financial packages with the EU. The IMF has also issued a Code of Good Practices on Fiscal Transparency.

Conclusion

This discussion by no means exhausts the relevant international organizations, as will be apparent later. In the analysis of UK institutions there was a bewildering collection of different domestic institutions concerned with economic management. The same is true at the international level. It is also true that the different types of institution may have a very different position in the economic constitution as a result of the varied degrees of binding force of their decisions. The EU is of course by far the most important in this respect owing to the doctrines of direct effect and supremacy; the WTO and GATS also have a major role, though their coverage is much more limited and major areas of governmental action and of the supply of public services are not covered by negotiated commitments. Other bodies such as the

[97] *Recommendation of the Council on Regulatory Policy and Governance* (Paris: OECD, 2012).

[98] For a critical analysis of the work of the institutions, see J. Stiglitz, *Globalization and its Discontents* (London: Penguin, 2002).

OECD have a facilitative and advisory role, and in this have been of considerable importance in spreading liberalization and regulatory reform whilst the conditionality of IMF support has also been a major international lever for liberalization. In all cases, international obligations may be a constraint on governments (for example, in state aid and procurement) or a resource for policy implementation (notably in the liberalization process).

Although the arrangements are complex and often permit more flexibility than is apparent at first sight, it is obvious that, at least in the context of EU law, there are more restrictive constitutional principles acting as constraints on economic decision-making than at the UK domestic level. This is most striking in the attempt to constitutionalize substantive budgetary constraints for the eurozone countries; in an institutional form, it is also evident in the restrictions on the use of regulatory agencies by the EU, an extreme contrast with UK flexibility.

At best, the range of different international institutions may secure that a collaborative learning process may take place and may permit a more coordinated response to a crisis; after a bad start there are now signs of this in the response to the sovereign debt crisis. Concern about accountability and transparency of the international institutions remains, although there have been improvements in recent years largely due to pressure from NGOs, and advances have been made in understanding possible means of accountability through work on 'Global Administrative Law'.[99] At worst, not only will complexity result in policy incoherence, but international obligations with an inadequate democratic pedigree may impose major limitations on the capacity of national governments to choose and implement policies. This has long been an important EU issue, and is of particular current importance given the severity of the conditions imposed on eurozone countries' economic management after the sovereign debt crisis.

[99] See e.g. S. Cassese, 'Administrative Law Without the State? The Challenge of Global Regulation' (2005) 37 *New York University Journal of International Law and Politics* 663–94; B. Kingsbury, N. Krisch, and R.B. Stewart, 'The Emergence of Global Administrative Law' (2005) 68 *Law and Contemporary Problems* 15–61.

4

'Getting and Spending' 1: Taxation and Public Borrowing[1]

Introduction

Tax law is, of course, a major academic and professional discipline in the UK. However, despite the great constitutional importance of the processes by which governmental fund-raising is facilitated, constrained, and scrutinized, there has been little discussion from a public law viewpoint: '[a]lthough the power to tax has been at the very centre of some of our major constitutional law disputes, including the execution of a King, there is a lack of engagement with public law issues.'[2] In this chapter I shall examine taxation using the public law concepts of scrutiny and accountability. I shall also examine public borrowing, which has existed almost completely outside parliamentary control; the lack of scrutiny has become particularly striking given the new centrality given to the reduction of the public deficit in government policy. The discussion will concentrate on central government, though it should be noted that the Scottish Government will gain important additional powers to set income tax and to borrow under the Scotland Act 2012, and local government taxation and borrowing have long been a controversial area of relations between the centre and localities.

[1] The phrase 'getting and spending' is from Wordsworth, 'The World is Too Much With Us' (1807): 'Getting and spending, we lay waste our powers . . . ' It has been used frequently to refer to the process of public finance and spending.

[2] J. Tiley and G. Loutzenhiser, *Revenue Law*, 7th edn (Oxford: Hart Publishing, 2012), 2.1. The major recent public law contribution is John Snape's highly original *The Political Economy of Corporation Tax* (Oxford: Hart Publishing, 2011), esp. 32–44, 166–72; I am grateful to the late John Tiley for drawing this to my attention. On the role of constitutional principle here, see E. Simpson, 'The *Ramsay* Principle: A Curious Incident of Judicial Reticence?' [2004] *British Tax Review* 358–74.

Taxation

UK constitutional principle

There is no doubt that the parliamentary scrutiny of the raising of funds by government is a basic requirement of constitutional principle. Indeed

> [t]he original need to summon a House of Commons arose from the financial requirements of the Crown, and the House's authority and influence sprang from its powers to consider those needs before approving taxation and government expenditure. Before granting supply, the Commons would seek the redress of grievances.[3]

Matters came to a head in the seventeenth century around the question of whether the Crown had the prerogative power to levy certain forms of taxation without parliamentary approval.[4] This was one of the causes of the Civil War; the issue was finally settled after the Glorious Revolution by the Bill of Rights, Article 4 of which states that 'levying money for or to the use of the Crown, by pretence of prerogative, without grant of Parliament for longer time, or in other manner than the same is or shall be granted, is illegal'.

This provision has resulted in important case law applying limits on the Crown's powers to levy taxes; for example, in *Bowles v Bank of England*[5] it was held that a resolution of the House of Commons was not sufficient in itself to authorize taxation; an Act of Parliament is needed. In *Attorney-General v Wilts United Dairies*[6] the House of Lords held that, even in wartime, payment of a levy of money could not be required unless it was done in the form of a tax authorized by legislation. In *Congreve v Home Office*[7] it was held that the early revocation of a television licence in order to maintain government revenues was unlawful. All these cases could probably have been decided on the basis of conventional principles of judicial review, but nevertheless the principle that taxation can only be levied on the basis of statute approved by Parliament was central to them.

The constitutional principle is not, however, reflected in the realities of parliamentary scrutiny. We shall see later in this chapter and in the next that parliamentary powers are particularly weak in relation to borrowing and public expenditure; in the case of taxation there is some greater degree of

[3] R. Blackburn and A. Kennon, *Griffith and Ryle on Parliament: Functions, Practice and Procedures*, 2nd edn (London: Sweet and Maxwell, 2003), 6-176.

[4] See e.g. *R v Hampden* (1637) 3 St Tr 825 (the Ship Money case, reversed by the Ship Money Act 1640).

[5] [1913] 1 Ch 57. [6] (1922) 91 LJKB 897; 38 TLR 781 (HL). [7] [1976] QB 629.

scrutiny. Key principles are that all charges (proposals for expenditure or taxation) must be demanded or recommended by the government before they can be considered, and all charges must first be considered by the House of Commons and must also be included in legislation for approval by both Houses.[8] These principles have two major political consequences; the government will treat its taxation proposals as matters of confidence and so, if defeated on them, will be obliged to resign, and only the government may propose taxes or tax increases. This limits backbenchers to proposing tax decreases, which of course would be treated as matters of confidence.

More detailed criticisms may also be made of the parliamentary procedures in relation to taxation. Permanent authority is provided by statute for some taxes, including VAT, but the key event in relation to taxation is the annual budget followed by the Finance Act which re-imposes liability for other taxes such as income tax and corporation tax. In the past the budget was preceded by a pre-budget report allowing consultation on proposed tax changes (and indeed this was required by statute[9]), but this has now been replaced by an Autumn Statement including a response to updated economic and fiscal forecasts published by the new Office for Budget Responsibility. As we shall see later in this chapter, new arrangements have been made for improved consultation on detailed tax policy.[10]

The Chancellor presents his budget to Parliament in the spring, followed by motions to give immediate provisional effect to urgent tax changes. The budget is then debated for four or five days, and resolutions will be passed under the Provisional Collection of Taxes Act 1968 which permits temporary authorization of tax changes where necessary. A lengthy Finance Bill is then introduced; under recent reforms, clauses will have been made available in advance in draft after the budget, for inclusion in the Bill in the following year. Major changes will be discussed after second reading by a committee of the whole House and a standing committee. These procedures do enable there to be discussion of tax policy changes, and debate may be well-informed.[11] However, some major constraints on the process remain. For example, the Hansard Society has criticized the process as follows:

[8] Blackburn and Kennon, *Griffith and Ryle on Parliament* (n 3) 6-178. For detailed coverage of parliamentary procedures on taxation, see T. Erskine May, *Erskine May's Treatise on the Law, Privileges, Proceedings and Usage of Parliament*, 24th edn (London: LexisNexis, 2011), ch. 35.

[9] Finance Act 1998, s 156.

[10] HM Treasury and HM Revenue and Customs, *Tax Policy Making: a New Approach* (2010).

[11] See Blackburn and Kennon, *Griffith and Ryle on Parliament* (n 3) 6-185–6-188, 8-038–8-040.

> [i]n theory, the committee stage of the Finance Bill allows Parliament an opportunity to scrutinise and improve the quality of the legislation. However, in practice, as with much legislation, the debate is generally divided along party lines, and the government's majority in the committee ensures that its proposals are passed in the form it wishes. It has been argued that the government may in fact be more determined to ensure that the Bill is passed with few changes, given its impact on government finances and activity. In addition, the defects that many commentators have identified with the legislative process—notably haphazard scrutiny resulting in key clauses being undebated—are particularly evident. However, perhaps the greatest challenge to effective scrutiny is the increasingly complex and lengthy nature of the Bill itself, which runs to many hundreds of pages.[12]

There is also a time constraint; the Provisional Collection of Taxes Act requires that the Finance Act becomes law within seven months of resolutions made under it (increased from four months by the Finance Act 2011).[13]

The key constitutional principle requiring parliamentary approval of taxation, as enforced by the courts, is clearly of central importance in limiting the powers of government to tax through prerogative. What it does not offer, however, is any guarantee of effective scrutiny of the making of tax law, and in this respect the centrality of the grant of supply to the survival of government in office may actually militate against such scrutiny. Later in this chapter I shall examine the extent to which other procedures do provide scrutiny, but first I need to turn to other constitutional dimensions of taxation.

The European Union constitutional dimension

The position of tax in EU competence is a complex one. Indirect taxation in the form of VAT is subject to the requirement in the Treaty to consider how the legislation of turnover taxes could be harmonized, and is also subject to the VAT Directive which imposed a common base for VAT throughout the EU and sets a VAT minimum rate.[14] However, wide derogations to the provisions still exist. Direct taxation is one of the areas which Member States (and, in particular, the UK) have insisted on keeping within their own national powers. Nevertheless, even in relation to direct taxation, principles of EU law have done much to provide a framework of constitutional

[12] A. Brazier and V. Ram, *The Fiscal Maze: Parliament, Government and Public Money* (London: Hansard Society, 2006), para. 3.7. See also Snape, *The Political Economy of Corporation Tax* (n 2) 70–6 emphasizing the role of select committees and their limitations.

[13] S 1(3).

[14] See now art. 113 TFEU and Directive 2006/112EC on the common system of value added tax [2006] OJ L347/1.

principle (of course, by no means an exhaustive one) based on principles of non-discrimination and the four freedoms.[15] Thus

> [i]n principle, the general free movement provisions of the EC Treaty apply in exactly the same way to Member States' direct tax rules as to non-tax rules. This is expressed in the classic formula found at the beginning of virtually all the Court's judgments in the area: 'although direct taxation falls within their competence, the Member States must none the less exercise that competence consistently with Community law'.[16]

This is clearly not the place to get into the detail of the complex and often conflicting case law in this area, but three points need making here. First, the relevant principles are Treaty-based, thereby enhancing their fundamental constitutional status. Secondly, they are interpreted frequently by the European Court of Justice, thereby also emphasizing their role as part of the economic constitution as identified in Chapter 1 of this book. Thirdly, they are based around the concept of what does and does not constitute acceptable discrimination, a matter which is of course familiar from the decisions of constitutional courts elsewhere. Although there is controversy about the extent to which the cases are based only on the Treaty's prohibition of discrimination on grounds of nationality or whether the four fundamental freedoms themselves provide a justification for finding a breach of the Treaty, nevertheless other characteristically constitutional values and tests come into play, notably citizenship and proportionality.[17] Moreover, the UK courts have now applied some of the European jurisprudence on freedom of establishment in tax matters in a way analogous to their application of human rights principles to construe domestic legislation to make it compliant with international obligations.[18] The role of the EU is also important in developing solutions to tax avoidance by multinational companies, and action is also being taken for this purpose by the G8, the G20, and through the OECD.

The European Convention on Human Rights

The European Convention on Human Rights also has major importance in setting out a constitutional framework for taxation decisions, especially since

[15] For a summary, see Tiley and Loutzenhiser, *Revenue Law* (n 2) 2.3.

[16] S. Kingston, 'A Light in the Darkness: Recent Developments in the ECJ's Direct Tax Jurisprudence' (2007) 44 *Common Market Law Review* 1321–59, 1321. The quotation is from the European Court of Justice in Case C-524/04 *Test Claimants in the Thin Cap Group Litigation v Commissioners of Inland Revenue* [2007] ECR 1-2107, para. 25.

[17] See Kingston, 'A Light in the Darkness' (n 16) esp. 1328–9, 1335, 1341, 1355, 1359.

[18] *Vodafone 2 v Revenue and Customs Commissioners (no. 2)* [2009] EWCA Civ 446, [2010] 2 WLR 288.

it was made enforceable in UK courts by the Human Rights Act 1998; in 2009–10 human rights arguments were used in 22 reported cases involving HM Revenue and Customs.[19] Once more, an important substantive principle is that of non-discrimination, and this was illustrated vividly in the case of *R (Wilkinson) v Inland Revenue Commissioners*.[20] The House of Lords accepted that discrimination against widowers through a tax reduction available only to widows was in breach of the prohibition on discrimination in the enjoyment of Convention rights under article 14, in conjunction with the right to peaceful enjoyment of possessions under the First Protocol. On a point to which further reference will be made later, the House of Lords also held that the discretion of the tax authorities did not extend to the ability to grant such an allowance through an extra-statutory concession. The discrimination had in fact already been removed by statutory amendment.

Other principles derived from Convention rights are also of considerable importance in relation to taxation.[21] These include non-retroactivity,[22] and the prohibition of interference with the right to family life under article 8 or with the right to peaceful enjoyment of possessions under the First Protocol, although it will be recalled from the previous chapter that this permits a considerable margin of appreciation to national governments and indeed is expressed not to impair the state's right to secure the payment of taxes.[23] Another relevant Convention right would seem to be that to a fair trial before an independent and impartial tribunal under article 6. However, except in the case of criminal proceedings, this applies to decisions which determine 'civil rights and obligations', and, in a much-criticized decision, the European Court of Human Rights held that this did not include a pecuniary obligation derived from tax legislation.[24] The effect of this is reduced by the fact that, as we shall see later in this chapter, the arrangements for independent review of taxation decisions in individual cases are well-developed and unlikely to fall foul of the requirements under article 6. Moreover, the imposition of tax penalties will count as a 'criminal charge' making article 6 applicable.[25]

[19] Sweet and Maxwell, *Use of Human Rights Act By Businesses Jumps 63%* at: <http://www.sweetandmaxwell.co.uk/about-us/press-releases/Arguments%20use%20of%20Human%20Rights%20Act.pdf>.

[20] [2005] UKHL 30, [2005] 1 WLR 1718.

[21] For a summary, see Tiley and Loutzenhiser, 'Revenue Law' (n 2) 2.4.

[22] For a decision giving considerable leeway to the UK on this issue, see *National Provincial Building Society v UK* (1997) 25 EHRR 127.

[23] See e.g. *R (Huitson) v Revenue and Customs Commissioners* [2011] EWCA Civ 893, [2012] QB 489 upholding as proportionate the use of retrospective legislation against tax avoidance.

[24] *Ferrazzini v Italy* (2002) 34 EHRR 45. For criticism, see P. Craig, 'The Human Rights Act, Article 6 and Procedural Rights' [2003] *Public Law* 753–73.

[25] *King v UK* [2004] STC 911.

The basic UK constitutional principle of no taxation without parliamentary approval is thus supplemented by a number of more substantive principles derived from EU law and the European Convention on Human Rights. Central to both of these is the principle of non-discrimination. Later in this chapter I shall consider the extent to which a similar principle can be found in the domestic law of judicial review.

Policy-making and administration

The roles of the Treasury and of Her Majesty's Revenue & Customs (HMRC) have already been discussed in Chapter 2. The creation of HMRC by the Commissioners for Revenue and Customs Act 2005, combining the previously separate Customs and Excise and Inland Revenue, was the result of the O'Donnell Report reviewing those departments.[26] A central principle is that ministers should be distanced from tax decisions in individual cases. However, this has created problems of accountability which have arisen both where the minister has been expected to take responsibility for decisions of which he was not informed, and where he has not been able to take action to bring about changes. As the Treasury Select Committee put it in the context of unacceptable performance by HRMC:

> [i]t is regrettable that the HMRC's relationship with HM Treasury can give rise to a situation where a Minister can recognise publicly that a problem exists in a department which is within his remit, but tell Parliament that he is powerless to take action to bring about improvement.[27]

Conversely, as noted in Chapter 2, the then Chancellor was angered by having to be responsible before Parliament for a catastrophic loss of private data by HMRC of which he had not been informed.[28] The House of Lords Economic Affairs Committee has proposed the establishment of a special joint committee with private access to settlements with multinational companies.[29]

Alongside the merger of the departments, a particular matter of concern in the Review was allocation of responsibility for tax policy-making between

[26] HM Treasury, *Financing Britain's Future: Review of the Revenue Departments* (Cm 6163, 2004).

[27] Treasury Committee, *Closing the Tax Gap: HMRC's Record at Ensuring Tax Compliance* (HC 2010–12, 1371), para. 90.

[28] A. Darling, *Back from the Brink: 1,000 Days at Number 11* (London: Atlantic Books, 2011), 49–53).

[29] House of Lords Select Committee on Economic Affairs, *Tackling Corporate Tax Avoidance in a Global Economy: is a New Approach Needed?* (HL 2013–14, 48), paras 119–24.

different institutions.[30] The Review considered the options of maintaining the status quo, of consolidating all strategic, policy development, and maintenance work in the Treasury with the new department focusing on delivery, and of shared responsibility. It opted for the latter, concluding that;

> [t]he Treasury would lead on strategic work and policy development, and the new department would lead on policy maintenance and delivery. To ensure continued joining up and partnership working, both departments would assist the other in the discharge of its duties. As part of this, the Treasury's capacity to advise on tax policy should be enhanced. For the operational policy that remains in the revenue department, the creation of the new department will help to ensure coherence across the tax system.[31]

The new arrangements were also intended to increase accountability through a clearer definition of policy-making roles set out in a new framework document (though, as we shall see, this has in fact never been issued).[32] It was also the intention that the new department be more outward-facing to stakeholders and that it should have a clearer published remit issued by the Chancellor: '*[t]his should be focussed on what should be achieved, and why, rather than how, which should be a matter for the new department*'.[33] The proposed merger was also reviewed by the Treasury Select Committee, which came to similar conclusions to those in the O'Donnell Review.[34]

The reform was implemented quickly and the new body was established by the 2005 Act; like its predecessors it takes the form of a non-ministerial government department. It is headed by Commissioners for Her Majesty's Revenue and Customs, who are civil servants and who act on behalf of the Crown in exercising their functions.[35] Of particular interest is section 11 of the Act setting out the legal basis for relations with the Treasury, which requires the Commissioners to comply with general directions from the latter. This is reminiscent of the standard provision applying to UK nationalized industries, although, unlike in the latter case, there is no requirement for publication of directions. The effect was summarized by the responsible minister in standing committee:

[30] HM Treasury, *Financing Britain's Future* (n 26) paras 1.25–31 and Ch. 5.

[31] HM Treasury, *Financing Britain's Future* (n 26) para. 1.28.

[32] HM Treasury, *Financing Britain's Future* (n 26) paras 1.31, 6.23, 6.44 and see generally Chapter 6.

[33] HM Treasury, *Financing Britain's Future* (n 26) para. 6.33 (emphasis retained).

[34] Treasury Committee, *The Merger of Customs & Excise and the Inland Revenue* (HC 2003–04, 556).

[35] Commissioners for Revenue and Customs Act 2005, s 1.

> Revenue and Customs is, first and foremost, a Government department. The clause is essential in setting the limits of ministerial control, because of the important sets of obligations that the Department needs to discharge to the taxpayer, to the law and to the Minister in assisting in the development of policy. Ministers are accountable to Parliament for that Department. Therefore they require powers—I hesitate to use the word, but I cannot think of an appropriate substitute—over the way in which commissioners exercise their functions. Without such control, HMRC would be autonomous and the important link of accountability to this House... would be broken. While ministerial control is essential, right and proper, and [*sic*] it is important to ensure that Ministers' control is at arm's length so that they cannot intervene in the affairs of individual taxpayers.[36]

The Treasury issues a remit for the department annually; this sets out the priorities for HMRC, currently of raising revenue through improving tax collection and reducing the tax gap, cost reduction, improving service for customers, and managing the transition to a Universal Credit.[37] The remit is, however, brief, running to little over four pages. With the abolition of public service agreements there are no centrally driven targets; however, the HMRC Business Plan includes the priorities of the Coalition Government, and progress in meeting the Coalition's Programme for Government commitments is reported through regular Structural Reform Plans.[38] HMRC also adopted a new governance structure in 2008 differing from that recommended in the O'Donnell Report. It is similar to private sector practice, with a Chairman and Board responsible for governance, whilst running the department is the responsibility of a Chief Executive and Executive Committee. The Board includes six non-executive directors as well as the members of the Executive Committee. According to a review by the Cabinet Office Capability Review Team, the arrangements have improved financial management and business planning.[39]

Despite these reforms, it is clear that some serious problems remain around the operation of HMRC. The first concerns the division of responsibility for policy development and implementation with the Treasury. A highly critical examination of this area by the Institute for Fiscal Studies in June 2010 noted the existence of 'numerous problems' in the relationship. In particular:

[36] The Paymaster General (Dawn Primarolo), HC Standing Committee E, 1st Sitting, col 26 (11 January 2005).

[37] HM Treasury, *Remit for HM Revenue & Customs 2012–13* (2012) at: <http://webarchive.nationalarchives.gov.uk/+/http://www.hmrc.gov.uk/news/cx-remit-letter.pdf>.

[38] HMRC, *Business Plan 2012–2015* (2012) at: <https://www.gov.uk/government/uploads/system/uploads/attachment_data/file/89203/2012-business-plan.pdf>.

[39] Cabinet Office, *HM Revenue & Customs: Progress and Next Steps* (2009).

> [t]here is a disconnect between those responsible for tax policy and those operating in the field, meaning that policies can suffer in terms of being inappropriately targeted. Too often, this means a need for stakeholders internally and externally to work to address the resulting problems before the legislation gives effect to the policy properly—or that the legislation is left as defective and/or burdensome.

It also found a less unified approach to the tax system, with tax policy becoming 'increasingly disjointed' and a lack of clarity of responsibility for policy, which affected stakeholders. Technical tax knowledge was undervalued, which caused problems with the effective development of tax policy.[40] The same points had been made earlier in reviews by parliamentary committees.[41] One striking contributor to this is the fact that the framework document, which was central to the O'Donnell Review's recommendations for the clarification of relations and improved accountability, has never been drawn up.

This problem may in part be addressed by the 'New Approach' reforms setting out a fresh framework for tax consultation, to be discussed later. Apart from problems of policy-making, however, there are serious administrative problems in HMRC. A capability review published at the end of 2009 found that:

> [s]taff morale and engagement are very low.... In the 2009 staff survey, only 25 percent of HMRC staff compared with 61 per cent of its Senior Civil Servants were proud to work for the Department. Current efforts by the senior leadership team to tackle poor staff engagement and improve visibility and communications are not working and this is affecting the productivity of staff. HRMC has a very high rate of sickness absence.[42]

Similarly, the Treasury Select Committee expressed itself in the following year as '*deeply concerned about employee engagement at HMRC and its effect on performance.... we are deeply troubled by the apparent absence of any detailed plan to ameliorate the situation*'.[43] Further criticisms were made by the Committee in 2011, which was once more highly critical about the lack of clarity in the role of the minister.[44] At the end of 2012 the National Audit

[40] T. Bowler, *Tax Policymaking in the UK*, Institute for Fiscal Studies Tax Law Review Committee Discussion Paper No. 8 (2010).

[41] See e.g. House of Lords Select Committee on Economic Affairs, *The Finance Bill 2008* (HL 2007–08, 117).

[42] Cabinet Office, *HM Revenue & Customs: Progress and Next Steps* (n 39) 8.

[43] Treasury Committee, *Administration and Expenditure of the Chancellor's* Departments, 2008–09 (HC 2009–10, 156), para. 66 (emphasis retained).

[44] Treasury Committee, 'Administration and Effectiveness of HM Revenue and Customs' (HC 2010–12, 731), esp. para. 73.

Office also identified serious problems in customer service.[45] The problems remain unresolved and indeed may be made worse by cuts in staffing; as part of the Spending Review settlement, HMRC must make efficiently savings of 25 per cent by 2014–15.

HMRC law-making

The process for the making of primary legislation imposing tax liability was noted at the beginning of this chapter. The resulting legislation has been heavily criticized for its opacity and complexity, so much so that the UK Tax Law Rewrite Project was launched in 1996 to make direct tax legislation clearer and easier for users to understand; it benefited from special parliamentary procedures for the implementation of its work, but was criticized for its own lack of clarity and has ceased work.[46] Nor has there been lack of criticism at the level of principle, for example in the Mirrlees Review established by the Institute for Fiscal Studies.[47]

It is important to remember that statute is not, of course, the only determinant of tax liability. The tax authorities have made important use of their own policy-making powers, through the form of extra-statutory concessions and other important rules and guidance; whilst settlements in individual cases also rely on the use of their extensive discretionary powers. Both these areas are of interest not only to the taxpayers directly the subject of the decision, but also to others, both taxpayers and users of public services, who wish to ensure that there is a fair balance between taxpayers in funding services. This concern is particularly strong, of course, at a time when problems of the public finances are resulting in substantial cuts in public services.

The balance between statutory rules and administrative rules is a difficult one to draw; as the Treasury Select Committee has noted, giving HMRC greater powers to issue binding guidance or a wider range of non-statutory concessions would not be acceptable as its decisions should be subject to reasonable challenge in the courts for breach of statutory provisions. On the other hand, according to the Committee it would be unrealistic to expect that all tax law should be contained in primary legislation; directions and concessions are needed. '*However, if details are to be left to secondary legislation, or to directions, scrutiny is important.*'[48] An interesting new approach to rule use is

[45] National Audit Office, *HM Revenue & Customs: Customer Service Performance* (HC 2012–13, 795).

[46] See Tiley and Loutzenhiser, *Revenue Law* (n 2) 3.1.2.

[47] See <http://www.ifs.org.uk/mirrleesReview>.

[48] Treasury Committee, *Principles of Tax Policy* (HC 2010–11, 753), paras 42–3 (emphasis retained).

contained in the general anti-abuse rule announced in the 2012 budget. This is statutory but accompanied by guidance notes with an advisory panel to approve non-binding guidance on its interpretation which forms a published database for future tax planning, as a way of combining flexibility with evolving clarity of interpretation.[49]

The most well-known examples of HMRC rule-making are extra-statutory concessions. They have been described as 'few, tightly written and almost legislative in form' and a booklet gathering them together is published annually.[50] Their directly binding effect is limited; the publication notes that their application may be withdrawn or restricted where an attempt is made to use them for tax avoidance.[51] The courts have accepted the legality of the concessions but only on a narrow basis; according to the House of Lords in the case of *Wilkinson* they can be used to 'formulate policy in the interstices of the tax legislation, dealing pragmatically with minor or transitory anomalies, cases of hardship at the margins or cases in which a statutory rule is difficult to formulate or its enactment would take up a disproportionate amount of parliamentary time.'[52] However, they cannot be used to provide an allowance which Parliament could have granted but did not, even if failing to do so contravenes a right under the European Convention. In response to this decision, statute now provides that concessions may be given binding effect through a statutory instrument.[53] Any reliance on a concession not given statutory effect would depend on the doctrine of legitimate expectation, which will be considered more fully later.[54] In addition to extra-statutory concessions, HMRC also publishes statements of practice, interpretations and decisions, and manuals, which have similar effect.[55]

Apart from rule-making, settlements with individual taxpayers have been of considerable importance. They raise some difficult questions as they are not made public as a result of the strong general principle of taxpayer confidentiality; however, the question of equal treatment between taxpayers may arise, as may the related question of whether individual settlements are too generous when overall tax yield needs to be maximized. The courts have clearly recognized the legality of such settlements:

[49] See HM Treasury, *GAAR Study: Report by Graham Aaronson QC* (2011).

[50] Tiley and Loutzenhiser, *Revenue Law* (n 2) 3.3.1; see now HMRC, *Notice 48 Extra Statutory Concessions* (2012).

[51] See also *Al Fayed v Advocate General for Scotland* 2004 SC 745.

[52] *R (Wilkinson) v Inland Revenue Commissioners* (n 20) para. 21, per Lord Hoffmann.

[53] Finance Act 2008, s 160.

[54] Tiley and Loutzenhiser, *Revenue Law* (n 2) 3.3.1; A.K. Rowland, 'Is the Revenue Being Fair? Revenue Statements and Judicial Review' [1995] *British Tax Review* 115–21.

[55] Tiley and Loutzenhiser, *Revenue Law* (n 2) 3.3.1–3.3.4.

> [t]he commissioners, of course, have no power to agree to take a smaller sum for tax than is lawfully due upon the information before the commissioners. They can, however, make a decision in their management functions as to the extent of the information which they can reasonably expect to get and then make an agreement on that basis as to the tax payable.[56]

The issue came before the House of Lords in a celebrated case involving an agreement not to investigate back tax liability of Fleet Street print workers. It was complicated by the fact that the challenge was brought by a third party, the National Federation of Self-Employed, and the case is a leading authority on standing to seek judicial review. However, the central point was that the agreement was lawful as it was undertaken for reasons of good management rather than for any improper purpose, although the exercise of this power was subject to a general duty of fairness and non-discrimination.[57] More recently, the courts also considered a challenge brought by a pressure group to a deal with Goldman Sachs. The challenge was unsuccessful, though the group was held to have standing. The admittedly irrelevant consideration of potential embarrassment to the Chancellor of withdrawal from the deal had not, in the view of the court, determined the outcome, and it was not irrelevant for HMRC to take into account future relations with the taxpayer.[58] By contrast, the courts have held that a forward tax agreement, renouncing HMRC's right to investigate in the future, is unlawful.[59]

The administration of settlements has become highly controversial, especially in relation to multi-national businesses. The Treasury Committee has once more been critical, noting that '*the processes by which large tax cases are settled must be in a relationship based on openness and transparency and it is vital that appropriate checks be in place so that other taxpayers can be sure that all taxpayers are receiving the same treatment from HMRC*'.[60] Such transparency was hindered by the principle of taxpayer confidentiality and the reluctance of ministers to intervene. Scathing criticism was also made repeatedly by the Public Accounts Committee, claiming that HMRC had tried to avoid scrutiny in such cases, and that there had been fundamental failures of governance. As a result, large companies had been treated more favourably

[56] *Inland Revenue Commissioners v Nuttall* [1990] 1 WLR 631, per Ralph Gibson LJ.

[57] *R v Inland Revenue Commissioners, ex parte National Federation of Self-Employed and Small Businesses Ltd.* [1982] AC 617.

[58] *UN Uncut Legal Action Ltd v Commissioners of Her Majesty's Revenue and Customs* [2013] EWHC 1283 (Admin).

[59] *Al Fayed v Advocate General for Scotland* (n 51).

[60] HM Treasury, *Closing the Tax Gap* (n 27) para. 71 (emphasis retained). For further detailed criticism, see the House of Lords Economic Affairs Committee, *Tackling Corporate Tax Avoidance in a Global Economy* (n 29).

than had other taxpayers. Some reforms were in place, including an independent assessor to review settlement proposals, but further steps would be needed to secure accountability, including greater acceptance of responsibility by senior staff and a less 'cosy' relationship with large companies.[61] The Committee took the matter up in further highly critical reports, notably criticizing avoidance by multinational companies such as Starbucks which paid little or no corporation tax in the UK; tackling this required 'a change of mindset' from HMRC and a major improvement in transparency.[62] The Treasury has taken some steps to tackle avoidance, including the provision of extra resources for HMRC and entering into international agreements for exchange of information and adopting a general anti-abuse rule, but the issue is likely to remain a high-profile one, especially in an environment of major cuts to public expenditure.

Consultation and the 'New Approach'

Turning now to procedures, the first issue to be considered is that of consultation.[63] There may be justifiable limitations on consultation in the tax field for two reasons. The first is once more that the confidentiality of individual tax matters will preclude public consultation on individual settlements. The second is that the prior announcement of proposed tax changes may result in 'forestalling' in an attempt to make arrangements for avoiding payment of a new liability, and substantial losses to public funds may result. This has influenced the highly ritualized budget secrecy in which budget proposals are not discussed in advance with other government departments through cabinet committees, let alone with outside interests. The closed nature of the process is enhanced by the fact that the nature of UK governance has in the past made it unnecessary for proposals to be agreed between members of a governing coalition, and there are no effective veto powers on the part of Parliament or a constitutional court.[64] Nevertheless, many important issues are not subject to this sort of sensitivity and the importance of consultation has been increasingly stressed, for example in the HMRC

[61] Public Accounts Committee, *HM Revenue & Customs 2010–11 Accounts: Tax Disputes* (HC 2010–12, 1531).

[62] Public Accounts Committee, *HM Revenue & Customs: Annual Report and Accounts 2011–12* (HC 2012–13, 716).

[63] See Snape, *The Political Economy of Corporation Tax* (n 2) 142–6.

[64] See J. Alt, I. Preston, and L. Subieta, 'The Political Economy of Tax Policy' in J. Mirrlees (ed.), *The Mirrlees Review—Dimensions of Tax Design* (London: Institute for Fiscal Studies, 2010), 1205–79, 1212–14 (available at: <http://www.ifs.org.uk/mirrleesReview/dimensions>).

Review of Links with Large Business in 2006.[65] The reality has, however, been extremely uneven. The House of Lords Select Committee on Economic Affairs has examined the practice in a number of reports examining the annual Finance Bill. In 2008 the Committee was highly critical of consultation on Capital Gains Tax and on Residence and Domicile, finding that it had been late and ineffective, and had failed to be even-handed as regards different participants: '*a review which starts with consultation, continues in a desultory way and appears to have petered out, only to be followed by the announcement of wide-ranging proposals which bear little relation to the matters previously under discussion, tends to devalue consultation.*'[66] In 2009 the Committee found that consultation on foreign profits had been well conducted, although consultation had been inadequate on other measures.[67]

The Coalition Government responded to this and other concerns through the publication of *Tax Policy Making: A New Approach*.[68] It proposed a clearer strategy for the tax system with greater predictability and stability. This included greater consultation on tax policy, and a new convention that the majority of changes to tax law be confirmed no later than three months before the tax year in which they come into effect or publication of the Finance Bill in which they are to be included, accompanied by draft primary legislation and significant statutory instruments. A minimum of eight weeks would be given for comments on draft legislation. There would also be improved impact analysis and supporting documentation. One consequence would be that major tax changes announced in one year's budget would not be legislated until the following year's Finance Bill. A final version of the Tax Consultation Framework was published on Budget Day 2011 and set out commitments to consultation at five separate stages in the development and implementation of tax policy.[69]

These extremely significant reforms were widely welcomed and, in accordance with the New Approach, draft clauses for the Finance Bill in 2011 were published three months in advance for consultation.[70] According the House

[65] HMRC, *2006 Review of Links with Large Business* (2006), paras 3.22–3.27.

[66] House of Lords Select Committee on Economic Affairs, *The Finance Bill 2008* (HL 2007–08, 117), para. 38 (emphasis retained).

[67] House of Lords Select Committee on Economic Affairs, *The Finance Bill 2009* (HL 2008–09, 113).

[68] HM Treasury and HM Revenue & Customs, *Tax Policy Making: A New Approach* (2010).

[69] Treasury Committee, *Administration and Expenditure of the Chancellor's Departments, 2008–09* (n 43); HM Treasury and HMRC, *The Government's Tax Consultation Framework: Summary of Responses and Finalised Framework* (2011).

[70] See Treasury Committee, *Principles of Tax Policy* (n 48) para. 64 and for the new legislative timetable, see paras 78–9.

of Lords Economic Affairs Committee, most of the measures in the Finance Bill 2011 had been carried out in accordance with the principles of the New Approach, and it commended the Government for this; however, in two areas there had not been sufficient consultation, and there remained a problem of a 'severe, and worrying, disconnect' between the Treasury and HMRC and their customers on how well the policy partnership between the two departments was working.[71] Once more, this issue of institutional relationships seemed to be the Achilles heel of reform. Other changes include a new Office of Tax Simplification to provide independent advice to the Chancellor on simplifying the tax system, and an attempt by the Treasury Select Committee to set out general principles of tax policy, both procedural and substantive.[72]

Parliamentary scrutiny of administration

Turning now to arrangements for the scrutiny of the administration of tax matters by HMRC, apart from the procedures for making tax law referred to in this chapter, the work of the Treasury Select Committee is of considerable importance, especially as it established a sub-committee to examine the administration and expenditure of departments falling under the responsibility of the Chancellor of the Exchequer. Several examples of its critical reports have already been referred to. The Committee has been a major continuing source of scrutiny of HRMC, and of course this scrutiny goes beyond administration to include policy-making. However, the Hansard Society, quoting former members of the Committee, has pointed to the need for more detailed scrutiny of tax legislation through the establishment of a separate HMRC committee, as the Treasury Committee has a wide sphere of responsibility of which tax is only a small part.[73] Scrutiny of Finance Bills and other matters has also been carried out by the House of Lords Economic Affairs Committee, and the 'New Approach' discussed in the previous subsection may result in enhanced parliamentary scrutiny.[74]

It will be recalled from Chapter 2 that a further means of scrutiny of government departments is through the work of the National Audit Office (NAO). This has been particularly far-reaching in relation to HMRC, with no fewer than 40 reports on the department having been published during

[71] House of Lords Economic Affairs Committee, *The Finance Bill 2011* (HL 2010–12, 158), paras 52–7, 75.

[72] Treasury Committee, *Principles of Tax Policy* (n 48).

[73] Brazier and Ram, *The Fiscal Maze* (n 12) paras 3.13–3.15.

[74] See the Economic Affairs Committee, *The Finance Bill 2011* (n 71) paras 21–2.

the years 2005–11.[75] They have included extensive work on compliance and enforcement, including recommending stronger action on the hidden economy. One limitation of the work of the NAO is, as noted in Chapter 2, that it is limited to value-for-money audit and cannot question policy goals; however, this still enables very detailed examination of administration to take place. Reports may be considered further by the House of Commons Public Accounts Committee, and this also looks frequently at HMRC matters, most notably in its recent forthright criticisms of the arrangements for settling tax disputes with large companies and lack of action on avoidance by multinational companies.[76] Despite the very wide responsibilities of the NAO and the Committee on other matters, of which tax only forms a small part, and despite their limitations on policy matters, their work (with that of the Treasury Committee) represents the most sustained means of scrutiny of tax administration.

Grievances

Other forms of scrutiny concern the treatment of individual decisions in relation to taxpayers; arrangements here reflect developments in public sector consumerism. Thus HMRC is obliged by statute to publish and review regularly a Charter setting out service standards and values.[77] There is an internal process for handing complaints; no fewer than 77,166 complaints were received in 2011–12.[78] Complaints are handled by the Adjudicator after internal remedies have been exhausted to provide an element of independent assessment. In 2011–12 the Adjudicator's office handled 15,264 inquiries and resolved 1,133 complaints.[79] Of course, the general arrangements for examining grievances and improving the quality of public administration also apply to HRMC. Thus in 2010–11 the Parliamentary Ombudsman received 1,671 complaints about HRMC, the second highest level for any government department. This did, however, represent a decline compared to previous years, and only 12 were accepted for full investigation.[80] In 2005 the

[75] They are summarized in National Audit Office, *The NAO's Work on HM Revenue & Customs: A Short Guide* (National Audit Office, 2010), and for more recent work, see *A Summary of the NAO's Work on HM Revenue & Customs* (National Audit Office, 2012).

[76] Public Accounts Committee, *HM Revenue & Customs 2010–11 Accounts: Tax Disputes* (n 61); *HM Revenue & Customs: Annual Report and Accounts 2011–12* (n 62).

[77] Finance Act 2009, s 92; HMRC, *Your Charter* (nd) at: <http://www.hmrc.gov.uk/charter/charter.pdf>.

[78] HMRC, *Departmental Report 2011–12* (HC 2012–13, 38), 15.

[79] Adjudicator's Office, *Annual Report 2012* (2012), 5.

[80] Parliamentary and Health Service Ombudsman, *A Service for Everyone: Annual Report 2010–11* (HC 2010–12, 1404), 14.

Ombudsman issued a special report on tax credits, an area of serious administrative shortcomings also examined by the Treasury Committee. Drawing on the complaints referred to her, the Ombudsman made 12 specific recommendations for change in the future, including the introduction of a statutory test for recovery of excess payments and a different model for delivery with more sustained and informed communication with customers.[81]

These remedies are concerned with administrative failings such as mistakes, delays, and poor advice. There are also clear procedures for challenging decisions of substance. Thus internal review is required by statute, and a new procedure for review on a consistent basis across taxes was introduced in 2009.[82] Appeal used to lie to the General and Special Commissioners of Income Tax or the VAT Tribunal. However, under the Tribunals, Courts and Enforcement Act 2007 they have now been incorporated into the new unified tribunal system. The First-Tier Tribunal has a specialist Tax Chamber, and the Upper Tribunal a Tax and Chancery Chamber to which appeal may be made with leave on point of law from the First-Tier Tribunal. Further appeal on point of law lies with leave to the Court of Appeal or Court of Session.[83] The Upper Tribunal hears some particularly complex appeals at first instance and may also exercise a judicial review jurisdiction on transfer from the High Court, and provision exists for extending this jurisdiction to further categories of cases to enable them to go directly to the Tribunal; however, the normal route for judicial review is to the High Court, and this may have to be taken in parallel with an appeal.[84]

Judicial review

Judicial review has had an important role to play in taxation issues. As the earlier part of the chapter showed, extra-statutory concessions and settlements have given rise to particular concern. The most celebrated case is *National Federation of Self-Employed* discussed earlier in the chapter, which concerned a challenge by a pressure group of a settlement relating to back tax granted to a different group of taxpayers. The case has been important in developing the rules relating to standing in judicial review cases; it was also important both in confirming the extent of the Inland Revenue's managerial powers to settle

[81] Parliamentary and Health Service Ombudsman, *Tax Credits: Putting Things Right* (HC 2005–06, 124).

[82] Finance Act 2008, s 119.

[83] Tribunals, Courts and Enforcement Act 2007, ss 13–14.

[84] Tribunals, Courts and Enforcement Act 2007, ss 15, 18–19.

and the existence of an overall duty of fairness when it did so.[85] Important issues of vires were determined in the *Wilkinson* case, which also showed the potential scope of human-rights based review, though also suggesting limitations on the ability to use extra-statutory methods to remedy contraventions of the European Convention on Human Rights.[86]

A related concern with fairness has also been shown in tax cases relating to legitimate expectations.[87] Thus in *R v Inland Revenue Commissioners, ex parte Preston*, the House of Lords held that in certain circumstances the tax authorities could not go back on an undertaking where to do so would be so unfair as to represent an abuse of power.[88] Similarly, in *R v Inland Revenue Commissioners, ex parte MFK Underwriting Agencies Ltd*, according to Lord Bingham the authorities could not withdraw from an undertaking if this would cause substantial unfairness, where the full information had been given by the taxpayer and a clear and unambiguous ruling had been made by the Revenue on which it was reasonable to rely.[89] In both these cases the applicants failed on the facts, but in the *Unilever* case, strictly not one of legitimate expectation, the Court of Appeal held that the treatment of a claim as time-barred when previous claims had consistently been accepted out of time did amount to an abuse of power and was unlawful.[90] It should also be added that judicial review is not, of course, the only possible judicial remedy. An action in tort for negligence might arise in limited circumstances.[91] In a case which attracted enormous attention from both public and private lawyers, it was held that a right in restitution arose for the repayment of moneys paid by a building society to the Revenue as the result of an ultra vires demand.[92] The decision was reversed retrospectively by legislation insofar as it had application to other building societies.[93]

The developing law of judicial review clearly has considerable potential. It may be possible to see in the cases, particularly those on fairness in the context of legitimate expectation and on the scope of extra-statutory concessions,

[85] *R v Inland Revenue Commissioners, ex parte National Federation of Self-Employed and Small Businesses Ltd* (n 57); for the duty of fairness, see esp. the opinion of Lord Scarman.

[86] *R (Wilkinson) v Inland Revenue Commissioners* (n 20).

[87] For detailed treatment of the concept of legitimate expectation, see P. Craig, *Administrative Law*, 7th edn (London: Sweet and Maxwell, 2012), ch. 22.

[88] [1985] AC 835.

[89] [1990] 1 WLR 1545.

[90] *R v Inland Revenue Commissioners, ex parte Unilever plc* [1996] STC 681.

[91] *Neil Martin Ltd v Her Majesty's Revenue and Customs* [2007] EWCA Civ 1041, [2007] STC 1802.

[92] *Woolwich Equitable Building Society v Inland Revenue Commissioners (no. 2)* [1993] AC 70. For repayment of tax wrongly paid on the basis of a mistake of law, see *Deutsche Morgan Grenfell Group v Inland Revenue Commissioners* [2006] UKHL 49, [2007] 1 AC 558.

[93] Finance Act 1991, s 53; Finance (No 2) Act 1992, s 64.

an appeal to a more general principle of equal treatment and non-discrimination.[94] This in turn mirrors the major European decisions outlined at the beginning of this chapter from both the EU and under the European Convention on Human Rights in which non-discrimination has played a major role. It can only increase as the use of Convention rights becomes further embedded in the grounds for judicial review. However, judicial review also has its limitations, and cannot be a means of ensuring substantive fairness in the allocation of tax burdens, which will remain a task for government and Parliament.[95]

Overall, then, in relation to taxation, there is a limited degree of scrutiny through Parliament for major decisions which are announced following full budget procedures, whilst the New Approach has the potential to improve the consultative process. At the other extreme, reflecting the effect of taxation on private property rights and the growth of consumerism in relation to government services, there are well-developed procedures for dealing with individual grievances. There is also extensive scrutiny of administration and value for money by the NAO and select committees. However, serious problems remain about the institutional design of HMRC and in particular its relations with ministers and their responsibility for correcting administrative failings. It is now time to turn to public finance through borrowing, where there is far less scrutiny than in tax matters.

Government borrowing

UK borrowing and its scrutiny

In addition to taxation, public expenditure is of course funded by government borrowing. This has now become of enormous significance given its major role in financing government, and in particular, because of concerns about the budget deficit. Thus in the UK in 2012/13 public sector net borrowing was £116.5 billion. Net debt was £1,202.8 billion, equivalent to 74.9 per cent of gross domestic product. By contrast, in 2002 net debt had been £348.1 billion, 31.5 per cent of GDP. [96] As we shall see in the following chapter, reducing the budget deficit has become the major aim of government fiscal policy, and has contributed to a large number of other policy decisions and constraints. Moreover, the reaction of the international

[94] For general discussion of such developments, see Craig, *Administrative Law* (n 87) ch. 23.

[95] For discussion, see the Treasury Committee, *Principles of Tax Policy* (n 48) paras 20–3.

[96] Office for National Statistics, *Statistical Bulletin: Public Sector Finances* (June 2013).

financial markets in setting the terms on which government can borrow has become a major political as well as economic concern, both in the UK and in other EU Member States, particularly in the context of the sovereign debt crisis.

The management of debt is for the UK Debt Management Office (DMO), which is an executive agency of the Treasury. It issues gilts and engages in cash management operations in the sterling money markets, and also carries out the statutory functions of the Commissioners for the Reduction of National Debt in the investment and management of government funds. Currently more important than this everyday management is the amount of borrowing. This has traditionally not been subject to any special form of outside scrutiny. Thus borrowing is not undertaken under statutory powers but rather under the inherent powers of the Crown, so challenge on the basis of ultra vires has not been available. Parliamentary scrutiny has also been limited; 'supply procedure gives Parliament no direct means of examining either the amount of government borrowing or its sources...'.[97] This absence of scrutiny is quite extraordinary given the importance of borrowing for overall fiscal policy.

However, in recent years there has been some attempt to give internal government controls on borrowing some binding force. From 1998 Gordon Brown, as Chancellor, developed two fiscal rules; the Golden Rule, that over the economic cycle the Government will borrow only to invest and not to fund current spending; and the Sustainable Investment Rule, that net public debt would be held over the economic cycle at a stable and prudent level. Other things being equal, it would be maintained below 40 per cent of GDP. These were supplemented by the Code for Fiscal Responsibility, which committed the Government to principles of transparency, stability, responsibility, fairness, and efficiency in fiscal matters; it also provided for the laying before Parliament of key financial documents accompanied by an independent report on them by the Comptroller and Auditor-General. Drawing up and publication of the Code was required by statute.[98] Controversy occurred in relation to application of the Golden Rule with several changes being made to the beginning and end dates of the economic cycle, making compliance easier.[99] From 2008 events were overtaken by the need to respond to the international financial crisis; near the end of the Labour Government a more substantive binding statement of policy appeared in

[97] I. Harden and N. Lewis, *The Noble Lie: The British Constitution and the Rule of Law* (London: Hutchinson, 1986), 95.

[98] Finance Act 1998, ss 155–6.

[99] See Treasury Committee, *The 2006 Pre-Budget Report* (HC 2006–07, 115), paras 27–39.

the form of the Fiscal Responsibility Act 2010. This legislation imposed a number of duties on the Treasury, including that for each financial year up to 2016 public borrowing be reduced, halving by 2014, and a specified reduction in public sector debt; further duties were imposed by order. The limited importance accorded to the statute by the then Chancellor was mentioned in Chapter 1.[100]

The Coalition Government replaced both this legislation and the Code for Fiscal Responsibility by a Charter for Budget Responsibility required by the Budget Responsibility and National Audit Act 2011.[101] The Charter includes objectives and a mandate for fiscal policy and objectives for debt management and debt management reporting.[102] Finally, that Act also establishes an independent Office for Budget Responsibility, previously set up on a non-statutory basis (described in Chapter 2). The Office examines and reports on the sustainability of the public finances, and has a broad remit to investigate the impact of trends and policies relating to them, although it may not provide normative commentary on the particular merits of government policies, as is made clear in the guidance for the Office in the Charter. It is unlikely that there will be any extensive role for judicial enforcement in relation to the new arrangements.[103] Nevertheless, they are important in requiring a greater degree of transparency in fiscal policy, including government borrowing.

Government borrowing and the European Union

The financial crisis was an international phenomenon and had particularly disastrous effects on the economies of EU Member States with a very high rate of government borrowing, culminating in the sovereign debt crisis discussed in Chapter 3. A Stability and Growth Pact was adopted in 1997, together with an Excessive Deficit Procedure now contained in article 126 TFEU.[104] This is based around a reference value for the existence of an excessive deficit of 3 per cent of gross domestic product and a debt-to-GDP ratio of 60 per cent. As noted in Chapter 3, scrutiny of national fiscal performance is undertaken by the Commission, and the ECOFIN Council can determine that an excessive deficit exists in a Member State. However, no

[100] Fiscal Responsibility Act 2010, ss 1–2. [101] Fiscal Responsibility Act 2010, s 1.

[102] HM Treasury, *Charter for Budget Responsibility* (2011).

[103] See *R (Luton Borough Council and Nottingham City Council) v Secretary of State for Education* [2011] EWHC 217, esp. para. 8.

[104] See also Protocol No. 12 TFEU on the Excessive Deficit Procedure and Council Regulation 1467/97 on speeding up and clarifying the implementation of the excessive deficit procedure [1997] OJ L209/6.

sanctions can be issued in relation to the UK because of its opt-out from full monetary union, although it will still 'endeavour to avoid an excessive government deficit' and the Commission has scrutinized its performance and may issue a report to the Council. The Stability and Growth Pact was breached in 2003 by Germany and France which had been able successfully to avoid sanctions; by 2012 almost all eurozone countries had been made subject to the excessive deficit procedure, and it had been initiated for the UK with a report by the Commission in 2008.

As described in Chapter 3, there were reforms to the Pact in 2011 as a result of the sovereign debt crisis, and the new Treaty on Stability, Coordination and Governance was adopted to impose much stricter fiscal discipline on eurozone countries, including a demanding fiscal compact. Of course, it does not apply to the UK, which remains subject to the 'Europe 2020' strategy providing for enhanced economic policy coordination within the Stability and Growth Pact and for greater coordination of national fiscal frameworks and budgetary procedures. There is also to be greater reflection of EU priorities in national fiscal frameworks.[105] A concrete measure to achieve this is the adoption of a 'European Semester' a six-month cycle permitting unified surveillance of budgetary and structural policies through a horizontal review by the Commission before Member States prepare Stability and Convergence Programmes and National Reform Programmes.[106] These measures apply to all Member States, not just those in the eurozone, and provide a further means of scrutiny of overall UK public borrowing. All Member States including the UK prepare National Reform Programmes outlining structural reform plans; the first was submitted in 2011.[107] A Convergence Programme must also be submitted commenting on the economy and public finances, as has been done as part of the Stability and Growth Pact since 1999. A further restriction on national policy is that article 123 TFEU applies to the UK (apart from a minor saving for the role of the Bank of England's 'ways and means' facility). It prohibits national central banks from providing overdraft or other credit facilities to national governments or other public authorities. This restricts the ability to use direct monetary financing of deficits.[108]

[105] Communication from the Commission, Reinforcing Economic Policy Coordination, COM (2010) 250 final, 12.5.2010.

[106] For Council approval, see Press Release 13161/10 *Economic and Financial Affairs* (7 September 2010).

[107] HM Government, *Europe 2020: UK National Reform Programme 2011* (2011).

[108] See C. Giles, 'Turner Defends Permanent Printing of Money', *The Financial Times*, 6 February 2013.

Private regulation: the credit rating agencies

Of course, the major determinants in setting the terms for public borrowing are the financial markets, and crucial to their operation is the work of the private credit rating agencies. As the European Commission has put it:

> [t]hey issue creditworthiness opinions that help overcome the information asymmetry between those issuing debt instruments and those investing in these instruments. CRAs have a major impact on the financial markets. It is essential, therefore, that they consistently provide high-quality, independent and objective credit ratings.[109]

They provide an important example of the phenomenon of private regulation, which has become increasingly subject to academic study.[110]

As a result of the financial crisis, the United States took action to regulate credit rating agencies as part of the reforms in the Dodd-Frank Act through the creation of an Office of Credit Rating Agencies within the Securities and Exchange Commission with which they must register.[111] No such action has been taken at the UK level, but in 2009 the EU passed a Regulation imposing mandatory registration of agencies issuing credit ratings in the EU.[112] The Regulation requires disclosure of their rating methodologies and ongoing supervision by national competent authorities. It also sets conditions for the endorsement by EU registered agencies of ratings issued in third countries. An amending Regulation has given the responsibility for oversight of credit agencies operating in the EU to the European Securities and Markets Authority (ESMA), the financial services regulator to be discussed in Chapter 7; it has powers to demand documents, to conduct on-site inspections and to impose fines for infringements.[113] Further rules were adopted at the beginning of 2013 to strengthen Regulation to reduce reliance on ratings agencies, to set up a calendar for publication of sovereign debt ratings limited to three per year, to increase the liability of agencies for their ratings, and to reduce conflicts of interest, for example through disclosure rules.[114]

[109] European Commission, *Public Consultation on Credit Rating Agencies* (5 November 2010), 3.

[110] See C. Scott, 'Private Regulation of the Public Sector: A Neglected Facet of Contemporary Governance' (2002) 29 *Journal of Law and Society* 56–76; C. Scott, F. Cafaggi, and L. Senden, 'The Conceptual and Constitutional Challenge of Transnational Private Regulation' (2011) 38 *Journal of Law and Society* 1–19.

[111] Public Law 111–203, July 21 2010, ss 931–939H.

[112] Regulation (EC) 1060/2009 on credit rating agencies [2009] OJ L302/1.

[113] Regulation (EU) 513/2011 on credit rating agencies [2011] OJ L145/30.

[114] Regulation (EU) 462/2013 on credit rating agencies [2013] OJ L146/1.

Conclusions

The first and pre-eminent UK constitutional principle relating to taxation is that it can only be lawfully imposed after parliamentary approval. However, this does not translate into effective parliamentary scrutiny. Although the unveiling of budget proposals in the Chancellor's budget day speech represents high theatre, their treatment as issues of confidence ultimately means that any change as a result of scrutiny is highly unlikely, and this is reinforced by the convention of strong budget secrecy. Similarly, the timetable for the annual Finance Act has limited debate on its highly technical content. The publication of draft clauses in advance under the 'New Approach' will do something to improve scrutiny, and this is linked to improved consultation. It may also result in more developed parliamentary scrutiny through select committees. A further, important, source of scrutiny of administration of tax matters is through the work of the Public Accounts Committee and, in particular, the many detailed reports of the NAO.

Taxation raises other constitutional principles as well; the Treasury Committee has made a start in developing a basis for further discussion of these issues in a report suggesting basic principles of fairness and economic welfare and growth, together with procedural principles of certainty, stability, and practicability.[115] In a more explicitly constitutional sense, the EU has developed principles based on the four freedoms and non-discrimination; the latter also has a major part to play in the role of the European Convention on Human Rights in relation to tax matters. Indeed, principles of non-discrimination and equal treatment may also provide a basis for scrutiny by the courts through judicial review; they are apparent in the concept of fairness used as the basis for review for breach of a legitimate expectation and in the more restrictive approach adopted in relation to the discretionary power to grant extra-statutory concessions. Finally, rights to challenge individual decisions, either because they are wrong in substance or because they involve some form of maladministration, are particularly well-developed in the tax field, reflecting taxation's effect on traditional property rights and the development of public-sector consumerism.

This still leaves some gaps in constitutional protection. The confidentiality of individual tax affairs necessarily results in limits to the ability to challenge the generous treatment of others. This increases the general importance of the sharing of tax burdens fairly, one of the basic principles identified by the

[115] Treasury Committee, *Principles of Tax Policy* (n 48).

Treasury Committee, especially in the context of conditions of great fiscal stringency. In one sense this involves fundamental political choices which can be subject only to political control; for example, the balance between a progressive income tax and other, less progressive, forms of taxation. However, given the discretionary powers of HMRC, it also raises concerns about enforcement and settlement policies, which have been examined by the parliamentary committees in highly critical terms. Indeed, the issues of discretionary settlements and the use of aggressive avoidance schemes have now become a major concern of the Public Accounts Committee. This also raises questions of equal treatment, and it is possible to see the beginnings of both the courts and the Committee acting to implement common concerns.

A major problem is the serious difficulty in establishing clear and accountable relationships between the Treasury and HMRC, and in ensuring the accountability of the latter. This has led to repeated criticism by select committees and others, and applies both in relation to ministers having to accept responsibility for problems of which they have not been informed, and difficulties for ministers seeking to put right administrative failings. It is linked also to problems of low morale in HMRC. One lesson of this chapter is that the framework of mutual responsibilities has to be set out in a much clearer and more transparent way with a much greater degree of specification of who is responsible for what. As will often be the case in the areas examined in this book, deficiencies of institutional interrelationships are a major constitutional inadequacy.

The biggest gaps exist in relation to public borrowing, which escapes the parliamentary and judicial forms of scrutiny applicable to taxation. There have been important improvements in transparency, notably through the creation of the Office for Budget Responsibility, and the amount of public borrowing is now at the centre of public debate. More structured forms of accountability have been created at the EU level, both for national borrowing and for the regulation of credit agencies. In both the national and European cases, it is the financial crisis and the sovereign debt crisis which have been responsible for the development of improved scrutiny and monitoring. In the following chapter I shall examine the question of public expenditure and its control, another area which has achieved greater prominence as a result of the financial crisis after a history of weak constitutional scrutiny.

5

'Getting and Spending' 2: Public Expenditure

Introduction

No area covered in this book is of greater current importance than that of the scrutiny and control of public expenditure. It became the central plank of the economic policy of the UK Coalition Government elected in 2010, providing the main means of attempting to achieve its original goal (later modified) of eliminating the structural deficit by 2014–15. It is also more than this; restricting public expenditure represents a new paradigm of regulation, using not command and control but access to resources. Thus the 2010 Spending Review states that it provides 'an opportunity to take a more fundamental look at the role of government in society and how it can perform that role'; it is part of 'a radical programme of public sector reform'.[1]

Scrutiny and control of public expenditure occur at a number of different levels. Political headlines often concern the overall total amount of public expenditure, reflecting, for example, the speed of deficit reduction, and this was a central issue of the 2010 UK general election. Just as important is the allocation of expenditure between departments and programmes, the subject of the 2010 Spending Review after the election. Finally, scrutiny of expenditure examines after the event whether spending has been legal and proper, and whether it has succeeded in achieving value for money. Both are carried out by the National Audit Office (NAO) and the Public Accounts Committee.

The complexity is increased by the fact that the process of expenditure control is multi-levelled. Thus the devolved jurisdictions have their own arrangements for expenditure allocation and audit, as mentioned in Chapter 2. The Scottish budgetary procedures are of particular interest and will be discussed in this

[1] HM Treasury, *The Spending Review Framework* (Cm 7872, 2010), para. 2.2; *Spending Review 2010* (Cm 7942, 2010), 7–9 and e.g. paras 1.18, 1.60, 1.76–77, 1.91. For fuller discussion of the relationship between the Spending Review and regulation, see T. Prosser, '"An Opportunity to Take a More Fundamental Look at the Role of Government in Society": The Spending Review as Regulation' [2011] *Public Law* 596–610.

chapter.[2] Similarly, EU expenditure is of great importance and is highly controversial at a number of levels, including the overall EU budget, determined by the Council on the basis of a multi-annual financial framework, and the use of funds, subject to scrutiny by the European Court of Auditors.[3] There is also scrutiny by the European Union Committee of the House of Lords. The grant of funds to the EU by the UK Government may also raise controversial questions, and is outside the scope of the supply procedure by which Parliament authorizes most other forms of public expenditure. This chapter will not cover EU procedures in detail, although they do provide an interesting model of a very different form of oversight of the use of public resources. Nor will it look in detail at two other highly controversial areas of public expenditure; the use of the private finance initiative and defence procurement, as these will be discussed extensively in Chapter 9. First I shall examine the constitutional principles relating to the control and scrutiny of public expenditure in the UK.

The Constitution: Parliament

As in the case of taxation, parliamentary control of government expenditure is at the heart of traditional constitutional principle. Although there is no equivalent to the provision in the Bill of Rights requiring parliamentary consent to taxation, a similar principle is based on the historic recognition that grievances should be redressed before the approval of supply. There has been some judicial recognition of this principle; thus in *Auckland Harbour Board v R*, the Privy Council stated that:

> it has been a principle of the British Constitution now for more than two centuries... that no money can be taken out of the consolidated Fund into which the revenues of the State have been paid, excepting under a distinct authorization from Parliament itself. The days are long gone by in which the Crown, or its servants, apart from Parliament, could give such an authorization or ratify an improper payment. Any payment out of the consolidated fund made without Parliamentary authority is simply illegal and ultra vires, and may be recovered by the Government.[4]

[2] See A. Brazier and V. Ram, *The Fiscal Maze: Parliament, Government and Public Money* (London: Hansard Society, 2006), ch. 7.

[3] For an introduction, see Brazier and Ram, *The Fiscal Maze* (n 2) ch. 9, and for fuller discussion of the Court of Auditors, F. White and K. Hollingsworth, *Audit, Accountability and Government* (Oxford: Clarendon Press, 1999), ch. 8 and C. Harlow, *Accountability in the European Union* (Oxford: Oxford University Press, 2002), ch. 5.

[4] [1924] AC 318, 326–7.

This constitutional norm is implemented through the parliamentary supply procedures. These are highly complex, and only a summary need be given here because it will soon be apparent that other processes are now of greater practical importance.[5] The major principle is that 'the government must seek the approval of the House of Commons for specific amounts of expenditure on particular purposes ("estimates") in each financial year and that approval must be expressed in legislation'.[6] Thus estimates are presented to Parliament (after being provided in draft to select committees) and are approved by a resolution of the House of Commons. Three 'estimates days' are provided each year for debate linked to select committee reports on the estimates; however, the debates are normally more focused in issues of administration than on the details of the estimates themselves, which are approved in bulk after little or no debate. Approval of the estimates is not in itself enough to provide parliamentary authority for expenditure, as this must be given by legislation. It normally takes the form of a Consolidated Fund Act and two Appropriation Acts each year, providing authority for the use of moneys from the Consolidated Fund. The bills which become these Acts are passed without debate at any of their formal stages, the assumption being that there will have been an earlier opportunity for debate in consideration of the estimates. An inquiry by the Hansard Society observed that '[t]he majority of people who gave evidence to this inquiry were of the view that the supply process as it currently operates, while being very complex, is little more than a "rubber stamp"'.[7] No estimate has been rejected since 1919 (referring to the provision of a second bathroom for the Lord Chancellor).

It should also be noted that a considerable proportion of public expenditure (around a third) falls outside the supply procedure. This includes that for Consolidated Fund standing services which do not require annual approval; examples are payments to the EU budget, the Sovereign Grant payments to the monarch, and judicial salaries. A further example, a result of the financial crisis, is in the Banking Act 2009. It provides that if the Treasury is satisfied that the need for expenditure on financial assistance to banks and other financial institutions is too urgent for arrangements to be made for the

[5] For more detailed coverage, see T. Daintith and A. Page, *The Executive in the Constitution* (Oxford: Oxford University Press, 1999), 155–64; J. McEldowney, 'Public Expenditure and the Control of Public Finance' in J. Jowell and D. Oliver, eds, *The Changing Constitution*, 7th edn (Oxford: Oxford University Press, 2011), 334–64, 341–5, 355–61; Brazier and Ram, *The Fiscal Maze* (n 2) ch. 4. The authoritative account is T. Erskine May, *Erskine May's Treatise on the Law, Privileges, Proceedings and Usage of Parliament*, 24th edn (London: LexisNexis, 2011), chs 33–4.

[6] R. Blackburn and A. Kennon, *Griffith and Ryle on Parliament: Functions, Practice and Procedures* (London: Sweet and Maxwell, 2003), para. 6-178.

[7] Brazier and Ram, *The Fiscal Maze* (n 2) para. 4.7.

provision of money by Parliament, it may be made from the Consolidated Fund. The Treasury must then report the amount of payment to Parliament, though not the identity of the recipient, although even reporting is not required if the Treasury considers this to be against the public interest.[8] Finally, the existence of the Contingencies Fund should be noted. This permits payments for urgent services in anticipation of parliamentary approval of expenditure. It has been used for a wide variety of purposes, including the building of the first atomic bomb, and for the temporary payment of funds held illegal in the 'Pergau Dam' case to be discussed later in the chapter. Although payments from the fund may not exceed 2 per cent of the previous year's estimates, they may still be substantial and, as McEldowney has noted:

> [n]o select committee directly monitors the use of the Fund and there are no satisfactory means to inquire into the policy behind the Government's use of the Fund prior to the Fund being used... Parliament has, in effect, through inactivity allowed an exception in the form of the Contingencies Fund to the principle that Parliament should vote money before expenditure is incurred.[9]

Perhaps most importantly of all, the supply procedures have not been coordinated with the arrangements for determining the total amount of public expenditure and its allocation between departments and programmes, despite the fact that the estimates are largely determined by the Spending Review process (to be discussed later). This was noted and strongly criticized by select committees. For example, the House of Commons Liaison Committee, comprised of the Chairs of the departmental select committees, pointed to the extreme complexity of the UK Government's financial arrangements and reporting resulting in a lack of transparency, largely because they brought together three different financial frameworks created at different times for different purposes. These frameworks were, first, departmental budgets largely set in spending reviews as administrative controls rather than authorizing expenditure; second, the estimates to seek annual parliamentary authority for expenditure; and third, resource accounts reporting expenditure departments have actually made. Each was prepared on a different basis, making it extremely difficult to read across from one to the other.[10] As a result, the estimates approved by Parliament reflected decisions already taken in the Spending Review process, which had received hardly any parliamentary scrutiny; the

[8] Banking Act 2009, s 228.

[9] 'Public Expenditure and the Control of Public Finance' (n 5), 345.

[10] House of Commons Liaison Committee, *Parliament and Government Finance: Recreating Financial Scrutiny* (HC 2007–08, 426), paras 27–8.

2007 Spending Review had been debated for only an hour and a half in the Chamber. Thus '[h]ad such a system been deliberately designed, it could fairly be assumed that it had been set up with the specific purpose of making it impossible to hold the Government and Departments to account'.[11]

Since this report, considerable progress has been made in reform through the Alignment Project, also known as the Clear Line of Sight project, which aimed to create a relatively simple system with a single set of numbers through aligning budgets, estimates, and accounts and the timing of financial reporting.[12] Necessary legislative changes were made in the Constitutional Reform and Governance Act 2010; the project was approved by the House of Commons in July 2010.[13] For the first time, the main supply estimates for 2011–12 were presented on a budgetary basis. This should provide a clearer basis of information for parliamentary scrutiny of spending plans. Moreover, the move to resource accounting and budgeting, to be discussed later in this chapter, has also contributed to the provision of more effective and meaningful financial information. However, none of this will change the fundamental point that supply procedures are not capable of providing effective scrutiny of either the total amount of public expenditure or of its allocation. Much more important will be the role of select committees, both in relation to the Spending Review process and, in particular, through the examination of expenditure which has already taken place so drawing lessons for the future.

The Constitution: the courts

The courts have assumed a major constitutional role in scrutiny of *local* government expenditure. This has taken a number of forms, including strict application of the rules of ultra vires and the development of a common law 'fiduciary duty' emphasizing local authority requirements to have regard to the interests of those providing funding.[14] Such scrutiny has been facilitated by the fact that all local authority spending must be undertaken under

[11] House of Commons Liaison Committee, *Parliament and Government Finance: Recreating Financial Scrutiny* (n 10) para. 30.

[12] HM Treasury, *Alignment (Clear Line of Sight) Project* (Cm 7567, 2009). For analysis, see the House of Commons Liaison Committee, *Financial Scrutiny: Parliamentary Control over Government Budgets* (HC 2008–09, 804).

[13] Constitutional Reform and Governance Act 2010, ss 43–44; HC Debs 5 July 2010, vol. 513, cols 85–108.

[14] Major cases include *Hazel v Hammersmith London Borough Council* [1992] 2 AC 1; *Bromley London Borough Council v Greater London Council* [1983] 1 AC 768.

statutory powers (which until recently, imposed major constraints on innovative initiatives), by the absence of direct parliamentary scrutiny, and by the former existence of the penalty of personal surcharge for unlawful expenditure.[15] By contrast, in relation to central government, where expenditure powers have been much wider and there has been no surcharge, the courts have taken a much more restricted role. A suggestion of greater judicial activism appeared in the 'Pergau Dam' case, which involved the provision of funding from the Aid and Trade Provision budget to build a dam in Malaysia.[16] The Overseas Development Agency had appraised the scheme and determined that it was uneconomic and should not be implemented for the foreseeable future, and the accounting officer (the civil servant with ultimate financial responsibility) had required a ministerial direction before authorizing the expenditure. The High Court held that the statutory power under which the aid was granted, whilst expressed as being 'for the purpose of promoting the development or maintaining the economy of a country', had to be interpreted as limited to the power to support sound development projects.[17] They did not cover a project such as the one in question where the contemplated project was so economically unsound that there was no economic argument in its favour. Despite losing the case, the Government provided temporary funding from the Contingencies Fund, with permanent authority obtained under another Act of Parliament and a supplementary estimate.

Commentators have suggested that the decision provides the basis for a new constitutional principle that '*the proposed spending by the Executive of money voted by Parliament is unlawful if, in relation to the object for which the money has been provided, no reasonable minister could think that the proposed spending represented value for money*'.[18] This principle might have provided a further limit on governmental discretion on expenditure matters, albeit one limited to extreme cases of bad spending; it has not been applied since the 'Pergau Dam' case itself. Other general principles of judicial review might also be relevant of course, and were successfully used to challenge the decision of the Coalition Government to cancel a major schools building

15 For a recent widening of local authority spending powers, also referred to in Chapter 2, see the Localism Act 2011, ss 1–8.

16 *R v Secretary of State for Foreign and Commonwealth Affairs, ex parte The World Development Movement Ltd* [1995] 1 All ER 611, discussed in detail in I. Harden, F. White, and K. Hollingsworth, 'Value for Money and Administrative Law' [1996] *Public Law* 661–81.

17 Overseas Development and Co-operation Act 1980, s 1(1).

18 Harden, White, and Hollingsworth, 'Value for Money and Administrative Law' (n 16) 662 (emphasis retained).

programme.[19] It should be emphasized that this decision was taken on procedural grounds of failure to consider the merits of individual cases in exercising a statutory discretion, and of failure to consult resulting in unfairness; illegality also resulted from a failure to consider statutory equalities duties. The court emphasized that it would be extremely reluctant to grant judicial review on grounds of substantive irrationality in the case of 'a very major decision with a patently political and heavy macro-economic content, made at the highest level in the immediate aftermath of a general election and change of government, and patently intended to help achieve economic demands from the Treasury'. To examine the reasons of the minister in detail would 'be a grave and exorbitant usurpation by the court of the minister's political role'.[20] The role of the courts is thus likely to remain marginal in relation to the substance of spending decisions by central government, although procedural challenges have a greater chance of success.

Planning public expenditure

The Comprehensive Spending Review

Of far greater importance than the parliamentary procedures is the process of the Spending Review (SR). The overall figure for public expenditure will be fixed in advance and announced in the budget, but the SR will determine how this is applied to different departments and programmes. It is now at the very centre of British politics, and merits description in detail.

The SR was introduced in its present form by the Labour Government as a way of instilling greater rationality and predictability into government spending decision through the process of a Comprehensive Spending Review (CSR). This succeeded other attempts to plan expenditure on a longer-term basis, most of which had met with only limited success, and formed part of the Public Expenditure Survey system first articulated by the Plowden Committee in 1961.[21] The system aimed to move beyond a single year time horizon in spending plans and to take a more comprehensive view of the level of expenditure; it was supplemented by a system of cash limits in 1976, and from 1981 was conducted on a cash basis rather than a real resource basis,

[19] *R (Luton Borough Council and Nottingham City Council) v Secretary of State for Education* [2011] EWHC 217 (Admin), [2011] BLGR 553.

[20] *R (Luton Borough Council and Nottingham City Council) v Secretary of State for Education* (n 19) para. 48, per Holman J; see also paras 7–8, 17, 47.

[21] HM Treasury, *Report of the Committee (Plowden) on the Control of Public Expenditure* (Cmnd 1432, 1961).

thus emphasizing its control function at the expense of that of planning.[22] Until 1992 the process involved bilateral negotiations between Departments and the Treasury; from 1981–92 disputes were resolved through the 'Star Chamber', an ad hoc Cabinet Committee of senior non-spending ministers. In 1992 a new Control Total was introduced as an aggregate providing a clearer and more controllable figure for expenditure planning, and a Cabinet Committee on public expenditure was established with the role not of settling bilateral disputes but of presenting a package of spending allocations to the Cabinet.[23]

These developments formed the basis for the CSR introduced in 1998, with overall totals announced in an Economic and Fiscal Strategy Report.[24] Three elements were of particular importance. The first was that, instead of determining expenditure for a single year, multi-year limits were to be set for three years ahead and rolled over every three years. A distinction was made between these Departmental Expenditure Limits (DEL) and other expenditure such as social security benefits, payments to EU institutions, and debt repayments which would remain subject to annual control, termed Annually Managed Expenditure (AME). Secondly, in relation to DEL the system was intended to be zero-based with all expenditure needing justification, although this was not always the approach taken in practice. Thirdly, spending allocations were to be linked to Public Service Agreements (PSAs) between each spending department and the Treasury, incorporating new objectives and detailed and measurable efficiency and effectiveness targets against which departments would be required to report annually.[25] The adoption of the CSR process was accompanied by other reforms, notably the move to resource accounting and budgeting for departments (to be considered later in this chapter), the publication of new fiscal rules in the form of the Golden Rule and the Sustainable Investment Rule referred to in Chapter 4, and the publication of a Code for Fiscal Stability committing the Government to publication of more information on the Spending Review process.[26] In principle, then, the CSR provided important opportunities for both greater rationality in the allocation of expenditure and increased transparency.

The second SR (not CSR as it was not zero-based) took place in 2000, covering the three years 2001–02 to 2003–04. In this case the Treasury Select

[22] Daintith and Page, *The Executive in the Constitution* (n 5) 143.

[23] Daintith and Page, *The Executive in the Constitution* (n 5) 146–9.

[24] See HM Treasury, *Stability and Investment for the Long Term: Economic and Fiscal Strategy Report 1998* (Cm 3978, 1998) and Treasury Select Committee, *The New Fiscal Framework and the Comprehensive Spending Review* (HC 1997–98, 360).

[25] HM Treasury, *Public Services for the Future: Modernisation, Reform, Accountability—Comprehensive Spending Review: Public Service Agreements 1999–2002* (Cm 4181, 1998).

[26] Finance Act 1998, ss 155–7; HM Treasury, *A Code for Fiscal Stability* (1998).

Committee made two criticisms of the process. The first was that, whilst it welcomed improvements in transparency in the way in which increases in expenditure were broken down, it was critical (as it had been in the case of the first CSR) of the failure to publish a consultative document on departmental totals and the division of expenditure within them in advance of the final figures. The Committee contrasted this with the innovation of a pre-budget report allowing consultation on proposed tax changes. Secondly, the Committee recommended that there be external validation by the NAO and the Audit Commission of the performance of public services against PSA targets.[27] Neither proposal was accepted by the Government. Further SRs took place in 2002 and 2004; in the latter case allocations had been made in advance of the SR to health and education through five-year plans in the budget and other announcements, thereby pre-empting a major part of the process.

There was a return to the full CSR system from a zero base in 2007, although this was constrained by the fact that there had been an 'unprecedented range' of earlier settlements, including for the Home Office, the Department for Work and Pensions, and the Department for Education and Skills.[28] The number of PSAs had been reduced from 250 to 110 since 2002, and a further reduction to 30 cross-departmental targets was announced in the Review, although these were accompanied by 103 new Departmental Strategic Objectives, casting doubt on the extent to which there would be a coherent framework for performance assessment. The Treasury Committee was critical of the failure of the Government to take forward wider national debate on the issues raised in the Review.[29] Overall, the SR process up to 2007 did seem to have succeeded in bringing greater predictability and openness to the allocation of public expenditure, although this was limited by the pre-empting of spending decisions on major services, and, as the Treasury Committee repeatedly emphasized, there was little sense of the process forming part of a wider debate on national priorities.

The 2010 Spending Review

The 2010 Review was conducted against a very different background to that of the earlier reviews. There had just been a general election in which the extent, and timing, of expenditure cuts had been a major issue. The Review

[27] Treasury Committee, *Spending Review 2000* (HC 1999–2000, 485), paras 5, 23.

[28] See Treasury Committee, *The 2007 Comprehensive Spending Review: Prospects and Processes* (HC 2006–07, 279), para. 11.

[29] Treasury Committee, *The 2007 Comprehensive Spending Review: Prospects and Processes* (n 28) paras 96–100.

no longer represented the management of growth but the allocation of major cuts across budgets. Moreover, it formed part of the new Coalition's plans to recast the role of the public sector, as noted earlier, and was considerably more politicized than were the earlier reviews.

The stage was set for the Review in an emergency budget on 22 June 2010.[30] The budget was based on forecasts of the public finances and the economy by the interim Office for Budget Responsibility (discussed in Chapter 2), and set out the path for public expenditure and fixed envelopes for current and capital expenditure. The framework for the SR was set out in a White Paper, and it included a number of major innovations.[31] Thus it was to cover expenditure for the entire Parliament, starting from a baseline of 2010–11 with plans for each of the succeeding four financial years, and was to include not only DEL but also significant parts of AME, including social security. It was accompanied by a number of other reviews, most controversially a Strategic Defence Review covering defence spending, published the day before the SR itself, and a White Paper on welfare reform shortly afterwards.[32] The system of PSAs was ended; instead departmental business plans would be required.

In terms of process, the Prime Minister had appointed a Public Expenditure Committee (PEX, or colloquially the 'Star Chamber') of senior ministers, chaired by the Chancellor and with the Chief Secretary to the Treasury as Deputy Chair, thus securing representation for both Coalition parties. Further ministers were added as they settled their departmental allocation, thereby providing an incentive for earlier settlements. Although it was initially intended to be the central institution in the process, in practice final decisions on the large spending departments and the Review as a whole were taken by the quadrilateral steering committee of the Coalition, composed of the Prime Minister, the Deputy PM, the Chancellor, and the Chief Secretary to the Treasury. Several major announcements were made outside the formal SR process. Thus the BBC was told that there would be extra social security cuts of £4 billion, and an announcement was made without prior Cabinet discussion to the Conservative Party Conference that child benefit would no longer be paid to higher rate taxpayers. Nevertheless, the Treasury Committee was able to conclude that the final SR position had been based on a collective decision-making process.[33] Other procedural innovations included scrutiny by a Spending Challenge Review Group with

[30] HM Treasury, *Budget 2010* (HC 2010–11, 61).

[31] HM Treasury, *The Spending Review Framework* (n 1).

[32] HM Government, *Securing Britain in an Age of Uncertainty: The Strategic Defence and Security Review* (Cm 7498, 2010); Department for Work and Pensions, *Universal Credit: Welfare that Works* (Cm 7957, 2010).

[33] Treasury Committee, *Spending Review 2010* (HC 2010–11, 544), para. 30.

38 members, mainly from the civil service but with four external members, to act as independent challengers and champions for departments; publication of improved raw spending data; and the organization of a series of events and meetings to discuss and debate public expenditure. Suggestions for possible expenditure savings were also sought from public sector workers and the general public via the internet.

The outcome of the 2010 SR was announced by the Chancellor on 20 October 2010, and set out in a 104-page White Paper.[34] The planned effect was to reduce public sector net borrowing from a peak of 11 per cent of GDP in 2009–10 to 1.1 per cent of GDP in 2015–16; to eliminate the structural current deficit by 2014–15; and to place public sector net debt on a downward path from 2014–15. Adjustments were made to the capital envelop to protect projects with long-term value, for example in transport, but overall £81 billion of savings were required by 2014–15. Although the headline figure for cuts in departmental budgets was for 19 per cent over four years, this disguised major variations between different departments and types of expenditure, in part reflecting decisions taken before the SR. Thus the DEL for the Department for Communities and Local Government was to be reduced by 51 per cent (communities) and 27 per cent (local government), for Environment, Food and Rural Affairs by 29 per cent, and for Business, Innovation and Skills by 25 per cent, whilst that for education was to fall by 3.4 per cent and that for the NHS to rise by 1.3 per cent. For AME spending, mainly on social security, over £10.5 billions of savings were to be achieved by the end of the 2014–15 financial year. Capital DEL also varied substantially between departments. Throughout the SR document, the link between the cuts and the Government's public sector reform process was made explicit, especially in relation to social welfare. The SR was not merely an exercise in allocating money, but part of a major rethinking of the role of the state. A SR process for 2015–16 (election year) took place in 2013. This planned a further cut in current spending of £11.5 billion whilst increasing capital spending plans by £3 billion per year; it was constrained by the 'ring-fencing' of expenditure on health and schools, protecting expenditure on them in real terms.[35]

Scrutiny of the Spending Review

The broad-ranging and controversial nature of the Review makes it all the more important to examine the means of scrutiny to which it was subjected.

[34] HC Debs 20 October 2010, vol. 516, cols 949–65; HM Treasury, *Spending Review 2010* (n 1).
[35] HM Treasury, *Spending Round 2013* (Cm 8639, 2013).

It has already been suggested that the role of Parliament in examining decisions on the allocation of public expenditure has been weak, and this point was made repeatedly by both the Treasury Select Committee and the Liaison Committee (comprised of the Chairs of the departmental select committees). One particular subject of criticism mentioned above was the fact that financial reporting arrangements bring together three different financial frameworks created at different times for different purposes; this has been addressed by the Alignment Project discussed earlier. Other criticisms from the Committees went much further. Thus the Liaison Committee recommended that information about the framework within which spending negotiations were taking place should be published, including draft PSAs and Departmental Strategic Objectives. It also endorsed an earlier recommendation of the Treasury Committee, rejected by the Government, that each department should inform the relevant select committees about 'the Government's emerging views on those past objectives which have been achieved and those supporting programmes from which spending is potentially available for reallocation'. The Committee noted that the 2007 CSR was debated for only an hour and a half in the Chamber, and recommended that debate be for a full day after reports had been published by select committees.[36] These proposals were not taken up by the Government, which simply made reference to existing departmental reports and welcomed parliamentary scrutiny in principle.[37]

After the 2010 SR, there was a debate of almost five hours in the House of Commons, although this fell short of the Liaison Committee's recommendations.[38] The Treasury Committee also quickly undertook an inquiry, which inter alia examined the process used for the Review.[39] It reported in generally positive terms on the publication for the first time of analysis of the distributional impact of the budget and the SR as a basis for further debate.[40] However, it was critical of the attempts to encourage wider input into the Spending Review process. This had been undertaken through the group of experts mentioned earlier, and through the 'Spending Challenge' process which enabled public sector employees and the general public to make suggestions for reducing the public sector deficit. In the case of suggestions

[36] House of Commons Liaison Committee, *Parliament and Government Finance: Recreating Financial Scrutiny* (n 10) para. 66.

[37] Liaison Committee, *Parliament and Government Finance: Recreating Financial Scrutiny: Government and National Audit Office Responses to the Committee's Second Report of Session 2007–08* (HC 2007–08, 1108), 6.

[38] HC Debs 28 October 2010, vol. 517, cols 499–582.

[39] Treasury Committee, *Spending Review 2010* (n 33) ch. 3.

[40] Treasury Committee, *Spending Review 2010* (n 33) paras 75–83.

from employees, after moderation these were passed to departments for consideration, whilst in the case of other suggestions members of the public were asked to rate them, with the top 2,000 ideas then being reviewed by officials. Over 100,000 suggestions were made, including 44,000 from the public. In the SR there was reference to 25 ideas which would be taken forward, for example a more preventative approach to public health and closer links across health and social care; further suggestions were said to be contributing other priorities for reform.[41] The Treasury Committee was critical of 'Spending Challenge'. Thus it was sceptical of the extent of the savings the suggestions would produce, and those who had given evidence to the Committee had described the Challenge as 'tokenistic and half-hearted'. The Committee also noted that 'there was no straight-forward method for interest groups to put their ideas and evidence forward'. It concluded that '*[s]hort-term e-consultation can be useful but it cannot be a substitute for longer engagement with public sector employees and responsiveness to input from stakeholder groups*'.[42]

Of much greater importance in achieving transparency was the role of the interim Office for Budget Responsibility, which is responsible for making independent and published assessments of public finances and the economy, and these formed part of the underlying basis of the SR. The Office was established on a permanent basis with important guarantees of independence by the Budget Responsibility and National Audit Act 2011, although it should be noted that it must have regard to relevant government policies and must not consider the effect of alternative policies, thereby limiting its ability to engage in wider debate.[43] Each year it produces a report on the economic and fiscal outlooks, and a Fiscal Sustainability Report with long-term projections of tax and expenditure. That issued in 2012 reported that the medium-term outlook for public sector net debt had actually deteriorated in the previous year, and that the budget deficit would widen over the long term, primarily because of an aging population, putting net debt on a continuously rising trajectory, which would clearly be unsustainable.[44] Such findings were hardly palatable to the Treasury. The Office has bi-partisan support, and indeed the opposition Labour Party has proposed that it audit the Party's fiscal policies before the 2015 election.

A further detailed and important examination of the SR came from the Equality and Human Rights Commission, which reported on the extent to

[41] HM Treasury, *Spending Review 2010* (n 1) 21.

[42] Treasury Committee, *Spending Review 2010* (n 33) paras 33–8 (emphasis retained).

[43] Budget Responsibility and National Audit Act 2011, s 5(3).

[44] Office for Budget Responsibility, *Fiscal Sustainability Report 2012* (2012).

which the Treasury had complied with the public sector equality duties then in force.[45] This was a substantial report running to 172 pages, and benefited from extensive cooperation from the Treasury, from which it had received detailed written and oral evidence. The Commission concluded broadly favourably, finding that there had been a serious attempt by ministers and officials to comply with the equality duties, and in six out of nine areas studied had acted fully in accord with them. In the three others the Commission could not come to a conclusion because of lack of clarity as to where the true site of the decisions lay and as to whether they were the responsibility of departments or of the Government as a whole. Despite the generally positive findings, the Commission noted that 'decision-making functions would benefit from a greater degree of institutional clarity and formal allocation of responsibilities' and was critical of the lack of analysis of the cumulative effect of separate measures in the SR.[46] It also criticized lack of consultation on proposals which were associated with the SR and an associated lack of transparency.[47]

Overall, then, the effect of efforts to achieve a more transparent SR process seems modest, and they suffered from a major defect; the process was a passive one dependent on the submission of ideas by public employees and members of the public rather than engaging in debate.[48] What was absent was any real opportunity for reflection, to develop ideas in a continuing process of mutual debate. The 2013 SR did not have any special arrangements for receiving outside inputs and the Institute for Fiscal Studies described the quality of the documentation and explanation given as 'woeful', although it did include distributional analysis and an assessment of the impact on equalities.[49]

The absence of arrangements for wider debate was particularly striking given the potential importance of the SR as a means of making decisions across government as a whole. It provided an important opportunity to limit the fragmentation of government identified in Chapter 2, yet the SR appears to have been weakest in addressing the cumulative effects of different measures; according to the Equality and Human Rights Commission:

[45] Equality and Human Rights Commission, *Making Fair Financial Decisions: An Assessment of HM Treasury's 2010 Spending Review Conducted under Section 31 of the 2006 Equality Act* (2012).

[46] Equality and Human Rights Commission, *Making Fair Financial Decisions* (n 45) 16, 22, 105–12.

[47] Equality and Human Rights Commission, *Making Fair Financial Decisions* (n 45) 90–1, 103, 108–9.

[48] For similar views in relation to the 2013 SR, see P. Johnson, 'Britain Needs a Broader Debate as Cuts Reshape the Nation', *The Financial Times*, 20 May 2013.

[49] Institute for Fiscal Studies, *The 2015–16 Spending Round* (2013) at: <http://www.ifs.org.uk/projects/418>.

> there was limited cross-government work during the Spending Review. . . . The level of confidentiality required throughout the Spending Review process meant that departments were making bids to HM Treasury in isolation. . . . This level of confidentiality made it difficult for departments to have an understanding of the full impact their measures might have on protected groups when combined with other departmental measures.[50]

Determining public expenditure in Scotland

One example of a more reflexive process can be found in that of the devolved Scottish Parliament and Government.[51] There a spending review takes place in three stages. The first originally took the form of the publication by 31 March of an Annual Evaluation Report as a long-term strategy document setting the scene for the Review but there were problems of linkage with the UK SR and the timing of Scottish elections; new arrangements have been adopted in the form of a 'strategic budget scrutiny phase' to be undertaken at least once in every Parliament.[52] In the special circumstance of 2010 where the prospect of substantial cuts in public expenditure was already clear, the Government commissioned an Independent Budget Review by three highly respected experts. This was a lengthy published document of 174 pages, and, during its development, meetings were held with stakeholders and submissions received from the public.[53] When the Review was published an online consultation website was set up, supplemented by a programme of budget consultation meetings in a number of locations in Scotland and meetings with stakeholders; a summary of the responses was published.[54] The Finance Committee of the Scottish Parliament held a 'Budget Strategy Phase' inquiry into issues raised by reduced budgets and had issued a Strategic Budget Scrutiny Report in the previous year.[55] Thus the first phase includes both a degree of public scrutiny and detailed involvement by an expert parliamentary committee, supported

[50] Equality and Human Rights Commission, *Making Fair Financial Decisions* (n 45) 107–8.

[51] See Brazier and Ram, *The Fiscal Maze* (n 2) 30–1 and the extremely useful summary of the process in Scottish Parliament Information Centre, *Financial Scrutiny Unit Briefing: Guide to the Scottish Budget—Subject Profile* (2011) at: <http://www.scottish.parliament.uk/S4_FinanceCommittee/General%20Documents/ScottishBudgetGuide.pdf>.

[52] See the recommendations of the Scottish Parliament Finance Committee, *Report on the Review of the Budget Process* SP 315 (2009).

[53] Independent Budget Review Panel, *Independent Budget Review 2010* (2010).

[54] The Scottish Government, *Public Spending in Scotland: Engaging with the People of Scotland* (2010).

[55] Scottish Parliament Finance Committee, *Budget Strategy Phase* SP 455 (2010); *Strategic Budget Scrutiny* SP 283 (2009).

by a small Financial Scrutiny Unit which also coordinates reports from other subject committees.

Stage 2 commences with the publication of a draft budget for the following year in September (November in 2010 because of the need to wait for the UK SR). This sets out the Scottish Government's detailed spending plans.[56] There is consultation of parliamentary committees and the public once more, and the Finance Committee may put forward alternatives so long as it keeps within the overall spending limit in the draft budget. The Committee makes a report bringing together recommendations from other committees, and this is debated in December or January.[57] Stage 3 begins when the Budget Bill is laid before the Scottish Parliament, setting out spending plans and taking into account comments made at stage 2. The Bill is subject to debate in Parliament; only members of the Scottish Government may propose amendments.

This process clearly permits much greater outside input and, indeed, parliamentary influence over the spending process. Admittedly, Scotland is a much smaller jurisdiction without the major commitments to social security and defence spending of the UK Government, but its expenditure is still substantial and covers areas of considerable political controversy, including health, education, and social care; it will also acquire important new taxation and borrowing powers under the Scotland Act 2012.[58] The process has the advantage of leaving the ultimate decision to the Scottish Government with no opportunity for the Parliament to block expenditure outright, whilst giving the Parliament a much greater stake in it.[59] In this respect it promotes parliamentary scrutiny more effectively than does the UK SR process, and also permits greater public involvement. It is now appropriate to turn to the processes where the UK Parliament has been more successful in developing effective scrutiny; the *ex post facto* scrutiny of spending and the use of audit.

Audit and scrutiny of spending

The audit and scrutiny of expenditure which has already taken place is a subject which has attracted considerably greater academic attention than have decisions on the total amount of public spending and its allocation in

[56] Scottish Government, *Scottish Budget; Draft Budget 2013–14* (2012).

[57] Scottish Parliament Finance Committee, *Report on Draft Budget 2013–14* SP 231 (2012).

[58] For the effects on the budget process, see Scottish Parliament Information Centre, *Financial Scrutiny Unit Briefing: Guide to the Scottish Budget—Subject Profile* (n 51), 15–16.

[59] Brazier and Ram, *The Fiscal Maze* (n 2) 31.

advance.[60] In this section I shall begin by discussing the key audit institution for central government and related bodies—the NAO—concentrating on its independence, the bodies which it is able to examine, and the types of audit it undertakes. I shall then briefly discuss the House of Commons Public Accounts Committee, and then look at the adoption of resource accounting and budgeting in government, both as a means of improving information used for outside scrutiny and to improve internal managerial accountability arrangements. Finally, a little will be said on the role of departmental reports as successors to reporting against PSAs and detailed targets.

It is important to recall, of course, that these formal mechanisms supplement the central role of the Treasury in the control of public expenditure.[61] Indeed, as part of the emphasis on controls over public spending, Treasury control has been strengthened, for example through the requirement of the provision of monthly spending information by departments.[62] As Daintith and Page have emphasized (and analyzed in detail), this forms the basis for a highly-developed set of internal controls within the executive.[63]

The National Audit Office

The NAO has a long history, having been established as the Exchequer and Audit Office in 1866, and re-established under its present title by the National Audit Act 1983, with further institutional reforms implemented by the Budget Responsibility and National Audit Act 2011. It works on behalf of the Comptroller and Auditor-General, and describes its major aims in the audit of central government as scrutinizing public spending on behalf of Parliament, helping it to hold government departments to account, and helping public service managers to improve performance and service delivery.[64] This points to the important distinction, to be discussed fully in this section, between financial audit to ensure that money has been properly spent, and value for money audit.

[60] See notably White and Hollingsworth, *Audit, Accountability and Government* (n 3) and for a more up-to-date summary, Brazier and Ram, *The Fiscal Maze* (n 2) paras 5.1–5.23. For the NAO's recent work on regulatory reform, see E. Humpherson, 'Auditing Regulatory Reform' in D. Oliver, R. Rawlings, and T. Prosser (eds), *The Regulatory State: Constitutional Implications* (Oxford: Oxford University Press, 2010), 267–82.

[61] For the Treasury rules relating to the scrutiny of expenditure, see HM Treasury, *Managing Public Money* (2007), available at: <https://www.gov.uk/government/uploads/system/uploads/attachment_data/file/179695/mpm_whole.pdf.pdf>.

[62] HM Treasury, *Improving Spending Control* (2012).

[63] Daintith and Page, *The Executive in the Constitution* (n 5) esp. ch 12.

[64] National Audit Office, 'What We Do', at: <http://www.nao.org.uk/about-us/role-2/what-we-do/>.

The NAO and the Comptroller and Auditor-General are guaranteed a considerable degree of constitutional independence.[65] Thus the latter is a corporation sole and an officer of the House of Commons; he is not to be regarded as a servant or agent of the Crown or to enjoy any Crown status.[66] Appointment is by the Crown but with the agreement of the Chair of the Public Accounts Committee, by convention a senior member of the Opposition, thereby securing cross-party acceptability, and removal may only be through an address of both Houses of Parliament.[67] The legislation also makes it clear that the Comptroller and Auditor-General has complete discretion in the carrying out of his functions, including as to whether to carry out a value for money audit and the manner in which such audit is carried out.[68] The NAO is established as a body corporate, and under the 2011 Act the model is adopted of a board comprised of non-executive and employee members; the Comptroller and Auditor-General acts as Chief Executive.[69] NAO employees are not civil servants, and independence is symbolically expressed by its location in Victoria, some distance away from government offices in Whitehall.

Within government departments and executive agencies, the crucial role in accounting for expenditure is played by the accounting officer, who is normally the permanent head of the department or the agency Chief Executive. As the Public Accounts Committee has described, the accounting officer 'is personally responsible for the regularity and propriety of expenditure, robust evaluation of different mechanisms for delivering policy objectives, value for money, the management of risk and accurate accounting for the use of resources'.[70] It is the accounting officer who will appear before the Public Accounts Committee to account for expenditure. As was mentioned in the discussion of the 'Pergau Dam' case, the minister may overrule the advice of the accounting officer; in this situation, the officer must be given a written instruction and must inform the Treasury and the Public Accounts Committee of what has occurred; since 'Pergau Dam' this also applies to value for money matters.[71] The role of the accounting officer thus offers both high-level scrutiny of the procedures and internal controls within departments and some independence from ministerial preferences in controversial decisions.

[65] For a detailed account of this independence and its place within the networks of other institutions, see White and Hollingsworth, *Audit, Accountability and Government* (n 3) 91–119.

[66] Budget Responsibility and National Audit Act 2011, s 12, repeating earlier provisions.

[67] Budget Responsibility and National Audit Act 2011, ss 11(5), 14(2).

[68] Budget Responsibility and National Audit Act 2011, s 17(1).

[69] Budget Responsibility and National Audit Act 2011, s 20 and sch. 2.

[70] Public Accounts Committee, *Accountability for Public Money* (HC 2010–11 740), para. 2.

[71] White and Hollingsworth, *Audit, Accountability and Government* (n 3) 69. For the detailed rules, see HM Treasury, *Managing Public Money* (2007).

The NAO has wide powers of access to information; thus the Comptroller and Auditor-General has free access to the books of account and other documents relating to the accounts of departments and other bodies which are held by government.[72] Similar access is provided for the purposes of value for money audit.[73] The availability of information has also been extended by administrative means in recent years.[74] The most important problems have arisen in relation to access to documents held by public companies acting on behalf of government in providing public services, and this raises the larger and controversial question of the extent of the Comptroller and Auditor-General's powers in relation to bodies other than government departments or executive agencies. This is of considerable importance given the fragmented nature of government discussed in Chapter 2.

There were two arrangements adopted for the audit of non-departmental bodies which were not companies. In some cases the minister appointed an external auditor; in other cases the legislation establishing the body appointed the Comptroller and Auditor-General as auditor, thereby opening up NAO scrutiny. Where the body took the form of a company, company law prevented such audit, however. The Comptroller and Auditor-General also had inspection rights over specified public bodies he did not audit, for example universities, acting alongside a private sector auditor. In the case of value for money audit, the National Audit Act 1983 provides for such audit by the Comptroller and Auditor-General of any body appearing to him to have received in any financial year more than half its income from public funds, so long as the body was appointed by the Crown. There are specified exclusions to this power, notably the nationalized industries.[75] The requirement of ministerial appointment would also prevent examination of companies.

However, more recent legislation permits the Treasury to provide by regulation for audit by the Comptroller and Auditor-General of non-departmental bodies which 'exercise functions of a public nature', and the law has been changed to permit this where the body takes the form of a company.[76] The Government announced in spring 2002 that it planned to extend such audit to all departmental public bodies, including the (previously excluded) Environment Agency and Housing Corporation, and a number of orders have been made to this effect. Further relaxation was made by the 2011 Act, by permitting use of the simpler procedure of an order subject to

[72] Government Resources and Accounts Act 2000, s 8. For a fuller discussion of access to information, see White and Hollingsworth, *Audit, Accountability and Government* (n 3) 111–14.

[73] National Audit Act 1983, s 8.

[74] White and Hollingsworth, *Audit, Accountability and Government* (n 3) 111–14.

[75] National Audit Act 1983, s 7 and sch. 4.

[76] Government Resources and Accounts Act 2000, s 25(6–10); Companies Act 2006, s 482.

annulment by Parliament to extend audit powers.[77] The powers of the NAO in relation to bodies exercising public functions have thus been extended, but in a piecemeal fashion falling short of a general right of access to them; the Public Accounts Committee has expressed serious concern that it has not been given audit rights in relation to Railtrack, despite government provision to it of over £3 billion each year and the underwriting of £25 billion of its debt.[78] The Coalition Government's so-called 'localism' agenda, which will involve the use of a wide range of different institutions, including GP consortia and free schools, raises serious questions which the Public Accounts Committee has started to examine.[79]

The NAO, as mentioned, undertakes two different types of audit. The first is certification audit, which is concerned with whether money has been spent properly, applying standards of regularity, propriety, and probity. Thus the auditor will consider whether accounts present 'a true and fair view' and are 'properly presented'. In particular, he will also determine whether the money has been used for the purposes intended by Parliament and that payments and receipts accord with the relevant legislation.[80] If satisfied, he will issue a certificate to this effect; if not he may qualify the accounts, which may lead to a hearing before the Public Accounts Committee.

Value for money audit undertaken by the NAO is now of considerable importance; a large number of such audits are undertaken each year. Statutory provision for this audit is provided by the National Audit Act 1983, which permits the Comptroller and Auditor-General to undertake examinations into the economy, efficiency, and effectiveness with which a department or other body has used its resources.[81] An important qualification is that this 'shall not be construed as entitling the Comptroller and Auditor-General to question the merits of the policy objectives of any department, authority or body in respect of which an examination is carried out'.[82] An amendment contained in the 2011 Act requires that, in determining whether to carry out such an examination, the Comptroller and Auditor-General must have regard to any proposals made by the Public Accounts Committee.[83]

77 Budget Responsibility and National Audit Act 2011, s 19.

78 Public Accounts Committee, *Reducing Costs in the Department for Transport* (HC 2010–12, 1760), paras 5–11.

79 See Public Accounts Committee, Accountability for Public Money (n 70).

80 For a detailed account, see White and Hollingsworth, *Audit, Accountability and Government* (n 3) 61–74.

81 National Audit Act 1983, s 6(1).

82 National Audit Act 1983, s 6(2).

83 National Audit Act 2011, s 18, inserting a new s 7A into the National Audit Act 1983.

It will be evident that these provisions offer very wide scope for examination of matters which go beyond tradition financial audit.[84] Thus the Office defines value for money as the optimal use of resources to achieve the intended outcomes, and issues detailed recommendations for achieving improved value for money in the future. The '3Es' have been explained as follows:

> 'economy' is about minimizing the costs of resources acquired or used, having regard to appropriate quality ('spending less'), 'efficiency' means achieving the maximum output from a given input ('spending well'), whilst 'effectiveness' is concerned with the extent to which outputs of goods, services or other results achieve policy objectives ('spending wisely').[85]

In undertaking value for money audit the NAO employs a wide range of techniques, including financial analysis and analysis of management information, documentary review, interviews or focus groups with staff, literature reviews, surveys of practitioners or users, and benchmarking against other organizations or other countries. The statutory prohibition on questioning policy objectives does not appear to have caused any major problems in the carrying out of far-reaching studies, not only of government departments but also of major regulatory bodies and of the process of regulatory reform; indeed, the prohibition has not prevented the NAO from studying how policy is formulated and aspects of the policy-making process itself. These techniques have also contributed to the important input of the NAO into the regulatory reform process, for example through examining the role and success of regulatory impact assessments and monitoring the extent to which public bodies have complied with principles of regulatory reform, including risk analysis.[86]

An example of such work in a controversial area is that of the wide-ranging studies of the NAO on the Private Finance Initiative (PFI). The initiative itself will be examined in Chapter 9, and it has been the subject of inquiry by a number of departmental select committees, including a major study by the Treasury Committee.[87] However, there have been some problems with examinations by these committees; although they may now be assisted by

[84] For more details, see White and Hollingsworth, *Audit, Accountability and Government* (n 3) 74–7. For a useful recent summary of the techniques used, see National Audit Office, *What is a Value for Money Study?* at: <http://www.nao.org.uk/about-us/role-2/what-we-do/value-for-money-programme/what-is-a-value-for-money-study/>.

[85] White and Hollingsworth, *Audit, Accountability and Government* (n 3) 74–5, referring to NAO, *A Framework for Value for Money Audits* (nd).

[86] For full discussion of this work, see Humpherson, 'Auditing Regulatory Reform' (n 60).

[87] Treasury Committee, *Private Finance Initiative* (HC 2010–12, 1146).

the NAO, they do not have the sustained support which it offers the Public Accounts Committee, moreover, there have been problems of commercial confidentiality limiting access by the committees to information about private finance deals.[88] Special arrangements are, however, in place for the NAO to see information about private finance schemes on a confidential basis, and it had published no fewer than 72 reports on PFI schemes by September 2009, with more reports in later years. Many of these studies have examined value for money issues in individual projects, but a number of reports have drawn general lessons.

The Public Accounts Committee

As this discussion has suggested, the NAO is much more than a mere provider of information to the Public Accounts Committee of Parliament; its many reports have great importance in their own right. However, most, though not all, reports will be considered by the Committee, on both financial and value for money audit, and, as commentators have noted, the hearing is important in securing both a degree of democratic public accountability and managerial accountability for spending and administrative systems.[89] The Public Accounts Committee is the oldest and most prestigious of the departmental select committees. In view of its special role, it examines more issues and publishes more reports each year than other select committees; it published not less than 88 reports in the 2010–12 session, and many of these include forceful criticism of departments and other public bodies. The Committee has also examined PFI deals in detail and issued highly critical reports, for example on PFI in housing and hospitals in January 2011.[90] As mentioned in Chapter 4, tax avoidance by multinationals and through settlements with HMRC has become a further subject of high-profile examination by the Committee.

The Government responds to the Committee's report within two to three months through a Treasury Minute setting out which recommendations it will accept. In addition, the Committee issues an annual report to Parliament forming the basis of a debate focusing on selected reports and the Government responses to them. This debate is not required in the case of the other select committees, and once more highlights the special status of the Public

[88] See Brazier and Ram, *The Fiscal Maze* (n 2) paras 8.3–8.4; House of Commons Liaison Committee, Parliament and Government Finance: Recreating Financial Scrutiny (n 10) para. 56.

[89] White and Hollingsworth, *Audit, Accountability and Government* (n 3) 122; the work of the Committee is examined at 122–7.

[90] Public Accounts Committee, *PFI in Housing and Hospitals* (HC 2010–11, 631).

Accounts Committee. By its very nature, the Committee is not able to make binding recommendations for improvement. However, the Treasury Minutes and the annual debate do go some way to creating both an opportunity for dialogue and pressure for improvement in the management of public expenditure. The influence which the Committee can exercise rests on both its prestige and the support it is given by the NAO, resulting in far more detailed scrutiny of spending which has taken place than is available to Parliament when expenditure is being planned.

Resource accounting and budgeting

Of course, scrutiny of expenditure involves much more than external audit on behalf of Parliament. The internal procedures for accounting are of the utmost importance for two reasons. The first is that the bodies engaged in external scrutiny need to have information presented to them in a way which makes it possible to identify clearly any problems and potential for increasing efficiency. Secondly, given that audit is largely concerned with systems rather than attempting to check individual transactions, the role internal systems play is crucial;

> [w]hen the C&AG and the NAO audit the accounts of central government bodies, they report on the observance of rules: rules which are not so much imposed on government from outside but which government uses to control itself. The system uses *democratic accountability* to Parliament to reinforce self-regulation within government; in particular to enable the Treasury to control departments and to reinforce *managerial accountability* within departments.... The same is true for value for money (*vfm*) reports. The NAO provides an independent external evaluation to Parliament of the *vfm* achieved by government. At the same time, *vfm* is a criterion government increasingly uses to evaluate itself.[91]

Thus external audit systems and those for internal audit are mutually reinforcing.

A major development with considerable importance in improving the quality of information was the move from cash accounting to resource accounting and budgeting (RAB) implemented under the Government Resources and Accounts Act 2000. Resource accounts are closer to private sector accounts and are prepared under GAAP (Generally Accepted Accounting Practice). Most importantly, they follow the concept of accruals accounting. This means that

[91] White and Hollingsworth, *Audit, Accountability and Government* (n 3) 9–10 (emphasis retained).

expenditure is matched to revenues earned and obligations incurred in the same period:

> For example, a department may have used electricity and received an electricity bill in the year, but may pay it after the financial year ends. The cost would be recognised in resource accounts in the financial year in which the cost was incurred. It is referred to as an accrual. The same cost would only have been recognised in cash-based accounts in the following year, when it was actually paid.[92]

Secondly, the cost of capital assets is matched to the period in which they are used or consumed by charging depreciation on them: '[i]n resource accounts assets are recorded in the balance sheet and depreciation is charged as a cost. Previous cash accounts did have an assets and liabilities statement but did not charge depreciation, which means that they did not reflect wear and tear of assets.'[93] Thus the cost of capital is spread across its lifetime.[94] Resource accounting is accompanied by resource budgeting, through which budgets are also prepared on an accruals basis; as was mentioned earlier, this has been supplemented by the Alignment Project to simplify and clarify the budgetary regime through aligning estimates with budgets set in the Spending Review.[95]

The Government Resources and Accounts Act 2000 requires government departments for which an estimate was approved by the House of Commons to prepare resource accounts in accordance with directions issued by the Treasury.[96] The system was implemented from April 2001 and as a result accounts are now comprised of a number of documents including an Annual Report (with a Management Commentary), a statement of internal control, a statement of parliamentary supply, an operating cost statement, a balance sheet, and a cash flow statement.[97] In 2008 the Public Accounts Committee reported that accruals-based accounting and budgeting systems were well-established after an initially slow start; 92 per cent of departments had now implemented RAB.[98] Further progress had been made by 2011.[99] Although others problems of financial management remained, RAB has

[92] Committee Office Scrutiny Unit, *Financial Scrutiny Uncovered: How the Government Manages its Finances and how Parliament Scrutinises Them* (House of Commons, 2007), 20.

[93] Committee Office Scrutiny Unit, *Financial Scrutiny Uncovered* (n 92) 20.

[94] For a more detailed account resource accounting and its role in the public sector, see White and Hollingsworth, *Audit, Accountability and Government* (n 3) 16–18, 132–4.

[95] For further discussion of resource budgeting, see Daintith and Page, *The Executive in the Constitution* (n 5) 166–8.

[96] Government Resources and Accounts Act 2000, s 5.

[97] For further details, see *Financial Scrutiny Uncovered* (n 92) 21–2.

[98] Public Accounts Committee, 'Managing Financial Resources to Deliver Better Public Services' (HC 2007–08, 519).

[99] NAO, *Progress in Improving Financial Management in Government* (HC 2010–11, 487).

been successfully implemented, and will be of further value in creating greater transparency with the completion of the Alignment Project.

Whole of government accounts

A further reform in relation to government accounting has been the adoption of 'whole of government' accounts. These are accounts which are prepared in a way similar to private sector practice and which cover, so far as practicable, the whole of the public sector in a consolidated form. The Government Resources and Accounts Act 2000 requires the preparation of such accounts for bodies which exercise functions of a public nature or are entirely or substantially funded from public money.[100] The Treasury designates each year the bodies to which the requirement applies by statutory instrument; a large number of such bodies is covered, including not only central government departments and national non-departmental public bodies but also local authorities and police authorities.[101] Given the amount of information required it is not surprising that implementation has taken some time, but whole of government accounts were drawn up fully for the first time for the year 2009/10 and published in 2011. They were welcomed by the Public Accounts Committee as 'a major step forward in improving transparency and accountability'; however, it was critical of the time taken to prepare them (20 months) and of the fact that the Comptroller and Auditor-General had qualified his opinion on them because of inconsistent application of generally accepted accounting practice, in particular because of the exclusion of Network Rail, the publicly-owned banks, and higher education institutions.[102]

Departmental reports and business plans

In addition to the more formal accounting information, there has been a succession of other types of reporting requirements applied to government departments and some other bodies, most recently in the form of departmental business plans. It was mentioned earlier that the CSR was linked to the issuing of PSAs which would include a system of targets for public bodies against which performance would be measured, and these were to form a substantial part of the departmental reports. Even before the introduction of this system, each department had been required annually to produce a

[100] S 9(1).

[101] S 9(2) and the Whole of Government Accounts (Designation of Bodies) Order 2010, SI 2010/1051.

[102] Public Accounts Committee, *Whole of Government Accounts 2009–10* (HC 2010–12, 1696).

document reporting on activity over the previous year and the year in progress, and presenting its spending plans; Treasury guidance specified a core of information to be included.[103] However, the system of reporting against targets proved controversial from the beginning. In 1998 the Treasury Committee questioned the effectiveness of quantitative targets in improving services, especially when the sanctions to back them up were unclear.[104] In a particularly important report, the Public Administration Committee undertook a detailed examination of the role of targets and criticized the lack of integration between the 'measurement culture' based around them and the developing of a 'performance culture' to improve services.[105] After further criticisms, the number of PSAs was reduced, from 250 to 110 by 2004, and it was announced that only 30 would be set for the 2007 Spending Review. However, alongside them arrangements for monitoring delivery would be strengthened and 103 new Departmental Strategic Objectives would be set, with further outcome-focused indicators.[106] A further source of controversy was the extent to which there should be external validation of performance against the targets, for example by the NAO.[107]

The Coalition Government in 2010 ended the system of PSAs, claiming that the previous Government's approach 'relied on top-down performance management and too many politically-motivated targets'. Instead, departmental business plans would be required:

> showing the resources, structural reforms and efficiency measures that they will need to put into place to protect and improve the quality of key frontline services whilst spending less. These plans will also include the key statistics and data that the public can use to hold departments to account for spending money efficiently and effectively.[108]

Thus the business plans published in 2010 included the department's vision and priorities to 2014–15; a structural reform plan; and key indicators to show the cost and impact of public services and departmental activities. Each month, departments publish a brief report on progress towards meeting the commitments, and the plans are updated annually.

[103] See Daintith and Page, *The Executive in the Constitution* (n 5) 154–5.

[104] Treasury Committee, *The New Fiscal Framework and the Comprehensive Spending Review* (HC 1997–98, 460), paras 42–5.

[105] Public Administration Committee, *On Target? Government by Measurement* (HC 2002–03, 62).

[106] See Treasury Committee, *The 2007 Comprehensive Spending Review* (HC 2007–08, 55).

[107] See e.g. Treasury Committee, *Spending Review 2000* (HC 1999–2000, 485), para. 23.

[108] HM Treasury, *The Spending Review Framework* (n 1), para. 2.7; see also *Spending Review 2010* (n 1), 34.

The departmental business plans were, according to the Prime Minister, part of a fundamental power shift from government to communities and people; however, it has also been pointed out that they really represent more continuity than change, with many targets appearing under another name, such as 'impact indicators' or 'outcomes', though in less quantified form.[109] Perhaps the most important role of the plans will be to offer substantial assistance to parliamentary select committees in examining the performance of departments. This has already represented a very significant part of the committees' work, and has been assisted by the creation of the Scrutiny Unit as a source of specialist information and assistance to the committees, especially on financial matters and draft bills, resembling on a much smaller scale the role of the NAO in relation to the Public Accounts Committee.[110] Once more, *ex post facto* scrutiny by committees has been the most effective means of holding public expenditure to account.

Conclusion

It was suggested in Chapter 2 above that a major problem with the UK economic constitution is its fragmented nature with little attempt to ensure coherence in the organization or scrutiny of government as a whole. One theme which has emerged from recent developments is greater emphasis on examination of government spending rather than that of individual departments, and this is evident in the SR process (although the Equality and Human Rights Commission was still critical of a failure in practice to look at the cumulative impact of different cuts). The introduction of whole of government accounts may also have contributed to a more holistic assessment of government spending. The advantages of such an overview mean that the SR process is clearly here to stay; the Labour Opposition plans to implement a fundamental SR should it gain power in 2015, and indeed a similar process has been adopted in other countries including France and Italy. These measures may do something to counteract the effects of the fragmentation of government. This is a point to which I shall return in the conclusion to this book.

Although some improvements are being made to the advance scrutiny of budgets, notably through the role of the Alignment Project in relating the estimates more directly to the planning of expenditure, Parliament has had

[109] N. Timmins, 'Coalition Creates Rod for its Own Back', *The Financial Times*, 9 November 2010.

[110] See also Brazier and Ram, *The Fiscal Maze* (n 2) paras 4.15–4.18.

only a very limited role in such advance scrutiny, and this is likely to remain the case. Indeed, commentators have stressed that giving Parliament powers of *control* of expenditure decisions (as opposed to improved powers of *scrutiny*) would be positively undesirable; as the Liaison Committee put it:

> [i]mproving financial scrutiny is not about finding ways to force through major changes to the Government's overall revenue-raising and spending plans . . . What improving financial scrutiny *is* about is making the Government, individual Departments and other public bodies accountable for their financial decisions—in other words, requiring them to justify their revenue-raising and spending plans and, later, to explain whether the expenditure achieved its objectives and, if not, why not.[111]

However, other mechanisms for advance scrutiny of spending decisions are very limited; the use of the internet to receive suggestions in the 2010 spending review process hardly represented a commitment to wider debate, although the role of the Office for Budget Responsibility does create greater transparency and independent forecasting and examination of economic performance, and the detailed examination by the Equality and Human Rights Commission was an important and innovative form of scrutiny of social impact. Although the 2010 Spending Review may be exceptional in that it followed a general election in which the amount of public expenditure was a major issue, that did not extend to the central question of how the cuts in expenditure should allocated. The experience in Scotland provides a striking example of a more open and participative process for taking these hard decisions. If the role of Parliament in advance scrutiny is inherently limited, it could be supplemented by other techniques for public involvement. Reforms proposed by select committees include the publication of fuller information in advance on draft business plans and on the achievement of past objectives.

There has been much more effective scrutiny of expenditure *ex post facto*. Here the most important role has been that of the NAO, which has engaged in sustained and detailed examination of many aspects of public expenditure, and this has been supplemented by the role of the Public Accounts Committee. The departmental select committees have an important role which has been aided by the creation of the Scrutiny Unit and the move to resource accounting and budgeting providing more useful financial information. The overall picture is thus one of improvement in scrutiny of spending itself, alongside only limited scrutiny of the process of expenditure planning, despite the increased political importance of the latter.

[111] House of Commons Liaison Committee, *Parliament and Government Finance: Recreating Financial Scrutiny* (n 10) paras 7–8 (reference omitted).

6

Monetary Policy and the Bank of England

Introduction

Monetary stability is one of the two objectives of the Bank of England, alongside financial stability. It is implemented through the Government setting an inflation target which the Bank seeks to meet through the monthly meetings of its Monetary Policy Committee (MPC) setting interest rates. Since March 2009 this has been supplemented by the process of quantitative easing through which money is directly injected into the economy to compensate for the very low level of the Bank rate and to increase the availability of corporate credit.[1] This chapter will concentrate on the institutional arrangements through which these processes (especially setting interest rates) take place; they offer a particularly useful case-study of legislative and institutional change through the creation of an independent MPC under the Bank of England Act 1998. The Bank of course also has other major functions in the economy, including acting as lender of last resort and as a key player in financial services regulation, a role now substantially increased. This will be considered separately in Chapter 7.

Constitutional Background

Domestic law and the history of the Bank of England

In 1997 Daintith observed that:

> [m]onetary policy is a central concern of governments of market economy states, yet it is an area that both public policy scientists and public lawyers have been reluctant to penetrate. This is hardly surprising. Everything important about it appears to be in dispute.[2]

[1] For a very accessible description of the role of the Bank in monetary policy see its website at: <http://www.bankofengland.co.uk/monetarypolicy/index.htm>.

[2] T. Daintith, 'Regulation' in International Association of Legal Science, *State and Economy* (Dordrecht: Martinus Nijhoff Publishers, 1997), vol. XVII, para. 10–109.

This must now be qualified. One reason for an increasingly high visibility of monetary policy is precisely the new arrangements introduced in the late 1990s, which have substantially increased transparency, especially when compared to other areas of economic policy. A second is the role of the European Central Bank (ECB) which is in charge of monetary policy for the eurozone, and whose decisions have a substantial impact on other economies such as that of the UK. However, since the financial crisis, interest rates have been at extremely low levels, requiring the use of other monetary tools.

Reflecting an earlier lack of interest in the institutions and processes of monetary policy, there was little concern with constitutional principle in this area in the UK. Before the 1998 Act the Bank of England had a shadowy constitutional status. It had been founded as a piece of private speculation to raise money for government in 1694, and remained a private company until it was nationalized in 1946. Its relations with government were sometimes obscure and changed considerably over time.[3] At times it claimed independence from government; in 1929 it maintained to a Committee of Inquiry that its obligations to the Government were no more than 'the ordinary duties of banker to client' and instead it owed to the community as a whole the principal duty to maintain the stability of the currency, and it claimed the right to act independently on interest rates.[4] In that year the Government had agreed that rates were a technical matter to be left to the Governor of the Bank; however, even during the 1930s, it vetoed increases in interest rates. Over the following 20 years responsibility for interest rates moved to the Treasury and the Bank lost any independent responsibility for policy, whilst retaining considerable autonomy in the execution of monetary policy through its daily operations in the money markets. The constitutional relationship of the Bank and the Treasury remained unclear; as one MP put it in 1940;

> I said to the [Governor] one day, 'The Chancellor of the Exchequer tells me that he does not control the Bank Rate' and the reply I got was 'I regret to tell you . . . that the Chancellor of the Exchequer did not tell you the truth'.[5]

[3] For an excellent summary, see M. Moran, 'Monetary Policy and the Machinery of Government' (1981) 59 *Public Administration* 47–61.

[4] See Moran, 'Monetary Policy and the Machinery of Government' (n 3) 49. The quotation is from Committee on Finance and Industry: Minutes of Evidence (London, 1931), Vol. I 1–2 and Vol. II 275.

[5] HC Debs 29 May 1940, vol. 361 col 264, quoted in Moran, 'Monetary Policy and the Machinery of Government' (n 3) 50.

The formal responsibility of the Governor could also be used as means for ministers to avoid parliamentary scrutiny. The result was a framework characterized as 'high on discretion, low on transparency'.[6]

Given this background, the nationalization of the Bank in 1946 was of limited importance. It was irrelevant to the question of control, and indeed the Bank of England Act simply took the assets of the Bank into public hands without changing its status; it remains a chartered rather than a public corporation. Section 4 of the Act gave the Treasury power to issue directions to the Bank and gave the Bank power to give directions to bankers with the approval of the Treasury. Neither of these powers has ever been used. Nor were any objectives for the Bank set out in the Act. In practical terms, there was a further decline in the Bank's independence in the 1980s with the Thatcher Governments placing a much greater stress on the importance of monetary policy as an instrument of economic policy. As the then Chancellor, Nigel Lawson, put it in the late 1980s, '[w]hen I think [interest rates] ought to go up they go up and when I think they should come down they come down' and '[w]e take the decisions but they [the Bank] do the work'.[7] Nevertheless, the first signs of change came when Lawson in 1988 presented a secret plan for Bank independence to Mrs Thatcher; he repeated the proposal in his resignation speech, and it later gained the support of another former Chancellor, Norman Lamont. In 1993, in response to this proposal, the Prime Minister stated that '[w]ere a way to be found to get the benefits of an independent central bank without the loss of parliamentary accountability, my views would be very close to those of my right hon. Friend'.[8] The background to the Bank of England Act 1998 and its provisions will be discussed further in this chapter; the Act sets out a much clearer and transparent set of relations between the Bank and government. First the European context needs consideration.

European Union law and the European System of Central Banks

Inevitably, there is a much clearer constitutional dimension to the implementation of monetary policy at the EU level, due to the creation of the ECB and the European System of Central Banks (ESCB) by the Maastricht Treaty

[6] T. Daintith, 'Between Domestic Democracy and an Alien Rule of Law? Some Thoughts on the "Independence" of the Bank of England' [1995] *Public Law* 118–32, 122.

[7] See Treasury and Civil Service Committee, *The Role of the Bank of England* (HC 1993–94, 98), para. 16.

[8] See Treasury and Civil Service Committee, *The Role of the Bank of England* (n 7), para. 8.

in 1992. Key features are a clear mandate set out in the Treaty for the ECB which is responsible for setting interest rates and the inflation target; the prohibition of interventions by national governments; and a system of national central banks which are independent of their national governments. As Daintith has emphasized, two elements of the new structure were particularly foreign to traditional UK constitutional arrangements. The first was their essentially federal character, evident in the ESCB itself and in the representation of the governors of national central banks in the governing council of the ECB.[9] The second major characteristic was the establishment of a strong normative framework for monetary policy in the Treaty rather than relying only on political direction and supervision.[10] The position is however complicated by the exclusion of the UK from many, but not all, of the relevant provisions owing to its decision not to join the eurozone or to participate in stage 3 of monetary union which passed monetary policy to the ECB.[11] The Treaty provisions implementing the opt-out are of considerable complexity but an overview can be given here.

Title VII of the TFEU deals with economic and monetary policy; article 119 sets common objectives, though the UK is excluded from the single monetary and exchange rate policy; it is however committed under article 119(3) to stable prices, sound public finances and monetary conditions, and a sustainable balance of payments. As noted in Chapter 4 on borrowing, it was also made subject to the excessive deficit procedure, though no formal sanctions could be brought against it. The UK is a member of the ESCB, which is composed of the ECB and the central banks of all Member States; however, it does not participate in decisions relating to the single monetary policy and the mandate of the ESCB does not apply to it. This is set out in article 127 TFEU, and is to maintain price stability; without prejudice to this, the system is to support the general economic policies in the Union and it is to act 'in accordance with the principle of an open market economy with free competition, favouring an efficient allocation of resources and in compliance with the principles set out in Article 119'. Article 282 TFEU also states that the primary objective of the ESCB is to maintain price stability (this does not apply to the UK). The Statute of the ECB once more sets out its primary objective as being to maintain price stability.[12] However, the UK derogation states that '[t]he United Kingdom shall retain

9 Daintith, 'Between Domestic Democracy and an Alien Rule of Law?' (n 6) 121.

10 Daintith, 'Between Domestic Democracy and an Alien Rule of Law?' (n 6) 125–30.

11 The details of the opt-out can be found in Protocol 15 to the TFEU, *On Certain Provisions Relating to the United Kingdom of Great Britain and Northern Ireland*.

12 Protocol 4, *On the Statute of the European System of Central Banks and of the European Central Bank*, art. 2.

its powers in the field of monetary policy according to national law' and the Statute of the ESCB states that central banks of countries with a derogation shall retain their powers in the field of monetary policy according to national law.[13] As discussed in Chapter 3, the UK has remained outside the fiscal pact contained in the Treaty on Stability, Coordination and Governance.

Further provisions of considerable importance relate to the independence of central banks. Thus article 130 TFEU, which does not apply to the UK, states that neither the ECB nor any national central bank shall seek or take instructions from Union institutions, any government of a Member State, or from any other body; under article 131 (again not applying to the UK) Member States are to ensure that their national legislation is compatible with this. Similar provision is made in the Statute.[14] The Treaty also makes provision for independence of the ECB in article 282(3), which does apply to the UK. At least every two years, the Commission and the ECB must report to the Council on the progress by Member States with a derogation on the achievement of economic and monetary union; this includes examination of the compatibility of their national legislation with the independence requirements applying to national banks which have entered the final stage of monetary union.[15]

These complex provisions thus have the result that, despite the Bank of England's membership of the ESCB, the constitutional and institutional framework for EU monetary policy does not apply to it. Moreover, it is inconceivable that the UK will enter the final stage of EU monetary union in the foreseeable future, and the problems of the eurozone in relation to the weak economies of Ireland and southern Europe have raised serious questions about the ability of the system to cope with widely different standards of economic performance. Nevertheless, given the importance of the eurozone in relation to UK monetary policy, and given the partial acceptance by the UK of its monetary objectives, something needs to be said about accountability issues which it raises.

Accountability of the European Central Bank

There has been a considerable degree of controversy around the question of the accountability of the ECB.[16] As mentioned, the federal nature of the

[13] Protocol 15, art. 3; Protocol 4, art. 42.2. [14] Art. 7, 14. [15] Art. 140(1).

[16] For discussion of this in greater details, see C. Harlow, *Accountability in the European Union* (Oxford: Oxford University Press, 2002), 47–51 and the essays in M. Adenas, L. Gormley, C. Hadjiemmanuil, and I. Harden (eds), *European Economic and Monetary Union: The Institutional Framework* (London: Kluwer, 1997).

system through which national central banks participate in the ESCB and in the Governing Council of the ECB is something largely foreign to UK practice. Here the appointment of the MPC is in practice a matter for the Chancellor of the Exchequer on behalf of the Government, whilst in the European system membership is a means of ensuring that a variety of different interests participate in the Bank's decisions, whilst being mandated by the Treaty to act in the interests of the Union as a whole. The EU system is much more closely in line with Continental traditions, especially the position in Germany.[17]

The importance of moulding different national interests into a collective viewpoint has influenced the major difference in accountability mechanisms from the current arrangements in the UK. Perhaps the most important and innovative aspect of the accountability of the UK MPC is the publication of its minutes, including the individual voting records, two weeks after each monthly meeting to set interest rates. The ECB consistently refused to publish its minutes or voting records in this way, claiming that this would undermine its collegiate character and would lead to national pressure being put on individual members.[18] Instead the Bank has pointed to the holding of a press conference after the first Governing Council meeting of the month, and the publication of a monthly bulletin (going beyond the quarterly report it is required to publish). It also publishes an annual report presented to the European Parliament, before which the President and member of the Bank's executive board regularly give evidence. For example, the President appears four times a year before the Parliament's Committee on Economic and Monetary Affairs to explain the Bank's policy decisions and to answer questions. Other members of the Governing Council are not held individually accountable by the European Parliament as they are appointed according to national procedures for the head of the national central bank. Otherwise, accountability has been assumed to work through the results or outcomes of the decision-making process, through asking whether monetary stability has been achieved. Unsurprisingly, this approach to accountability, and especially the failure to publish the minutes and voting records, has been severely criticized, not least by a member of the Bank of England MPC as 'typical of a central banking tradition that was, until very recently, dominant across the world, which views central banking as a sacred, quasi-mystical vocation, a cult whose priests perform the holy sacraments far from the prying eyes of the

[17] Daintith, 'Between Domestic Democracy and an Alien Rule of Law?' (n 6) 121, 130–2. The appointments mechanisms for the MPC will be considered in more detail later.

[18] See e.g. 'The Accountability of the ECB', *ECB Monthly Bulletin* (November 2002), 45–57.

non-initiates'.[19] This system is coming under increasing strain owing to the pervasive effects of the sovereign debt and banking crises and growing calls for the prioritization of growth alongside the maintenance of price stability. In July 2013 the Bank provided very limited forward guidance through stating that it did not intend to increase interest rates 'for an extended period of time', and in the following month it promised to prepare proposals for fuller explanations of it decisions, though whether this would involve publication of minutes was unclear.[20]

The Bank of England and monetary policy

As we saw earlier, by the early 1990s the autonomy of the Bank of England had been further restricted, largely due to the growing centrality of monetary policy. On the other hand, greater independence for the Bank was debated as a means of keeping interest rate decisions insulated from short-term political considerations, and this was also influenced by the Maastricht Treaty and the process of European Monetary Union. Some reforms to increase the role of the Bank were implemented after the UK's withdrawal from the Exchange Rate Mechanism in 1992; these included the publication by the Bank of a quarterly inflation report and power to determine the precise timing of interest rate changes.

In 1993 two major calls were made for a much greater degree of Bank independence in setting interest rates. The first was from an unofficial committee chaired by Lord Roll, a former director of the Bank.[21] It recommended that, in order to establish the credibility of monetary policy through a process of pre-commitment, the structure should be closer to that of the German Bundesbank. The Bank should have a single objective of price stability; there should be no role for government in setting inflation targets and no powers of routine government control over the Bank. However, there should be provision for a temporary suspension of the objective with parliamentary approval in exceptional circumstances.

A highly influential report was published by the Treasury Select Committee.[22] It included a fundamental review of the arguments for and against

[19] W.H. Buiter, 'Alice in Euroland' (1999) 37 *Journal of Common Market Studies* 181–209, 198.

[20] ECB, *Introductory Statement to the Press Conference, 1 August 2013* at: <http://www.ecb.europa.eu/press/pressconf/2013/html/is130801.en.html>.

[21] Centre for Economic Policy Research, *Independent and Accountable: A New Mandate for the Bank of England* (London: Centre for Economic Policy Research, 1993).

[22] Treasury Committee, *The Role of the Bank of England,* (n 7).

greater independence and an examination of overseas experience. On the first, it described the argument for greater independence as 'disarmingly simple'; that there was no long-term trade-off between growth and employment on the one hand and inflation on the other, but there was a short-term trade-off which could lead to political manipulation of rates and undermine the credibility of monetary policy.[23] On the other hand, witnesses before the Committee had challenged the basic premise that control of the rate of inflation should always be the primary aim of economic policy, and argued instead that it was one of a number of different objectives which conflicted and so trade-offs should be resolved in the political arena.[24] A central question was also that of the lack of transparency in the existing arrangements, on which the Committee was scathing.[25] The Committee concluded that the objectives of the Bank should be defined clearly in statute, with price stability the principal objective. A separate MPC should be established to set interest rates; this should be strong and independent with published minutes. The Government should agree public targets for the achievement of the objective of price stability, and would have the power to override the objective in exceptional circumstances. The proposed model was thus somewhat different from that of the Bundesbank and closer to that adopted for New Zealand.[26]

In its response, the Government agreed to consider the recommendations, though it remained concerned about the problem of accountability of a more independent Bank. In the meantime, the minutes of the meetings of the Chancellor and Governor would be published around six weeks after the meetings had taken place.[27] These minutes made it clear that it was the Chancellor who summed up and took the decision on interest rates.

The Bank of England Act 1998

On 6 May 1997, four days after the general election resulting in a Labour Government, the new Chancellor announced a major reform reflecting the Treasury Committee proposals. The Treasury would continue to set the inflation target but the Bank would be given immediate operational responsibility for setting interest rates. Interim arrangements to secure this would be put into place before legislation was passed, including the establishment of

[23] Treasury Committee, *The Role of the Bank of England* (n 7) para. 24.
[24] Treasury Committee, *The Role of the Bank of England* (n 7) para. 36.
[25] Treasury Committee, *The Role of the Bank of England* (n 7) paras 62, 79.
[26] For the Committee's conclusions, see paras 72–82.
[27] Treasury and Civil Service Committee, *The Role of the Bank of England: The Government's Response* (HC 1993–94, 338).

the MPC, to meet monthly with published minutes. The overriding objective would be to deliver price stability as defined by the inflation target. The remit of the MPC would be set through an annual letter from the Chancellor to the Governor, which would include the inflation target; the letter would be published. There would be an override power for the Chancellor for use in exceptional circumstances. The Court of the Bank of England would also be reformed to review the performance of the Bank and ensure that proper regional and sectoral information was collected for monetary policy formation. The Bank would report to the Treasury Select Committee and there would be a debate in the House of Commons on its annual report.

The Bank of England Act 1998 fully implemented the reforms. The Act reformed the Court of Directors of the Bank, which was given the role of managing the Bank's affairs other than the formulation of monetary policy and determining its strategy; in relation to monetary policy the Court was to keep the procedures of the MPC under review and to determine whether the latter had collected regional, sectoral, and other data for the purposes of formulating monetary policy.[28] The key provisions on monetary policy are set out in Part II of the Act. The power of the Treasury to give directions to the Bank (which was never used) is removed in relation to monetary policy.[29] The Act then provides that the objectives of the Bank in relation to monetary policy shall be:

(a) to maintain price stability; and
(b) subject to that, to support the economic policy of Her Majesty's Government, including its objectives for growth and employment.[30]

The Treasury is given the power to specify 'what price stability is to be taken to consist of' and 'what the economic policy of Her Majesty's Government is to be taken to be', and must do so at least annually.[31]

The setting of the remit by the Treasury is thus at the heart of the system. The initial remit given was to set the target for monetary policy as an underlying inflation rate based on the Retail Price Index of 2.5 per cent, later changed to 2 per cent as measured by the Consumer Prices Index. The economic policy objective was stated as being to achieve strong, sustainable, and balanced growth that is more evenly shared across the country and between industries. Changes in the remit were made in the 2013 budget. The inflation target and the economic objective remained unchanged, but there was a greater emphasis on the trade-offs involved in setting monetary

[28] Bank of England Act 1998, ss 2, 16.
[29] Bank of England Act 1998, s 10.
[30] Bank of England Act 1998, s 11.
[31] Bank of England Act 1998, s 12.

policy to meet the target, in particular with output and avoidance of financial imbalances. The Committee was also invited to set intermediate thresholds in the form of policy commitments conditional on future economic developments, as adopted elsewhere, notably by the US Federal Reserve linking its pledge to keep inflation low to a target for lower unemployment.[32] The MPC then issued forward guidance, committing itself not to raise interest rates until the unemployment rate had fallen to 7 per cent, subject to conditions relating to future inflation forecasts and expectations, and to a judgment by the Financial Policy Committee on whether monetary policy posed a risk to financial stability.[33] Despite criticisms of its complexity, this detailed guidance is itself a major contribution to the transparency of monetary policy.

The Act provided for the establishment of the MPC, comprised of the Governor and Deputy Governor of the Bank appointed by the Crown on the advice of the Prime Minister, two members appointed by the Governor after consultation with the Chancellor, and four other members appointed by the Chancellor; in the latter case he must be satisfied that the person has relevant knowledge or experience.[34] This is used to appoint the independent members, initially academic economists with a specialism in monetary economics; more recent appointments have included appointees from a wider range of backgrounds, for example from business. There are thus three different means of appointment to the Committee. The Act required that a statement of the decisions taken by the MPC is published after each meeting, and, crucially, that minutes are published within six weeks of the meeting; in practice, they are published after two weeks. The minutes are required to show the voting preferences of the members who took part in the vote.[35] The Bank is also under the duty to publish a quarterly report reviewing its monetary policy decisions and developments in relation to inflation; this takes the form of its quarterly inflation report, first published in 1993.[36] Reserve powers are provided for the Treasury to give the Bank directions by order with respect to monetary policy if it is satisfied that these are required in the public interest and by 'extreme economic circumstances'. Such an order must be laid before Parliament and will lapse if not approved by a resolution of each House within 28 days; it can last for a maximum of three months, though the order may be renewed after this.[37] Unsurprisingly in view of the likely market reaction, a direction of this kind has never been given. Finally,

[32] HM Treasury, *Remit for the MPC* (2013) at: <https://www.gov.uk/government/uploads/system/uploads/attachment_data/file/221566/chx_letter_to_boe_monetary_policy_framework_200313.pdf>.

[33] Bank of England, *Monetary Policy Trade-offs and Forward Guidance* (2013).

[34] Bank of England Act 1998, s 13.

[35] Bank of England Act 1998, s 14–15.

[36] Bank of England Act 1998, s 18.

[37] Bank of England Act 1998, s 19.

the 1988 Act also removed the Bank's powers of supervision of the financial system; as we shall see in Chapter 7, important powers of such supervision have now been returned to the Bank.

Accountability for monetary policy: parliamentary scrutiny

As has been noted, the question of the accountability of an independent body setting interest rates was central to the debate on reform. Although ritual claims were made to the effect that such important economic decisions could only be made by a politically accountable minister, the Treasury Committee in 1993 was scathing about such a view, pointing out that it remained unclear whether the Chancellor was acting in accordance with the Bank's advice or not, and that neither the Chancellor nor the Governor would answer questions before the Committee about the content of their discussions.[38] The main means of holding the Bank accountable, apart from the work of the Treasury Select Committee, was said to be the annual report to Parliament; this had, however, never been debated.

In practice, parliamentary accountability has been secured largely through sustained examination of the work of the MPC by parliamentary select committees. Although the Treasury Committee had examined monetary policy on a number of occasions before 1997 (with evidence being given to the Committee by the Governor no less than 49 times between 1979 and 1997), the new institutional structure was subject to a succession of detailed inquiries by the Committee in its early years. The Committee issued a report in 1997, after the Chancellor's announcement of the change to a more independent MPC but before the passage of the Act.[39] This report was broadly optimistic about the reforms which had taken place and the new arrangements, pointing to the important potential role of the Committee in relation to them. Thus it was able to call members of the MPC to give evidence, and would hold hearings on the quarterly inflation report. Importantly, it also intended to hold confirmation hearings when new independent members of the Committee were appointed, although these had no basis in statute and a recommendation would not be binding on the Chancellor. A further means of accountability was through the open letter system, under which, should inflation be more than 1 per cent above or below target, the Governor would send a letter to the Chancellor explaining the reasons for this together with the action the Bank would take (to be considered shortly). The

[38] Treasury Committee, *The Role of the Bank of England* (n 7) para. 79.

[39] Treasury Committee, *Accountability of the Bank of England* (HC 1997–98, 282).

Committee intended to question the Governor after such a letter had been sent. A similarly upbeat report was issued by the Committee a year later.[40] It noted the high standard and openness of the minutes, though it observed that as the contributions are not identifiable the role of the Treasury representative who attends the meeting (without voting rights) was unclear. A year later a follow-up report concluded that '*[t]he Chancellor's decision to transfer day to day control of monetary policy to an independent Bank of England has been vindicated so far in the transparency and technical quality of the process of decision making*'.[41] An 'end of term report' at the end of the Parliament by the Committee also praised the transparency of the monetary framework and the dissemination of information. It recommended that confirmation hearings should have a statutory basis (an interesting comparison is now the case for the Office for Budget Responsibility, where statute provides that appointments must have the consent of the Treasury Committee). This reflected experience in a couple of cases where the Committee had doubts about candidates and in one case had refused to approve a nomination; nevertheless the Chancellor had gone ahead with it.[42] Although no such statutory basis was provided, 20 hearings were held between 1998 and 2003 and they have continued as new appointments have been made, and hearings are also held for appointments to the Bank's Financial Policy Committee. The hearings have been concerned with the two criteria of professional competence and personal independence of nominees rather than with party political matters.[43]

The sheer volume of reports in relation to the performance of the MPC in its first few years illustrates vividly how seriously the Treasury Select Committee took its job of scrutiny. The pace slackened later somewhat, but a report on the Committee 10 years on in 2007 also reached favourable conclusions, noting that the framework has been broadly successful and that there was no reason to accord legislative change high priority.[44] Prophetically, the Committee noted that the economic climate over the next 10 years might not be as benign as that over the last decade.[45] Specific

[40] Treasury Committee, *Bank of England: Operation of Accountability—One Year On* (HC 1997–98, 993).

[41] Treasury Committee, *The Monetary Policy Committee—Two Years On* (HC 1998–99, 505) (emphasis retained).

[42] Treasury Committee, *The Monetary Policy Committee—An End of Term Report* (HC 2000–01, 42), paras 50–2.

[43] Treasury Committee, *The Monetary Policy Committee of the Bank of England: Appointment Hearings* (HC 2005–06, 525).

[44] Treasury Committee, *The Monetary Policy Committee of the Bank of England: Ten Years On* (HC 2006–07, 299), para. 7.

[45] Treasury Committee, *The Monetary Policy Committee of the Bank of England: Ten Years On* (n 44) para. 18.

improvements suggested were that the length of the term of members of the MPC could be increased from three years to six, that a pool of candidates be set up (the Government had already reformed the appointment procedures in 2007 to create a clearer timetable and to use advertising based around clearer criteria), and that confirmation hearings be replaced by pre-appointment hearings. The Committee also recommended that there should be immediate publication of the outcome of votes in the MPC, indicating how members had voted; there should also be reference in the minutes to the names of individuals taking particular positions in the debates.[46] In a further report, the Treasury Committee was highly critical of the arrangements for corporate governance of the Bank and of the role of the Court, though it made only relatively limited recommendations for change on monetary policy issues.[47]

Rather unusually for the area of economic policy, House of Lords select committees have also played an important role, enabling a different form of expertise to be brought to play from that of MPs on the Commons Committee. A specialist select committee to establish the work of the MPC was established for the 1998–99 and 2000–01 sessions, and issued two detailed reports.[48] These reports reached similar conclusions to those of the Treasury Committee, commenting, for example, that '[b]oth the Chancellor and the Governor have committed themselves fully to a policy of transparency which is unprecedented in this country or, as far as we know, elsewhere'.[49] Relatively minor recommendations for improvement were made, also broadly similar to those of the Treasury Committee, whilst the reports contained useful extended analysis of the remit of the MPC and of the policy framework within which it operates. There was also detailed discussion of technical issues around monetary policy. However, to avoid duplication of the work of the Treasury Committee, the House of Lords Committee did not examine specific interest rate decisions. After these two sessions, the Committee was succeeded by the House of Lords Economic Affairs Committee. Although the new Committee obviously has a wider remit, it has continued to examine periodically the work of the MPC; indeed it benefits from being able to put this into a broader context. For example, in a report issued in 2004 on monetary and fiscal policy, the Committee looked in detail at matters

[46] Treasury Committee, *The Monetary Policy Committee of the Bank of England: Ten Years On* (n 44) paras 82, 112, 116.

[47] Treasury Committee, *Accountability of the Bank of England* (HC 2010–12, 874).

[48] House of Lords Select Committee on the Monetary Policy Committee of the Bank of England, *Monetary Policy Committee of the Bank of England* (HL 1998–99, 96); *Monetary Policy Committee of the Bank of England* (HL 2000–01, 34).

[49] 'House of Lords Select Committee on the Monetary Policy Committee of the Bank of England, *The Monetary Policy Committee of the Bank of England* (1998–99) (n 48) para. 7.24.

concerning the substance of the MPC's work within the general context of different aspects of government economic policy, and was critical of some recent appointments to the Committee.[50]

The open letters

The MPC has thus been subject to detailed and repeated examination by select committees, and the outcome has been extremely positive, especially as regards transparency and the Committee's procedures. However, an important caveat must be entered here. The bulk of the examination took place in favourable economic circumstances, and since the financial crisis of 2008–09 the climate has been far less benign. Indeed, for reasons largely outside the MPC's control, the inflation targets have not been met, and up to spring 2012 the Governor had to issue no less than 14 quarterly open letters to the Chancellor explaining why inflation has been more than 1 per cent above the target (the first being issued in 2007). For example, in January 2012 inflation was 3.6 per cent against the target of 2 per cent. The open letter explained the reasons for this (mainly the effects of an increase in VAT rates, higher energy prices, and increases in import prices). The Governor noted that further increases were likely, but that inflation should fall back to near the target by the end of 2012. The Bank for the moment intended to keep the Bank Rate at 0.5 per cent and to undertake asset purchases (discussed later) with a view to meeting the target over the longer term. The Chancellor replied welcoming this approach.[51]

The Chancellor has emphasized that the open letter system should not be regarded as a sanction but as a communication tool, a view shared by the Treasury Select Committee.[52] Given that it is published, as is the reply from the Chancellor, it can be seen as a further means of transparency and dialogue alongside the inflation report and the publication of the minutes. The new remit in 2013 provided for later publication of the open letter alongside the minutes of the first MPC meeting after the publication of the inflation data, communicating the MPC's plans to return inflation to the target after considering trade-offs.

Accountability and the remit of the Bank

It is quite clear that there is far greater accountability for the setting of interest rates by the independent MPC than was the case when the decision was

[50] House of Lords Select Committee on Economic Affairs, *Monetary and Fiscal Policy: Present Successes and Future Problems* (HL 2003–04, 176).

[51] Bank of England, *Letter from the Governor to the Chancellor, 13 February 2012* (2012).

[52] Treasury Committee, *The Monetary Policy Committee of the Bank of England: Ten Years On* (n 44) paras 100-104–4.

taken by the Chancellor on the advice of the Bank. The Committee, as an independent body, has a relatively clear remit; it also has reporting requirements which are highly developed, and in particular the publication of minutes has greatly increased the information available and opportunities for debate by the specialist press and the interested public. In addition, the inflation report and the open letter system have been important contributors to openness, and parliamentary scrutiny through select committees of both Houses has been intense. This is particularly important in showing that a public body need not be headed by a minister to be subject to detailed scrutiny by Parliament; indeed, when decisions were taken directly by the Chancellor, parliamentary scrutiny was minimal in comparison.

Although the secondary statutory objective of the Committee is to support the economic policy of the Government, including its objectives for growth and employment, in practice the Committee concentrated almost exclusively on inflation control, more recently supplemented by quantitative easing.[53] Given the low rate of economic growth and repeated very low interest rates, a limited approach of this kind has proved inadequate, as illustrated by the repeated missing of targets and resort to the open letters. This raises the question of widening the objectives and remit of the MPC to increase the importance of objectives other than price stability. There has indeed been a tentative move towards this in the 2013 remit for the Committee, and the appointment from 2013 of a new Governor more open to the use of a wider range of instruments for monetary policy. Would a change to the remit remove the legitimacy of a non-elected body taking such fundamental economic decisions by changing them from essentially technical ones to policy ones involving the balancing of different priorities, a task only appropriate for elected politicians? Two arguments can be raised in response to this. The first is that, even with its earlier objectives and remit, the work of the MPC was not merely technical and had extensive scope for the use of informed judgment, as illustrated vividly by the frequency of dissenting voices and votes in the Committee, and by its reluctance to raise interest rates in the short term where this would affect the longer-term chances of meeting the target. The second point is that the developed accountability arrangements here are appropriate for the balancing of a wider range of objectives; indeed, whilst increasing transparency, they do not undermine ministerial responsibility, given that the Chancellor remains responsible for setting the overall remit, and the major objectives are included in legislation passed by Parliament.

[53] See Committee on the Monetary Policy Committee of the Bank of England, *Monetary Policy Committee of the Bank of England* (2000–01) (n 48) para. 50.

However, a modified remit of the MPC to include a wider range of top-level objectives alongside that of price stability would mean that two other issues need addressing. The first is that of coordination of monetary policies with fiscal and other economic policies; the 2013 remit addresses coordination with the Bank's Financial Policy Committee, to be discussed in Chapter 7. The second is the membership of the Committee itself. There would need to be a move away from technical expertise in monetary policy as the major qualification, moving closer to what Daintith has termed a 'balanced constitution'. This could involve a membership representative of regional interests as in the case of the governing body of the Bundesbank, or other interests such as manufacturing industry, through mixed forms of appointment as in France, where appointments are made from nomination by the Senate, the National Assembly, and the relevant minister rather than all lying in the hands of the executive. This is not of course incompatible with requiring relevant expertise.[54] However, it is difficult to envisage a system of such representation of interests given the highly centralized UK Constitution and its hostility to corporatist interest representation. This question also raises the highly contentious issue of the role and composition of the Court of Directors of the Bank, discussed in Chapter 2.

The Asset Purchase Facility and quantitative easing

Setting interest rates is not the whole of monetary policy. The interest rate set by the MPC is the so-called 'repo rate' representing the rate of interest implied by the difference between the sale and repurchase price of assets bought briefly by the Bank from counterparties in the financial markets. It is supported by further operations in the sterling money markets by the Bank, conducted on an ordinary contractual rather than statutory basis.[55] Transactions have taken place through the Sterling Monetary Framework, published in the Bank's 'Red Book'.[56] However, when the Bank rate was set at a mere 0.5 per cent from March 2009, the main instrument of policy changed from

[54] Daintith, 'Between Domestic Democracy and an Alien Rule of Law' (n 6) 131–2; the issue was also discussed by the House of Lords Select Committee which was concerned at the limited range of experience of MPC members; see *Monetary Policy Committee of the Bank of England* (1998–99) (n 48) paras 2.7–2.10, 7.12; 'Monetary Policy Committee of the Bank of England' (2000–01) (n 48) para. 90.

[55] For discussion of monetary policy as the deployment of wealth instruments, see Daintith, 'Regulation' (n 2) 10-109–10-113. Further details of the Bank's market operations can be found in its *Annual Report 2013* (2013), 14–17.

[56] Bank of England, *The Framework for the Bank of England's Operations in the Sterling Money Markets* (2012).

the rate at which money could be borrowed to the quantity of money provided, and the Framework was partly suspended. In January 2009 the Chancellor had authorized the Bank to set up an Asset Purchase Facility to improve liquidity in private credit markets.[57] This purchased sterling commercial paper and sterling corporate bonds on a large scale (£2.4 billion of paper and £1.5 billion of bonds at their peak in 2009).

The Asset Purchasing Facility also provided a means for the MPC to add liquidity directly into the economy through the purchase of large quantities of assets, including gilts and private sector debt, in the form of quantitative easing. This aims to compensate for the very low level of Bank rate, and is a way in which the Committee can inject money into the economy on a massive scale; the Chancellor authorized up to £150 billion of purchases, of which up to £50 billion was to purchase private sector assets, and the limit was increased at the Committee's request, to £175 billion and then to £200 billion; further purchases were agreed in 2012, bringing the total to £375 billion. The transactions are undertaken by a Bank subsidiary, the Bank of England Asset Purchase Facility Fund Limited (BEAPFF), and do not involve any statutory authority, instead being based on ordinary contractual capacity. However, the structure of the arrangements is not dissimilar to that for other aspects of monetary policy. The Chancellor is responsible for authorizing a total figure, but decisions on quantitative easing are taken by the MPC itself and are recorded in its published minutes. Literature is also published by the Bank on the process, including a quarterly report. Thus some of the mechanisms of accountability associated with setting interest rates are applicable also in relation to quantitative easing. The Bank was reluctant to administer credit easing to ease the flow of credit to small and medium-sized companies, considering that this would suggest that it had a political role in the allocation of credit. It does, however, administer the 'Funding for Lending' scheme to encourage banks to increase their loan books, and this will be discussed in Chapter 8.

Foreign exchange and the reserves

It should be mentioned briefly that one other related area of Bank of England policy has a statutory basis, though it is not implemented by the MPC. This is that of foreign exchange and the reserves, through management of the Exchange Equalisation Account. This account is used to conduct exchange rate interventions, as well as for foreign currency liability management, and is

[57] For details see Bank of England, *Annual Report 2010* (2010), 16.

underpinned by the Exchange Equalisation Account Act 1979. This legislation is, however, very different from the Bank of England Act 1998, and merely offers a loose framework for the use of the account with no institutional or procedural arrangements specified. There is a framework agreement between the Treasury and the Debt Management Office, and a Treasury remit; an annual report and accounts are published on a non-statutory basis so providing some degree of transparency.

Conclusions

Monetary policy has thus been conducted in a framework very different from that which existed for other operations of the Bank of England, including those relating to financial stability. The latter, as we shall see in Chapter 7, were conducted mainly through contractual powers, notably as lender of last resort, although the Banking Act 2009 imported a greater degree of statutory underpinning, whilst still raising major issues of public accountability.[58] By contrast, the statutory framework for monetary policy was highly successful in creating increased transparency. This occurred through clarifying the Bank's mandate and the role of the Chancellor, establishing a MPC with clearer objectives, requiring the publication of detailed minutes of its meetings and of regular reports, and sustained and detailed examination by select committees of both Houses of Parliament. Indeed, a similar framework has now been adopted for financial stability through the new Financial Policy Committee of the Bank to be discussed in Chapter 7. What is certain is that the framework for the MPC has finally disproved the simplistic view of ministerial responsibility which assumed the illegitimacy of all decisions related to economic policy taken by a public body other than a minister; transparency can be maximized through other institutional and procedural arrangements.

Two questions remain to be more fully considered. The first is that, as noted earlier, there may have been a failure of constitutional imagination in relation to the composition of the MPC.[59] Seeing its role as essentially a technical one to be performed by experts in the science of monetary policy underplays the need for a representation of a wider range of views in a

[58] See J. Black, 'The Credit Crisis and the Constitution' in D. Oliver, T. Prosser, and R. Rawlings (eds), *The Regulatory State: Constitutional Implications* (Oxford: Oxford University Press, 2010), 92–18, 118–19.

[59] This point was made strongly by Daintith, 'Between Domestic Democracy and an Alien Rule of Law' (n 6) 131–2.

committee which clearly performs more than merely a technical role; this is particularly the case with the tentative moves towards an extended remit for the Committee in which it will concentrate on trade-offs between the control of inflation and support for economic growth. It reflects the broader criticisms made by the Treasury Committee of the corporate governance arrangements of the Bank and, in particular, the role of its Court, and with similar concerns about the remit and accountability of the ECB.[60] Secondly, these arrangements exist in isolation from other aspects of government economic policy, in particular fiscal policy, as emphasized by the House of Lords Select Committee on Economic Affairs, and financial stability, a major concern of Treasury Committee.[61] Although, as the House of Lords Committee emphasized, fiscal policy is too heavily politicized to entrust to an independent agency, nevertheless procedural lessons on specification of remits and transparency are equally applicable to this field, and this may also result in greater coordination between the two different sets of policies. One move in this direction is that of the steps taken to improve coordination between the Monetary Policy and Financial Policy Committees of the Bank under the Financial Services Act 2012, through cross-membership and requirements in their remits for each to have regard to the policies and forecasts of the other.

This chapter began by noting the contrast between the strongly constitutional dimension of monetary policy at the EU level and the lack of such constitutional concerns in the UK. It is perhaps ironic that the former now faces serious problems, both because of the substantive failure of the eurozone to deal with the effects of the financial crisis uniformly across highly diverse economies, and the lack of transparency of the ECB. By contrast, the UK has, through the Bank of England Act 1998, something closer to a formal economic constitution in the area of monetary policy than in any other area examined in this book. This has resulted both in improved substantive decisions (within the limits of a remit prioritizing price stability) and, especially, in massively increased transparency.

[60] Treasury Committee, *Accountability of the Bank of England* (n 47).

[61] House of Lords Select Committee on Economic Affairs, Monetary and Fiscal Policy: Present Successes and Future Problems (n 50) paras 63–85; Treasury Committee, *Accountability of the Bank of England* (n 47) paras 121–32.

7

The Regulation of Financial Services

Introduction

No reminder should be necessary of the importance of the regulation of financial services in examining the economic constitution, especially after the financial crisis of 2008 and the problems of bank misconduct in 2012–13. The subject is of course an enormous one, and no attempt will be made to cover it all even in outline; there will be discussion only of those aspects with an important constitutional dimension.

There are a number of major constitutional issues raised here. The division of power between national and trans-national bodies, in particular those of the EU, has proved highly controversial, especially where decisions have important effects on the expenditure of public funds, a key component of national sovereignty. At the international level the relationship between 'hard' and 'soft' law, and at national level the role of self-regulation, co-regulation, or 'light-touch' regulation, are also central to the debates. At both levels the design and powers of regulatory agencies have been much debated, as has the relationship between central banks and other regulatory bodies. The accountability of the different institutions has raised fundamental questions, particularly accountability to those outside the financial services industry who have had to carry the costs of its failures and of failures of regulation. Finally, in such a complex regulatory terrain the question of how to coordinate the different agencies and to ensure communication between them and with government has become of pressing importance.

International regulation

There are many important actors at the international level; it would be tempting to dismiss them as merely concerned with the development of 'soft law' as opposed to the 'hard' legislation of national bodies. This would be a profound mistake for two reasons. The first is that 'soft law' may itself be hugely influential, with behavioural effects greater than those of 'hard law'.[1] It may be backed both by pressure from government and, of particular importance, pressure from the markets. Secondly, as we shall see, standards developed in international fora which are not capable of producing immediate legal effects may be nevertheless incorporated through binding requirements both in EU law and in domestic law, thus making them effectively part of national law. From a large number of such international bodies, I shall examine three of particular importance.

The Financial Stability Board

After its London summit in April 2009, the G20 announced that the Financial Stability Forum would be re-established with a stronger institutional basis and enhanced capacity as the Financial Stability Board.[2] Its functions include assessing vulnerabilities in the financial system, promoting coordination and information exchange, reviewing the work of international standard-setting bodies, setting guidelines for the establishment and functioning of supervisory colleges of national regulators to deal with cross-boundary issues, and conducting early warning exercises in relation to macroeconomic and financial risks. It reports to the IMF, the OECD, and the G20. The Board is composed of national and regional bodies responsible for maintaining financial stability (including ministries of finance, central banks, and supervisory and regulatory authorities) and international standard-setting and regulatory bodies; thus for the UK, the Treasury, the Bank of England, and the Financial Conduct Authority are represented. Particularly important work the Board has undertaken includes the development of 12 key standards for sound financial systems and supporting the establishment of more than 30 supervisory colleges of different national regulators for large financial institutions. In 2012 the G20 accepted Board proposals that its mandate be enhanced to give it standard-setting powers and to increase transparency, and that it should be given its own legal personality and guaranteed multi-year financial support. Although it is responsible for the development of 'soft law',

> [t]he endorsement of certain standards by the FSB (itself a 'soft' organization but one with a strong mandate from economically-developed countries to act as the

[1] See e.g. J. Scott and D. Trubek, 'Mind the Gap: Law and New Approaches to Governance in the European Union' (2002) 8 *European Law Journal* 1–18, and in the financial services context E. Ferran and K. Alexander, 'Can Soft Law Bodies be Effective? The Special Case of the European Systemic Risk Board' (2010) 35 *European Law Review* 751–76, esp. 754–7.

[2] G20, *Declaration on Strengthening the Financial System—London, 2 April 2009* at: <http://www.g20.utoronto.ca/2009/2009ifi.pdf>.

global overseer of the financial markets) gives them particular authority, which is now reinforced by the commitment of FSB member countries to submit to periodic peer review.[3]

The Basel Committee on Banking Supervision

An international body which has achieved a particularly high level of visibility during the financial crisis is the Basel Committee on Banking Supervision. It provides a forum for international cooperation on financial matters and is best known for its standard-setting role (in particular the Basel international standards on capital adequacy), its core principles for effective banking supervision, and its concordat on cross-border banking supervision.[4] The capital adequacy standards were introduced from 1988; from 1999 a revised version was developed (Basel II) which was widely blamed as having contributed to the financial crisis through the inadequacy of its standards, through their being based on risk-weighted assets which had risen in value during the boom, and through giving insufficient weight to microprudential and liquidity risk. New standards were announced at the end of 2010 (Basel III) with enhanced capital requirements and further regulatory requirements on leverage and liquidity, and these are now in the process of implementation.

It is particularly important to note that the Basel standards are incorporated into EU law, and so into the law of Member States, through the Capital Requirements Directive.[5] A Regulation and Directive to implement Basel III were agreed in 2013.[6] The Basel standards thus originate as 'soft law' but achieve binding legal effect.

The International Accounting Standards Board

A further international standard making body whose norms are transferred into hard law is the International Accounting Standards Board (IASB).[7] The Board operates under the aegis of the International Financial Reporting

[3] Ferran and Alexander, 'Can Soft Law Bodies be Effective?' (n 1) 754–5 (footnote omitted).

[4] For more information, see its website at: <http://www.bis.org/bcbs/about.htm>.

[5] Directive 2006/49 on the capital adequacy of investment firms and credit institutions [2006] OJ L177/201 as amended.

[6] Regulation 575/2013 on prudential requirements for credit institutions and investment firms [2013] OJ L176/1; Directive 2013/36/EU on access to the activity of credit institutions and the prudential supervision of credit institutions and investment firms [2013] OJ L176/338.

[7] For details and an account of some of its work, see C. Villiers, 'A Global Framework for Management Commentary Disclosure?' (2009) 60 *Northern Ireland Legal Quarterly* 63–84.

Standards Foundation (IFRS) and both develops standards and approves their interpretation. Since 2001 it has been a full-time, professional body. The IASB places a particularly strong emphasis on transparency and accountability.[8] For example, it has a Monitoring Board of public capital market authorities, consults widely on new standards (normally publishing a discussion paper), and holds all its meetings in public; they are also webcast and meeting notes are made publicly available. It has drawn up a public Due Process Handbook setting out in detail its consultative arrangements.[9] These extensive procedures for participation make it stand out compared to other international organizations where it is extremely rare to find any structured arrangements of this kind; in 2007 the IASB topped global rankings in an examination of the transparency of 30 global organizations, and a detailed academic analysis of its deliberative procedures concludes that:

> while we find evidence of significant deviations from the normative benchmark, it is fair to say that the IASB has put into place an ambitious and, in some aspects, innovative set of due process practices that emulate but, crucially, also adapt domestic cultural models to the more complex environment of transnational standard-setting.[10]

Once more, the standards developed by the IASB are incorporated into EU law, in this case through the 2002 Regulation on the Application of International Standards requiring all listed EU-based companies to prepare their accounts in accordance with the standards.[11] Market considerations and the effect of market scandals also have an important effect in creating incentives for the adoption of the standards elsewhere in the world.[12]

EU regulation of financial services

Turning now to regulatory institutions of the EU, they are of particular constitutional importance for a number of reasons.[13] The first is the most

[8] For detailed examination of this, see A.J. Richardson and B. Eberlein, 'Legitimating Transnational Standard-Setting: the Case of the International Accounting Standards Board' (2011) 98 *Journal of Business Ethics* 217–45.

[9] International Accounting Standards Board, *Due Process Handbook* (2008, updated 2013), at: <http://www.ifrs.org/DPOC/Documents/2013/Due-Process-Handbook-February-2013.pdf>.

[10] Richardson and Eberlein, 'Legitimating Transnational Standard-Setting' (n 8) 236.

[11] Regulation 1606/2002 on the application of international accounting standards [2002] OJ L243/1 as amended.

[12] Villiers, 'A Global Framework for Management Commentary Disclosure?' (n 7) 65–7.

[13] For an excellent summary of the institutions, see E. Ferran, 'Understanding the New Institutional Architecture of EU Financial Market Supervision' in E. Wymeersch, K.J. Hopt, and

obvious; the division of regulatory responsibilities between the EU and Member States.[14] On the one hand, the effect of the financial crisis has been to fuel calls for stronger trans-national regulation, but, on the other, national concern to protect key industries remains strong. This is particularly the case in the UK, where failure to achieve a Treaty protocol protecting the City of London was the ostensible reason why the Prime Minister vetoed the proposed Treaty changes addressing the eurozone crisis in December 2011. A further important problem is that, as we shall see, crises brought on by mismanagement of the financial services industry and ineffective regulation may impose a huge burden on public funds, and such fiscal matters are at the heart of national sovereignty.

A further constitutional issue at the EU level does not have a UK equivalent. This is the restriction of the delegation of powers to independent agencies as a result of the *Meroni* decision in 1958, which has already been mentioned in Chapter 3.[15] In this case the Court of Justice decided that, whilst it was acceptable for the Commission to delegate to an agency 'clearly defined executive powers the exercise of which can . . . be subject to strict review in the light of objective criteria determined by the delegating authority', it was not lawful to delegate 'a discretionary power, implying a wide margin of discretion which may, according to the use which is made of it, make possible the execution of actual economic policy'. There has been a degree of controversy on the extent to which the decision still prevents any such delegation, and whether it is possible to compensate for any lack of accountability through delegation by enhanced procedural safeguards.[16] Nevertheless, the decision still offers a strong disincentive to granting European agencies discretionary powers to take binding regulatory decisions, and thus limits EU regulatory capacity. However, it has been in tension with the requirement of enhanced European-level supervision after the banking crisis.[17]

G. Ferrarini, *Financial Regulation and Supervision: A Post-Crisis Analysis* (Oxford: Oxford University Press, 2012), ch. 5.

[14] See P. Schammo, 'EU Day-to-Day Supervision or Intervention-based Supervision: Which Way Forward for the European System of Financial Supervision?' (2012) 4 *Oxford Journal of Legal Studies* 771–97.

[15] Case 9/56 *Meroni & Co. Industrie Metallurgiche S.p.A. v High Authority of the European Coal and Steel Community* [1957–58] ECR 133.

[16] See, e.g. S. Griller and A. Orator, 'Everything Under Control? The "Way Forward" for European Agencies in the Footsteps of the *Meroni* Decision' (2010) 35 *European Law Review* 3–35.

[17] See P. Schammo, 'The European Securities and Markets Authority: Lifting the Veil on the Allocation of Powers' (2011) 48 *Common Market Law Review* 1879–914.

The de Larosière Report

Despite this restriction, three EU-level committees of financial market supervisors were established between 2001 and 2003, referred to as the 'Lamfalussy' or 'Level 3' committees. These were the Committee of European Securities Regulators, the Committee of European Banking Supervisors, and the Committee of European Insurance and Occupational Pensions Supervisors. It is important to note that they had no powers to issue binding rules nor to impose binding decisions on authorities in Member States; '[i]nstead, they played a more indirect role by seeking to foster consistent, cooperative practices and open relations among the frontline national supervisors and marshalling peer pressure forces in respect of areas of divergence.'[18] They also issued non-binding interpretative guidance, recommendations, and standards, and their role became more important and visible with time; nevertheless, the Committees remained very different from the national model of regulators with binding powers to make rules and supervise compliance. This lack of powers was thrown into sharp relief by the financial crisis.

In response to the crisis the Commission established a high-level group chaired by Jacques de Larosière to make proposals for reform of the regulatory and supervisory arrangements. As well as proposing changes of substance in EU law, the report made major suggestions for reforming the institutional framework.[19] The lesson which it drew from the crisis was that there had been 'real and important regulatory failures'; these included lack of adequate micro-prudential supervision, ineffective early warning mechanisms, weaknesses in supervision of individual institutions, and failures to challenge supervisory practices on a cross-border basis with extensive reliance on the judgments and decisions of the home supervisor. Further difficulties had been caused by lack of cooperation between supervisors, the weaknesses of the 'Level 3' committees, and the lack of a means for supervisors to take common decisions.[20] The report instead proposed that a new European Systemic Risk Council be set up chaired by the European Central Bank President, with a new risk warning system.[21] For micro-level supervision, a new European System of Financial Supervision should be established, consisting of a network of financial authorities independent from political or national influence, accompanied by three new authorities replacing the 'Level 3' committees,

[18] Ferran, 'Understanding the New Institutional Architecture of EU Financial Market Supervision' (n 13) 5.12.

[19] European Commission, *The High Level Group on Financial Supervision in the EU Chaired by Jacques de Larosière* (2009), ch. III.

[20] de Larosière Report (n 19) paras 162–6.

[21] de Larosière Report (n 19) paras 162–6 173–82.

having responsibility for coordinating the application of supervisory standards and ensuring cooperation between national regulators. The European authorities would have a special role in relation to cross-border institutions, and would have new competences to carry out legally binding mediation between national supervisors, to adopt binding supervisory standards and technical decisions, and to license and supervise specific EU-wide institutions, though national supervisory authorities should continue to be responsible for the day-to-day supervision of firms.[22] The legally binding powers would thus give the European-wide authorities more of the attributes of independent regulatory agencies.

The European System of Financial Supervision

After some controversy and negotiation with the European Parliament, the Regulations to set up the new arrangements were agreed in September 2010 to become effective in early 2011; they comprise the European System of Financial Supervision (ESFS).[23] The Regulations established, first, a European Systematic Risk Board to oversee systemic risk in the European financial system. It was not given legal personality, and has no legally binding powers; nevertheless, it is a powerful source of 'soft law' through powers of recommendation and warning and as part of a broader system.[24] In addition, the Regulations set up three other bodies with legal personality: the European Banking Authority (EBA), the European Securities and Markets Authority (ESMA), and the European Insurance and Occupational Pensions Authority (EIOPA). These walk a narrow line between the need to ensure stronger and more effective market supervision and to respect the limits imposed under the *Meroni* doctrine.[25]

To summarize a complex set of powers, the new bodies have responsibility for developing technical standards; however, these need endorsement by the

[22] de Larosière Report (n 19) paras 162–6 183–214.

[23] Regulation 1092/2010 on European Union macro-prudential oversight of the financial system and establishing a European Systematic Risk Board [2010] OJ L331/1; Regulation 1093/2010 establishing a European Supervisory Authority (European Banking Authority) [2010] OJ L331/12; Regulation 1094/2010 establishing a European Supervisory Authority (European Insurance and Occupational Pensions Authority) [2010] OJ L331/48; Regulation 1095/2010 establishing a European Supervisory Authority (European Securities and Markets Authority) [2010] OJ L331/84.

[24] For full discussion, see Ferran and Alexander, 'Can Soft Law Bodies Be Effective?' (n 1).

[25] For full discussion of this issue, see Ferran, 'Understanding the New Institutional Architecture of EU Financial Market Supervision' (n 13), and E. Fahey, 'Does the Emperor Have Financial Crisis Clothes? Reflexions on the Legal Basis of the European Banking Authority' (2011) 74 *Modern Law Review* 581–95.

Commission before acquiring binding force as directly applicable Regulations. They must not involve policy choices or strategic decisions. Unlike their predecessors, the new agencies do have power to ensure compliance with clear and unconditional obligations in EU financial markets law; however, '[t]he power applies only in a quite narrow range of circumstances and it involves following a rather time-consuming and laboured process'.[26] In brief, it involves a four-stage process of investigation by the new agencies; a recommendation for compliance addressed to the national supervisor; a formal compliance opinion from the Commission; and a compliance decision from the agency in conformity with the Commission's opinion addressed directly to the financial market participant. Thus for the first time the agencies have an enforcement role, but one which must be in compliance with the Commission's opinion.[27] Special powers exist for emergency situations, where the agencies have a general power to facilitate and coordinate national supervisory responses, and may formally intervene where the Council has determined that an emergency situation exists and that there are exceptional circumstances which may jeopardize the orderly functioning and integrity of the financial markets or the stability of all or part of the EU financial system. The agencies may then adopt decisions addressed to national supervisors and in limited circumstances address an individual decision to a financial market participant.[28] Finally, the agencies may impose binding settlements on national supervisors in certain cross-border situations and address a decision to a financial market participant.[29] This is the nearest thing to a direct regulatory power similar to that of national regulatory agencies; however, as has been pointed out, 'it is hard to envisage circumstances—other than a catastrophic breakdown in the ESFS—in which a national supervisor would maintain its defiance to the point where the last resort option has to be pursued'.[30] ESMA has also acquired more direct powers to regulate credit ratings agencies under amendments to the credit ratings agencies regulation; these include registering agencies and the power to conduct investigations and on-site inspection, and to impose

[26] Ferran, 'Understanding the New Institutional Architecture of EU Financial Market Supervision' (n 13) 5.64 (footnote omitted).

[27] Ferran, 'Understanding the New Institutional Architecture of EU Financial Market Supervision' (n 13) 5.65–68.

[28] Ferran, 'Understanding the New Institutional Architecture of EU Financial Market Supervision' (n 13) 5.69–71.

[29] Ferran, 'Understanding the New Institutional Architecture of EU Financial Market Supervision' (n 13) 5.72–5.75.

[30] Ferran, 'Understanding the New Institutional Architecture of EU Financial Market Supervision' (n 13) 5.75.

financial penalties on them.[31] Further powers are included in other areas, including regulation of OTC derivatives under the European Market Infrastructure (EMIR) Regulation agreed in 2012, by which ESMA is required to identify contracts subject to a clearing obligation and to supervise trade repositories, and short selling.[32] In the case of the latter, ESMA is empowered, where there is a threat to the orderly functioning of markets or to financial stability, to impose notification requirements, and to prohibit transactions; these provisions are being challenged by the UK Government before the European Court of Justice.

In an attempt to avoid the accountability deficits identified in *Meroni* as a reason for limiting delegation to agencies, a number of requirements for transparency and accountability apply to the new bodies. They thus have reporting requirements to the EU institutions, they must employ consultation and cost-benefit analysis in drafting standards, and standards are subject to the new rule-making procedures under the Lisbon Treaty before adoption by the Commission, which involve either veto powers by the Parliament and the Council or the comitology procedures using committees from the Member States, also now with a veto power.[33] Individual decisions can be appealed to a Joint Board of Appeal of the agencies and are subject to judicial review by the EU courts.

It is of course too early to assess the effectiveness of the new system, especially given the challenge imposed by the continuing financial crisis in the EU. They raise two major constitutional issues. The first is that of the legitimacy of delegation to independent agencies, where tentative steps now seem to have been made away from the narrow constraints imposed under the *Meroni* decision.[34] The second is the potentially incendiary relationship between the role of EU regulation and national powers. The latter are particularly important in relation to fiscal issues; indeed, according to Ferran,

> the main immediate stumbling block to the further transfer of direct supervisory powers to the [agencies] is not so much technicalities arising from the position of

[31] Regulation 513/2011 on credit rating agencies [2011] OJ L145/30.

[32] Regulation 648/2012 on OTC derivatives, central counterparties and trade repositories [2012] OJ L201/1; Regulation 236/2012 on short selling and certain aspects of credit defaults [2012] OJ L86/1. For an important analysis of its powers and the *Meroni* doctrine, see the opinion of the Advocate-General in Case C-270/12 *United Kingdom v Council of the European Union and European Parliament*, 12 September 2013.

[33] For full discussion, see R. Schütze, '"Delegated" Legislation in the (New) European Union: A Constitutional Analysis' (2011) 74 *Modern Law Review* 661–93.

[34] For detailed discussion, see Schammo, 'The European Securities and Markets Authority' (n 17) esp. 1892–9.

> the agencies in EU law and governance, because pragmatic solutions to address these issues are emerging, but rather fiscal considerations; where taxpayers' money is at risk... the 'he who pays the piper calls the tune' principle for now mandates a national supervisory approach.[35]

Recognizing this principle, the Regulations applying to each of the new agencies provide that actions taken in emergency situations must not impinge in any way on the fiscal responsibilities of a Member State.[36] However, the sensitivity of EU regulatory competence was shown in December 2011 when the UK Government vetoed a new treaty to rescue the eurozone in an attempt to gain concessions limiting regulation of the City of London.

Continuing banking problems, especially the need to rescue Spanish banks, took the debate further, creating support for a European banking supervisor covering all the eurozone, with binding powers, as was agreed by the eurozone summit at the end of June 2012. Prudential regulation for the eurozone will be passed to the ECB in collaboration with other authorities, avoiding the *Meroni* problem by using powers vested directly in the Bank by articles 127(6) and 132 TFEU.[37]

Financial services regulation in the UK

In examining the development of the domestic institutions, recently subject to major reform, there are a number of key issues of principle to be considered. These include the extent to which regulation is 'de-centred' and the role of self-regulation, and the degree to which 'light-touch' regulation contributed to the failure to control the activities of banks during the financial crisis. A further issue is that of the accountability of the institutions involved; as we shall see, a very different constitutional approach has been adopted from that of the EU with extensive delegation permitted to regulatory agencies in Britain. Finally, as discussed in Chapter 2, the coordination of the system of regulation as a whole is crucial, as the lack of such coordination and inadequacies of communication were widely credited as major regulatory failures in the management of the financial crisis.

[35] Ferran, 'Understanding the New Institutional Architecture of EU Financial Market Supervision' (n 13) 5.83 (footnote omitted).

[36] See art. 38(1) of the Regulations.

[37] See European Commission, *Proposal for a Council Regulation Conferring Specific Tasks on the European Central Bank*, COM(2012) final.

The Financial Services Authority and the tripartite system

Financial services was long the classic area for self-regulation, initially through 'club-like' arrangements in a closed and cartelized City of London, and then, after the liberalization of Big Bang in 1986 through a group of 'self-regulatory organizations' loosely supervised by the Securities and Investment Board under the Financial Services Act 1986.[38] This system proved unstable and ineffective through failing to provide public reassurance as to the trustworthiness of the industry, failing to avoid major financial scandals, for example in relation to the mis-selling of private pensions, and failing to provide adequate procedural protections for those affected. Over time, it moved to become closer to a system of public regulation with self-regulatory elements downgraded.[39]

The Labour Government elected in 1997 was pledged to replace this with a new and more coherent system of public regulation through a new integrated financial regulatory body, the Financial Services Authority (FSA), established under the Financial Services and Markets Act 2000.[40] The Authority, although given the legal status of a company limited by guarantee, was made subject to considerable legal control; in the words of one leading commentator:

> [i]n the arrangements that have emerged one can discern the outlines of an alternative model or theory of regulatory accountability, one that is not over-reliant on fictions about ministerial responsibility. Key elements of that model include the FSA's statutory objectives, which provide the basis for a 'positive' system of accountability, due process and oversight.[41]

Thus the Act set out a system of statutory objectives and principles, something which did not appear in earlier legislation.[42] Extensive consultation was required before rules were made, including the publication of draft rules accompanied by a cost-benefit analysis, and publication of the representations received and a general response to them with the finalized rules.[43] The FSA

[38] For an excellent summary, see M. Moran, 'Politics and Law in Financial Regulation' in C. Graham and T. Prosser (eds), *Waiving the Rules: The Constitution Under Thatcherism* (Milton Keynes: Open University Press, 1988), 56–72.

[39] See the Treasury and Civil Service Committee, *The Regulation of Financial Services in the UK* (HC 1994–95, 332).

[40] For detailed discussion of the background, see the essays in E. Ferran and C. Goodhart (eds), *Regulating Financial Services and Markets in the 21st Century* (Oxford: Hart Publishing, 2001).

[41] A. Page, 'Regulating the Regulator—A Lawyer's Perspective on Accountability and Control' in E. Ferran and C. Goodhart (eds), *Regulating Financial Services and Markets in the 21st Century* (n 40) 127–49, 128.

[42] Financial Services and Markets Act 2000, s 2.

[43] Financial Services and Markets Act 2000, s 155.

was also required to set up Practitioner and Consumer Panels to represent those interests. More structured provision for adjudication was also provided compared to earlier legislation, partly to ensure compliance with the requirements of the European Convention on Human Rights. This included establishing a separate Regulatory Decisions Committee and an appeal right to the Financial Services and Markets Appeals Tribunal (now the Upper Tribunal).[44] A Financial Ombudsman Service was also established to deal with consumer complaints.[45] These mechanisms served to provide accountability to the regulated profession, and were extensively used (as was judicial review) in a highly litigious industry, whilst there was some degree of accountability to consumers for individual problems through the Ombudsman. What turned out to be lacking, as became increasingly apparent with the financial crisis, was any system of accountability to wider public interests or concern with the systemic effects of the development of new financial instruments.

The FSA was associated with a particular style of regulation, often characterized as 'light-touch'. Although this was not a phrase used by the regulator itself, it was used by Government to characterize its preferred regulatory approach; indeed on one occasion the Prime Minister characterized this as '[n]ot just a light touch but a limited touch'.[46] Two elements in the FSA approach were particularly important and contributed to a perception of light touch regulation. The first was the adoption of 'principles-based regulation', which it defined as 'moving away from dictating through detailed, prescriptive rules and supervisory actions how firms should operate their businesses. We want to give firms the responsibility to decide how best to align their business objectives and processes with the regulatory outcomes we have specified'.[47] The second was a strongly risk-based approach, using a sophisticated risk assessment model known as ARROW (Advanced, Risk-Responsive, Operating Framework).[48] Both these key regulatory approaches received a battering in the financial crisis. As memorably put by the then FSA Chief Executive, Hector Sants: '[a] principles-based approach does not work with people who have no principles'.[49] Risk regulation meant prioritizing

[44] Financial Services and Markets Act 2000, ss 395(2), 132–3, 208(4).

[45] Financial Services and Markets Act 2000, sch. 1, para 7.

[46] Quoted in FSA, *The Failure of the Royal Bank of Scotland* (2011), 262.

[47] FSA, *Principles-based Regulation—Focusing on the Outcomes that Matter* (2007), 4.

[48] For an introduction, see FSA, *The FSA's Risk-Based Approach* (2006). More detailed discussion of ARROW in its successive manifestations can be found in FSA, *The Failure of the Royal Bank of Scotland* (2011), 271–2, 293.

[49] 'Delivering Intensive Supervision and Credible Deterrence', Speech delivered to the Reuters Newsmakers Event, 12 March 2009, quoted in J. Black, *Designing Regulation: Lessons from the*

some forms of regulatory problems over others, and the financial crisis showed that there was inadequate understanding of both systemic risk and risk at the level of the individual firm to enable this to be done convincingly. The complex modelling also created a false ethos of economic and managerial rationality in coping with political and social uncertainties; thus 'qualifications and hesitancies are lost in the confident exposition of risk identification, assessment and validation; in the apparently neat and more or less elegant solutions to complex and often intractable problems'.[50]

Of course, the FSA was not the only body involved in financial services regulation, forming part of the tripartite system alongside the Treasury and the Bank of England. As noted in Chapter 2, this was set up by a memorandum of understanding signed by the three parties in 1997, updated in 2006.[51] The memorandum set out four guiding principles of clear accountability, transparency, avoidance of duplication, and regular information exchange, and summarized the responsibilities of each party. Coordination was to be secured through cross-board membership and the role of the Standing Committee on Financial Stability, chaired by the Treasury and with members from each of the three institutions. The division of responsibilities was, however, heavily criticized even before the financial crisis, and was seen as a major contributor to the lack of an earlier effective response to it, for example through giving the Bank a de facto veto over proposed Treasury action.[52]

Regulation and the financial crisis

It is universally agreed that financial services regulation did not perform well during the financial crisis. This is very apparent from a number of reports detailing the problems, including highly critical reports produced by the FSA itself; the Parliamentary Commission on Banking Standards summarized the history as '[m]isconceived and poorly-targeted regulation has been a major

Financial Crisis, paper delivered at the Warwick Law School and Law Commission Symposium, 13–14 September 2011.

[50] J. Black, 'The Development of Risk-based Regulation in Financial Services: Just "Modelling Through"?' in J. Black, M. Lodge, and M. Thatcher (eds), *Regulatory Innovation—A Comparative Analysis* (Cheltenham: Edward Elgar, 2005), 156–80, 179.

[51] *Memorandum of Understanding Between HM Treasury, the Bank of England and the Financial Services Authority* (2006) at: <http://www.bankofengland.co.uk/financialstability/mou.pdf>.

[52] See Treasury Select Committee, Accountability of the Bank of England (HC 2010–12, 874), paras 21–29. See also J. Black, 'The Credit Crisis and the Constitution' in D. Oliver, R. Rawlings, and T. Prosser (eds), *The Regulatory State—Constitutional Implications* (Oxford: Oxford University Press, 2010), 92–128, 97–8, 114–16.

contributory factor across the full range of banking standards failures . . . the scale and breadth of regulatory failure was shocking'.[53] A general overview of performance is contained in the Turner Review, produced by the Chair of the FSA in 2009 at the request of the Chancellor.[54] The Review found major reforms to be necessary; these included the need for a more systematic approach to banking regulation and supervision, fundamental changes in approaches to capital, accounting, and liquidity regulation, changes to institutional and geographic coverage of regulation to reflect economic substance rather than legal form, better arrangements for deposit insurance and bank resolution, and detailed changes in relation to the role of credit rating agencies, executive remuneration, and derivatives trading.[55] Like other reports, it was critical of the failures of the tripartite system, and noted that the FSA had focused too much on the supervision of individual institutions, and insufficiently on wider sectoral and system-wide risk.[56] The report was also highly critical of the FSA's regulatory approach based on a philosophy that markets are in general self-correcting and that risk management should take place at the level of the individual firm. This resulted in supervision of individual institutions rather than the entire system, a focus on ensuring that systems and processes were correctly defined rather than challenging business models or strategies, and a balance between conduct of business regulation and prudential regulation that was biased towards the former. Thus

> [t]he combination of these features, underpinned by the then dominant philosophy of confidence in self correcting markets, meant that even in the many cases where the FSA did meet high standards in the execution of its regulatory and supervisory approach, it was not with hindsight aggressive enough in demanding adjustments to business models which even at the level of the individual institution were excessively risky and which pursued simultaneously by several banks, contributed to the build-up of system-wide risks.[57]

The FSA, however, operated a new more intrusive and more systemic approach of 'intensive supervision' after the crisis. For example, it vetted appointments to senior roles in major firms on competence as well as probity grounds.[58]

[53] Parliamentary Commission on Banking Standards, *Changing Banking for Good; Summary and Conclusions and Recommendations* (2013–14, HL 27-I, HC 175-I), paras 21, 181.

[54] FSA, *The Turner Review: a Regulatory Response to the Global Banking Crisis* (2009).

[55] FSA, *Turner Review* (n 54) ch. 4.

[56] FSA, *Turner Review* (n 54) 84.

[57] FSA, *Turner Review* (n 54) 86–8.

[58] See E. Ferran, 'The Break-up of the Financial Services Authority' (2011) 31 *Oxford Journal of Legal Studies* 455–80, 472.

The FSA also produced detailed reports into the failures in its handling of Northern Rock and of Royal Bank of Scotland. The former (issued before the Turner Review) was highly critical of the supervision team's implementation of the supervisory framework.[59] The latter was originally not to be published. After forceful criticism, particularly from the Treasury Select Committee which sent in special advisers to ensure that the report was a fair and balanced summary of the relevant evidence and that it fairly reflected the findings of the FSA investigation, a detailed report did emerge near the end of 2011.[60] This report was highly critical of the supervisory approach which had been adopted by the FSA; thus, apart from the failure of the framework of regulatory standards,

> many aspects of the FSA's approach to the supervision of systematically important firms in the pre-crisis period were inadequate. This reflected the fact that the FSA's overall philosophy and approach was flawed. There was insufficient focus on the core prudential issues of capital and liquidity, and inadequate attention given to key business risks and asset quality issues. Too much reliance was placed on assessments that appropriate decision-making processes were in place, with insufficient challenge to management assumptions and judgements. And a flawed concept of a 'regulatory dividend' rewarded firms with less intensive supervision if they could demonstrate effective controls and displayed a degree of cooperation with the FSA that ought to have been a non-negotiable minimum.[61]

The heavily criticized FSA philosophy included the risk-based and principles-based approaches, which had provided the basis for the 'regulatory dividend' granted to RBS despite its high-risk activities.[62] Further problems included the Government's pressure for 'light-touch' regulation; ironically, after criticism of supposedly heavy-handed regulation by the Prime Minister in 2005,

> the then Chairman of the FSA sought to correct this view by replying in a letter that the FSA was efficient and proportionate and, by way of example, noted that the FSA devoted only six staff to the supervision team responsible for HSBC. This allocation was similar to that for RBS . . . and a level of resource that we now consider severely deficient.[63]

Finally, the Treasury Select Committee also undertook an inquiry into regulation and supervision in the banking crisis, published in 2009. Whilst critical, and describing the FSA as having 'failed dreadfully', it took heart

[59] FSA, *The Supervision of Northern Rock: A Lessons Learned Review* (2008).
[60] FSA, *The Failure of the Royal Bank of Scotland* (2011).
[61] FSA, *The Failure of the Royal Bank of Scotland* (n 60) 27.
[62] FSA, *The Failure of the Royal Bank of Scotland* (n 60) 255–8.
[63] FSA, *The Failure of the Royal Bank of Scotland* (n 60) 262.

from the changes in the regulator's philosophy and operation since the crisis.[64] It was also highly critical of the tripartite system.[65] However, the Coalition Government elected in 2010 proposed more radical reforms.

The Coalition reforms: from tripartite to 'twin peaks'

The reforms were first announced by the Chancellor of the Exchequer in his Mansion House speech in June 2010, and then developed in more detail in three successive consultation papers, the last in June 2011 containing a draft Financial Services Bill amending the Financial Services and Markets Act 2000.[66] This approach was preferred to drafting a completely new piece of legislation, although the amendments are very extensive and the resulting mix of provisions is hardly user-friendly. It should be mentioned that the proposals operated alongside the major substantive reforms recommended by the Independent Commission on Banking and accepted by the Government; these include 'ring-fencing' to separate retail and investment banking and so avoid the need for state rescue if the latter fails.[67] These will be implemented through separate legislation.[68]

The basic regulatory structure is changed fundamentally, with an end to both the tripartite system and the FSA. Macro-prudential regulation passes to a new Financial Policy Committee (FPC) of the Bank of England; prudential regulation of firms to a new Prudential Regulation Authority (PRA), a subsidiary of the Bank of England, and consumer protection and markets regulation to the Financial Conduct Authority (FCA), adopting the existing legal corporate entity of the FSA. Thus the tripartite structure is replaced by 'twin peaks', in which prudential regulation of financial services is separate from the oversight of consumer protection and market conduct, with new overall macro-prudential regulation of the sort that had been badly lacking under the previous arrangements. The Treasury retains responsibility for decisions on the use of public funds, and the Bank of England regulates systematically important infrastructure such as payment and settlement systems. The new PRA was to adopt a more 'judgment-led' approach to regulation than the FSA.

[64] Treasury Committee, *Banking Crisis: Regulation and Supervision* (HC 2008–09, 767), para. 22.

[65] Treasury Committee, *Banking Crisis: Regulation and Supervision* (n 64) paras 103–20.

[66] HM Treasury, *A New Approach to Financial Regulation: Judgement, Focus and Stability* (Cm 7874, 2010); HM Treasury, *A New Approach to Financial Regulation: Building a Stronger System* (Cm 8012, 2011); HM Treasury, *A New Approach to Financial Regulation: The Blueprint for Reform* (Cm 8083, 2011). For useful background, see Ferran, 'The Break-up of the Financial Services Authority' (n 58).

[67] Independent Commission on Banking, *Final Report Recommendations* (2011).

[68] See the Financial Services (Banking Reform) Bill introduced in May 2013.

The proposals were subject to an unprecedented degree of parliamentary scrutiny, with four detailed reports from the Treasury Committee as well as pre-legislative scrutiny by a Joint Select Committee. The Treasury Committee took the highly unusual step of issuing a report to inform the House of Lords debates of its view of the Bill's defects and possible remedies.[69] There were many detailed criticisms, but what stand out are three central ones closely related to the main constitutional themes of this book. They were the questions of institutional coordination, of institutional design and accountability, and of regulatory style and culture. Given that the new structure is as yet untested, it is worth looking at the criticisms in some detail as they may anticipate future problems.

The first question of regulatory coordination is of course particularly important both as regards relations with the Treasury, especially in the case of the FPC, and coordination between the new authorities, given that the 'twin peaks' structure loses the previous advantage of a single coordinated regulator for financial services.[70] In its early examination of the proposals, the Treasury Committee noted that the institutional changes would move more powers away from the Government itself and that 'financial stability' is a broad and debatable concept, raising questions about the circumstances in which firms should be allowed to fail and of access to credit in the wider economy. This made it very different from the inflation target implemented by the Monetary Policy Committee of the Bank; the Committee wanted the Government to provide a detailed view of what the financial stability 'target' should be.[71] It also recommended a reserve veto power over the FPC by the Treasury.[72] In its response to the Committee the Government agreed to include a discretionary power for the Treasury to issue remit letters similar to those for the Monetary Policy Committee, and to issue a statutory memorandum of understanding on crisis management in an attempt to avoid the weaknesses of the tripartite system.[73]

This raises questions about Treasury powers over the Bank of England where public funds are at risk. In the financial crisis relations between the Treasury and the Bank had been confused, and the latter had, according to the then Chancellor, an effective veto on putting funds into the banking

[69] Treasury Committee, *Financial Services Bill* (HC 2012–13, 161).

[70] See Ferran, 'The Break-up of the Financial Services Authority' (n 58).

[71] Treasury Committee, *Financial Regulation: a Preliminary Consideration of the Government's Proposals* (HC 2010–11, 430), paras 34–8, 62–7.

[72] Treasury Committee, *Financial Regulation: a Preliminary Consideration of the Government's Proposals* (n 71) para. 184.

[73] Treasury Committee, *Financial Regulation: a Preliminary Consideration of the Government's Proposals: Government Response* (HC 2010–12, 958).

system. The Committee recommended that the proposed memorandum of understanding be strengthened by specifying more clearly the circumstances in which the Bank had to inform the Treasury of a 'material risk' to public funds, and that there should be a new power for the Chancellor to direct the Bank in the event of such a notification having been made. This would help ensure that once the Bank had notified the Chancellor of such a risk, the Chancellor would be in charge of all decisions involving public funds and liabilities. The Bank of England and the Government accepted that such a power was necessary, but only in relation to some instruments of crisis management, notably provision of financial assistance. The Treasury Committee continued to argue for a general power of direction.[74]

The Committee was also concerned about the adequacy of a memorandum of understanding in coordinating the three new institutions, and recommended that:

> *[g]iven previous unsatisfactory experience of regulators operating within a Memorandum of Understanding, we recommend that the relationship between the FCA, PRA and FPC be set out more explicitly in primary legislation and in as much detail as possible in secondary legislation. This can help to avoid regulatory gaps or overlap. This will also provide greater clarity and should limit the scope for institutional bickering about obligations under the MoU, although with the risk of some loss of flexibility.*[75]

It was also critical of the proposed use of a memorandum of understanding to coordinate the new bodies in relation to their representation in the European regulatory institutions.[76]

Finally, there were problems over the veto powers of the PRA over actions of the FCA where the latter might threaten financial stability. The Treasury Committee was doubtful whether such a veto was appropriate as it might result in the FCA being seen as subordinate to the PRA; if it was provided, it should be given to the FPC instead and only available in exceptional circumstances.[77] The proposed arrangements for institutional coordination were thus highly complex and, according to the Treasury Committee, unsatisfactory.

On the second issue, that of accountability and institutional design, there was fundamental criticism of the suitability of an unreformed Bank of England for performing its enhanced role, especially as it is not, of course, a government department and so does not have direct ministerial accountability to Parliament, yet is not an independent regulatory agency with the

74 Treasury Committee, *Financial Services Bill* (n 69) paras 30–4.

75 Treasury Committee, *Financial Conduct Authority* (HC 2010–12, 1574), para. 90 (emphasis retained).

76 Treasury Committee, *Financial Conduct Authority* (n 75) para. 106.

77 Treasury Committee, *Financial Conduct Authority* (n 75) paras 91–7.

procedural protections usually afforded such bodies. The Joint Select Committee made a number of proposals for clarifying the objectives of the new bodies, and increasing the accountability of the Bank of England.[78] The Treasury Committee issued a similarly critical report on the Bank's governance and accountability, as mentioned in Chapter 2.[79] This noted that, unlike in the case of the FSA, there had been no transparent and public review of the Bank's performance in the financial crisis, and the Bank had refused to give minutes of its governing Court during this period to the Committee.[80] The Committee recommended that the Court be transformed into a smaller supervisory board with greater expertise in prudential policy; its minutes should be published and it should conduct published reviews of the Bank's action.[81] These recommendations were rejected by the Government and the Bank, as was a recommendation for a pre-appointment hearing before the Treasury Committee for the Governor, although they did accept that a weaker internal oversight committee should be set up and minutes of the Court published. The accountability of the Bank was one of the most controversial issues during the passage of the Bill through the House of Lords. In addition, problems remained relating to internal coordination; thus the former deputy governor of the Bank has pointed to the difficulties likely to result from decision-making in the Bank being divided between different committees, each with different external members and different remits.[82] The Joint Committee and Treasury Committee also made extensive recommendations for increasing the accountability of the FCA, including publication of full minutes of meetings, pre-appointment scrutiny of the Chief Executive by the Treasury Committee, and that Parliament be empowered by legislation to request retrospective reviews of the FCA's work.[83]

Both the Joint Committee and the Treasury Committee were also critical of the confused statutory objectives for the new regulatory institutions. One issue concerned the extent to which the objectives of the FPC should include a secondary objective of supporting the economic policy of the government, thereby enabling it to support growth; another was the extent to which it

[78] Joint Committee on the Draft Financial Services Bill, *Draft Financial Services Bill* (2010–12, HL 236, HC 1447).

[79] Treasury Committee, *Accountability of the Bank of England* (HC 2010–12, 874).

[80] Treasury Committee, *Accountability of the Bank of England* (n 79) paras 74–7, 86–7. The Bank did conduct an internal review later.

[81] Treasury Committee, *Accountability of the Bank of England* (n 79) paras 165–70.

[82] J. Gieve, 'A Better Blueprint for the Bank of England's Governance', *The Financial Times*, 19 December 2011.

[83] Treasury Committee, *Financial Conduct Authority* (n 75) ch. 3.

should have an objective of promoting competition.[84] In the case of the FCA, the role of the over-arching strategic objective, amended to 'ensuring relevant markets function well', was unclear.[85]

Turning finally to the regulatory approach and culture of new bodies, the Joint Select Committee noted that '[a]lthough ministers and regulators have been very vocal about the importance of the new judgement-led approach, the term is not referred to or defined in the legislation and no specific powers are given'.[86] As regards the PRA, in the second consultation paper the Government stated that it 'will make greater use of principles in its approach and will enforce a "purposive" application, and enforcement, of PRA rules requiring compliance with the "spirit" as well as the letter of the rules . . .'. It remains to be seen how far this will differ from the discredited principles-based approach of the FSA, although the PRA was to take a 'whole firm' approach to authorizations and would only grant them where it was comfortable that the firm would be prudently managed with a viable business model. [87] In the case of the FCA, it had issued a document setting out how the new Authority would approach regulation, emphasizing the need for early preventative action, for tackling causes rather than symptoms of problems, and for taking a more thematic and differentiated approach to regulating firms. It would also enhance its enforcement activity. However, the document was criticized by the Treasury Committee as outlining '*an inappropriate culture for the FCA, one that may allow some old and inappropriate practices and culture from the FSA to be replicated... Its lack of detail and substance demonstrates the amount of work required to get the legislation right*'.[88] An interesting clue to a new approach was provided by an interview with the FCA Chairman suggesting that it would reject the pre-crisis assumption that markets had an inherent tendency towards efficient and stable risk diversion, and instead recognize 'human myopia and imperfect rationality'.[89]

[84] See C. Jones and B. Masters, 'Change of Heart Puts Growth on New Stability Panel's To-do List', *The Financial Times*, 19 June 2012; Treasury Committee, *Financial Services Bill* (n 69) para. 57.

[85] Treasury Committee, *Financial Services Bill* (n 69) paras 55–6.

[86] Joint Committee on the Draft Financial Services Bill, *Draft Financial Services Bill* (n 78) para. 189.

[87] HM Treasury, *A New Approach to Financial Regulation: Building a Stronger System* (n 66) para. 3.32.

[88] FSA, *The Financial Conduct Authority: Approach to Regulation* (2011); Treasury Committee, *Financial Conduct Authority* (n 75) para. 137 (emphasis retained).

[89] B. Masters, 'We Will be Looking at Things from a Consumer Perspective', *The Financial Times*, 25 January 2012.

The Financial Services Act 2012

These well-informed and comprehensive criticisms did not bode well for the new system; understanding the reforms is also made more difficult by the approach adopted of complex amendments to the Financial Services and Markets Act 2000 rather than enacting a new legislative code. Further changes were made by the Government during the passage of the legislation. The effect was the adoption of some, but by no means all, of the criticisms made by the Committees.

The question of communication and coordination within the system was addressed briefly in Chapter 2. On relations between the Bank of England and the Treasury and political responsibility for public expenditure, provision is made for a new duty on the Bank to notify the Treasury of a possible need for public funds, for example to provide financial assistance to a bank, and for a power of direction by the Treasury to the Bank requiring the latter to exercise its powers of financial assistance, its stabilization powers, or its powers of bank administration.[90] A memorandum of understanding was also to be drawn up between the Treasury and the Bank (and the PRA), including guidance on what is to be regarded as a risk requiring notification of the Treasury and the respective roles of the institutions where a public funds notification has been given.[91] This sets out the responsibilities of each institution; thus the Bank has primary operational responsibility for crisis management whilst the Treasury has sole responsibility for decisions on the use of public funds. It provides more details of notification requirements, of the handling of crisis management, and of the Treasury power of direction over the Bank.[92] A further memorandum of understanding sets out coordination of international functions.[93]

Importantly, the Treasury is also empowered to specify to the FPC what the Government's economic policy is to be taken to be (as in the case of the Monetary Policy Committee remit) and issue recommendations to the Committee; both must be published.[94] This is done through the publication of a remit, to be repeated annually, similar to that issued to the Monetary Policy Committee; the remit highlights the need to make trade-offs between supporting economic growth and addressing sources of systemic risk and

[90] Financial Services Act 2012, ss 58–63. [91] Financial Services Act 2012, s 65.

[92] HM Treasury and Bank of England, *MOU on Financial Crisis Management* (nd) at: <http://www.bankofengland.co.uk/about/Documents/mous/moufincrisis.pdf>.

[93] Financial Services Act 2012, s 66.

[94] Financial Services Act 2012, s 4, inserting new ss 9D and 9E into the Financial Services and Markets Act 2000.

notes the importance of the former.[95] The Bank must consult the Treasury in drawing up its financial stability strategy and there must be meetings (with a published record) between the Governor and Chancellor after each Financial Stability Report is published.[96] The FPC is able to give directions to both the other regulatory institutions requiring macro-prudential measures to be taken.[97] The PRA has a right of veto over actions of the FCA which might threaten the stability of the UK financial system.[98] A further memorandum of understanding covers relations between the PRA and the FCA; a draft was published in advance to inform parliamentary debate.[99] Collaboration is also promoted through cross-membership of the different bodies; thus the Chief Executive of the FCA must be a member of the boards of both the FPC and the PRA.[100]

On institutional design, the changes made to the Bank of England were described in Chapter 2; they go some way to meeting the Treasury Committee's requirements, notably through the establishment of the Oversight Committee, though they fall far short of a fundamental reform to the Bank's structure, and the role of the Governor remains central. The Parliamentary Commission on Banking Standards remained highly critical in 2013 of the accountability and corporate governance arrangements of the Bank, though its recommendations were not taken up.[101] The FPC is subject to a similar requirement to the Monetary Policy Committee to publish a record of its meetings within six weeks, and it is also under a duty to publish explanations for decisions to exercise its key powers, including making directions to the other regulators.[102] As with the Monetary Policy Committee, it has four independent members appointed by the Chancellor.[103] The combination of

95 HM Treasury, *Remit and Recommendations for the Financial Policy Committee* (2013) at: <https://www.gov.uk/government/uploads/system/uploads/attachment_data/file/207473/remit_fpc_290413.pdf>.

96 Financial Services Act 2012, s 4, inserting new ss 9A and 9X.

97 Financial Services Act 2012, s 4, inserting new s 9H into the Financial Services and Markets Act 2000.

98 Financial Services Act 2012, s 6, inserting new s 3I into the Financial Services and Markets Act 2000.

99 Bank of England, *Memorandum of Understanding Between the Financial Conduct Authority and the Prudential Regulation Authority* (nd) at: <http://www.bankofengland.co.uk/about/Documents/mous/moufcapra.pdf>.

100 Financial Services Act 2012, s 4 inserting new s 9B into the Financial Services and Markets Act 2000; sch. 3 inserting new sch, 1ZB, para. 3 into the Financial Services and Markets Act 2000.

101 Parliamentary Commission on Banking Standards, *Changing Banking for Good* (2013–14, HL 27-II, HC 175-II), paras 1082–1093.

102 Financial Services Act 2012, s 4, inserting new ss 9S and 9U into the Financial Services and Markets Act 2000.

103 Financial Services Act 2012, s 4, inserting new s 9B into the Financial Services and Markets Act 2000.

a form of remit from the Treasury for the new Committee and published minutes will, from experience in monetary policy, represent a substantial increase in the clarification of responsibilities and of transparency. The Treasury Committee has however expressed concern about the FPC's independence and the Government's refusal to grant it power to set the baseline leverage ratio for banks as recommended by the Parliamentary Commission on Banking Standards; such a ratio would prevent banks pursuing aggressive growth strategies.[104] The Government, however, has kept to its original plan to use the Basel III standard which will come into effect in 2018, and which was criticized by the Commission as too low. In the meantime, the PRA has set capital adequacy requirements for individual firms. Overall, the Commission concluded that 'the future accountability to Parliament of the new bodies . . . appears to have been treated as an afterthought'.[105]

As mentioned, there was uncertainty about the objectives and transparency of the FCA, especially in view of the serious mistakes made by its predecessor, the FSA. The Government had initially rejected Treasury Committee recommendations that minutes of FCA meetings be published and that legislation should increase its accountability to the Select Committee, for example through requiring pre-appointing scrutiny of its members. During passage of the Bill, it was amended to require the publication of a record of each FCA meeting within six weeks, and it seems that this will be similar to minutes.[106] Transparency will be important given the highly complex objectives of the FCA.[107] It has a strategic objective of securing that markets function well; there are also three operational objectives. These are the consumer protection objective of securing an appropriate degree of protection for consumers; the integrity objective of protecting and enhancing the integrity of the UK financial system, and the competition objective of promoting effective competition in the interests of consumers. This is only a bare summary of objectives that are specified in considerable detail. The Parliamentary Commission on Banking Standards recommended that they be simplified through removing the strategic objective, though this recommendation was rejected

[104] Treasury Committee, *Treasury Committee to Conduct Inquiry into Appointment Processes for Bank of England bodies and the Independence of the FPC*, news release, 10 June 2013; Parliamentary Commission on Banking Standards, *Changing Banking for Good* (n 101) paras 1003–13.

[105] Parliamentary Commission on Banking Standards, *Changing Banking for Good* (n 101) para. 1106.

[106] Financial Services Act 2012, sch. 3, inserting new sch. 1ZA into the Financial Services and Markets Act 2000, para 10.

[107] Financial Services Act 2012, s 6, inserting new s 1B-L into the Financial Services and Markets Act 2000.

by the Government.[108] Both the FCA and the PRA are also required to apply a set of regulatory principles, including using resources efficiently and effectively, only imposing proportionate burdens, the desirability of sustainable growth, and transparency.[109] The use of potentially conflicting general duties is familiar from the role of the utilities regulators in the UK.[110] However those applying to the Authority are far more complex and their balancing will be extraordinarily difficult.

Finally, there is the question of the regulatory approach to be adopted by the new institutions and to what extent it can be differentiated from the failed approach of the FSA discussed in this chapter. Only time will provide an answer to this, but there are some early indications of what we can expect. Thus the Bank of England has stated that the approach of the PRA will be based on judgment, weighting its supervision towards those issues and firms which it judges to pose the greatest risk to the stability of the UK financial system. It will be forward-looking, considering future risks. This will also require judgment, but it will be based on evidence and analysis. It will use a structured risk framework, and the intensity of its supervision will vary across firms.[111] None of this seems to differ very much from the FSA's approach pre-crisis. In the case of the FCA, it is proposed that it will concentrate more on wholesale conduct than did its predecessor, and that it will adopt a more issues- and supervisory-based approach. It will be more prepared to intervene early to take preventative action to protect consumers, and will try to tackle root causes rather than symptoms of problems through a deeper understanding of underlying commercial and behavioural drivers and the often multiple causes of poor outcomes for consumers. It will tailor its approach more effectively to risk, engaging in more thematic work but with intensive institution-specific supervision of institutions which can cause significant consumer or market detriment. It will engage more effectively with consumers and be more transparent.[112] Again, only experience will show whether this represents a radical shift from the past; in particular, the reliance on

[108] Parliamentary Commission on Banking Standards, *Changing Banking for Good* (n 101) para. 1074.

[109] Financial Services Act 2012, s 6 inserting new s 3B into the Financial Services and Markets Act 2000.

[110] See T. Prosser, *The Regulatory Enterprise: Government, Regulation and Legitimacy* (Oxford: Oxford University Press, 2012), ch. 9.

[111] Bank of England, *The Bank of England, Prudential Regulation Authority: The PRA's Approach to Banking Supervision* (2012). For further discussion of the PRA's approach and its problems, see the Parliamentary Commission on Banking Standards, *Changing Banking for Good* (n 101) paras 935–42.

[112] Financial Services Authority, *The Financial Conduct Authority: Approach to Regulation* (2011). See also *Journey to the Financial Conduct Authority* (2012).

risk-based models was shown by earlier FSA experience to be itself highly risky. The Parliamentary Committee on Banking Standards was sceptical about the FCA's ability to adopt a radically different approach from its predecessor.[113]

Conclusions

Financial services regulation in the UK has been subject to substantial reform. Although we have a clear idea of the institutional architecture to be adopted, we know far less about the new regulatory approaches to be taken and whether they will improve on the disastrous experience of the past. In the EU there is even greater uncertainty as a result of the sovereign debt crises and banking crises and a continuing lack of clarity on the extent to which European-wide or national solutions will be the way forward. The EU has been particularly affected by constitutional questions of the legitimacy of delegation to agencies; although these seem to have been resolved pragmatically in the establishment of the ESFS, uncertainties still remain.[114] In the UK, there has not been a serious problem of the constitutional legitimacy of independent regulatory agencies, and this model was adopted for financial regulation in the form of the FSA. However, the UK arrangements gave rise to other problems. The first was that of lack of coordination of the regulatory system as a whole; as we have seen, the tripartite system failed during the crisis. Major uncertainties surround the arrangements for the coordination of its successor system. The Financial Services Act 2012 certainly takes a number of steps to avoid the problems through a greater clarification of institutional responsibilities and through creating requirements for increased communication between the different authorities. However, it still has to be said that the result of the reforms is to create more institutions rather than fewer, and the danger still remains that the measures required by the Act may break down under the pressures of financial crisis.

The FSA also failed for a number of reasons concerned both with its regulatory style, emphasizing the principles-based and risk-based nature of its supervision, and its relative openness to the industry without a corresponding degree of openness to other interests or any form of public interest. This was seriously exacerbated by pressure from the Government to adopt a 'light-touch' style of regulation. Once more, it is still uncertain to what extent

[113] Parliamentary Commission on Banking Standards, *Changing Banking for Good* (n 101) paras 943–6.

[114] See Schammo, 'The European Securities and Markets Authority' (n 17).

the reform will change this. There are some welcome increases in transparency in the new model, which may also do something to clarify the different responsibilities of each of the institutional actors involved. It is clear that lessons have been learned from the largely successful experience with the Monetary Policy Committee of the Bank of England described in Chapter 6. However, that Committee had the advantage of a clear remit and a single overriding objective; things are much more complex in promoting financial stability and regulating financial services, as the multiple objectives of the FCA vividly illustrate. Despite the heavy criticism of the FSA approach, it is still unclear what the 'judgment-led' approach to regulation will actually mean and the extent to which a risk-based model can be reconfigured to avoid the over-confidence of the past. The new institutional arrangements are extremely complex; this itself may limit transparency, and their success or otherwise will depend on how effectively institutional collaboration is achieved between them. Other chapters of this book, and past experience in times of financial crisis, suggest that this will not be an easy task.

8

State Aid, Government Shareholdings, and Industrial Policy

Introduction

The UK has never had a clear or coherent industrial policy. Of course, there have been many government interventions aimed at steering or supporting the economy, for example nationalization and systems of industrial support, but these have been ad hoc and have not represented any developed form of economic planning. Indeed, it is doubtful to what extent even the post-war nationalizations under the Attlee Government represented a serious attempt to use the industries as a tool of industrial policy; certainly the reality was far from this.[1] Nevertheless, as we shall see in this chapter, the various more limited forms of state intervention provide interesting lessons in themselves about the working of our economic constitution.

There have been signs of greater ambition in industrial policy. The most important of these was the Industry Act 1975. Although this was 'a gelded creature' both compared to the Labour Government's original plans and in its very restricted implementation, in a celebrated article Winckler saw the Act as a sign of a major transformation in the British economy from a liberal form of capitalism to corporatism characterized by detailed control over the decision-making of firms, control not made explicit by law but through informal agreement and directed to the end of economic success rather than respect for legal rights. 'Full realisation of a corporatist economic system in Britain would therefore mean the end of the rule of law as traditionally known.'[2] Winckler envisaged three alternative options to such corporatism; the reversion to a market economy, muddling through, or 'a socialist revolution of

[1] For detailed discussion, see T. Prosser, *Nationalised Industries and Public Control* (Oxford: Basil Blackwell, 1986), chs 2–3.

[2] J.T. Winckler, 'Law, State and Economy: The Industry Act 1975 in Context' (1975) 2 *British Journal of Law and Society* 103–28.

either a workers' controlled or authoritarian type'.[3] The former decisively won out; industrial policy has not become an explicit area of government policy, and indeed opportunities to implement it are seriously restricted by EU state aid law, as we shall see. Nevertheless, suggestions for some limited form of industrial strategy are still made, most notably in the form of the 'comprehensive strategy for national wealth creation' proposed in the Heseltine Report of 2012, including a new National Growth Council chaired by the Prime Minister.[4]

The downgrading of industrial policy does not mean that there has been no state intervention; most recently, the involuntary nationalization or part-nationalization of the banks has resulted in a massive increase in government shareholding. There is an irony here. Earlier nationalizations were criticized from the political left as ignoring the 'commanding heights of the economy' and from several political directions as being concerned only with failing enterprises which required government support to prop them up rather than to achieve any public purposes. The bank rescues cut across both of these; financial services, not manufacturing industry, are the new 'commanding heights', whilst the reason for the massive government support was their failure under private management. The intention of the Government is that its shareholdings in the banks will be temporary; however, the powers used to acquire them are permanent.

Apart from the absence of a clear industrial policy, we also have a remarkable lack of relevant domestic constitutional norms, a point which may give some limited support to Winckler's claims. It is well-documented that law was largely irrelevant to public ownership in the form of the old nationalized industries.[5] As we shall see in this chapter, in the case of government shareholdings, it is not public law but company law which has the most important role, both in providing a vehicle for public ownership and in limiting the opportunities to use the holdings as a means of wider public interest interventions. At the international level, the WTO rules limit state aid, and act as a constraint on the implementation of a developed industrial policy. However, they are relatively weak in that they do not apply to services, do not involve *ex ante* control or scrutiny, and have limited institutional arrangements for their enforcement.[6] Far more important is the state aid law

[3] Winckler, 'Law, State and Economy' (n 3) 113.

[4] The Rt Hon the Lord Heseltine of Thenford CH, *No Stone Unturned in Pursuit of Growth* (Department for Business Innovation and Skills, 2012).

[5] See Prosser, *Nationalised Industries and Public Control* (n 1) for a sustained demonstration of this point.

[6] For an outline, see C-D. Ehlermann and M. Goyette, 'The Interface between EU State Aid Control and the WTO Disciplines on Subsidies' [2006] *European State Aid Quarterly* 695–718.

of the European Union. This provides the major constitutional constraint on the implementation of industrial policy in the UK, and I shall begin this chapter by outlining its scope and key provisions.

The EU state aid regime

Introduction

The basic law of state aid is contained in articles 107 and 109 TFEU. Article 107(1) provides that:

> [s]ave as otherwise provided in the Treaties, any aid granted by a Member State or through State resources in any form whatsoever which distorts or threatens to distort competition by favouring certain undertakings or the production of certain goods shall, in so far as it affects trade between Member States, be incompatible with the internal market.

Article 107(2) then goes on to list categories of aid which are compatible with the common market, and in Article 107(3) those categories of aid which may be considered by the Commission to be compatible. Examples of the former are aids with a social character granted directly to consumers (not undertakings) and aid to make good damage caused by natural disasters or 'exceptional occurrences'; examples of the latter are aid to promote the economic development of areas where the standard of living is abnormally low or to 'remedy a serious disturbance in the economy of a Member State'.

Article 108 provides for the supervision of state aid by the Commission, including, crucially, imposing a duty on Member States to notify the Commission in advance of any plans to grant or to alter aid.[7] In the case of public enterprises, the system is reinforced by a Directive requiring transparency in their financial relations with governments.[8]

The state aid regime has been subject to simplification and streamlining under the Commission's 2005 State Aid Action Plan. Notable measures have included the General Block Exemption Regulation of 2008.[9] It applies to a range of types of state aid, including some aid to SMEs, aid for environmental

[7] Art. 108(3).

[8] Directive 2006/111/EC, Transparency of financial relations between Member States and public undertakings as well as on financial transparency within certain undertakings (Codified version) [2006] OJ L318/17.

[9] Commission regulation 800/2008 declaring certain categories of aid compatible with the common market in application of Articles 87 and 88 of the Treaty (General Block Exemption Regulation) [2008] OJ L214/3.

protection, employment aid, and regional aid. It does not cover capital injections or many types of risk capital measures, which are dealt with under separate guidelines. The effect of the Regulation is to exempt such aid from the requirement of prior notification, replacing it with summary notification and reporting obligations. The exemption has been used extensively, with the Commission being informed of 414 such new measures in 2010. Further reform is currently planned, with a proposal for a more focused framework announced in 2012. This would set out more clearly common principles, revise and streamline the many guidelines in this area, focus enforcement on cases with the biggest impact on the single market through limiting notification requirements and through a new block exemption, and would clarify the notion of a state aid and make the Commission's procedures more flexible.[10]

The law of state aid is highly complex, and cannot be covered in detail here.[11] However, there are a few issues of relevance which deserve a little more comment.

Acquisition of property in a company and state guarantees

The acquisition of state holdings or other forms of property in companies has been a major subject of controversy in the state aid regime for a considerable time. Article 345 TFEU provides that:

> [t]he Treaties shall in no way prejudice the rules in Member States governing the system of property ownership.

This prevents any explicit finding that nationalization is in itself contrary to EU competition provisions. However, substantial limitations have been imposed on the ability of Member States to engage in traditional forms of nationalization or support for public enterprises.[12] In 1984 the Commission issued guidelines setting out its approach to this subject.[13] On the one hand, a simple acquisition of a holding without the injection of fresh capital would not constitute state aid, nor would the contribution of fresh capital in circumstances that would be acceptable to a private investor operating under normal market conditions. However, there would be state aid where the contribution would not be acceptable to a private investor under those

[10] European Commission, *EU State Aid Modernisation*, COM(2012) 209 final.

[11] A useful summary can be found in C. Quigley, *European State Aid Law and Policy*, 2nd edn (Oxford: Hart Publishing, 2009).

[12] For further details, see Quigley, *European State Aid Policy* (n 11) 110–26.

[13] European Commission, 'Application of Articles 92 and 93 of the EEC Treaty to public authorities' holdings', *Bulletin EC* 9-1984.

conditions. This approach was applied by the European Court of Justice in *Belgium v Commission*, where the Court accepted the test for state aid of whether the undertaking would be able to obtain the finance on the private capital markets.[14] This has been criticized on the basis that '[f]orcing public ownership into the mould of the private sector prejudices the system of property ownership in the Member States—the very thing that Article 345 seeks to prohibit'.[15]

In the case of guarantees, the Commission issued a notice in 2008 on the application of state aid law.[16] In brief, to avoid characterization of an individual guarantee as state aid the borrower must not be in financial difficulty (as defined in the Commission's guidelines), the extent of the guarantee must be precisely measurable and linked to a specified transaction, the guarantee must not cover more than 80 per cent of the outstanding loan, and a market-oriented price must be paid for it. Similar conditions apply to guarantee schemes, and simplified provision is made for aid to SMEs which establishes safe harbours for premiums below a set amount. Once more, the effect is largely to mimic the effect of the private financial markets.

Payment for services of general economic interest

The state aid arrangements just discussed assume that enterprises being supported operate in what are essentially normal markets. However, as we saw in Chapter 3, special provision is made where public services are supplied on a non-market basis in the form of services of general economic interest. Important and difficult questions were raised about the extent to which public compensation for the delivery of such services would constitute state aid, and the leading case is the *Altmark* decision of 2003.[17] The Court of Justice held that such compensation would not constitute state aid so long as four conditions were met. These are that the public service obligation must be clearly defined; that the parameters for calculating the compensation must be established in advance in an objective and transparent manner; that compensation must not exceed the costs of providing the service (including a reasonable profit); and that either the undertaking is selected through a public procurement procedure based on the lowest cost, or the compensation

[14] Case 234/84 *Belgium v Commission* [1986] ECR 2236, paras 14–17.

[15] D. Nicol, *The Constitutional Protection of Capitalism* (Oxford: Hart Publishing, 2010), 118.

[16] Commission Notice on the application of Articles 87 and 88 of the EC Treaty to State aid in the form of guarantees [2008] OJ C 155/02, and see Quigley, *European State Aid Policy* (n 11) 119–23.

[17] Case C-2800/00 *Altmark Trans GmbH* [2003] ECR I-7747.

payable must be assessed on the basis of the costs of a notional efficient undertaking. Of course, even if the payments are held to constitute state aid, they may still be held to be compatible with the common market if they are necessary to avoid obstructing the performance of a service of general economic interest.

The Commission issued the 'Altmark Package' of rules as part of the simplification and streamlining of state aid law in 2005. This included a Decision specifying the conditions, as laid down in the *Altmark* judgment, under which compensation to companies for the provision of public services is compatible with the state aid rules and does not require advance notification[18] The Commission also issued a framework specifying the conditions under which compensation not covered by the Decision is compatible with state aid rules, emphasizing the need for notification and that compensation which exceeds the costs of the public service, or is used by companies in other markets open to competition, will not be compatible with the rules.[19] Finally, the Directive on transparency in relations with public enterprise referred to earlier was amended to require the keeping of separate accounts for public service and other markets. A further package was adopted in 2011–12, comprising a new Decision on exemption from notification, a revised framework for compensation for services with a more commercial character, a general Communication clarifying the rules on compensation, and new *de minimis* rules applying to small services. The Decision exempts from notification aid to all social services in relation to health and social care, child care, access to and reintegration in the labour market, social housing, and the care and social inclusion of vulnerable groups; this is irrespective of the amount of aid granted. It also exempts companies that provide small-scale air or maritime transport services.[20] There has thus been extensive work to clarify the application of the state aid rules to the granting of public service compensation, and substantial exemptions have been granted. Moreover, in line with the *Altmark* decision, the requirements are now largely procedural and require transparency rather than imposing major substantive restrictions on the granting of compensation.

[18] Commission Decision 2005/842/EC on the application of Article 86(2) of the EC Treaty to State aid in the form of public service compensation granted to certain undertakings entrusted with the operation of services of general economic interest [2005] OJ L312/67.

[19] Community framework for State aid in the form of public service compensation, 2005/C 297/04 [2005] OJ C 297/4.

[20] Commission Decision 2012/21/EU on the application of Article 106(2) of the Treaty on the Functioning of the European Union to State aid in the form of public service compensation [2012] OJ L7/3.

State aid, rescues, and the financial crisis

The state aid rules of course played a major part in the resolution of the financial crisis from 2008. At first sight they appeared to be simply a restriction on the ability to rescue financial institutions, and the Commission was faced with considerable pressure from Member States to relax the rules. New guidelines on rescuing and restructuring firms in difficulty had been issued in 2004, and these were extended because of the crisis.[21] They were based on the principles that the beneficiary must finance a considerable proportion of its restructuring costs, and that no additional rescue or restructuring aid could be granted for a period of 10 years; detailed conditions were also laid down for authorizing aid. The Treaty power used at first for authorizing aid in the financial crisis was article 107(3)(c) TFEU: 'aid to facilitate the development of certain economic activities or of certain economic areas, where such aid does not adversely affect trading conditions to an extent contrary to the common interest.' Given the strict conditions attached to such aid, it was clear that a more generous approach was needed.

The main actions of the Commission in this context were taken under article 107(3)(b) TFEU: 'to remedy a serious disturbance in the economy of a Member State.'[22] This provided the basis for a temporary framework for support, and the approval of a large number of schemes in the financial sector. Four Communications were issued on banks, concerning the application of state aid rules to measures taken in relation to financial institutions in the context of the global financial crisis; the recapitalization of financial institutions in the financial crisis; the treatment of impaired assets in the banking sector, and restructuring measures in the financial sector.[23] These were partially replaced and amended by a further Communication in 2013, which placed a considerably greater emphasis on burden sharing through contributions to restructuring by banks and their investors, as well as taxpayers.[24] A general Communication was also issued providing a temporary framework for measures to support access to finance, including for non-bank

[21] Communication from the Commission—Community guidelines on state aid for rescuing and restructuring firms in difficulty [2004] OJ C 244/2.

[22] For a general account of the approach, see P. Marsden and I. Kokkoris 'The Role of Competition and State Aid Policy in Financial and Monetary Law' (2010) 13 *Journal of International Economic Law* 875–92.

[23] These are summarized in the Communication on the application, from 1 January 2011, of State aid rules to support measures in favour of banks in the context of the financial crisis [2010] OJ C329/07.

[24] Communication from the Commission on the application, from 1 August 2012, of State aid rules to support measures in favour of banks in the context of the financial crisis [2013] OJ C216/1.

enterprises.[25] This set out provision for aid under existing instruments and explained that the Commission would consider some categories of aid granted before the end of 2011 as justified as a result of the crisis.[26]

The rules were applied very generously, at least initially. Thus according to commentators '[t]he EU largely rubber-stamped almost all of the interventions made by Member States to support their domestic banking industries' and by December 2009 of 81 Decisions by the Commission only six were conditional after a full investigation process. The level of state aid almost quintupled in 2008 and in the year from October 2008 around 3,632 billion Euro of state aid schemes were approved.[27] The Commission was indeed proud of its ability to decide quickly, approving the rescue of the UK bank Bradford and Bingley in a mere 24 hours.[28] Approval often came well after the rescues had taken place. However, a tougher approach was taken in general to the rescue of the UK banking sector given the sheer scale of the financial packages. Thus, according to Julia Black, after the immediate crisis, 'the Commission did not simply act as a rubber stamp'. In particular, support for the Royal Bank of Scotland (amounting to a state recapitalization of £20 billion) was subject to 'long detailed and hard-fought negotiations' and the Commissioner noted that, should the bank not deliver on its balance sheet reduction targets, the Commission could intervene once more and require further divestments.[29] After a drop in UK state aid applications from 2009, they have increased once more through attempts to deal with the continuing recession.[30] The state aid rules may create problems for any restructuring of the Royal Bank of Scotland to prepare it for privatization, especially as a result of the new requirements for burden-sharing.

The state aid rules are thus of fundamental importance in providing a basic constitutional framework for industrial policy, including the taking of stakes in enterprises and refinancing them. They do not go so far as to prohibit or prevent public ownership of industry as that would contradict article 345

[25] Temporary Community framework for state aid measures to support access to finance in the current financial and economic crisis [2009] OJ C16/1.

[26] Communication of the Commission—Temporary Union Framework for State aid measures to support access to finance in the current financial and economic crisis [2011] OJC 6/5.

[27] Marsden and Kokkoris, 'The Role of Competition and State Aid Policy in Financial and Monetary Law' (n 22) 875 and fn 2.

[28] Commissioner N. Kroes, 'Competition Policy and the Crisis—the Commission's Approach to Banking and Beyond' (2010) *Competition Policy Newsletter*, 4.

[29] J. Black, 'The Credit Crisis and the Constitution' in D. Oliver, T. Prosser, and R. Rawlings (eds), *The Regulatory State: Constitutional Implications* (Oxford: Oxford University Press, 2010), 92–128, 123.

[30] B. Groom, 'Surge in Requests to EU for Approving State Aid', *The Financial Times*, 25 March 2013.

TFEU; however, they impose major constraints on the action which can be taken to give public enterprises a distinctive role. It is important, however, that the effects of these constraints are not exaggerated. In particular, the response to the financial crisis showed a considerable degree of flexibility in the system, and the approach to public service compensation has shown that the primary goal is transparency with the development of procedural protections, rather than simply imposing substantive limitations. This is not to say that a government wishing to implement a more interventionist industrial policy may not face difficulties as a result of the state aid regime, but it is to acknowledge that the reality is a complex one, with plenty of room for manoeuvre dependent on the political context.

Public ownership

Public corporations

Of course, public ownership of parts of industry, notably the public utilities, played a major role in the UK up to the Thatcher revolution of the 1980s. The most important institutional means for such ownership was the public corporation at 'arm's length' from government departments. This arrangement was seriously deficient in a number of important respects, most notably through the absence of a framework for coherent communication with government, and in the very rudimentary arrangements for industry accountability.[31] It is unnecessary to go into detail here, however, as the public corporation form is now of very limited importance as a means of the delivery of industrial policy. Of course, this is largely due to the effect of privatization, but another reason for its decline, not just in the UK, is the effect of the state aid rules. The Commission decided in 2010 that the legal form of the French postal service, an entity governed by public law and not subject to the ordinary law on compulsory administration and the winding up of firms in difficulty, amounted to an implicit guarantee by the state of its debts and so was in breach of the state aid requirements. This was not a result of its public ownership as such, but of the legal form chosen for it. As a result of this Decision, La Poste was converted into a public limited company.[32] This does not mean that all public corporations automatically infringe state aid

[31] These problems are discussed in developed form in Prosser, *Nationalised Industries and Public Control* (n 1).

[32] Commission Decision on State aid C 56/07 granted by France to La Post [2010] OJ L274/1; the conversion was implemented by Loi No 2010-123 du 9 février 2010 relative à l'entreprise publique La Poste et aux activités postales.

law as the case was largely concerned with the specific character of French law on putting enterprises into administration, but it does create a further reason for EU Member State governments to be wary of the use of this institutional form.

There are virtually no remaining public enterprises in the form of public corporations in the UK, and none of major strategic importance. To give some examples, Scottish Water remains a body corporate.[33] The other major Scottish public enterprise, CalMac Ferries, is now a wholly owned subsidiary of David MacBrayne Ltd, itself a company wholly owned by the Scottish Ministers. Until 1990 it was part of a public corporation, the Scottish Transport Group, but was then vested in government and assumed its present form largely owing to the need to comply with EU tendering requirements for ferry services. In London, London Underground Ltd is a company wholly owned by Transport Trading Ltd, itself wholly owned by Transport for London, a body corporate but required by statute to act through subsidiary companies.[34] British Waterways, which owns and maintains the canal and much of the navigable river systems, has recently been transformed from a public corporation into a charitable trust, with the exception of its Scottish operations.[35]

Government shareholding

Such public ownership as exists is mainly implemented through shareholdings in public limited companies. Acquisition of shares has been important, of course, in the rescue of the failed banking sector; the most important example outside the financial sector was until recently that of the Royal Mail where the state had a 100 per cent holding.[36] A majority stake in the Royal Mail was sold in 2013 under the Postal Services Act 2011, and the process was aided by state aid approval for the transfer of its huge pension liabilities to the Government, and a debt reduction of £1,089 million.

There is nothing new about the use of government shareholdings as a means of public ownership; companies wholly owned by government or 'mixed enterprises' with both public and private holdings has been extensively used in many countries. Advantages over the public corporation form included flexibility, the ability to influence industrial sectors through relatively small holdings, the possibility of dispensing with the need for legislation when

[33] See the Water Industry (Scotland) Act 2002, s 20.
[34] Greater London Authority Act 1999, ss 154, 157.
[35] The British Waterways Board (Transfer of Functions) Order, SI 2012/1659.
[36] See the Postal Services Act 2000, pt IV.

acquiring stakes, and easy privatization. In the UK, nineteenth-century examples included the acquisition of shares in the Suez Canal Company, and most important of all was the purchase by the Government in 1914 of a substantial shareholding in the Anglo-Persian Oil Co, which later became BP, in order to protect the Royal Navy's supply of oil and to provide competition with the international cartel of Standard Oil and Shell. More recent examples included British Nuclear Fuels Ltd and the National Nuclear Corporation.

This form of public ownership did not resolve the difficulties associated with the use of the public corporation. In principle, government control was to be exercised through its voting power as shareholder and the power to appoint directors, though in practice these were supplemented by additional powers in legislation, in the articles of association of the company, or through using contractual techniques to make the provision of aid dependent on further governmental powers. A particular problem was caused by the position of the Government-appointed director under company law. He or she was responsible to the company itself to promote the commercial advantage of the members of the company as a whole, and this would come into conflict with any desire by government to represent the public interest and to implement general economic policy.[37] The position has been eased only slightly by the Companies Act 2006, which requires directors to promote the success of the company for the benefit of its members as a whole, having regard to a number of considerations including the interests of employees, impact on the community and the environment, and the need to act fairly between the members of the company.[38] On this basis, it is hardly surprising that the BP Treasury directors, who had power to veto any resolution of the board, were not used as a means of imposing government policy, and indeed the veto was never employed, although BP had a well-known record of opposition to government.[39] The relevant company law causes particular difficulty where there are private shareholders alongside government, as in the case of the two large nationalized banks, to be discussed later in the chapter.

A somewhat different technique used by the Labour Government in the late 1970s was that of a state holding corporation with shares in a number of companies: the National Enterprise Board.[40] The Board was created by the Industry Act 1975 as part of the broader 'corporatist' attempts to influence the broader economy; however, its role in practice was limited and was dominated by its responsibility for ailing concerns which government had

[37] See *in re Smith and Fawcett, Ltd* [1942] Ch 304.

[38] Companies Act 2006, s 172.

[39] Prosser, *Nationalised Industries and Public Control* (n 1) 33.

[40] Prosser, *Nationalised Industries and Public Control* (n 1) 47–52.

been forced to rescue and had transferred to the Board; notably Rolls-Royce (1971) Ltd and British Leyland. Nor was it any more successful at resolving problems of accountability; despite repeated pressure from the Public Accounts Committee for access to its books by the Comptroller and Auditor-General, this was never granted, and the Committee also seriously criticized the quality of departmental monitoring of the Board.[41] It was wound down after the 1979 change of government.

The Shareholder Executive

More recently, government shareholdings have been managed by the Shareholder Executive. Unlike the National Enterprise Board, it is not a public corporation with a separate legal personality but an executive agency of the Department for Business, Innovation and Skills. This means that the NAO has access to its books. The Executive was created in 2003, according to the NAO because of '[t]he recognition of the difficulties inherent in balancing public policy and ownership objectives and thereby ultimately in preserving and enhancing the value of public businesses'.[42] Thus '[b]alancing the need to increase shareholder value against . . . other objectives requires transparency so that they are assessed with full knowledge of their expected impact on value. This enhances decision-making'.[43] It was originally located in the Cabinet Office, but was transferred to BIS in 2004.

The Shareholder Executive has a portfolio of 19 businesses which are wholly or partly owned by the Government. It agrees strategic plans with the board of each business and appoints the Chairman. An important area of its activity recently has been arranging asset sales; one example was the sale of QinetiQ, which carries out research for the Ministry of Defence, advises on procurement, and manages the testing and evaluation of equipment. This took place through a private sale of a minority stake in 2003 and flotation of the rest in 2006. The sale proved controversial on value for money grounds, but the Public Accounts Committee praised the role of the Shareholder Executive in providing expertise and protecting the Department's interests.[44] In the case of the sale of the Government's stake in British Energy, the Committee was more critical, pointing to the Executive's reliance on expensive external advice and the payment of a £4 million success fee to a bank which had significantly underestimated what a buyer would pay; it was also

[41] The reports are summarized at Prosser, *Nationalised Industries and Public Control* (n 1) 50.
[42] NAO, *The Shareholder Executive and Public Sector Businesses* (HC 2006–07, 255), para. 1.3.
[43] NAO, *The Shareholder Executive and Public Sector Businesses* (n 42) para. 1.12.
[44] Public Accounts Committee, *The Privatisation of QinetiQ* (HC 2007–08, 151).

critical of a lack of concern with competition and the failure to carry out a timely risk assessment.[45] The Executive also offers extensive advice on corporate finance across government. Further asset sales are likely in the future.

The Executive is accountable to the permanent secretaries of government departments owning shareholdings. It originally reported to a stakeholder group consisting of a senior official from each department and held regular meetings with the Cabinet Secretary. After criticism by the Public Accounts Committee of the lack of independent representation in these arrangements, a non-executive Chairman and an advisory group of external members were introduced; a Shareholder Executive Board has now been established with external directors. A memorandum of understanding has been agreed with the devolved administrations in relation to their own shareholdings. From 2010, the annual report of the Executive has been produced in only a brief summary form in order to save costs, which restricts the amount of information available on its work.

A further important criticism was that '*reconciling public policy with shareholder value objectives can be difficult because the cost of meeting the former can have a negative effect on the latter*'.[46] The NAO had noted that 'in the past government departments struggled to balance these important responsibilities—often with the result that long-term shareholder value was not protected adequately' and that the problem was compounded in the cases where government-owned businesses sustained large losses.[47] This was particularly strongly the case in relation to the Royal Mail where the future of the industry has been a highly politicized issue; responsibility for postal services policy was moved to the Department from the Executive in 2007, though the Executive still manages the portfolio.

Clearly the Shareholder Executive does not have a major public policy role; however, its decisions may impinge on important policy matters and there has been no resolution of the earlier difficulties in the relationship between public policy and the role of government as shareholder. The Executive's main role is to act as a manager of share portfolios and to organize disposals, and also to provide financial expertise and advice across government. In the case of the bank rescues as a result of the 2008 financial crisis, the Executive provided advice and initially managed assets acquired by the Government.

[45] Public Accounts Committee, *The Sale of the Government's Interest in British Energy* (HC 2009–10, 356).

[46] Public Accounts Committee, *The Shareholder Executive and Public Sector Businesses* (HC 2006–07, 409) (emphasis retained).

[47] NAO, *The Shareholder Executive and Public Sector Businesses* (n 42) para. 1.2.

However, responsibilities in this area were gradually transferred to a new specialist body, UK Financial Investments Ltd (UKFI), and this is important enough to merit separate discussion.

UK Financial Investments Ltd

UKFI is the offspring of the bank failures and the Government's bank rescues.[48] It manages government holdings of two types; the 'market investments' comprising 66 per cent of voting shares (82 per cent of economic ownership) of the Royal Bank of Scotland and 33 per cent of the total share capital of Lloyds; and the 'wholly-owned companies', formerly including 100 per cent holdings in Northern Rock plc and still including UK Asset Resolution Ltd. The latter company was formed in 2010 to integrate Northern Rock (Asset Management) plc and Bradford and Bingley plc, and comprises the closed mortgage books of these companies with outstanding debts of around £47 billion. The size of the holdings dwarfs other government investments in companies.

A major role of UKFI was to dispose of the holdings as market conditions improved; initially it seemed merely a temporary holding body. In June 2011 the Chancellor announced that a sale process for Northern Rock plc would commence; indeed this disposal was mandated by the state aid agreement for the former Northern Rock business. A successful sale was completed to Virgin Money at the end of 2011.[49] However, disposal of the market investments will take much longer; although disposal of the Lloyds shareholding started in 2013, RBS is unlikely to be sold before the 2015 general election. As a result, UKFI has 'evolved into a kind of internal public sector investment banking resource' advising the Government on banking matters, including regulatory reform.[50] It remains a small organization, with only 12 staff, less than a tenth of those of the Shareholder Executive.

UKFI takes the form of a wholly-owned Government company, although the Treasury Committee argued for a statutory body:

> *[g]iven the importance of the task entrusted to it and the vast sums of public money involved, we believe that UKFI should be established, at the earliest opportunity on a proper statutory basis. While the current ad hoc administrative arrangements persist we*

[48] For details, see Black, 'The Credit Crisis and the Constitution' (n 29) 98–104, and Treasury Committee, *Banking Crisis: Dealing with the Failure of the UK Banks* (HC 2008–09, 416), chs 3, 6.

[49] For details, see National Audit Office, *The Creation and Sale of Northern Rock plc* (HC 2012–13, 20).

[50] P. Jenkins and S. Goff, 'Sell-off Unit Proves Worth with Advice on Regulation', *Financial Times*, 3–4 September 2011.

have no confidence that UKFI will have the real operational independence that is necessary.[51]

This recommendation was ignored by the Government in its response. However, UKFI is audited by the Comptroller and Auditor-General and the NAO has examined the stewardship of the banks and other aspects of the management of the bank rescues.

The Treasury Select Committee was also critical of what it termed the 'enigmatic' nature of UKFI in the absence of a published investment mandate and government strategy.[52] This problem has been partly resolved by the publication of some key documents. There is a published framework document setting out the role of UKFI and its relations with the companies in which it owns shares; the emphasis is strongly on a commercial approach, and in particular the development of a strategy for the disposal of the holdings by sale, redemption, buy-back, or other means. It also emphasizes the importance of investee company independence; '[t]he Company will manage the Investments on a commercial basis and will not intervene in day-to-day management decisions of the Investee Companies' save as provided in the investee company framework documents, which themselves emphasize a commercial approach.[53] UKFI does, however, act as an 'active shareholder', voting the Government's shares on all resolutions put to shareholders and holding frequent meetings with other institutional shareholders. As regards relations with the Treasury, the latter appoints the UKFI chair and two directors, and authorizes the appointment of other board members. It also determines high-level objectives and approves the budget, although the company is given commercial freedom to adhere to its business plan and the activities set out in the Framework Document and Investment Mandate, which has also been published.[54] It envisages quarterly meetings between the UKFI board and the Treasury to review strategic options, and provides more details of relations with investee companies.

In a manner reminiscent of public enterprises in the past, the Treasury has a power of direction; thus:

[51] Treasury Committee, *Banking Crisis: Dealing with the Failure of the UK Banks* (n 48) para. 223 (emphasis retained).

[52] Treasury Committee, *Banking Crisis: Dealing with the Failure of the UK Banks* (n 48) para. 212.

[53] UK Financial Investments Ltd, *UKFI Shareholder Relationship Framework Document* (revised edn, 2010) at: <http://www.ukfi.co.uk/releases/UKFI_FD_180110v2.pdf>.

[54] UKFI, *UKFI Investment Mandate* (2010) at: <http://www.ukfi.co.uk/releases/UKFI_IM_180110.pdf>.

> [i]n view of HM Treasury's broader functions, including its functions in relation to financial stability and financial and economic policy, it may be necessary for HM Treasury to give the Board directions of a general or specific nature from time to time. The Board will comply with such directions or resign.[55]

The direction is to be published promptly except where financial stability requires that publication is delayed or withheld. Clearly this is a potentially far-reaching power, notable for permitting both general and specific directions and so wider than the power of general direction which existed in relation to the old nationalized industries. The Treasury Committee noted that, although it was a 'nuclear option', it could undermine the arm's length relationship with investee companies and invited the Treasury to set out the precise circumstances in which it would be used; the Treasury declined this invitation.[56]

Once more, the role of UKFI raises difficult problems of the relationship between the approach of a commercial shareholder and the implementation of broader policy. As Julia Black has put it;

> trying to manage this unique relationship within a company law framework is far from satisfactory, and does not give UKFI particularly refined regulatory tools at its disposal. UKFI is required to use a corporate governance relationship to achieve conflicting commercial, regulatory, and political ends, and it is not a comfortable fit.[57]

The difficulties arose first in relation to commitments made by the banks in return for recapitalization and other support measures, and which later evolved to form part of the so-called 'Project Merlin', which included RBS and Lloyds alongside private sector banks. These required them to maintain competitively priced lending to homeowners and small businesses, to introduce support schemes to avoid home repossessions, and to address the remuneration of senior executives; further detailed conditions were also laid down.[58] The lending conditions proved controversial. Monitoring was by a lending panel appointed by the Chancellor and the Business Secretary with annual reporting to Parliament, the political sensitivity of the issue making it inappropriate for UKFI. According to the Chancellor:

[55] *UKFI Shareholder Relationship Framework Document* (n 53) para. 924.

[56] Treasury Committee, *Banking Crisis: Dealing with the Failure of the UK Banks* (n 48) para. 222.

[57] Black, 'The Credit Crisis and the Constitution' (n 29) 108.

[58] The conditions are summarized by the Treasury Select Committee in *Banking Crisis: Dealing with the Failure of the UK Banks* (n 48), paras 147, 191–3. For further details and criticism of the role of government and banking support for businesses, see Business, Innovation and Skills Committee, *Government Assistance to Industry* (HC 2010–11, 561), paras 28–76.

> as the major shareholder, through UKFI acting independently on our behalf, we have insisted that, actually, [RBS] do change their business model and they do shrink their investment bank much more than they had previously wanted to do and proposed doing, and we make sure that they become a UK-focused corporate and retail bank.[59]

This hardly clarifies responsibilities, and serious criticism of the low lending levels of the banks continued; 'Project Merlin' was replaced by the Funding for Lending scheme to be discussed in the next section.

Secondly, remuneration conditions are overseen by UKFI; the latter had characterized its approach as one of a 'very engaged institutional investor' acting not for political reasons but to express shareholder concerns, whilst the Treasury Committee argued that UKFI '*should use this opportunity to fundamentally change the bonus culture provided by current banking remuneration practices*'.[60] In a later report, the Treasury Committee noted 'considerable public resentment and anger' at continuing bonus payments to staff in the two part publicly-owned banks, and was highly critical of the lack of transparency in bonus payments by the banks, whilst accepting that some bonuses would continue to be needed to recruit and retain staff.[61] This came to a head with the granting of a bonus of almost £1 million to the Chief Executive of RBS after a substantial fall in its share price, on which UKFI had been consulted. The decision of the Chief Executive to waive the bonus voluntarily did nothing to clarify relations with government.[62] Further controversy arose with the dismissal of the Chief Executive of RBS, a decision in which both the Chancellor and UKFI had played important parts. The Parliamentary Commission on Banking Standards was highly critical of government interference in the running of the banks, and concluded that '*UKFI will increasingly be perceived as a fig-leaf to disguise the reality of direct Government control*'. The Commission recommended that UKFI be wound up, a proposal quickly rejected by the Chancellor because of its expertise and experience.[63]

It is thus clear that the nationalization of the banks has not been employed as a means of implementing public policy objectives. This appears to be the

[59] Parliamentary Commission on Banking Standards, *Changing Banking for Good: Oral Evidence* (2013–14, HL 27-III, HC 175-III), q. 4333.

[60] Treasury Committee, Banking Crisis: Dealing with the Failure of the UK Banks (n 48) paras 213–17 (emphasis retained).

[61] Treasury Committee, *Banking Crisis: Reforming Corporate Governance and Pay in the City* (HC 2008–09, 519), paras 83–6, 88, 94–5.

[62] See S. Goff, 'Hands-off Role of Ministers Put in Doubt', *The Financial Times*, 31 January 2012.

[63] Parliamentary Commission on Banking Standards, *Changing Banking for Good* (HL 2009–09, 27 II; HC 2009–09, 175 II), para. 451 (emphasis retained).

case even on the issues of lending to businesses and remuneration policy where clear commitments were entered into by the banks at the time of their rescue. There has been no attempt to adopt more ambitious plans for transforming nationalized banks into different types of enterprise; for example, to turn the Royal Bank of Scotland into a 'Royal Bank of Sustainability' with the Government through UKFI prioritizing social and environmental policies and reducing exposure to high carbon investments.[64] This did have an echo within government with the Business Secretary calling for the break-up of RBS to create a vehicle for lending to small companies on the line of the German KFW bank, but the proposal was rapidly rebuffed by the Prime Minister and Chancellor; it would have required buying out the private shareholders in the bank.

Public ownership has not been used as a means of implementing distinctive public purposes, being instead concerned with the maximization of value and in permitting a return to the private sector of distressed assets. This is partly because of the limits imposed by state aid law, partly because of the company law framework within which state shareholdings are managed, but most of all owing to the market-based predilections of successive governments; there has been little attempt to explore alternative models for implementing public policy through public ownership. Meanwhile, the relations between government and the nationalized banks remain opaque and unstructured, as exemplified by the problems of securing increased lending to business and more reasonable remuneration.

Government support for industry

Government financial support for industry has had a long history, though in practice arrangements have been complex and fragmented, with frequent changes to the various schemes. Once more, the Industry Act 1975 could have provided the basis for a more coherent approach, with support tied to the implementation of economic planning goals, but this was never properly implemented and support has never been clearly linked to wider industrial policy objectives. This has been particularly true recently, when the emphasis has been on limited support schemes to facilitate growth led by the private sector.

[64] N. Silver, *Towards a Royal Bank of Sustainability: Protecting Taxpayers' Interests; Cutting Carbon Risk* (London: Friends of the Earth Scotland, PLATFORM, World Development Movement, 2010).

Of course, support for industry will be covered by the EU state aid regime. Article 107(3)(a) TFEU provides that the aid may be compatible with the common market where it is 'to promote the economic development of areas where the standard of living is abnormally low or where there is serious underemployment, . . . in view of their structural, economic and social situation'. This has provided the basis for the development of a complex EU regional aid regime, identifying eligible areas and permissible aids, with the use of guidelines and block exemptions.[65] There is also European support, for example through the European Investment Bank and the European Regional Development Fund providing matching funding for economic development administered through national industrial development bodies. An Enterprise Europe Network of almost 600 business support organizations, including chambers of commerce and development agencies in the Member States, assists small businesses in accessing finance and to provide other services.

Turning to domestic provision, a major problem has been that of persuading banks to lend to industry, especially small businesses. The Business Select Committee was so disappointed by the Government's response to recommendations on this that it took the unusual step of publishing the response with critical comments and calling for the Secretary of State and Chancellor to appear before the Committee to explain how they would ensure sufficient access to finance for UK businesses.[66] The failure of 'Project Merlin' was discussed earlier, and it was replaced by the Funding for Lending Scheme administered by the Bank of England. It was set up on the basis of an exchange of letters between the Governor of the Bank and the Chancellor, and operates through financial transactions rather than the exercise of statutory powers. Banks are able to borrow Treasury bills at lower cost from the Bank at an amount up to 5 per cent of their loans to the UK non-financial sector, thereby creating an incentive for such loans. This also had disappointing results, at least initially.[67] The Government will also create a Business Bank working with the private sector from 2014 to support the development of finance markets for business and the provision of finance; it will function on commercial terms and will not lend directly to businesses.[68] The Government has provided guarantees for a small number of nationally significant infrastructure projects through its UK Guarantees scheme, operating on a

[65] The regime is summarized in Quigley, *European State Aid and Policy* (n 11) ch 8.

[66] Business Select Committee, *Government Assistance to Industry: Government Response to the Committee's Third Report of Session 2010–11* (HC 2010–12, 1038).

[67] HM Treasury, *The Funding for Lending* Scheme (2012); C. Jones, 'BoE Loan Scheme Fails to Impress', *Financial Times*, 4 December 2012.

[68] Department for Business, Innovation and Skills, *Building the Business Bank: Strategy Update* (2013).

commercial basis to kick-start projects which have stalled because of adverse credit conditions. Authority for the use of financial resources is provided by the Infrastructure (Financial Assistance) Act 2012.

Nationally, there are several schemes now in existence for business support.[69] The Business Select Committee has criticized the lack of a clear strategy, and the various schemes do appear something of a mish-mash.[70] The Government has attempted to move from individual support schemes towards macro-economic change, in particular regulatory reform. For example, the 2011 budget announced the creation of new Enterprise Zones, previously a creature of the Thatcher Governments, in which planning rules are simplified and a large discount granted on business rates. A Regional Growth Fund was established in 2010, aimed at encouraging private enterprise through support for projects with potential for economic growth, and to support the transition from dependence on the public sector to private sector-led growth, with funding of £2.6 billion. Money is allocated to bids competitively by a ministerial group, based on recommendations from an independent advisory panel and information from officials. The NAO found that it had resulted in 41,000 additional full-time equivalent jobs for seven years, at an average cost of £33,000 each; however, value for money was not optimized as a significant proportion of the Fund was allocated to projects that offered relatively few jobs for the public money invested.[71] Grant for Business Investment, which provided a capital grant to businesses to support sustainable investment, was closed for new investment from February 2011, apart from 'large exceptional projects' and applications from offshore wind equipment manufacturers. Other schemes run by the Department for Business, Innovation and Skills include the Enterprise Finance Guarantee Scheme, a loan guarantee scheme for lenders to enable them to provide additional lending to SMEs, and a number of other small schemes providing access to capital and support for training. The Government-funded Manufacturing Advisory Service provides support for manufacturing business, and further support is provided by UK Trade & Investment to develop UK-based companies' ability to trade and to maximize their international success, and also to support inward investment. The Export Credits Guarantee Department (now known as UK Export Finance) supports loans to

[69] For a summary, see Business, Innovation and Skills Committee, *Government Assistance to Industry* (n 66) Written Evidence from the Department for Business, Innovation and Skills, Ev 91–107.

[70] See Business, Innovation and Skills Committee, *Government Assistance to Industry* (n 66) paras 5–16, 24. Similar conclusions were reached more recently by the NAO; *Improving Access to Finance for Small and Medium-Sized Enterprises*, (HC 2013–14, 734).

[71] NAO, *The Regional Growth Fund* (HC 2012–13, 17).

overseas buyers to purchase goods and services from UK exporters and provides insurance to exporters and investors overseas against the risks of not being paid.

At the end of 2012 major reforms were proposed in the Heseltine Report, which recommended that funding be combined and localized, with the creation of a single fund of around £50 billion for which Local Enterprise Partnerships (LEPs) (see the next subsection) would bid, so decentralizing administration of business support.[72] These recommendations were accepted in principle by the Government, which is creating a single Local Growth Fund from 2015 with initial funding of £2 billion.

The Regional Development Agencies and Local Enterprise Partnerships

The most well-known institutions for business support outside central government were the Regional Development Agencies.[73] The Agencies were established by the Regional Development Act 1998 for London and for eight regions; they became the lead agencies for coordinating bids for EU regional funding. The membership was predominantly drawn from business, although a third of it was to be drawn from local government in the areas covered by the agencies. Ministers used their powers under the Act to designate Regional Chambers in the form of regional assemblies which had to be consulted by the Agencies. The assemblies were indirectly elected and drawn from local authorities, business, and other interests.

The Regional Development Agencies were criticized for a number of reasons, including 'mission creep' as their functions were expanded to include innovation, sectoral development, tourism, digital access, transport infrastructure, resource efficiency, social exclusion, and response to economic shocks. There were also problems relating to the extent to which they actually represented the views of business as a whole.[74] The most serious problem was the basic democratic deficit resulting from the failure of the Labour Government's plans to establish directly elected regional assemblies throughout the UK, thus resulting in a fundamental lack of accountability of the agencies at

[72] The Rt Hon the Lord Heseltine of Thenford CH, *No Stone Unturned in Pursuit of Growth* (n 4) ch 2; Department for Business Innovation & Skills, *Government Response to the Heseltine Review* (Cm 8587, 2013).

[73] For a brief history, see I. Leigh, 'The Changing Nature of Local and Regional Democracy' in J. Jowell and D. Oliver (eds), *The Changing Constitution*, 7th edn (Oxford: Oxford University Press, 2011), 237–59, 255–6.

[74] For a summary of the criticisms, see Business, Innovation and Skills Committee, *The New Local Enterprise Partnerships: An Initial Assessment* (HC 2010–11, 434), paras 13–22.

regional level (with the exception of the special case of London where the Greater London Assembly had been successfully established).

The Coalition Government announced that the agencies would be abolished, and provision was made for this in the Public Bodies Act and (for London) in the Localism Act.[75] They have been replaced by Local Enterprise Partnerships (LEPs). These are very different animals. There is no statutory basis for their creation, and instead bids were invited from consortia of businesses and councils, not corresponding to a regional structure. They are privately funded.[76] Some Regional Development Agency (RDA) functions, including responsibility for business support, have been transferred to the national level, whilst LEPs will undertake a diverse range of roles, including supporting high growth businesses and working with the Government to set out key investment priorities, including transport infrastructure. 39 such LEPs were approved, varying significantly in size and coverage. They will have strategic influence over at least £320 billion of resources in the years to 2021.

The Business Committee found considerable support for the introduction of the new system; however, it clearly raises major accountability issues. The Committee recommended that memoranda of understanding be published between Government Departments and the new LEPs; however, this recommendation was rejected by the Government.[77] The Committee had also stressed the need for proper performance and value for money review of the new Partnerships; thus:

> *[w]e strongly discourage the Government from recognising any LEP without insisting on full local scrutiny—including by publishing of accounts and minutes where appropriate and by giving local stakeholders the means to question LEP boards. Furthermore, where LEPs are in receipt of public funds we recommend that they be subject to an independent and transparent auditing process meeting the minimum standards required for NDPBs.*[78]

The Government in response stated that:

> [t]he development of local enterprise partnerships is a bottom up process and the days of centrally imposed dictates [*sic*] are over. It is for partnerships to work out their own relationships with member local authorities and Government will not

[75] Public Bodies Act 2011, s 30; Localism Act 2011, s 191.

[76] See Department for Business, Innovation and Skills, *Local Growth: Realising Every Place's Potential* (Cm 7961, 2010) and Business, Innovation and Skills Committee, *The New Local Enterprise Partnerships: An Initial Assessment* (n 74).

[77] Business, Innovation and Skills Committee, *The New Local Enterprise Partnerships: An Initial Assessment* (n 74) para. 147.

[78] Business, Innovation and Skills Committee, *The New Local Enterprise Partnerships: An Initial Assessment* (n 74) para. 151 (emphasis retained).

> impose a particular model. The Government has provided a framework that gives business the opportunity to have a defining role in these partnerships, and to create a new more creative and productive relationship with local authorities.

On the specific issue of financial scrutiny, it pointed to the need for private sector audit and the normal accountability of local authority members: 'local enterprise partnerships are not NDPBs like the RDAs were, and will not be funded or performance managed in the same way as RDAs.'[79] In a further report two years after the inception of the system, the Committee found that, though there were good examples of transparency and engagement with stakeholders, there was no actual mechanism by which LEPs could be held to account; there should be more active monitoring by the Department and the NAO should also take on this role. The report was also critical of confused relations between the LEPs and the two government departments to which they are responsible.[80] Echoing the select committee findings, a report by the Work Foundation based on interviews with LEP members also recommended that there should be enhanced accountability arrangements and that LEPs should consider establishing themselves as legal entities.[81]

As mentioned earlier, the responsibilities of the LEPs are likely to be substantially increased with the devolution of funding to them as a result of Government acceptance of the Heseltine recommendation. The danger, especially given the lack of a statutory basis for the new bodies, is that there will be no consistent approach to issues of accountability and that their private nature will get in the way of effective public scrutiny. Heseltine also proposed that local Chambers of Commerce would deliver business support services on behalf of the LEPs and should be given basic statutory functions, though this proposal was rejected by the Government.

Development agencies in Scotland

Different solutions have been adopted for the devolved nations of the UK. In Wales, the Welsh Development Agency (which had earlier been embroiled in financial scandal) had been abolished in 2006 as part of a plan to reduce the number of non-departmental public bodies in the Principality, its functions passing to the Welsh Government Department for Business, Enterprise,

[79] Business, Innovation and Skills Committee, *The New Local Enterprise Partnerships: An Initial Assessment* (n 74) paras 41, 44.

[80] Business, Innovation and Skills Committee, *Local Enterprise Partnerships* (HC 2012–13, 598), paras 29–35, 51–66.

[81] N. Cominetti, L. Crowley, and N. Lee, *The Business of Cities: The Private Sector, Local Enterprise Partnerships and Growth* (London: Work Foundation, 2012).

Technology and Science acting through a network of 12 regional centres. Similarly, in Northern Ireland, Invest Northern Ireland is part of the Department of Enterprise, Trade and Investment of the Northern Ireland Assembly.

However, Scotland has retained its two development agencies, Scottish Enterprise and Highlands and Islands Enterprise. These have a statutory base in the Enterprise and New Towns (Scotland) Act 1990, succeeding earlier bodies, and have a remit of furthering the development of Scotland's economy by a number of means including enhancing skills and promoting industrial efficiency and international competitiveness; Highlands and Islands Enterprise has an additional social remit of preparing and implementing proposals for social development.[82]

The problems of democratic accountability which bedevilled the English Regional Development Agencies are avoided in Scotland by the close linkage of the enterprise bodies to the Scottish Government and Scottish Parliament. Thus the work of the agencies forms part of the Scottish Government's Economic Strategy, and the Parliament scrutinizes their work; for example, the Parliament's Economy, Energy and Tourism Committee undertook such a review and published a detailed report in 2011.[83] Since devolution a number of changes have been made to the way in which the enterprise agencies carry out their work. Formerly, they worked through local enterprise companies (LECs), not dissimilar to the LEPs. The LECs were, however, abolished in 2007, and some of their services ('Business Gateway' for business start-up and support, local development, and local regeneration services) were transferred to local authorities. The result has been a more focused remit for the agencies, although the Parliamentary Committee noted a reduction in expertise and local engagement. Other recent developments have included the establishment of a Scottish Investment Bank as a division of Scottish Enterprise and a Scottish Loan Fund.[84] Indeed, concern has been expressed by the North of England at the competitive advantage of Scotland in attracting investment, especially as it continues to offer regional selective assistance whilst the Grant for Business Investment scheme in England had been largely closed in 2011.[85] However, some problems remain; the budget for the agencies has declined steadily since 2007, raising questions, according to the Committee, of whether they can continue to deliver a broad range of services to businesses as well as delivering on opportunities relating to

[82] Enterprise and New Towns (Scotland) Act 1990, ss 1, 5.

[83] Economy, Energy and Tourism Committee of the Scottish Parliament, *A Fundamental Review of the Purpose of an Enterprise Agency and the Success of Recent Reforms*, SP Paper 594 (2011).

[84] Scottish Enterprise, *Annual Report and Accounts for the Year Ended 31 March 2011* (2011).

[85] C. Tighe, A. Bounds, and A. Bolger, 'North Seeks Help to Rival Scotland for Job Creation', *The Financial Times*, 28 October 2011.

renewable energy and large infrastructure projects such as the roll-out of fast broadband.[86] The Committee also noted that there is still a plethora of different bodies at local and regional level; this had led to a lack of clarity as to accountability and leadership.[87] However, it is clear that the existence of devolved government and a devolved parliament in Edinburgh offer a resolution to the major problem in England of lack of democratic legitimacy for institutions at the crucial level below national government and above local government; it is noteworthy that the Committee rejected any change to make local authorities responsible for the delivery of all services.[88]

Local authorities in England

As this discussion has shown, there is an increased stress, especially in England, on the role of local authorities in delivering services for business, either through their role in the new LEPs or through using their own powers. This is an area in which there have been a number of problems with the existing powers of local authorities to engage in industrial and business activities.[89] Historically, the major difficulty was the absence of a power of general competence for local authorities. Such a power would mean that, rather than a specific power having to be identified for any action, it would be presumed to be lawful if it is considered by the authority to be for the benefit of the local area and did not otherwise constitute a crime, tort, or breach of contract.[90] An illustration of the effect of the absence of such a power can be found in the *Crédit Suisse* case.[91] Here a local authority had established a company to assist in the financing of a leisure centre, and had guaranteed its borrowings. The company failed, but the council resisted claims for reimbursement on the basis that it had had no power to enter into the contract. The Court of Appeal held that the contract was void and unenforceable as the council had had no power to enter into it.

Legislation was introduced to remedy this particular injustice,[92] and the Local Government Act 2000 took steps to widen the powers of local

[86] Economy, Energy and Tourism Committee of the Scottish Parliament, *A Fundamental Review of the Purpose of an Enterprise Agency and the Success of Recent Reforms* (n 83), para. 356.

[87] Economy, Energy and Tourism Committee of the Scottish Parliament, *A Fundamental Review of the Purpose of an Enterprise Agency and the Success of Recent Reforms* (n 83) paras 214–51.

[88] Economy, Energy and Tourism Committee of the Scottish Parliament, *A Fundamental Review of the Purpose of an Enterprise Agency and the Success of Recent Reforms* (n 83) paras 339–40.

[89] For a summary, see Leigh, 'The Changing Nature of Local and Regional Democracy' (n 73) 240–6.

[90] Leigh, 'The Changing Nature of Local and Regional Democracy' (n 73) 244.

[91] *Crédit Suisse v Allerdale Borough Council* [1997] QB 306.

[92] Local Government (Contracts) Act 1997.

authorities in economic and related areas. Thus the Act provided that local authorities were to have the power to do anything which they consider likely to promote or improve the economic, social, or environmental well-being of their areas.[93] This included the power to incur expenditure, to provide financial assistance to any person, to enter into arrangements or agreements with any person, or to cooperate with, or facilitate or coordinate the activities of, any person.[94] It did not, however, enable local authorities to avoid the effect of restrictions on other powers.[95] Local authorities were also required to prepare strategies for promoting or improving the economic, social, or environmental well-being of their areas and contributing to the achievement of sustainable development.[96] This power was on occasion interpreted narrowly by the courts,[97] and further steps have been taken as part of the Coalition Government's localism agenda. The Localism Act 2011 restricts the power in the Local Government Act 2000 to local authorities in Wales. For English authorities, it gives a broader power of general competence: a 'local authority has power to do anything that individuals generally may do'.[98] This is free of most of the restrictions associated with the power under the 2000 Act. Thus the powers of local authorities have been considerably extended in this area, and this fits with the more general agenda of localism at the expense of any regional dimension in England. However, it has yet to be seen what resources local authorities will have to engage in economic initiatives; the funding of local government has suffered particularly seriously in the Spending Review under the Coalition Government. An indication of a future approach can be found in the decision in July 2012 to devolve further powers to promote growth to eight large provincial cities (to which 20 more were added later), including powers to establish investment funds for priority projects and a venture capital fund. The powers were conditional on stronger and more accountable local leadership and more efficient spending.[99] The Heseltine Report recommended that local authorities should have an overarching legal duty to have regard to economic development in the exercise of all their activities and functions, though the Government rejected the proposal for new legislation.

[93] Local Government Act 2000, s 2(1).

[94] Local Government Act 2000, s 2(4).

[95] Local Government Act 2000, s 3(1).

[96] Local Government Act 2000, s 4.

[97] See esp. *Brent LBC v Risk Management Partners Ltd* [2009] EWCA Civ 490.

[98] Localism Act 2011, s 1(1).

[99] Department for Business, Innovation and Skills, *Cities' Economic Power Unlocked in Radical Power Shift*, Press Release 5 July 2012.

Conclusion

Although the UK has never had a developed industrial policy, let alone the full-blown corporatism suggested by Winckler in the work cited at the beginning of this chapter, it has been possible to identify a number of discrete and important initiatives. At a constitutional level, by far the most important regime has been that of EU state aid law and policy. This sets out detailed and sometimes complex constraints on actions of Member States, which have effectively ruled out many traditional techniques of industrial policy such as large-scale nationalization with open-ended financial support. However, the financial crisis revealed a considerable degree of flexibility in this regime in these unusual circumstances, permitting rescues of the banks at an expense to governments which dwarfs earlier types of financial support for industry. The role of the Commission and the European Courts has resulted in some outside scrutiny of interventions; after an initially liberal attitude to support schemes, scrutiny also occurred in relation to the bank rescues; 'it is the Commission, rather than the UK Parliament, which is the body outside the UK executive which has had the greatest involvement in determining how UK taxpayers' money will be spent'.[100]

Partly because of the state aid regime, but mainly because of ideological changes, there is now only a very limited role for the public corporation as a means of public ownership, and government shareholdings have become far more important. This shift has not resolved problems identified earlier of accountability of public enterprise and of their relations with government. Company law imposes restrictions on the use of public shareholdings for policy purposes, and even the limited policy goals of increasing bank lending to small businesses and restricting bankers' remuneration have proved difficult to achieve. Apart from company law, there is no clear constitutional structure through which these problems can be resolved; in particular, the current position of the banks in which there is a substantial state shareholding shows the problems of using state shareholding for any purpose other than temporary support of enterprises; yet their disposal to the private sector also raises difficulties. The role of UKFI remains ambiguous.

Industrial development and support are now relatively limited areas of government activity, and are focused on a role subsidiary to that of the market and of entrepreneurialism. The schemes are now centralized or at a local level; the ending of regional mechanisms for industrial development

[100] Black, 'The Credit Crisis and the Constitution' (n 29) 123.

point to a major constitutional absence, that of a means of holding accountable institutions in the English regions. Scotland provides a marked contrast to this, with development agencies responsible to the Scottish Government and Parliament. The arrangements for England, in the form of the LEPs, are not subject to clear arrangements for accountability and are small-scale and organized in an ad hoc way; similarly, although local government has gained increased powers, spending restrictions are likely severely to limit its role in supporting industry and the broader economy. The new arrangements set out in the Heseltine Report for decentralization of business support, whilst suggesting a real commitment to localism, will make the apparent lack of accountability and transparency of LEPs more rather than less pressing. The relative coherence of EU state aid law stands in marked contrast to the plethora of institutions at national level.

9

Government and Contract

Introduction

Procurement and the use of contract by government are areas of major importance and considerable controversy. Questions of particular constitutional salience are raised by the use of contracts as a means of regulation, the role of non-market 'secondary' objectives (notably industrial policy, equality, and sustainability) in procurement, transparency in procurement, and value for money. The relevant law and practice is complex, and will not be covered in detail here; readers are instead referred to the major treatises.[1] As will become evident in this chapter there is now also a substantial literature in the form of government guidance and studies and recommendations from the NAO, the Public Accounts Committee, and other select committees. Until recently the area was one relatively neglected by public lawyers, but it has now gained substantial coverage in the more sophisticated texts.[2]

Constitutional principle

Domestic law: 'government by contract'

The UK has no equivalent to the distinctive French corpus of administrative law relating to government contracts.[3] This is not to say that there has been no distinctive body of law relating to government contracts; as Harlow and Rawlings put it, '[b]ehind the scenes, a well-established "law of the contract" was in operation, a reservoir of standard terms and conditions on which

[1] E.g. S. Arrowsmith, *The Law of Public and Utilities Procurement*, 3rd edn (London: Sweet and Maxwell, 2013).

[2] P. Craig, *Administrative Law*, 7th edn (London: Sweet and Maxwell, 2012), ch. 5; C. Harlow and R. Rawlings, *Law and Administration*, 3rd edn (Cambridge: Cambridge University Press, 2009) chs 8–9.

[3] For an introduction, see N. Brown and J. Bell, *French Administrative Law*, 5th edn (Oxford: Oxford University Press, 1998), 202–12.

officials could draw when specifying performance and to anticipate disputes'.[4] It has never been the case that government contracts can simply be assimilated to those of private contractors. However, before the advent of the internet, the relevant internal law was often completely inaccessible to those outside the small group of specialist officials using it.[5] As with some other areas examined in this book, the role of statute has been limited, and there have been few relevant principles of the common law. This is partly due to the fact that, unlike in the case of local government, central government has inherent power to contract and need not point to direct statutory authority for entering into contracts. There is some dispute as to whether this power is part of the prerogative or not, but

> [i]t is unimportant whether we attach the label "prerogative" to the Crown's power to conclude contracts . . . [w]hatever the designation, the scope is the same; it is an arbitrary power, in that the common law does not impose, either in general or on the Crown in particular, any constraint in the choice of contractual partners, and is prepared to offer its aid in the enforcement of almost any contractual terms.[6]

In the case of local government, and other statutory bodies, the source of contracting power is statute, and its scope has given rise to important litigation.[7]

Moreover, the older cases have a strong air of unreality in modern conditions. An example is *The Amphitrite* in which it was held that an undertaking not to requisition a foreign ship in wartime was unenforceable, and that no compensation need be payable.[8] On this slender basis, a defence of 'executive necessity' for breach of contract by the Crown was alleged to exist. In practice, however, this is dealt with by the contractual terms: '[g]overnment contracts commonly contain variation clauses which make provision for compensation, as also so-called break clauses, permitting the authority to terminate the contract at any time.'[9] Similarly, the possibility that a contract for which the legislature had not appropriated funds would be unenforceable is 'largely academic because of the broad terms in which the votes in the Appropriation Act are nowadays drafted'.[10]

[4] Harlow and Rawlings, *Law and Administration* (n 2) 339 (footnote omitted).

[5] The author still recalls the bemusement created by a phone call to the Treasury in 1985 asking for the guidelines on public purchasing policy, which were stated in a prospectus to govern government-industry relations after privatization. Needless to say, they were not provided.

[6] T. Daintith, 'Regulation by Contract: The New Prerogative' [1979] 32 *Current Legal Problems* 41–64, 42.

[7] See e.g. *Credit Suisse v Allerdale Borough Council* [1997] QB 306.

[8] *Rederiaktiebolaget Amphitrite v The King* [1921] 3 KB 500.

[9] Harlow and Rawlings, *Law and Administration* (n 2) 345.

[10] Daintith, 'Regulation by Contract' (n 6) 44; for the doctrine, see *Churchward v R* (1865) LR 1 QB 173; *New South Wales v Bardolph* (1934) 52 CLR 455.

Most of the internal law produced by government itself is concerned with the mechanics of the contractual process and issues of value for money, and these will be discussed later in the chapter. However, first there needs to be discussion of the important role of contract as a means of regulation by government; this includes both the use of contract directly to impose regulatory norms, and requiring other bodies, such as local authorities and health bodies, to employ contractual techniques such as competitive tendering for the provision of services. On the first point, the pioneering study was that of Daintith; although the substance of much of his examination, the use of contract to implement a non-statutory anti-inflation policy, now seems dated, his conclusions are still extremely important. These were that, at the pre-contractual phase,

> the situation of the public authority . . . is in domestic law one of almost complete discretion. This is so whether the power to contract is based on common law or in statute. The discretion is large enough to permit the pursuit of a wide range of regulatory policies through the contractual process . . . [11]

His conclusion is a little more nuanced in relation to the exercise of powers under the contract, where a 'general policy of the contract' test might be employed by a court to mirror the tests used in administrative law.[12] Nevertheless, overall '[g]overnment enjoys far greater freedom and discretion in the elaboration of contractual schemes of regulation than it could reasonably hope to possess as the operator of a statutory scheme under powers conferred by Parliament.'[13] As we shall see, EU procurement law now qualifies this conclusion, and the courts have made some tentative steps towards greater willingness to grant judicial review of the exercise of statutory powers, but formal control of contracting by domestic law remains undeveloped compared to that of the direct exercise of statutory powers.

After the election of the market-oriented Thatcher Governments from 1979, we find a very different emphasis on contract as a means of governing. In brief, contracting was used as a means of reorganizing the provision of public services in a variety of different ways.[14] This was particularly important in relation to the health service, where there was an attempt (only partially successful) to reorganize it around an internal market with participants linked

[11] Daintith, 'Regulation by Contract' (n 6) 52.

[12] Daintith, 'Regulation by Contract' (n 6) 54–9.

[13] Daintith, 'Regulation by Contract' (n 6) 59.

[14] For developed discussion, see I. Harden, *The Contracting State* (Buckingham: Open University Press, 1992) and M. Freedland, 'Government by Contract and Private Law' [1994] *Public Law* 86–104.

by special 'NHS contracts' without legally binding status.[15] Similarly, non-binding 'contracts' can be detected as the basis for relations between core government departments and the 'Next Steps' agencies. For local government, the major emphasis was requiring them to engage in compulsory competitive tendering, initially through a Byzantine body of statute law and administrative requirements and, more recently, through the 'Best Value' process which permits greater flexibility in how services are provided. For central government itself there was an increasing emphasis on the use of 'market testing' to determine which governmental functions could be contracted out. Contracting out of services has increased further under the Coalition Government with over £20 billion of contracts awarded in 2012, and a greater role for contractual commissioning in the NHS under the Health and Social Care Act 2012.

In a detailed and valuable study, Vincent-Jones has examined the 'New Public Contracting' characterized by the delegation of power through various forms of contractual arrangement preserving central government control.[16] Within this he points to three types of contract; administrative contracts such as those associated with 'Next Steps'; economic contracts directed at improving public services through competition and the devolution of management powers to public purchasing or commissioning agencies, for example in the health service or through Private Finance Initiative (PFI); and social control contracts used in the regulation of relations between individuals and the state, for example jobseekers' agreements.[17] Like Daintith, he is concerned with issues of responsiveness and accountability, and finds

> while there exists a potential for contracts to serve responsively in the performance of a range of public service functions, in many cases contracting regimes have demonstrably failed or are at risk of failure . . . The legitimacy deficit in the New Public Contracting consists in the lack of adequate opportunities for public deliberation in policy and decision making on public service issues.[18]

An important point is that, although value for money has dominated the control mechanisms for public contracting, the constitutional issues raised are far wider than this.

[15] For details, see A.C.L. Davies, *Accountability: A Public Law Analysis of Government by Contract* (Oxford: Oxford University Press, 2001).

[16] P. Vincent-Jones, *The New Public Contracting: Regulation, Responsiveness, Relationality* (Oxford: Oxford University Press, 2006).

[17] For a summary, see Vincent-Jones, *The New Public Contracting* (n 16) 21–3.

[18] Vincent-Jones, *The New Public Contracting* (n 16) 347 (footnote omitted).

Domestic law: the courts and ombudsmen

The seminal work of Daintith referred to in the previous subsection noted the reluctance of the courts to apply public law standards and review procedures to the contractual process, especially in its pre-contractual phase.[19] This has now been in part qualified by the willingness of the courts to intervene through judicial review where there is some 'public law element' present distinguishing the situation from an ordinary contract; unfortunately, that element has been difficult to define with any precision.[20] It will not apply to all contracts to implement a public purpose; in the case of *Hibbit and Saunders* the High Court declined to intervene in a dispute concerning the proper scope of post-tender negotiations in the supply of court reporting services on the ground that no policy issues were raised and there was no public law element.[21] By contrast, in *Molinaro* the court held that the use of contractual provisions to implement a local authority's planning powers was reviewable; here

> the Council was not simply acting as a private body when it sought to give effect to its planning policy through the contract... In my view, the fact that a local authority is exercising a statutory function ought to be sufficient to justify the decision itself being subject in principles to judicial review if it is alleged that the power has been abused.[22]

However, *Hibbit and Saunders* was distinguished on the basis that it involved a common law, not statutory, power to contract, leaving some doubt as to the applicability of judicial review to non-statutory contracting by central government. As we shall see later, the courts have now been given a central role in the enforcement of remedies under the EU procurement regime, and this creates a distinct body of specialist law, as well as being likely to increase the willingness of the courts to intervene on the basis of the common law. Interesting further possibilities were opened up by *Smith v Ministry of Defence* in which the Supreme Court refused to rule out liability under the Human Rights Act or in negligence for damages for defence procurement decisions.[23]

Contractual techniques have also benefited from special treatment in relation to investigations by ombudsmen. It remains the case that the Parliamentary

[19] S. Arrowsmith, 'Government Contracts and Public Law' (1990) 10 *Legal Studies* 231–44.

[20] For discussion, see Craig, *Administrative Law* (n 2) 852–5; Harlow and Rawlings, *Law and Administration* (n 2) 375–6; Vincent-Jones, *The New Public Contracting* (n 16) 283–8.

[21] *R v Lord Chancellor's Department, ex parte Hibbit and Saunders* [1993] COD 336.

[22] *R (Molinaro) v The Royal Borough of Kensington and Chelsea* [2001] EWHC Admin 846, per Elias J at paras 63–5.

[23] [2013] UKSC 41, [2013] 3 WLR 69, paras 65, 76, 80, 99.

Ombudsman, who investigates complaints of maladministration against central government and many other statutory bodies, is precluded from investigating actions taken in matters relating to contractual or other commercial transactions by government departments or authorities, except for those relating to the compulsory acquisition or disposal of land.[24] This exclusion has been extensively criticized and is highly anomalous, particularly as the Health Service Ombudsman (the Parliamentary Ombudsman wearing a different hat), though subject to a similar exclusion, is able to investigate health services provided under contract by the private sector and matters arising from contracts between health authorities.[25] The equivalent restriction for the Local Government Ombudsman was abolished by legislation in 2007, and the restriction for the Scottish Public Services Ombudsman is much narrower; nor is the Welsh Public Services Ombudsman covered by such a restriction.[26] The exclusion does not prevent the Parliamentary Ombudsman investigating decisions taken on behalf of departments as a result of contracting out, but, as with judicial review, it means that the contracting powers of central government are subject to significantly less control and scrutiny than those of other public bodies.

Value for money

For value for money, the central monitoring institution is the NAO, which has issued a large number of reports on government contracting. Nor is this limited to scrutiny *ex post facto*, for it has also issued extensive guidance on good commissioning practice.[27] The many reports on PFI were referred to in chapter 5; we shall also see that the NAO has scrutinized in detail the serious problems of defence procurement. The Public Accounts Committee has also undertaken many examinations of procurement issues and has issued regular reports with detailed recommendations. It should be recalled from Chapter 5, however, that NAO and Public Accounts Committee scrutiny is limited to value for money issues (though these are widely defined in practice) and does not extend to questioning policy objectives. Other select committees have also

[24] Parliamentary Commissioner Act 1967, sch. 3, para 9; for discussion, see M. Seneviratne, *Ombudsmen: Public Services and Administrative Justice* (London: Butterworths, 2002), 106–9.

[25] Health Service Commissioners Act 1993, s 7(2); Seneviratne, *Ombudsmen* (n 24) 165.

[26] See the Local Government and Public Involvement in Health Act 2007, s 173; the Scottish Public Services Ombudsman Act 2002, sch. 4, para. 7, as amended by the Scottish Parliamentary Commissions and Commissioners etc. Act 2010; Public Services Ombudsman (Wales) Act 2005, sch. 2.

[27] See e.g. its guidance on successful commissioning at: <http://www.nao.org.uk/successful-commissioning/>.

played a part in examining both value for money and policy questions, as we shall see in the discussion of PFI and defence procurement. One important example was examination of IT procurement by the Public Administration Committee in 2011, concluding that 'government's overall record in developing and implementing new IT systems is appalling. The lack of IT skills in government and over-reliance on contracting out is a fundamental problem which has been described as a "*recipe for rip-offs*".' Unlike some other select committee reports, this resulted in a constructive response from government addressing the problems.[28]

European Union public procurement law

The major change since Daintith's seminal discussion of regulation by contract in 1979 has been the development of a complex body of binding EU rules on public procurement. These have clear constitutional status in providing the basic normative principles relevant to the procurement process; moreover, they provide remedies to disappointed contractors, and indeed in effect establish a special system of administrative law for this field.[29] They have not, of course, been free from controversy. A particular, and continuing, concern has been the extent to which they permit the incorporation of so-called 'secondary' policies in the form of non-market goals such as prevention or relief of unemployment, equal treatment of employees, and environmental considerations. The rules have been alleged to have resulted in highly individualized procedures which militate against a more relational set of contractual arrangements and continuing relationships with suppliers based on trust. Reforms are in the process of enactment to address some of these concerns.[30]

A brief outline of the EU principles

The underlying basis for the EU supervision of public procurement is of course the creation of a single market and the prohibition of discrimination against Member States. Thus Treaty principles may impose constraints on

[28] Public Accounts Committee, *Government and IT—'a Recipe for Rip-offs': Time for a New Approach* (HC 2010–12, 715); *Government and IT—'a Recipe for Rip-offs': Time for a New Approach: Further Report with the Government Response* (HC 2010–12, 1724).

[29] For this characterization of the EU rules, see Harlow and Rawlings, *Law and Administration* (n 2) 383–92.

[30] European Commission, *Proposal for a Directive of the European Parliament and of the Council on Public Procurement* COM(2011) 896 final.

the procurement process, whether or not it is covered in detail by the Procurement Directives. They impose on contracting authorities an obligation to ensure that there is a sufficient degree of transparency for the process to be reviewed to ensure non-discrimination. In the words of the ECJ, the 'obligation of transparency which is imposed on the contracting authority consists in ensuring, for the benefit of any potential tenderer, a degree of advertising sufficient to enable the services market to be opened up to competition and the impartiality of procurement procedures to be reviewed'. These requirements have been specified in greater detail by the Commission in an interpretative Communication.[31] Thus there must be advertising and a fair and transparent procedure for the award of contracts even outside the scope of the Directives.

The Directives themselves go considerably further. They were merged into two Directives in 2004 covering public works, supply and service contracts, and utility contracts; the last will not be covered here.[32] They are implemented by UK regulations.[33] Further reform is in progress, with final agreement on new Directives expected in early 2014, and implementation will be required by Member States within two years. The Directives and Regulations impose a number of important requirements at different stages of the contracting process, and in doing so make a distinction between the specification stage, where the requirements are established and published, the selection stage, where the contracting authority assesses the capacity and suitability of the potential bidders, and the award stage, when the offers are examined and the best selected. Requirements at the first stage relate, for example, to advertising in the EU Official Journal and to technical specifications in the tender documents, which must be such as to avoid discrimination in favour of or against particular suppliers; these may also include requirements relating to the performance of the contract. At the second stage, criteria will include the economic and financial standing of the potential bidder, and its technical knowledge and ability; the award stage must be based strictly on criteria concerning the products and services offered.

[31] Case C-324/98 *Teleaustria Verlags GmbH v Telekom Austria AG* [2000] ECR I-10745; Commission Interpretative Communication on the Community law applicable to contract awards not or not fully subject to the provisions of the Public Procurement Directives [2006] OJ C-197/2.

[32] Directive 2004/18/EC on the coordination of procedures for the award of public works contracts, public supply contracts and public service contracts [2004] OJ L134/114; Directive 2004/17/EC coordinating the procurement procedures of entities operating in the water, energy, transport and postal services sectors [2004] OJ L 134/1.

[33] The Public Contracts Regulations 2006, SI 2006/7; the Utilities Contracts Regulations, SI 2006/6.

Important provisions concern the choice of procedures for the award of the contract, in which a number of different pathways are specified which must be followed.[34] These are the 'open procedure', in which all interested firms may submit a tender; the 'restricted procedure', where tenders are invited from a list of firms selected by the procuring authority; the 'negotiated procedure', where, exceptionally, contractual terms may be negotiated with chosen contractors, and the 'competitive dialogue procedure', where a limited number of firms are invited to join in discussions on possible solutions for requirements and chosen bidders are then invited to tender. The last was an innovation in the 2004 Directive and is applicable only to exceptionally complex, long-term contracts, notably those under PFI. The Directive and Regulations also specify the grounds on which contractors may be excluded from the tendering processes, for example because of bankruptcy, criminal convictions, or inadequate economic or financial standing or technical capacity.

The award of the contract must be made on the basis of the lowest price or the 'most economically advantageous tender'. The 2004 Directive supplies criteria for the latter decision. These are stated to include (the list is not exhaustive) quality, price, technical merit, aesthetic and functional characteristics, environmental characteristics, running costs, cost-effectiveness, after-sales service and technical assistance, delivery date, and delivery period or period of completion. The criteria to be used must be set out in the contract notice and weighted or listed in order of importance.[35] Reasons for the contract award must also be given to unsuccessful tenderers; the domestic regulations require that these must include the 'characteristics and relative advantages' of the successful tenderer.[36]

A distinctive and important set of remedies is also provided under the Directives.[37] These are available for disappointed suppliers and contractors in the High Court, and are supplemented by the possibility of action against a defaulting Member State by the Commission in the European Court of Justice. Remedies available to the High Court include suspension of an incomplete contract and ineffectiveness or cancellation of the contract for a serious breach of the procedures; the Court may also award damages. The effectiveness of the remedies has been increased by the requirement of a compulsory 10-day standstill period after the provision of reasons for the

[34] For more details, see Harlow and Rawlings, *Law and Administration* (n 2) 384–7.

[35] Directive 2004/18/EC, art. 53.

[36] The Public Contracts Regulations 2006, SI 2006/5, reg. 32.

[37] See Directive 2007/66/EC on improving the effectiveness of review procedures concerning the award of public contracts [2007] JO L335/31, and the Public Contracts (Amendment) Regulations 2009, SI 2009/2992.

contract award to permit a challenge to be brought before the contract is concluded.

The 2004 Directive is thus of considerable complexity and of enormous importance in providing a more structured and open system for the award of public contracts. It does not, however, apply in full to all cases of the procurement of works, supplies, or services, although even the award of contracts not covered must comply with the general Treaty principles referred to earlier. First, 'in-house' provision is not covered. This has given rise to considerable controversy as to what constitutes such provision. In key cases, the Court of Justice decided that it only applies where a contracting authority has control over an entity similar to that which it exercises over its own departments, and where the entity provides the essential part of its activities to the controlling authority or authorities.[38] Very importantly, there must be no private capital whatsoever in the entity for it to qualify as 'in house'.[39] This clearly imposes serious limits on the potential for public/private cooperation through the use of a jointly-owned enterprise unless the public authority is content for the full rigour of the Directive to apply. The UK Supreme Court has, however, applied the test liberally, holding that a mutual insurer established jointly by a number of London local authorities was able to benefit from the exemption.[40] Here there was no private participation in the insurer, and the control test was held to include collective control by a number of public bodies.

Secondly, the Directive does not apply in full to concession contracts; these are more popular on the Continent than in the UK but may include some PFI procurement. The Directive defines a concession as a contract where the consideration for the provision of works or services 'consists either solely in the right to exploit the service or in that right together with payment'.[41] This would include, for example, a contract under which a private provider constructs infrastructure such as a road or bridge and recoups its expenditure through charging tolls. The Directive merely specifies advertising requirements and an obligation regarding the minimum time limit for the receipt of applications, with a view to ensuring that general Treaty requirements are met.[42] Given the importance of concession contracts, this represents a major gap in the system, and the reformed Directive will include more demanding requirements, though without specifying specific award procedures.[43]

[38] Case C-107/98 *Teckal Srl v Commune di Vaiano* [1999] ECR I-8121.

[39] Case C-26/03 *Stadt Halle* [2005] ECR I-1.

[40] *Risk Management Partners v Brent London Borough Council and others* [2011] UKSC 7, [2012] AC 34.

[41] Directive 2004/18/EC, arts 3–4.

[42] Directive 2004/18/EC, arts 56–9.

[43] European Commission, *Proposal for a Directive of the European Parliament and of the Council on the Award of Concession Contracts*, COM(2011) 897 final.

Thirdly, the Directive does not apply in full to so-called 'Part B' services, where only requirements relating to the publication of technical specifications and of an award notice will apply.[44] These services are listed in Annex II B to the Directive; the list is extensive, and includes education, health, and social services. Under the proposed reform this distinction will be removed and instead special provision made for social services (including health and education) with a higher threshold and imposing only the basic principles of transparency and equal treatment. An area of particular concern has been that of health services, which in the UK are increasingly part of a marketized system in which services are commissioned from public and private providers; marketization is further increased by the Health and Social Care Act 2012. Such services fall within the Annex and so are not subject to the full requirements of competitive tendering. Controversial regulations made under the 2012 Act require transparency and equal treatment and outlaw anti-competitive behaviour whilst not making competitive tendering obligatory in all cases.[45] Provision of other types of health supplies not falling within Annex B are of course subject to the normal procurement requirements. The reformed Directive will abandon the distinction between the two types of services, and instead provide a 'light touch' regime for social and health services, with a much higher threshold for coverage by the Directive.

Finally, the Directive makes provision for an accelerated procedure where urgency renders the normal time limits impracticable.[46] The Commission considered that, as a result of the financial crisis, the use of this procedure could be justified for conducting major public investment projects in 2009 and 2010.[47]

EU procurement rules and secondary policies

We have seen that there have often been attempts to use contractual techniques to implement policy objectives; indeed such policies were used extensively in Continental Europe as part of both industrial and social policy. A particularly striking and far-reaching domestic example was that of the Labour Government's anti-inflation policy in the 1970s; another example is that of attempts to support national industry through a 'Buy British' policy.

[44] Directive 2004/18/EC, art. 21.

[45] The National Health Service (Procurement, Patient Choice and Competition) (No. 2) Regulations 2013, SI 2013/500.

[46] Directive 2004/18/EC, art. 38(8).

[47] See Commission Press Release IP/08/2040 of 19 December 2008, *Public Procurement: Commission Recognises Need for Accelerated Procurement Procedure.*

The latter example would clearly be in breach of the EU Treaty requirements whose main *raison d'être* is the avoidance of discrimination on the ground of nationality in the supply of goods and services. However, the position of other socially-based policies has been less clear. Key examples would be attempts to relieve unemployment, especially in depressed regions, attempts to implement equal treatment of workers, and environmental policies, especially those relating to sustainability.[48] A particularly controversial case was the UK Government's preferential treatment of workshops employing the disabled and those in prison, which was abandoned in 1994 because of doubts as to its compatibility with the EU rules.[49] More recently, the Government faced serious criticism because of its award of a contract for rail rolling stock to Siemens, at the expense of the rival bidder, Bombardier, whose UK-based train manufacturing capability was placed at risk by the decision. The previous Government had excluded socio-economic factors from the criteria, a decision which now had 'few defenders', but it was too late to re-open the bidding.[50]

Originally, the EU procurement rules appeared seriously to limit the use of secondary policies in contracting for those works and services which they covered fully.[51] Moreover, the position of the Commission itself was strongly influenced by economic liberalism with 'almost implacable opposition' to secondary policies, especially during the mid-1980s to early-1990s. It thus interpreted 'most economically advantageous offer' as limiting the tender evaluation to economic or commercial grounds only, and as late as 1997 stated that '[t]here is widespread agreement that social policy and public procurement should not overlap'.[52]

Perhaps surprisingly in view of its commitment to market integration, the ECJ took a somewhat different view. In the case of *Beentjes* the Court held that there had been no breach of a Procurement Directive where the contract has not been awarded to the lowest bidder as it was unable to employ long-term unemployed persons; this had been stated as a necessary condition for selection. The Court considered that such a consideration was not precluded

[48] For a highly detailed account of this issue, concentrating on equality but also of relevance in relation to other policies, see C. McCrudden, *Buying Social Justice: Equality, Government Procurement and Legal Change* (Oxford: Oxford University Press, 2007).

[49] S. Arrowsmith, 'Public Procurement as an Instrument of Policy and the Impact of Market Liberalisation' (1995) 111 *Law Quarterly Review* 235–84, 244.

[50] See Transport Committee, *Thameslink Rolling Stock Procurement* (HC 2010–12, 1453).

[51] For an early detailed account, see Arrowsmith, 'Public Procurement as an Instrument of Policy' (n 49).

[52] McCrudden, *Buying Social Justice* (n 48) 332–3, quoting European Commission, 'Public Procurement in the EU: Special Sectoral Report No 1' (1997).

by the Directive, so long as the condition was transparent, non-discriminatory, and consistent with Treaty principles.[53] In a further case, where contracts were awarded on criteria including conditions relating to participation in a local project to combat unemployment, the ECJ considered that an award condition relating to the campaign against unemployment was permissible so long as it was not discriminatory and that the procedural rules, especially those on advertising, had been followed; the condition must also have been expressly mentioned in the contract notice.[54] The ECJ in a third case confirmed that non-economic criteria, including those relating to the protection of the environment, could be used so long as they related to the subject-matter of the contract and were not discriminatory; of course, the procedural requirements must be followed.[55]

When the Directives were merged and amended in 2004, changes were made to bring the new Directive more into line with the approach taken by the ECJ.[56] Thus the Directive specifies that technical specifications may include environmental characteristics and accessibility, and contracts may be reserved for sheltered workshops; it is made explicit that special conditions relating to the performance of the contract may concern social and environmental considerations.[57] These may also include conditions favouring vocational training and the fight against unemployment. As regards the criteria for the award of the contract, it is made clear that the criteria set out in the Directive are non-exhaustive and include environmental and other considerations; non-compliance with social legislation may also result in the disqualification of a bid as abnormally low.[58] Any criteria must, however, relate to the subject-matter of the contract and so, for example, a decision based on whether a gender-equal employment policy was in place or on the employment of quotas of particular groups would be precluded where these did not related to the contract in question. The proposed reforms increase flexibility further, for example by permitting the exclusion of bidders or tenders because of breaches of social, labour, or environmental law.

Thus it is now no longer true that the Procurement Directive leads to 'the economic dominating the social'.[59] Although the amendments to the Directive made in 2004 are relatively limited, they recognize that:

[53] Case 31/87 *Beentjes* [1988] ECR 4635.

[54] Case C-225/98 *Commission v France, Nord-Pas-de-Calais* [2000] ECR I-7455.

[55] Case C-513/99 *Concordia Bus Finland Oy Ab* [2002] ECR I-7213.

[56] For a summary, see J. Arnould, 'Secondary Policies in Public Procurement: the Innovations of the New Directives' [2004] *Public Procurement Law Review* 187–97.

[57] See Directive 2004/18/EC, recitals 28–9, 33; arts 19, 23, and 26.

[58] Directive 2004/18/EC, arts 53, 55(1)(d).

[59] McCrudden, *Buying Social Justice* (n 48) 574.

> Community legislation and the Court of Justice have already gone very far and, in reality, there are very few techniques that are by themselves contrary to the Directives. Contracting authorities and entities may take into account environmental and social considerations, on which the emphasis has been put in recent years, but also other objectives like competition policy or support for subcontracting.[60]

Indeed, the Commission has published a detailed guide on how to implement 'socially responsible public procurement'.[61] This is a very different approach from that of the Commission in the 1980s and 1990s, although an obviously discriminatory policy such as 'Buy British' is of course still unlawful, but reference to combating unemployment or sustainability does not in itself breach EU law, so long as it relates to the subject-matter of the contract. In the UK, the Public Services (Social Value) Act 2012, originating in a private member's bill, requires English contracting authorities to consider, before commencing the process, how what is proposed to be procured might improve the economic, social, and environmental well-being of their area so long as this is relevant to the procurement. A more recent invitation to negotiate for rail rolling stock, unlike the example discussed earlier, included requirements for 'responsible procurement', such as to provide opportunities for training, apprenticeships, and small and medium-size businesses, to establish a local presence to manage the contract, and to report on the source of each element of the contract.[62]

Individualization and relationality

A related criticism of the EU procurement rules has been that they promote a model of contracting which is highly individualized, and which discourages the use of other models, such as those based on 'partnering' or 'partnership sourcing' which involve the development of long-term cooperative relationships with a limited number of suppliers extending beyond individualized contracts.[63] Indeed, this reflects a major theme in current socio-legal debates

[60] Arnould, 'Secondary Policies in Public Procurement' (n 56) 197.

[61] European Commission, *Buying Social: A Guide to Taking Account of Social Considerations in Public Procurement* (2010).

[62] See HC Debs 28 February 2012, vol. 541, cols 29–30WS.

[63] See esp. S. Arrowsmith, 'The Way Forward or a Wrong Turning? An Assessment of the European Community Policy on Public Procurement in Light of the Commission's Green Paper' (1997) 3 *European Public Law* 389–411; 'The EC Procurement Directives, National Procurement Policies and Better Governance: the Case for a New Approach' (2002) 27 *European Law Review* 3–24.

on contracting, in which the emphasis has increasingly been on the role of relationality in contracts, characterized by norms promoting values including flexibility, reciprocity, and solidarity.[64] The absence of reference to such norms has been seen also as a weakness in the 'new public contracting'.[65] A related difficulty is the high procurement costs imposed by the requirements of the Directive, and their complexity. These problems have led a leading UK expert on public procurement to call for an approach based on the Treaty principles without the attempt to specify detailed transparency requirements and procedures through Directives. Compliance would be assessed through performance indicators based on import penetration or commercial performance with national enforcement authorities acting within an EU-level framework. In the meantime, exemptions could be made from the current requirements for contracting entities which can demonstrate compliance with Treaty principles.[66]

Such a major about-turn is unlikely in the foreseeable future; the new procedure of 'competitive dialogue' introduced in the 2004 reforms was intended partly to remedy this problem for highly complex contracts such as PFI schemes. It permits discussions with suppliers to develop suitable solutions, on the basis of which chosen suppliers are then invited to tender. However, the procedure has problems of its own. It can only be used for particularly complex contracts, and requires a greater degree of agreement on contractual terms before the appointment of a preferred bidder as only fine-tuning of the terms will be permitted after that; this increases the overall tendering costs for losing bidders. It is also likely to make it more common to reduce the number of bidders to two at an earlier stage, creating problems if one then drops out.[67] The current reforms will make further changes to increase flexibility, for example by replacing the negotiated procedure with new procedures, removing the need to justify the use of the competitive dialogue procedure, and relaxing documentation and publication requirements. Nevertheless, this individualization and lack of concern with relationality is likely to be a more serious problem with the EU procurement rules than that of limits on secondary policies.

[64] See Vincent-Jones, *The New Public Contracting* (n 16) 4–7. The major work in developing this concept is that of Ian Macneil; see e.g. *The New Social Contract* (New Haven: Yale University Press, 1980).

[65] Vincent-Jones, *The New Public Contracting* (n 16) 347–61.

[66] Arrowsmith, 'The EC Procurement Directives, National Procurement Policies and Better Governance: the Case for a New Approach' (n 63).

[67] For discussion, see National Audit Office, *Improving the PFI Tendering Process* (HC 2006–07, 149) and Public Accounts Committee, *HM Treasury: Tendering and Benchmarking in PFI* (HC 2006–07, 754).

The World Trade Organization and the Agreement on Government Procurement

This aspect of the international legal framework can be dealt with more briefly. At first sight there would appear to be little effect of WTO rules in relation to government procurement as GATT article II:8 and GATS article XIII exclude procurement by government agencies of services purchased for governmental purposes from the application of the principles of market access and national treatment. However, there has been an Agreement on Government Procurement (GPA) since 1979, and a new agreement was drawn up under the auspices of the WTO in 1994 which came into effect in 1995.[68] The GPA is plurilateral; it is not part of the 'single undertaking' of the WTO and many countries have not opted to join it (although the EU and the United States are members). It is also dependent on commitments by members as to which contracts, agencies, and services will be covered, though the EU Member States have made extensive commitments which bring under the Agreement a large range of contracting authorities and types of supplies, such as computer services and financial services.[69] The GPA contains non-discrimination requirements and sets out detailed obligations which are to be followed in relation to the procurement it covers; for example, publication of requirements for the qualification of suppliers (which must be limited to those relating to a firm's capability to perform the contract), and publication of the criteria for the award of the contract. It also sets out three basic methods for procurement (open, selective, or by negotiation), though it is possible other methods may be used if they are non-discriminatory. National remedies are also required for disappointed bidders. A new text for the GPA with relatively minor changes relating to transparency was agreed in 2006 and adopted in 2012; the new text refers explicitly to the permissibility of the use of technical specifications relating to protection of the environment, but not to other secondary policies.

Article XXIII of the GPA includes an exception for measures necessary to protect public morals, order, safety, or health or relating to the services of handicapped persons, philanthropic institutions, or prison labour; according to McCrudden, this can be interpreted in such a way as to leave considerable

[68] For discussion, see A. Reich, 'Legislative Comment: the New Text of the Agreement on Government Procurement: an Analysis and Assessment' (2009) 12(4) *Journal of International Economic Law* 989–1022.

[69] For details, see World Trade Organization, *Agreement on Government Procurement* (1994), Annexes 1–5.

scope for the use of secondary policies.[70] He is, however, critical of the lack of clarity in the system as to how conflicting principles relating to economic and social policies can be resolved; renegotiation of the provisions is politically very difficult and the WTO dispute panels and Appellate Body are not appropriate institutions for undertaking broad-ranging inquiries of this kind, for example relating to equality rights.[71] Arrowsmith has made similar criticisms of the GPA to those she made in relation to the EU procurement regime, notably in relation to cost and the limits on negotiations enabling suppliers to develop their proposals jointly with the contracting authority, and to select a preferred bidder early to limit costs for those excluded.[72] Thus the GPA raises similar issues of the role of secondary policies and of relationality to those raised by the EU Directives, though given its more limited effect these have not yet emerged in so serious a form.

Procurement in the UK

Institutional arrangements

The UK institutional arrangements for procurement have been subject to a number of recent changes. Historically the Treasury was responsible for developing procurement principles with responsibility for implementation lying with individual spending departments. In 1994 a Central Unit on Procurement was established within the Treasury and a Buying Agency set up within the Cabinet Office. In 1999 the Gershon Review on civil procurement found that responsibility for procurement was fragmented and that there was a lack of consistency between different departments with each using different rules; there was a wide gap between best and worst practice, and as a result the Office of Government Commerce (OGC) was established within the Treasury as a central resource for procurement skills, with a supervisory board headed by the Chief Secretary to the Treasury. The OGC was to set a common strategic framework for procurement by all departments, define a common process, and develop common performance measures. It would reduce the burden imposed on business by the additional cost of complex public procurement procedures.[73] It developed a range of procurement

[70] McCrudden, *Buying Social Justice* (n 48) 491–3, 573.

[71] McCrudden, *Buying Social Justice* (n 48) 586–94.

[72] S. Arrowsmith, 'Transparency in Government Procurement: The Objectives of Regulation and the Boundaries of the World Trade Organisation' (2003) 37 *Journal of World Trade Law* 283–303, esp. 289–90.

[73] HM Treasury, *Review of Civil Procurement in Central Government* (1999).

strategies and guidelines, and also established 'gateway reviews' as a means of helping departments improve their records in project delivery; these involved reviewing projects at key stages to determine whether they should proceed further and what changes were necessary, and over 1,500 reviews were carried out between 2001 and 2007, though not published. OGC Trading Solutions was established as the OGC trading arm.[74]

A further review took the form of the Treasury's paper *Transforming Government Procurement* in 2007.[75] This set out plans for transforming the OGC into a smaller, more focused, and higher calibre organization; to increase focus it would lose its responsibilities under the broader efficiency programme, and would now handle complaints from industry relating to procurement issues.[76] The Chief Executive of the OGC was to become the head of the procurement service, and there was to be greater collaboration between departments. In addition to implementing these reforms, the Government established a Major Projects Review Group, chaired by the Treasury and composed of commercial experts to ensure that the most important and complex projects are subject to effective review at key stages.

The Coalition Government moved the OGC from the Treasury to the Efficiency and Reform Group in the Cabinet Office; this was associated with some major improvements in the transparency of procurement, which will be discussed in the following section. Yet another review of the efficiency of procurement, this time conducted by Sir Philip Green on behalf of the Prime Minister, criticized the lack of coordination in procurement and of the use of economies of scale, as well as lack of necessary data on procurement matters.[77] In response, greater centralization was adopted with the establishment of the Government Procurement Service and the appointment of a Chief Procurement Officer. This has had some success in clarifying lines of responsibility and improving capability, though tensions between centralization and departmental accountability remain, with no sanctions for non-compliance with the central mandate.[78] The Heseltine Review (discussed in Chapter 8) recommended that each department recruit a chief procurement officer from the private sector and that the Cabinet Office should set common standards through a procurement strategy for all public bodies, backed up by legislation if necessary.[79] These recommendations were accepted by the Government,

[74] See Harlow and Rawlings, *Law and Administration* (n 2) 358–9.

[75] HM Treasury, *Transforming Government Procurement* (2007).

[76] HM Treasury, *Transforming Government Procurement* (n 75) para. 2.3.

[77] Cabinet Office, *Efficiency Review by Sir Philip Green: Key Findings and Recommendations* (2010).

[78] NAO, *Improving Government Procurement* (HC 2012–13, 996).

[79] BIS, *No Stone Unturned in Pursuit of Growth* (2012), paras 4.1–4.19.

though without reference to legislation, and procurement is to be further centralized with procurement of common services through a new agency, the Crown Commercial Service. The Scottish Government has prepared a Procurement Reform Bill to provide a clearer procurement framework and to support greater use of social and environmental considerations as part of a wider public procurement reform programme.

The procurement framework and transparency

As is to be expected both from the highly technical nature of much procurement and the plethora of attempts at reform, the framework of rules under which it operates is highly complex. No attempt will be made here to analyze it in any detail; however, the guidance and rules are available on the internet.[80] As already described, these provide a comprehensive body of law relating to government contracts, and include general best practice and guidance, templates, and model documentation. They are supplemented by extensive guidance from the NAO.[81]

The public availability of this material via the internet represents a considerable increase in transparency. Further attempts were made to increase accessibility by the Coalition Government shortly after its election. The Prime Minister announced that all new central government contracts were to be published in full from January 2011, including the original tender documents and contract information. These requirements apply to all central government departments including their agencies, all non-departmental public bodies, NHS bodies, and trading funds. This and other openness initiatives are overseen by a Public Sector Transparency Board in the Cabinet Office. The information is available through a new 'Contracts Finder' website.[82]

This represents a major advance in transparency. Indeed, a problem for the future is likely to be making sense of a mass of complex material rather than having difficulty in accessing it. Problems of commercial confidentiality remain; thus the Transport Committee was not allowed to see the tender documents submitted by the bidders in the controversial rail procurement discussed earlier; the publication of the terms of the contract does not extend to information on the bids. The Public Accounts Committee itself has

[80] See e.g. Cabinet Office, *Policy and Standards Framework—Best Practice Guidance* at: <https://www.gov.uk/government/publications/policy-and-standards-framework-best-practice-guidance>.

[81] For details, see the National Audit Office, *Successful Commissioning Toolkit* at: <http://www.nao.org.uk/report/successful-commissioning-toolkit/>.

[82] <http://www.contractsfinder.businesslink.gov.uk/>.

criticized lack of availability of data from private companies which provide public services owing to commercial confidentiality, for example in relation to the Private Finance Initiative and welfare-to-work contractors.[83]

The Private Finance Initiative

The Private Finance Initiative (PFI) has been a highly controversial means of procuring capital assets. The technique was introduced by a Conservative Government but was used extensively by the Labour Governments from 1997. The scale of PFI has been enormous with over 700 projects and private sector investment of around £55 billion. In brief, PFI takes the form of a public sector body, for example in the health or education sectors, contracting with the private sector to furnish a capital asset. The private sector, through a 'special purpose vehicle', will provide the asset for a substantial period (up to 35 years) and will be paid for doing so by the public sector purchaser over the course of the contract, or, in a few cases, directly by the users through charges or tolls. PFI has had the advantage for government of taking the immediate capital costs of a project off the public sector balance sheet, and also attempts to transfer the risk of delays in completion or failure to perform the contract properly from the public to the private sector (though, as we shall see, the extent to which this has been achieved in practice has been disputed).

Under EU procurement law, in the early days of PFI, in the relatively few cases where fees were paid directly by users, government policy was to treat these as concession contracts and so only subject to limited requirements under the Procurement Directive. Other PFI deals (the vast majority) were treated as works or services contracts for which the competitive dialogue procedure is now used. Institutionally, there is a large number of bodies involved in the negotiation of PFI deals, which are highly complex.[84]

Why has the PFI programme proved so controversial? There are a number of reasons. The first is the claim that it has been used inappropriately where traditional public procurement would have provided better value for money, and would avoid public bodies being tied into costly long-term commitments for the benefit of the private sector. This may have extra force in an era of public expenditure cuts when PFI contractual payments are fixed. The fact that most PFI deals were effectively 'off balance sheet', as the risk was treated

[83] Public Accounts Committee, *Implementing the Transparency Agenda* (HC 2012–13, 102).

[84] For an introduction, see Harlow and Rawlings, *Law and Administration* (n 2) 417–25.

as borne by the private sector, led to pressure for a PFI solution to be adopted for major capital projects where an alternative would have provided better value for money.

Indeed, from the early days of PFI there have been criticisms both of value for money and of the reality of risk transfer.[85] In one of the first PFI deals, that for the development of the Royal Armouries Museum in Leeds, after inadequate income from visitors to service its debts, the contractor had to renegotiate the deal so that risk was taken back by the public sector and extra grant aid had to be provided for this from the Department.[86] Although steps were taken to avoid a similar outcome in later contracts, the collapse of the major public/private partnership (not strictly a PFI project) for the maintenance and upgrading of the London Underground also showed how risk remained with the public sector, though this was an exceptional case where 95 per cent of the contractor's debt obligations had been guaranteed by Transport for London, costing the public purse around £2 billion.[87]

Refinancing and bundling of PFI contracts have raised major concerns of value for money. In the early days, a PFI to build, finance, and operate Fazakerley Prison had been refinanced in such a way as to increase returns to investors by 61 per cent with no commensurate return to the taxpayer as rights to share in refinancing benefits had not been included in the contract.[88] New terms were introduced into PFI contracts signed since 2002 to give the public sector the right to 50 per cent of the gains, rising to 70 per cent in some contracts signed since 2008. However, a secondary market has developed enabling PFI projects to be traded and specialist investment funds acquired portfolios of such projects. This permits investors to gain added value from economies of scale, with no commensurate benefit to taxpayers. A further potential issue is that of tax liability where PFI deals are calculated on a basis which includes tax liabilities and contractors then locate in overseas tax havens.

A final problem is that of complexity and lack of transparency. This contractual complexity was particularly great in relation to the London

[85] See e.g. Public Accounts Committee, *Getting Better Value for Money from the Private Finance Initiative* (HC 1998–99, 583); Treasury Committee, *The Private Finance Initiative* (HC 1999–2000, 147).

[86] National Audit Office, *The Re-negotiation of the PFI-type Deal for the Royal Armouries Museum in Leeds* (HC 2000–01, 103).

[87] See House of Lords Economic Affairs Committee, *Private Finance Projects and Off-balance Sheet Debt* (HL 2009–10, 63), paras 92–101, and for fuller analysis, Harlow and Rawlings, *Law and Administration* (n 2) 425–37.

[88] See National Audit Office, *The Refinancing of the Fazakerley PFI Prison Contract* (HC 1999–2000, 584).

Underground contracts; as Harlow and Rawlings note, the complexity of the legal documents was 'mind-boggling' and the original documentation ran to 28,000 pages and over two million words, employing complex mathematical formulae to calculate payments. The transaction costs of the deals for the London Underground contracts were some £500 million.[89] Some select committees had criticized the use of commercial confidentiality to deny them access to information about private finance deals, although the NAO benefits from special arrangements permitting it to see information on a confidential basis.[90]

The NAO issued a report in 2011 drawing general lessons from PFI and related projects, and concluded that the Government needs to act as a more intelligent customer in the procurement and management of projects, and that PFI may not be suitable for as many projects as it has been in the past, although lessons from it could be applied to other types of procurement.[91] Similar conclusions were reached by the Public Accounts Committee, which also criticized the lack of transparency because of the use of commercial confidentiality.[92] This was followed by a devastating report on PFI by the Treasury Committee.[93] The Committee concluded that there was no clear evidence to suggest that the savings from PFI were sufficient to outweigh the extra cost of private rather than public borrowing, which had become substantial after the financial crisis. It suggested a more limited role for PFI in the future, and that it should be used only sparingly until value for money concerns had been addressed. The Treasury undertook a review of PFI, concluding that there were indeed problems of inflexibility, lack of value for money, and of insufficient transparency. Limited reforms would be introduced, including equity participation by government and the private sector, more information on actual and forecast returns, reducing the number of services included in the contract to increase flexibility, and greater retention of some risks by the public sector.[94] PFI will continue to be used for the procurement of some major capital projects; and the liabilities relating to existing projects will continue for years into the future.

[89] Harlow and Rawlings, *Law and Administration* (n 2) 429, where there is a revealing example of such an impenetrable formula.

[90] See A. Brazier and V. Ram, *The Fiscal Maze: Parliament, Government and Public Money* (London: Hansard Society, 2006), paras 8.3–8.4; Liaison Committee, *Parliament and Government Finance: Recreating Financial Scrutiny* (HC 2007–08, 426), para. 56.

[91] NAO, *Lessons from PFI and Other Projects* (HC 2010–12, 920).

[92] Public Accounts Committee, *Lessons from PFI and Other Projects* (HC 2010–12, 1201).

[93] Treasury Committee, *Private Finance Initiative* (HC 2010–12, 1146).

[94] HM Treasury, *A New Approach To Public Private Partnerships* (2012).

Defence procurement

The EU

PFI has given rise to an unusual degree of public controversy for public procurement, and this has been even truer for defence procurement, in which there has been a toxic combination of enormous sums of money, limited competition, and mishandling of contracts on both the purchasing and the supplier sides. Here the international dimension is less developed than in most other areas of procurement. The GPA does not cover defence procurement. In the past EU law has been assumed to have had only limited applicability because of a wide interpretation of article 346 TFEU. This provides, inter alia, that:

> any Member State may take such measures as it considers necessary for the protection of the essential interests of its security which are connected with the production of or trade in arms, munitions and war material; such measures shall not adversely affect the conditions of competition in the internal market regarding products which are not intended for specifically military purposes.[95]

Although Member States treated this provision as giving a complete exemption from EU law for defence industries, there has been some doubt as to just how extensive this freedom given is, with a narrower approach taken by the ECJ and in an interpretative Communication from the Commission.[96]

In 2005 a voluntary code of conduct on defence procurement was produced under the auspices of the European Defence Agency, providing for fair and equal treatment of suppliers through transparent and objective selection and award criteria, with feedback for unsuccessful bidders.[97] In 2007 the Commission produced its 'defence package', which included a proposal for a Directive on public procurement of arms, munitions, war material, and related works and services, and the Directive was issued in 2009.[98] This

[95] For discussion, see P. Koutrakos, 'The Application of EC Law to Defence Industries—Changing Interpretations of Article 296 EC' in C. Barnard and O. Odudu (eds), *The Outer Limits of European Union Law* (Oxford: Hart Publishing, 2009), 307–27.

[96] See e.g. Case C-414/97 *Commission v Spain* [1999] ECR I-5585; European Commission, Interpretative Communication on the application of Article 296 of the Treaty in the field of Defence Procurement, COM(2006) final.

[97] European Defence Agency, *Code of Conduct on Defence Procurement of EU Member States Participating in the European Defence Agency* (2005).

[98] Directive 2009/81/EC on the Coordination of Procedures for the Award of Certain Works Contracts, Supply Contracts and Service Contracts by Contracting Authorities or Entities in the Fields of Defence and Security [2009] JO L216/76, implemented in the UK by the Defence and Security Public Contracts Regulations 2011, SI 2011/1848.

ousts the general Procurement Directives, and permits Member States to choose between the restricted procedure or the negotiated procedure with prior publication, and to use competitive dialogue for particularly complex contracts; there is also provision for remedies adapted from the general Remedies Directive. However, Member States will still be able to use article 346 TFEU to exempt specific contracts from the Directive's requirements.

UK defence procurement

This has long been an area of serious difficulty, as illustrated in the regular reports from the NAO and Public Accounts Committee on major projects. By the nature of the subject-matter of contracts for major projects, competition is limited. In addition, questions of value for money have often been subordinated to industrial policy in the form of the maintenance of a domestic defence industry. Non-competitive contracts have been remunerated on the basis of profit formulae set by the Review Board for Government Contracts, a surprisingly corporatist body comprised of members nominated by the Ministry of Defence and the Confederation of British Industry. The formula aims to give contractors a rate of return comparable to that earned by British industry as a whole over recent years, and is reviewed annually, with more wide-ranging general reviews usually every three years.[99] The Board is now to be replaced by a Single Source Regulations Office with power to oversee the efficiency and value for money of single-source purchasing.[100] Purchasing is undertaken by Defence Equipment and Support (DE&S), an executive agency of the Ministry of Defence and successor to the Defence Procurement Agency. A major reform considered by the Government was to turn DE&S into a 'GoCo', owned by the Government but operated by a private consortium, but this was dropped after attracting only one bidder.[101]

There have been successive attempts to reform the process of defence procurement. Thus in 1997 the policy was adopted of No Acceptable Price No Contract (NAPNOC) with equality of information rights between contractors and purchasers, and an objective of agreeing contract prices at the outset for the main stages of contract work rather than letting work proceed whilst objectives are firmed up. This was not successful, and 25

[99] For background, see I. Harden, 'Corporatism Without Labour: the British Version' in C. Graham and T. Prosser (eds), *Waiving the Rules: The Constitution Under Thatcherism* (Milton Keynes: Open University Press, 1988), 36–55, 44–6. The details of the Review can be found in Review Board for Government Contracts, *Report on the 2012 Annual Review of the Profit Formula for Non-Competitive Government Contracts* (2012).

[100] Ministry of Defence, *Review of Single Source Pricing Regulations* (2011).

[101] Ministry of Defence, *Better Defence Acquisition* (Cm 8626, 2013).

major projects in 1999 were forecast to cost more than £2.7 billion more than originally estimated, with an average in-service delay date of 47 months.[102] The Department then moved to policies of 'Smart Procurement' or 'Smart Acquisition' adopting a whole-life approach based around a single integrated project team bringing together the main stakeholders, more open trade-offs between performance and costs, and greater emphasis on risk reduction before major investment decisions were taken. However, serious problems continued; in its 2003 Major Project Report the National Audit Office found that projects had slipped an average of 18 months beyond their expected delivery dates, and costs had increased by £3.1 billion in the last year.[103] In a report highly critical of the failure of 'Smart Acquisition', the Defence Committee concluded that '*[t]he performance of the Defence Procurement Agency in 2002–03 can only be described as woeful*'.[104]

In 2002 the Department launched its 'Defence Industrial Policy' aiming to enhance the competitiveness and sustainability of the UK defence industry whilst improving value for money, in part through greater transparency from the early stages of a procurement project. It summarized the wider factors to be taken into account in acquisition decisions, including security of supply, export participation, industrial participation by UK industry, industrial capabilities, and foreign and security policy interests.[105] Once more, the Defence Committee was critical, pointing to a lack of clarity on the part of the Department as to which sectors of the defence industry it was vital to retain in the future, and noting that wider factors were considered too late in the procurement process.[106] Indeed, what was striking about the Policy was its vagueness; it rehearsed the different criteria to be used in procurement decisions but did not rank them clearly and provided little on the mechanisms for the resolution of conflict between them. The Policy was updated in a White Paper in 2005 which aimed to provide greater clarity on which industrial capacities needed retention and to provide a clearer focus, with more stress on upgrading and maintaining platforms rather than designing and building new equipment, with greater use of long-term partnering arrangements. It also gave fuller information on underlying principles and processes.[107] Reviews by the select committees were more positive; for example, in 2006 the Defence Committee welcomed it as providing greater

[102] National Audit Office, *Major Projects Report 1999* (HC 1999–2000, 613).
[103] National Audit Office, *Major Projects Report 2003* (HC 2003–04, 195).
[104] Defence Committee, *Defence Procurement* (HC 2003–04, 572), para. 12 (emphasis retained).
[105] Ministry of Defence, Policy Paper 5, *Defence Industrial Policy* (2002).
[106] Defence Committee, *Defence Procurement* (n 104) paras 115, 118.
[107] Ministry of Defence, *Defence Industrial Strategy: Defence White Paper* (Cm 6697, 2005).

clarity for the industry, although it was still concerned about lack of incentives in non-competitive contracts and of competition for underlying work.[108] It also noted better quality performance in 2006.[109]

However, serious problems were looming. In 2010 the Public Accounts Committee found that the defence budget was unaffordable by between £6 billion and £35 billion, largely because of deliberate decisions to delay projects to produce short-term annual savings which did not represent good value for money. The Treasury had permitted this to develop through concentrating only on whether the Department's books balanced each year.[110] This critique was developed in a devastating major report by the Defence Committee, taking account of the critical Gray Review of Acquisition carried out for the Secretary of State.[111] The Committee found that the costs of the 're-profiling' of expenditure by delaying projects in 2008–09 had added £733 million to the future costs of the core equipment programme, and that the 'frictional costs' of delays within the equipment programme were in the range £900 million to £2.2 billion per year.[112] Many other problems were identified, including a delay of at least three years in the delivery of the A440M military transport aeroplane. The Committee was also extremely critical of lack of transparency, in particular a lack of cooperation with the Committee on the part of the Department and the giving of misleading answers in the past.[113] The problems were not limited to major projects; the Public Accounts Committee found serious fault with the management of the defence budget and estate, where it concluded that the Accounting Officer had not discharged his responsibility to ensure that planned and committed expenditure across the defence budget represented value for money.[114]

The Coalition Government included defence in the Spending Review and almost simultaneously with it issued the Strategic Defence and Security Review.[115] The Ministry of Defence was to face cuts of at least £8.3 billion and a reduction in its resource spending of 8 per cent. The Strategic Defence Review did not consider procurement procedures in detail, but important decisions of substance had been made in an attempt to cut losses and a large

[108] Defence Committee, *The Defence Industrial Strategy* (HC 2005–06, 824), paras 81–2, 85, 92, 94.

[109] Defence Committee, *Defence Procurement 2006* (HC 2006–07, 56).

[110] Public Accounts Committee, *Ministry of Defence: Major Projects Report 2009* (HC 2009–10, 338).

[111] Defence Committee, *Defence Equipment 2010* (HC 2009–10, 99).

[112] Defence Committee, *Defence Equipment 2010* (n 111) paras 64–5.

[113] Defence Committee, *Defence Equipment 2010* (n 111), e.g. paras 20 and 43.

[114] Public Accounts Committee, *Managing the Defence Budget and Estate* (HC 2010–11, 503).

[115] HM Government, *Securing Britain in an Age of Uncertainty: The Strategic Defence and Security Review* (Cm 7948, 2010).

number of contracts were to be cancelled or renegotiated. Both the Public Accounts Committee and the Defence Committee were critical once more of the way in which these decisions had been taken.[116] The Government decided in the Strategic Defence Review to proceed with a delayed project to build two aircraft carriers, on which the overrun was £1.6 billion, although owing to a shortage of suitable aircraft one would be mothballed as soon as it was completed. To cancel the project would have produced relatively small savings owing to continuing contractual commitments to maintain industrial capacity. The decision was later revised to use a different form of aircraft, but the Public Accounts Committee was once more highly critical, both of the process and the costs of converting the carriers, which had risen by 150 per cent over 18 months.[117] Moreover, in 2009–10 the Department had had to commit an extra £2.7 billion to the Typhoon project to honour contractual commitments; the purchase cost of each aircraft had risen by 75 per cent.[118] One particularly devastating point was the Public Accounts Committee's finding that the Department was renegotiating contracts without properly understanding the contractual penalties for which it might be liable.[119] The Defence Committee noted that the Department now considered that the gap between the planned programme and budget was substantially in excess of £38 billion, though with the cuts in the Review there was now a prospect of bringing plans and budget into balance.[120] It recommended a system of 10-year budgeting to provide greater stability. The National Audit Office's 2011 Major Projects Report was more positive, noting that cost overruns had declined and were lower on newer projects, whilst the Public Accounts Committee was again critical of decisions to cancel or delay projects, adding significant long-term costs to the whole defence programme.[121]

In 2012 a further White Paper emphasized open procurement in the domestic and global market, for example by buying equipment 'off the shelf', except where it is necessary for national security to protect operational advantages and freedom of action, for example by retaining advanced

[116] Public Accounts Committee, *The Major Projects Report 2010* (HC 2010–11, 687); Defence Committee, *The Strategic Defence and Security Review and the National Security Strategy* (HC 2010–12, 761).

[117] Public Accounts Committee, *Carrier Strike: The 2012 Reversion Decision* (HC 2013–14, 113).

[118] Public Accounts Committee, *Management of the Typhoon Project* (HC 2010–12, 860).

[119] Public Accounts Committee, *The Major Projects Report 2010* (n 116) paras 4, 21.

[120] Defence Committee, *The Strategic Defence and Security Review and the National Security Strategy* (n 116) paras 198–205.

[121] NAO, *The Major Projects Report 2011* (HC 2010–12, 1520); Public Accounts Committee, *Ministry of Defence: The Major Projects Report 2011* (HC 2010–12, 1678).

technologies. Future requirements would be planned and defined more clearly.[122] The Defence Committee considered that the White Paper was not a substitute for a defence industrial strategy, the absence of which put the UK at a disadvantage against its competitors, and that greater clarity was needed on which capabilities must be protected as critical to national sovereignty.[123] One more promising sign was that the Defence Secretary was able to announce in May 2012 that the defence budget was now in balance with a small annual reserve built in; in future the equipment plan would be reviewed by the NAO to confirm its affordability.[124] In its review of major projects in 2012, the Office found cost variation and time slippage in 14 out of 16 of them, though much of the increased cost was outside the control of the Department.[125]

There is no simple explanation for this disastrous record. Contributing factors must be confusion about the role of industrial policy and a failure to balance this properly with value for money considerations. Government has clearly not been prepared to leave procurement only to the international market, but where a strategy has been attempted it has been inadequate and ambiguous. Lack of transparency in procurement procedures no doubt also contributed, though there have been important and regular *ex post facto* examinations by the NAO and select committees. A major factor has also clearly been poor organization in the Ministry of Defence and its executive agencies, and an apparent belief that defence procurement is somehow outside the constraints imposed on the rest of public spending. Credit must be given to the Coalition Government for tackling this issue in the strategic review through treating defence procurement as a major area for public expenditure control. However, given the failure of earlier reform attempts, it is hard to be optimistic about improvement in the future.

Conclusion

Some aspects of government contracting have clearly improved dramatically in recent years. This can be attributed in large part to the frequent detailed examination of decisions on a value for money basis by the NAO and the Public Accounts Committee, and on a wider basis by other select committees.

[122] Ministry of Defence, *National Security Through Technology: Technology, Equipment, and Support for UK Defence and Security* (Cm 8278, 2012).

[123] Defence Committee, *Defence Acquisition* (HC 2012–13, 9), paras 34–45.

[124] HC Deb 14 May 2012, vol. 545, cols 261–4.

[125] NAO, *The Major Projects Report 2012* (HC 2012–13, 684).

Procedures have been structured much more clearly by the EU Procurement Directives. These procedures are too restrictive in focusing on individual contracts at the expense of longer-term relations with contractors, but their existence is one reason why transparency is far greater than it was 25 years ago, and the use of the internet to make a wide range of information available has been most valuable of all. Indeed, a problem in taking advantage of transparency may be the difficulty of selecting useful information from a mass of material. As a result of these various arrangements, value for money of public procurement is now subject to extensive scrutiny, although it seems that the familiar difficulties of combining central standards and departmental accountability still exist.

However, contracting is not simply a matter of obtaining the best value for money. It may also raise issues relating to equality of treatment (in part dealt with by the EU Directives) and other social concerns; democratic rather than financial accountability. This is not so well-developed, and may go some way to explain both why PFI remains an object of suspicion, and the serious problems in defence contracting, where the role of industrial policy is both important and unclear. Should the Coalition implement its 'Big Society' programme, which envisages a greatly increased role for the commissioning of public services from competing providers, the problems of legitimacy are likely to become much more acute.[126]

At the beginning of this chapter, there was reference to Vincent-Jones' conclusion that '[t]he legitimacy deficit in the New Public Contracting consists in the lack of adequate opportunities for public deliberation in policy and decision making on public service issues'.[127] The challenge is now to build mechanisms for such responsiveness that go beyond study of value for money.

126 See HM Government, *Open Public Services White Paper* (Cm 8145, 2011), esp. ch. 5.
127 Vincent-Jones, *The New Public Contracting* (n 16) 347.

10

Conclusion: The Plural Constitution

In Chapter 1, I outlined a variety of different conceptions of an economic constitution, both descriptive and normative. Some, such as ordoliberalism and the new constitutionalism, saw economic constitutions as imposing substantive constraints on government linked to a particular vision of the limits of legitimate state action; others, including my own, adopted a much more open approach treating an economic constitution as providing an institutional framework for economic management and as inspired by process values of communication and deliberation rather than restrictions of substance. It is now time to consider the detailed analysis in the earlier chapters within this context. The first question to be considered will be the extent to which the UK has a constraining economic constitution (at domestic or international levels), followed by discussion of the role of the constitution in providing a framework for inter-institutional relations and a vehicle for deliberation.

The economic constitution as a substantive constraint

Does the economic constitution stifle politics through imposing a particular vision of legitimate economic intervention? It will be recalled from Chapter 1 that the 'new constitutionalists' have suggested that constitutional rules, mainly at a trans-national level, have had the effect of entrenching the position of private capital and the politics of neo-liberalism.[1] This is clearly a hugely important matter; one role of constitutions is to permit governments to get things done, and to implement positive programmes, including regulation of the economy. This has been emphasized in a number of accounts of public law, for example, the 'green light' conception of Harlow and Rawlings, which 'sees in administrative law a vehicle for political progress and welcomes

[1] For the UK, see esp. D. Nicol, *The Constitutional Protection of Capitalism* (Oxford: Hart Publishing, 2010).

the "administrative state"'. This is contrasted with the 'red light' theory in which the 'the primary function of administrative law should be to *control* excesses of state power and, more precisely, subject it to the rule of the law courts'.[2] An emphasis on the positive role of law in promoting public purposes can also be found in the French law of public service, inspired in part by the work of Duguit who saw it as ensuring the uninterrupted provision of activities indispensable to the realization and development of social solidarity.[3] Does the UK economic constitution represent a serious substantive constraint on such policies?

This book has not shown the economic constitution acting as a straitjacket on economic management which does not fit a particular socio-economic model. This is unsurprising in the case of domestic law given the essential openness of the constitutional arrangements, with no entrenched constitutional provisions. However, it is also true at an international level. As suggested in Chapter 1, EU law cannot be seen as an inherently neo-liberal project, but in fact is a mixed one, based on competing values and, indeed, with a number of different forms of underlying economic constitution. The WTO and GATS suffer from serious legitimacy problems but have not so far seriously impeded the implementation of social programmes. The European Convention on Human Rights has had a relatively limited role to play in this area, and one which has been mainly procedural, especially given the considerable deference accorded by the Strasbourg and national courts to states restricting property rights.

This is not to deny that EU law, in particular, is of fundamental importance in the areas of economic management considered in this book, and clearly it may form a constraint on governmental actions. In at least two areas, those of industrial policy and of public procurement, the key constitutional requirements are those of EU law in the form of state aid and procurement rules. However, these rules to a large degree impose procedural rather than substantive constraints, for example in relation to financial aid for the provision of a public service, and tendering for some public contracts. Moreover, there is more flexibility in these rules than is apparent at first sight. This is illustrated most clearly by the fact that they did not prevent a rapid, far-reaching, and costly response by national governments to the 2008 financial crisis. The provisions which come closest to imposing a substantive constraint are those limiting the ability to provide traditional modes of open-ended funding to public corporations; however, this has not prevented a

[2] C. Harlow and R. Rawlings, *Law and Administration*, 3rd edn (Cambridge: Cambridge University Press, 2009), 23, 31 (emphasis retained).

[3] L. Duguit, 'The Law and the State' (1917) XXXI *Harvard Law Review* 1–185.

continued use of other forms of public enterprise, as a look at France will quickly confirm. Nor did it prevent the use of public ownership to save the banks; the failure to use them for other policy purposes was the result of domestic, not European, political choices. It is true, of course, that strong industrial policies based on public ownership and limitations on private capital are off the agenda, but this failure of radicalism is the result of electoral politics, not of a constitutional straitjacket.

What is more apparent than substantive constraints on state action is something more subtle and more interesting; the interpenetration of public and private through, for example, the use of contractual techniques, the Private Finance Initiative, and Local Enterprise Partnerships. This has been well analyzed by governance theory; 'governance refers to the development of governing styles in which boundaries between and within public and private sectors have become blurred'.[4] There is thus an interaction of public and private rather than an imposition of a single substantive constitutional model. The 'new constitutionalism' exaggerates both the coherence of the economic constitution and its binding force. In fact, as we shall see in a moment, limits on the ability of government to get things done and to implement interventionist policies are more likely to be due to the incoherence of institutional arrangements than to the coherence of constitutional constraints.

Balanced budget rules

One subject of current European debate does, however, in principle involve a major substantive constraint on fiscal policies. This is the use of 'balanced budget' rules limiting the ability of governments to fund social and other programmes by borrowing. Readers will need no reminding that this has been a central issue in responses to the sovereign debt crisis in the EU and in the adoption of austerity programmes. As mentioned in Chapter 1, the German Constitution was amended in 2009 to limit the scope for running a deficit after 2016, and Italy also amended its constitution in 2012 to require a balance between revenues and expenditures.[5] Both rules contain exceptions to permit public borrowing with parliamentary approval to respond to the economic cycle and exceptional events. Most importantly, as outlined in Chapter 3, the Treaty on Stability, Coordination and Governance sets out a fiscal compact applying to the members of the eurozone requiring them to

[4] G. Stoker, 'Governance as Theory: Five Propositions' (1998) 50 *International Social Science Journal* 17–28, 17.

[5] Art. 81, amended by the Constitutional Law n. 1/2012. See T. Groppi, 'The Impact of the Financial Crisis on the Italian Written Constitution' (2012) 4 *Italian Journal of Public Law* 1–14.

achieve a balanced budget with a structural deficit not exceeding 0.5 per cent of GDP. The rules are to take effect in national law 'through provisions of binding force and permanent character, preferably constitutional, or otherwise guaranteed to be fully respected and adhered to throughout the national budgetary processes'.[6] By contrast the current UK requirements in the form of the Charter for Budget Responsibility under the Budget Responsibility and National Audit Act 2011 are limited and have little binding force; indeed, the procedural requirements relating to the Office for Budget Responsibility are much more important than the substantive provisions. An earlier attempt to impose substantive budgetary limitations through statute in the Fiscal Responsibility Act 2010 was ridiculed even by the then Chancellor.

In this respect the UK experience represents a much more appropriate approach to fiscal policy than would any more binding form of constitutional balanced budget rule. This is where the 'new constitutionalist' critique has force; such a rule, if it is actually effective, does limit the scope of democratic politics and risk over-judicialization of expenditure decisions. The position in relation to the eurozone is somewhat different; the Treaty forms a condition of a pact which was voluntarily entered into through the political process. It does not seem unreasonable that as part of their commitments members accept constraints which go along with the benefits of membership, however questionable particular austerity policies may be in themselves. To adopt a balanced budget rule as a free-standing constitutional principle rather than as a requirement of eurozone membership is to restrict policy choices in an illegitimate way. However, as noted in Chapter 3, even in the case of the eurozone, there are considerable qualifications to the rules, and the past history of the Stability and Growth Pact has shown that the larger Member States will be able to benefit from flexibility and may in effect be able to opt out. National constitutional rules are also highly qualified and have limitations; for example, the German rule does not cover deficits of the social security system. Thus there is doubt as to how binding the balanced budget rules will actually be.

If balanced budget rules are effective as constraints on governments, they not only exclude legitimate political choices, but encourage bad politics based on bargaining rather than deliberation, often against unrealistic deadlines, and may encourage 'pork-barrel' politics rather than an overview of what is needed to meet a broader public interest. In this context, Habermas has made an important distinction which is well summarized by Sandra Fredman:

[6] Treaty on Stability, Coordination and Governance in the Economic and Monetary Union (2012), art. 3(2).

> Interest governed co-ordination presupposes that each party comes to the bargaining table with fixed interests, the aim being to induce the other party to accept their claim. There is no challenge to the validity of those interests. Success depends on factual power, be it economic, political or collective, rather than the power of reasons. Correspondingly resolution lies in victory, surrender or compromise; but not a change in the parties' perceptions of their own interests. This contrasts with value-oriented or deliberative coordination. Here parties do not come to the table with fixed interests. They enter the process aiming to justify their positions by appeal to reasons that all parties can accept, while at the same time being open to persuasion. Thus, instead of taking preferences as given, deliberative democracy is capable of influencing preference formation itself.[7]

Of course, politics is characterized by both forms of decision-making, and bargaining is an essential element of the process of allocating resources. Nevertheless, allocation of resources under the shadow of a balanced budget rule is likely to be reduced to bargaining on shares rather than more deliberative attempts to assess a broader public interest.

This can be illustrated by experience in the United States which, although it has no federal constitutional balanced budget rule, has had since 1917 a statutory debt ceiling limiting total federal debt. The limit was routinely raised as necessary to meet new annual budgets. However, from 2011 it has created a succession of political crises.[8] The Republicans used the threat of refusal to increase the limit as a weapon in budget negotiation, engaging in 'political brinkmanship' to extract concessions.[9] A deal was reached, but this was to result in automatic spending cuts at the end of 2012 unless fresh deficit reduction legislation was enacted; further last-minute temporary measures extended that deadline into 2013 when the limit was temporarily suspended. In the autumn of 2013 the problems reasserted themselves; further last-minute negotiations resulted once more in a temporary extension of the debt limit, whilst a separate failure to appropriate funds, as a device to force withdrawal or delay of healthcare legislation already passed by Congress, resulted in a government shutdown for over two weeks. Failure to agree on the limit would result in the Federal Government falling off the 'fiscal cliff' and having to default on its obligations, with catastrophic results for the

[7] S. Fredman, 'From Dialogue to Deliberation: Human Rights Adjudication and Prisoners' Rights to Vote' [2013] *Public Law* 292–311, 294–5 (footnote omitted). See also J. Habermas, *Between Facts and Norms* (Cambridge: Polity Press, 1996), 139–41, 166–8.

[8] For details, see N.H. Buchanan and M.C. Dorf, 'How to Choose the Least Unconstitutional Option: Lessons for the President (and Others) from the Debt Ceiling Standoff' (2012) 112 *Columbia Law Review* 1175–1243; 'Nullifying the Debt Ceiling Once and for All: Why the President Should Embrace the Least Unconstitutional Option' (2012) 112 *Columbia Law Review Sidebar* 237–49.

[9] Buchanan and Dorf, 'How to Choose the Least Unconstitutional Option' (n 8) 1187–8.

world economy. Not only did this process raise serious constitutional problems; it created the exact opposite to the stability which such budgetary commitments are supposed to promote. It was the major reason why the US lost its triple A credit rating.

The open nature of the substantive rules of the UK economic constitution strongly reduces the force of the 'new constitutionalist' critique. However, other features have been much less successful, in particular those concerned with institutional coherence and opportunities for deliberation, and I shall now turn to discussion of some of the problems documented in earlier chapters.

The economic constitution and institutional coherence

One theme which has permeated the discussion in this book has been the lack of institutional coherence. Coherence refers both to institutional design which permits a clear allocation of responsibilities and to the ability of institutions to communicate effectively. Of course, this is not a new finding; as the governance literature has emphasized, despite the unitary assumptions of the 'Westminster model' of government responsible to Parliament, in practice '[i]n the modern world of government "what is" is complex, messy, resistant to central direction and in many respects difficult for key policy-makers let alone members of the public to understand'.[10] The same point can be made in relation to regulation, where there is a complex of institutions, sometimes with uncertain relationships between them.[11] Striking examples covered in this book have been the failure of the tripartite system of the Treasury, Bank of England, and the financial services regulator; the lack of a clear relationship between the Treasury and HMRC; the uncertainty about whether public ownership of the banks permits government to use them as means of implementing public policy, and the pervasive fudging of the relationship between defence procurement and industrial policy.

A related point has also been made forcefully by the Public Administration Select Committee in a report on strategic thinking in government.[12] Findings included '*[w]e have little confidence that policies are informed by a clear, coherent*

[10] Stoker, 'Governance as Theory: Five Propositions' (n 4) 19.

[11] See T. Prosser, 'Conclusion: Ten Lessons' in D. Oliver, T. Prosser, and R. Rawlings eds, *The Regulatory State: Constitutional Implications* (Oxford: Oxford University Press, 2010), 306–18.

[12] Public Administration Select Committee, *Strategic Thinking in Government: without National Strategy, can Viable Government Strategy Emerge?* (HC 2010–12, 1625).

strategic approach, informed by an assessment of the public's aspirations and their perceptions of the national interest'; '*[m]inisters and Senior Civil Service are alone in their complacency that cross-departmental working is adequate*'; '*[t]here remains a critical unfulfilled role at the centre of Government in coordinating and reconciling priorities, to ensure that long-term and short-term goals are coherent across departments*'.[13] Constitutional accountability through the Secretary of State to Parliament had locked departments into their own 'silos' preventing thinking across the whole of government.[14] Defence procurement was cited as a particularly striking example of policy incoherence.[15] The report met with a dismissive response from the Government, but the theme of policy incoherence due to institutional incoherence corresponds with the findings of this book.

The lack of institutional coherence is precisely where more developed constitutional thought would be helpful. It is due to inadequate institutional design and an over-reliance on informal networks and on personal relations, for example between the Chancellor and the Governor of the Bank of England. Such networks and relations are particularly vulnerable to breakdown at times of crisis. There are also deeper reasons for the lack of a more coherent set of institutional arrangements and the role of ministerial responsibility as creating institutional 'silos'. These relate to the lack of a developed concept of the state in the UK, as contrasted with the nations of Continental Europe. Dyson thus writes of

> an anthropological conception of government. The hitching of monarchical prerogatives on to parliamentarianism, combined with ministerial responsibility, meant that governments became personified in the 'over-life-size' role of ministers. Powers were conferred by statute on a named person, not on the impersonal state as a corporation, and were exercised in his, not the ministry's, name.[16]

State societies are characterized by 'a stress on the unitary character of the public power'; the UK by 'an anthropomorphic conception of politics and the personalised and private character of the executive'.[17]

Some examples of attempts to provide greater institutional coherence have been identified in this book. The first is, of course, that of the Spending

[13] Public Administration Select Committee, *Strategic Thinking in Government* (n 12) paras 58, 74, 81 (emphasis retained).

[14] Public Administration Select Committee, *Strategic Thinking in Government* (n 12) paras 100–4.

[15] Public Administration Select Committee, *Strategic Thinking in Government* (n 12) para. 34.

[16] K. Dyson, *The State Tradition in Western Europe: A Study of an Idea and Institution*, (Colchester: ECPR, 2009), 40–1 (originally published 1980).

[17] Dyson, *The State Tradition in Western Europe* (n 16) 51–2.

Review process. This does attempt to adopt a more holistic view of government spending and to allocate through a process which goes beyond bilateral bargaining. In this it has had some success, and the process has been paid the compliment of adoption in some other countries, for example in Italy and, in a somewhat different form, France.[18] Indeed, in its earlier form as a Comprehensive Spending Review linked to performance measurement through public service agreements, it was the most developed example in this book of a coordinated approach to the use of resources. The proliferation of targets under New Labour was clearly not the most successful way to improve service delivery, but at least there was a link between performance and resource allocation.

The Spending Review does, however, have its limitations. The Public Administration Committee report on 'Strategic Thinking in Government' found that spending allocation was not linked to strategic aims.[19] To start coordination with spending allocation is to ignore the need for a higher level set of priorities as a basis for such an allocation. Moreover, the analysis of the Spending Review by the Equality and Human Rights Commission discussed in Chapter 5 found that it was weakest in examining the cumulative effects of different measures across government, and that there had been only limited cross-government work carried out in it.[20] Most seriously, as analyzed in detail in Chapter 5, the Spending Review was weak on deliberation; such attempts as were made to secure wider public input were tokenistic and had little effect on the outcome.

Other attempts to secure greater institutional coherence throughout government are also subject to serious limitations. The new arrangements under the Financial Services Act 2012 to replace the Tripartite System do represent an attempt to allocate political and regulatory responsibilities more clearly, with an explicit Treasury role where public funds may be needed, and improved arrangements for communication between different regulatory bodies. However, they are highly complex and will need to be tested in a crisis for any assessment to be made of their effectiveness in practice, and a crisis is precisely where such arrangements are prone to breakdown and to being replaced by reliance on personal relationships, as was proved disastrously in

[18] La revisione delle spese (more usually, 'La spending review'); Loi organique no. 2001/692 relative aux lois de finances du 1 août 2001 (LOLF); La revue générale des politiques publiques (RGPP), now replaced by the Comité interministériel pour la modernisation de l'action publique (CIMAP).

[19] Public Administration Select Committee, *Strategic Thinking in Government* (n 12) para. 110.

[20] Equality and Human Rights Commission, *Making Fair Financial Decisions: An assessment of HM Treasury's 2010 Spending Review conducted under Section 31 of the 2006 Equality Act* (2012).

the 2008 financial crisis. The Heseltine proposals, discussed in Chapter 8, for the development of a strategy for growth and for reform and decentralization of industrial support represent an attempt to develop greater coordination of industrial policy, but the LEPs which will administer funding still raise fundamental questions of the effectiveness and accountability of private bodies with no clear legal structure handling public funds. The mandate of the Monetary Policy Committee of the Bank of England is the most promising development of all, especially as it has been linked to developed transparency requirements for the Committee. However, it may have been successful precisely because the mandate could be narrowly defined and addressed only a limited number of objectives, and will be difficult to apply where there are more complex conflicts of values requiring trade-offs, notably between financial stability and supporting economic growth, and in fiscal policy.

The economic constitution and deliberation

In Chapter 1 constitutions were linked to issues of legitimacy through procedures for deliberation in decision-making; within the concept of deliberation I include accountability through the giving of reasoned justifications for decisions. This is particularly important in the context of the complex institutional patterns described in this book, both in terms of the accountability of institutions to each other (for example, of the Monetary Policy Committee to the Treasury for fulfilment of the remit) and to outside interests.

In the past, it has been common to see accountability for economic management as occurring through ministerial responsibility to Parliament. In its traditional form, ministerial responsibility has been highly non-deliberative through shrouding discussions between civil servants and ministers in secrecy, and in hiding the role of debate behind the fiction of the minister as the anthropomorphic embodiment of the state. The secrecy associated with collective responsibility has also limited open debate about policy formation. The experience, described in Chapter 6, of the setting of interest rates before the establishment of the Monetary Policy Committee showed clearly that accountability through the minister was far less transparent or effective than that of a separate body with a clear mandate and publication duties.

Fortunately, quite apart from the breakdown of traditional notions of ministerial responsibility with the growing willingness to identify named civil servants when things have gone wrong, this book has revealed a much more diversified range of different accountability mechanisms.[21] The core truth to ministerial responsibility, that political decisions require political accountability, has been preserved, for example in the new specification of the role of the Treasury in financial crises set out in the Financial Services Act 2012. The role of select committees has continued to grow, and as all sections of this book have illustrated, they are now the central means of scrutinizing government; particularly striking examples are those of the Public Accounts Committee's work on payment of tax and on defence procurement, and the work of the Treasury Committee on a large number of economic matters including public expenditure, reform of financial services, and the Private Finance Initiative. The work of the committees has done much to replace with concrete institutional scrutiny the empty generalities of ministerial responsibility.

Other institutions have also developed to provide both scrutiny and a form of countervailing power to that of government, power in this sense referring primarily to the production of information. One is the Office for Budget Responsibility with its roles of independent forecasting and of assessing whether the government is on course to meet its financial targets and the underlying sustainability of public finances. Already it has had public conflicts with the Government, and is of great importance as a means of supplementing limited parliamentary scrutiny. Indeed, its role is similar to that of bodies in countries with a more developed economic constitution. Thus in France, projections from the Cour des Comptes have played a central role in the budgetary and Spending Review processes. For example, in its 2012 report on public finances the Cour was outspoken about the need to gain savings.[22] The role of the Cour was strengthened in 2012 with the establishment within it of the Haut Conseil des Finances Publiques, responsible for critically evaluating budget plans and government growth forecasts, as does the Office for Budget Responsibility.[23]

Other countervailing institutions include the Monetary Policy Committee of the Bank of England whose mandate has successfully combined a considerable degree of independence with political accountability through the Treasury Committee, and the plethora of new institutions in the area of financial services regulation; as mentioned earlier, there has been some attempt in the Financial Services Act 2012 to separate out political and

[21] For an important example of the breakdown, see the Transport Committee, 'Cancellation of the InterCity West Coast Franchise Competition' (HC 2012–13, 537).

[22] Cour des Comptes *La situation et les perspectives des finances publiques*, (Cour des Comptes, July 2012).

[23] Loi organique no. 2012-1403 du 17 décembre 2012 relative à la programmation et à la gouvernance des finances publiques, arts 11–22.

regulatory functions more clearly. This reflects a theme which has developed in other areas of regulation; that regulation is an essentially plural activity involving a range of different institutions, with complex relationships between them. They form networks which themselves raise major questions of coordination and accountability.[24] At best, the pattern of institutional development described here may result in a form of deliberation based on dialogue, in which a number of competing versions of the public interest and of economic prospects are made publicly available as a foundation for political and administrative decisions.

Although there has been a greater willingness to recognize economic management as best carried out through a complex of different institutions with competing capacities to produce information, less has been learned from experience of the design of regulatory institutions themselves. In recent years there has been a major growth of interest in both 'smart regulation' and in deliberative forms of regulatory procedure. Moreover, this has resulted in changes in the form of regulatory institutions which have moved away from a highly personalized model with legal powers granted to an individual director general to a model based on regulatory boards permitting a variety of views to shape decisions and debate to take place.[25] Less has been learned from such lessons in the areas covered in this book. Thus the Bank of England remains organized around the 'Sun King' personality of the Governor, despite proposals by the Treasury Select Committee to reduce his dominance, and, as documented in Chapter 5, there has been little attempt to adopt more participative procedures for the Spending Review process. Other areas still reflect the traditions of the old, opaque, forms of ministerial responsibility, for example the ritual of budget secrecy, even on matters which are neither market sensitive nor which may result in pre-emptive avoidance, although in practice considerable consultation now takes place on the detailed development of tax changes.

The plural constitution

It is evident from the discussion in this book that our constitution is a highly plural one. This is true in several senses. It was suggested above that the 'new constitutionalist' approach overestimates the extent to which the constitution is based on a single neo-liberal worldview; instead it has space for a number of

[24] See e.g. T. Prosser, *The Regulatory Enterprise: Government, Regulation and Legitimacy*, (Oxford: Oxford University Press, 2010), 233–5.

[25] See e.g. Prosser, *The Regulatory Enterprise* (n 24) chs 8–9.

different political and ideological approaches. It is plural in the sense that there is now a wide range of different institutions involved in the 'fragmented state' and in drawing up and implementing economic policy. Indeed, this fragmentation has increased since the financial crisis, and has advantages in permitting the testing of different views, whilst being weak on coordination. There is also a plurality of different means of accountability. Thus we have seen here a number of different institutions scrutinizing government; perhaps most important have been the parliamentary select committees, but the EU institutions have also had a major role to play, notably through the scrutiny of state aid. In some areas the courts have been important, though in relation to economic management it has been the EU courts which have assumed the greatest role rather than domestic courts or the European Court of Human Rights. The National Audit Office (NAO) has been a major source of scrutiny in a large number of the areas examined, and has gone far beyond acting as a source of information for the Public Accounts Committee, being an important source in its own right of models for administrative best practice. These multiple structures of accountability are of value in producing countervailing views and sources of information. However, once more there is only limited coordination between them; pluralism means a fragmented rather than a networked constitution.[26] One contrasting constitutional example mentioned in Chapter 1 was that of the German Federal Constitutional Court making the availability of parliamentary scrutiny of revenue and expenditure central to the constitutionality of guarantees for Greece and increased liabilities to the European Stability Mechanism.[27] This mutuality of constitutional and parliamentary scrutiny has no equivalent in the material examined here, precisely because of the absence of any overriding constitutional allocation of responsibilities.

One distinction which has been made over a number of years in the UK is that between a 'political' and a 'legal' constitution.[28] It is most usually made in discussions of the role of judicial review and the protection of individual rights, contrasting different methods for controlling government and identifying shifts towards a greater judicial role. In the areas examined in this book, we should expect to find a predominantly political constitution, with reliance on parliamentary mechanisms rather than the courts for the scrutiny of

[26] I am grateful to my colleague Julian Rivers for this distinction.

[27] Decision of 7 September 2011, BVerfG, 2 BvR 987/10 vom 7.9.2011, paras 104–7, 121–9, 141: Decision of 12 September 2012, BVerf G, 2BvR 13/90 vom 12.9.2012, paras 194–6. I n a different context cf. *A v HM Treasury* [2010] UKSC 2, [2012] 2 AC 534.

[28] For a useful brief survey, see A. Tomkins, 'In Defence of the Political Constitution' (2002) 22 *Oxford Journal of Legal Studies* 157–75. The seminal work was J. Griffith, 'The Political Constitution' (1979) 42 *Modern Law Review* 1–21.

economic management. To an extent this is true; we have found that parliamentary select committees have been a major source of information and accountability, aided by the NAO. However, there has also been a role for the courts. Although the 'Pergau Dam' case[29] did not, as some expected, result in a rapid expansion of judicial review of economic decision-making, there have nevertheless been some continuing examples of judicial intervention on issues of public spending, and of course judicial control has always been extremely well-developed in the tax field, supplemented by the developing principles of non-discrimination under EU law and the European Convention on Human Rights. Whilst a large number of challenges to government have been made using the Human Rights Act, the courts have been cautious in applying the Act to decisions on economic management and it has not created important new substantive constraints based on property rights. As noted earlier in this section, the most far-reaching decisions have been those of the EU courts, notably on competition law, procurement, and state aid; an example is that of the *Altmark* decision on public service compensation.[30] It is thus clear that even in economic management there is a mix between the political and legal constitutions; indeed, it is doubtful whether the distinction, useful as it is in showing trends over time, would make sense in any other constitutional regime where one central role of a constitution is precisely to define the allocation of both political and legal accountability.

This argument can be taken further. Political and legal constitutions do not exhaust the possible constitutional categories. Just as the EU has been characterized by shifting constitutional norms over time, so one can detect a number of different economic constitutions in these pages. Thus alongside the political and legal constitutions, there is an administrative constitution operating through informal and internal rules and controls. This has previously been identified by Daintith and Page as a central constitutional feature of the UK.[31] It is visible here in, for example, the frequent reliance on memoranda of understanding to structure relations, the mandate of the Monetary Policy Committee, and the complex administrative rules relating to tax liability and to procurement. A further example applying across government is that of the regulatory reform programme, for example through the requirement of regulatory impact analysis. This administrative constitution is

[29] *R v Secretary of State for Foreign and Commonwealth Affairs, ex parte The World Development Movement Ltd.* [1995] 1 All ER 611.

[30] Case C-2800/00 *Altmark Trans GmbH* [2003] ECR I-7747.

[31] T. Daintith and A. Page, *The Executive in the Constitution: Structure, Autonomy and Internal Control*, (Oxford: Oxford University Press, 1999), 17–19.

one area where further detailed empirical work is needed, updating that of Daintith and Page.

It is also apparent throughout this book that, alongside the domestic arrangements, there is also a European Constitution shaping key areas, notably those of procurement and state aid. This of course breaks down into the two different regimes of the EU and of the Council of Europe, of which the first is by far the more important. We thus have a plural constitution both in the sense that it accommodates a number of different social and economic values, and that it has a wide range of different institutional structures for its organization and accountability.

There is of course a formal legal hierarchy of these varieties of constitution; however, this book suggests that the reality of relations can be very different from what this suggests.[32] For example, public expenditure planning, currently the most important area of economic management in the UK, has been conducted with no reference to binding legal rules and with little reference to Parliament; the same applies to government borrowing. The sociological hierarchy of normative systems might be very different from what the legal hierarchy suggests, and it is here also that further, more detailed, empirical work will be useful. This constitutional pluralism has its merits; for example, through flexibility and through permitting multiple means of accountability which have the potential to be mutually reinforcing. However, as noted earlier in this section, the constitution is fragmented rather than networked. The price that has to be paid is the absence of any coherent framework allocating constitutional responsibilities, and this has led to collapse in time of crisis and serious problems of communication between different systems for managing the economy and for securing deliberation in, and accountability of, the processes of economic management.

[32] For discussion of a 'disorder of orders' in global terms, see N. Walker, 'Beyond Boundary Disputes and Basic Grids: Mapping the Global Disorder of Normative Orders' (2008) 6 *International Journal of Constitutional Law* 373–96, esp. from 385.

Bibliography

Adenas, M., Gormley, L., Hadjiemmanuil, C., and Harden, I. (eds), *European Economic and Monetary Union: The Institutional Framework* (London: Kluwer, 1997).

Adjudicator's Office, *Annual Report 2012* (2012).

Adlung, R., 'Public Services and the GATS' (2006) 9(2) *Journal of International Economic Law* 455–85.

Alt, J., Preston, I., and Subieta, L., 'The Political Economy of Tax Policy' in J. Mirrlees (ed.), *The Mirrlees Review—Dimensions of Tax Design* (London: Institute for Fiscal Studies, 2010), 1205–79, at: <http://www.ifs.org.uk/mirrleesReview/dimensions>.

Anderson, G., 'Beyond "Constitutionalism Beyond the State"' (2012) 39 *Journal of Law and Society* 359–83.

Arnould, J., 'Secondary Policies in Public Procurement: the Innovations of the New Directives' [2004] *Public Procurement Law Review* 187–97.

Arrowsmith, S., 'Government Contracts and Public Law' (1990) 10 *Legal Studies* 231–44.

Arrowsmith, S., 'Public Procurement as an Instrument of Policy and the Impact of Market Liberalisation' (1995) 111 *Law Quarterly Review* 235–84.

Arrowsmith, S., 'The Way Forward or a Wrong Turning? An Assessment of the European Community Policy on Public Procurement in Light of the Commission's Green Paper' (1997) 3 *European Public Law* 389–411.

Arrowsmith, S., 'The EC Procurement Directives, National Procurement Policies and Better Governance: the Case for a New Approach' (2002) 27 *European Law Review* 3–24.

Arrowsmith, S., 'Transparency in Government Procurement: The Objectives of Regulation and the Boundaries of the World Trade Organisation' (2003) 37 *Journal of World Trade Law* 283–303.

Arrowsmith, S., *The Law of Public and Utilities Procurement*, 3rd edn (London: Sweet and Maxwell, 2013).

Azoulai, L., 'Constitution Economique et Citoyenneté de l'Union Européene' (2011) XXV *Revue Internationale de Droit Economique* 543–57.

Bailey, S.H., 'The Structure, Powers, and Accountability of Local Government' in D. Feldman (ed.), *English Public Law*, 2nd edn (Oxford: Oxford University Press, 2009), 199–240.

Bank of England, *Annual Report 2010* (2010).

Bank of England, *Annual Report 2012* (2012).

Bank of England, *Letter from the Governor to the Chancellor, 13 February 2012* (2012).

Bank of England, *Review of the Bank of England's Framework for Providing Liquidity to the Banking System* (2012).

Bank of England, *The Bank of England, Prudential Regulation Authority: The PRA's Approach to Banking Supervision* (2012).

Bank of England, *The Framework for the Bank of England's Operations in the Sterling Money Markets* (2012).

Bank of England, *Monetary Policy Trade-offs and Forward Guidance* (2013).

Bank of England, *Memorandum of Understanding Between the Financial Conduct Authority and the Prudential Regulation Authority* (nd) at: <http://www.bankofengland.co.uk/about/Documents/mous/moufcapra.pdf>.

Barker, A., 'Political Responsibility for UK Prison Security—Ministers Escape Again' (1998) 76 *Public Administration* 1–23.

Barnard, C. and Odudu, O. (eds), *The Outer Limits of European Union Law* (Oxford: Hart Publishing, 2009).

Barnard, C. and Scott, J. (eds), *The Law of the Single European Market: Unpacking the Premises* (Oxford: Hart Publishing, 2002).

Black, J., 'Proceduralising Regulation' (2000) 20 *Oxford Journal of Legal Studies* 597–614 and (2001) 21 *Oxford Journal of Legal Studies* 33–58.

Black, J., 'The Development of Risk-based Regulation in Financial Services: Just "Modelling Through"?' in J. Black, M. Lodge, and M. Thatcher (eds), *Regulatory Innovation—A Comparative Analysis* (Cheltenham: Edward Elgar, 2005), 156–80.

Black, J., 'The Credit Crisis and the Constitution' in D. Oliver, T. Prosser, and R. Rawlings (eds), *The Regulatory State: Constitutional Implications* (Oxford: Oxford University Press, 2010), 92–128.

Black, J., Lodge, M., and Thatcher, M. (eds), *Regulatory Innovation—A Comparative Analysis* (Cheltenham: Edward Elgar, 2005).

Blackburn, R. and Kennon, A., *Griffith and Ryle on Parliament: Functions, Practice and Procedures*, 2nd edn (London: Sweet and Maxwell, 2003).

Boeger, N. and Prosser, T., 'United Kingdom' in M. Krajewski, U. Neergaard, and J. van de Gronden (eds), *The Changing Legal Framework for Services of General Interest in Europe* (The Hague: T.M.C. Asser Press, 2009), 357–82.

Bowler, T., *Tax Policymaking in the UK*, Institute for Fiscal Studies Tax Law Review Committee Discussion Paper No. 8 (2010).

Braithwaite, J., *Regulatory Capitalism: How it Works, Ideas for Making it Work Better* (Cheltenham: Edward Elgar, 2008).

Brazier, A. and Ram, V., *The Fiscal Maze: Parliament, Government and Public Money* (London: Hansard Society, 2006).

Brown, N. and Bell, J., *French Administrative Law*, 5th edn (Oxford: Oxford University Press, 1998).

Buchanan, J.M., 'The Constitution of Economic Policy' (1987) 77 *The American Economic Review* 243–50, 243.

Buchanan, J.M. and Tullock, G., *The Calculus of Consent: Logical Foundations of Constitutional Democracy* (Ann Arbor: University of Michigan Press, 1962).

Buchanan, N.H. and Dorf, M.C., 'How to Choose the Least Unconstitutional Option: Lessons for the President (and Others) from the Debt Ceiling Standoff' (2012) 112 *Columbia Law Review* 1175–1243.

Buchanan, N.H. and Dorf, M.C., 'Nullifying the Debt Ceiling Once and for All: Why the President Should Embrace the Least Unconstitutional Option' (2012) 112 *Columbia Law Review Sidebar* 237–49.

Buiter, W.H., 'Alice in Euroland' (1999) 37 *Journal of Common Market Studies* 181–209.

Business, Innovation and Skills Committee, *Government Assistance to Industry* (HC 2010–11, 561).

Business, Innovation and Skills Committee, *Government Assistance to Industry: Government Response to the Committee's Third Report of Session 2010–11* (HC 2010–11, 1038).

Business, Innovation and Skills Committee, *The New Local Enterprise Partnerships: An Initial Assessment* (HC 2010–11, 434).

Cabinet Office, *Executive Agencies: A Guide for Departments* (2006).

Cabinet Office, *HM Revenue & Customs: Progress and Next Steps* (2009).

Cabinet Office, *Efficiency Review by Sir Philip Green: Key Findings and Recommendations* (2010).

Cabinet Office, *Policy and Standards Framework—Best Practice Guidance* at: <https://www.gov.uk/government/publications/policy-and-standards-framework-best-practice-guidance>.

Caranta, R., Andenas, M., and Fairgrieve, D. (eds), *Independent Administrative Authorities* (London: British Institute of International and Comparative Law, 2004).

Cass, D., *The Constitutionalization of the World Trade Organization: Legitimacy, Democracy and Community in the International Trading System* (Oxford: Oxford University Press, 2005).

Cassese, S., 'Administrative Law Without the State? The Challenge of Global Regulation' (2005) 37 *New York University Journal of International Law and Politics* 663–94.

Cassese, S., *La Nuova Costituzione Economica*, 5th edn (Rome: Editori Laterza, 2012).

Centre for Economic Policy Research, *Independent and Accountable: A New Mandate for the Bank of England* (London: Centre for Economic Policy Research, 1993).

Cominetti, N., Crowley, L., and Lee, N., *The Business of Cities: The Private Sector, Local Enterprise Partnerships and Growth* (London: Work Foundation, 2012).

Committee on Monetary Policy Committee of the Bank of England, *Monetary Policy Committee of the Bank of England* (HL 1998–99, 96).

Committee on Monetary Policy Committee of the Bank of England, *Monetary Policy Committee of the Bank of England* (HL 2000–01, 34).

Committee Office Scrutiny Unit, *Financial Scrutiny Uncovered: How the Government Manages its Finances and how Parliament Scrutinises them* (House of Commons, 2007).

Cour des Comptes *La situation et les perspectives des finances publiques* (Cour des Comptes, July 2012).

Craig, P., 'The Human Rights Act, Article 6 and Procedural Rights' [2003] *Public Law* 753–73.

Craig, P., *Administrative Law*, 7th edn (London: Sweet and Maxwell, 2012), 86–91, 104–6.

Craig, P., 'The Stability, Coordination and Governance Treaty: Principle, Politics and Pragmatism' (2012) 37 *European Law Review* 231–48.

Cruz, J. Baquero, *Between Competition and Free Movement: The Economic Constitutional Law of the European Community* (Oxford: Hart Publishing, 2002).

Daintith, T., 'Between Domestic Democracy and an Alien Rule of Law? Some Thoughts on the "Independence" of the Bank of England' [1995] *Public Law* 118–32.

Daintith, T. and Page, A., *The Executive in the Constitution: Structure, Autonomy and Internal Control* (Oxford: Oxford University Press, 1999).

Daintith, T.C., 'Regulation by Contract: The New Prerogative' [1979] 32 *Current Legal Problems* 41–64.

Daintith, T.C., 'Legal Analysis of Economic Policy' (1982) 9 *Journal of Law and Society* 191–224.

Daintith, T.C.,'Regulation' in International Association of Legal Science, *International Encyclopedia of Comparative Law* (Dordrecht: Martinus Nijhoff Publishers, 1997), vol. XVII, ch. 10.

Darling, A., *Back from the Brink: 1,000 Days at Number 11* (London: Atlantic Books, 2011).

Davies, A.C.L., *Accountability: A Public Law Analysis of Government by Contract* (Oxford: Oxford University Press, 2001).

de Schutter, O. and Lenoble, J. (eds), *Reflexive Governance: Redefining the Public Interest in a Pluralistic World* (Oxford: Hart Publishing, 2010).

Defence Committee, *Defence Acquisition* (HC 2012–13, 9).

Department for Business, Innovation & Skills, *Local Growth: Realising Every Place's Potential* (Cm 7961, 2010).

Department for Business, Innovation & Skills, *Reducing the Impact of Regulation on Business* (2012) at: <https://www.gov.uk/government/policies/reducing-the-impact-of-regulation-on-business>.

Department for Business, Innovation & Skills, *Government Response to the Heseltine Review* (Cm 8587, 2013).

Department for Work and Pensions, *Universal Credit: Welfare that Works* (Cm 7957, 2010).

Department of Trade and Industry, *Liberalising Trade in Services: A New Consultation on the World Trade Organisation GATS Negotiations* (2002).

Dickens, C., *Little Dorrit* (Harmondsworth: Penguin, 1998, originally published 1857).

Drexl, J., 'La constitution économique européenne—l'actualité du modèle ordolibéral' (2011) XXV *Revue Internationale de Droit Economique* 419–54.

Duguit, L., 'The Law and the State' (1917) XXXI *Harvard Law Review* 1–185.
Dyson, K., *The State Tradition in Western Europe: A Study of an Idea and Institution* (Colchester: ECPR, 2009, originally published 1980).
Economic Affairs Committee, *Monetary and Fiscal Policy: Present Successes and Future Problems* (HL 2003–04, 176).
Economic Affairs Committee, *The Finance Bill 2008* (HL 2007–08, 117).
Economic Affairs Committee, *The Finance Bill 2009* (HL 2008–09, 113).
Economic Affairs Committee, *Private Finance Projects and Off-balance Sheet Debt* (HL 2009–10, 63).
Economic Affairs Committee, *The Finance Bill 2011* (HL 2010–12, 158).
Economic Affairs Committee, *Tackling Corporate Tax Avoidance in a Global Economy: is a New Approach Needed?* (HL 2013–14, 48).
Eeckhout, P., 'The Scales of Trade—Reflections on the Growth and Functions of the WTO Adjudicative Branch' (2010) 13(1) *Journal of International Economic Law* 3–26.
Ehlermann, C-D. and Goyette, M., 'The Interface between EU State Aid Control and the WTO Disciplines on Subsidies' [2006] *European State Aid Quarterly* 695–718.
Ehring, L., 'Public Access to Dispute Settlement Hearings in the World Trade Organisation' (2008) 11 *Journal of International Economic Law* 1021–34.
Equality and Human Rights Commission, *Making Fair Financial Decisions: An Assessment of HM Treasury's 2010 Spending Review Conducted under Section 31 of the 2006 Equality Act* (2012).
Erskine May, T., *Erskine May's Treatise on the Law, Privileges, Proceedings and Usage of Parliament*, 24th edn (London: LexisNexis, 2011).
European Central Bank, 'The Accountability of the ECB', *ECB Monthly Bulletin*, (November 2002), 45–57.
European Commission, *The High Level Group on Financial Supervision in the EU Chaired by Jacques de Larosière* (the de Larosière Report) (2009).
European Commission, *Buying Social: A Guide to Taking Account of Social Considerations in Public Procurement* (2010).
European Commission, *Public Consultation on Credit Rating Agencies* (5 November 2010).
European Commission, *Proposal for a Directive of the European Parliament and of the Council on Public Procurement*, COM(2011) 896 final.
European Commission, *Proposal for a Directive of the European Parliament and of the Council on the Award of Concession Contracts*, COM(2011) 897 final.
European Commission, *Proposal for a Council Regulation Conferring Specific Tasks on the European Central Bank*, COM(2012) 511 final.
European Defence Agency, *Code of Conduct on Defence Procurement of EU Member States Participating in the European Defence Agency* (2005).
European Union Committee, *The Euro Area Crisis* (HL 2010–12, 260).
Fahey, E., 'Does the Emperor Have Financial Crisis Clothes? Reflexions on the Legal Basis of the European Banking Authority' (2011) 74 *Modern Law Review* 581–95.

Fawcett, P., 'Metagovernance and the Treasury's Evolving Role within the British Core Executive, 1997–2007' (2010) at: <http://www.researchgate.net/publication/228538229_Metagovernance_and_the_Treasury's_Evolving_Role_within_the_British_Core_Executive_1997-2007?ev=sim_pub>.

Ferran, E., 'The Break-up of the Financial Services Authority' (2011) 31 *Oxford Journal of Legal Studies* 455–80.

Ferran, E., 'Understanding the New Institutional Architecture of EU Financial Market Supervision' in E. Wymeersch, K.J. Hopt, and G. Ferrarini, *Financial Regulation and Supervision: A Post-Crisis Analysis* (Oxford: Oxford University Press, 2012), ch. 5.

Ferran, E. and Alexander, K., 'Can Soft Law Bodies be Effective? The Special Case of the European Systemic Risk Board' (2010) 35 *European Law Review* 751–76.

Ferran, E. and Goodhart, C. (eds), *Regulating Financial Services and Markets in the 21st Century* (Oxford: Hart Publishing, 2001).

Feldman, D. (ed.), *English Public Law*, 2nd edn (Oxford: Oxford University Press, 2009).

Financial Services Authority, *The FSA's Risk-Based Approach* (2006).

Financial Services Authority, *Principles-based Regulation—Focusing on the Outcomes that Matter* (2007).

Financial Services Authority, *The Supervision of Northern Rock: A Lessons Learned Review* (2008).

Financial Services Authority, *The Turner Review: a Regulatory Response to the Global Banking Crisis* (2009).

Financial Services Authority, *The Failure of the Royal Bank of Scotland* (2011).

Financial Services Authority, *The Financial Conduct Authority: Approach to Regulation* (2011).

Financial Services Authority, *Journey to the Financial Conduct Authority* (2012).

Fredman, S., 'From Dialogue to Deliberation: Human Rights Adjudication and Prisoners' Rights to Vote' [2013] *Public Law* 292–311.

Freedland, M., 'Government by Contract and Private Law' [1994] *Public Law* 86–104.

Gerber, D., 'Constitutionalizing the Economy: German Neo-liberalism, Competition Law and the "New" Europe' (1994) 42 *American Journal of Comparative Law* 25–84.

Gerber, D., *Law and Competition in Twentieth Century Europe: Protecting Prometheus* (Oxford: Clarendon Press, 1998).

Gill, S., 'New Constitutionalism, Democratisation and Global Political Economy' in R. Wilkinson (ed.), *The Global Governance Reader* (London: Routledge, 2005), 174–86.

Graham, C. and Prosser, T. (eds), *Waiving the Rules: The Constitution Under Thatcherism* (Milton Keynes: Open University Press, 1988).

Griffith, J., 'The Political Constitution' (1979) 42 *Modern Law Review* 1–21.

Griller, S. and Orator, A., 'Everything Under Control? The "Way Forward" for European Agencies in the Footsteps of the *Meroni* Decision' (2010) 35 *European Law Review* 3–35.

Groppi, T., 'The Impact of the Financial Crisis on the Italian Written Constitution' (2012) 4 *Italian Journal of Public Law* 1–14.

Habermas, J., *Between Facts and Norms* (Cambridge: Polity Press, 1996).

Harden, I., 'Corporatism Without Labour: the British Version' in C. Graham and T. Prosser (eds), *Waiving the Rules: The Constitution Under Thatcherism* (Milton Keynes: Open University Press, 1988).

Harden, I., *The Contracting State* (Buckingham: Open University Press, 1992).

Harden, I. and Lewis, N., *The Noble Lie: The British Constitution and the Rule of Law* (London: Hutchinson, 1986).

Harden, I., White, F., and Hollingsworth, K., 'Value for Money and Administrative Law' [1996] *Public Law* 661–81.

Harlow, C., *Accountability in the European Union* (Oxford: Oxford University Press, 2002).

Harlow, C. and Rawlings, R., 'Promoting Accountability in Multilevel Governance: A Network Approach' (2007) 13 *European Law Journal* 542–62.

Harlow, C. and Rawlings, R., *Law and Administration*, 3rd edn (Cambridge: Cambridge University Press, 2009).

Hawkins, K., *Law as Last Resort: Prosecution Decision-Making in a Regulatory Agency* (Oxford: Oxford University Press, 2002).

Hayek, F.A., *The Constitution of Liberty* (London: Routledge and Kegan Paul, 1960).

Heseltine of Thenford CH, Lord, *No Stone Unturned in Pursuit of Growth* (Department for Business Innovation and Skills, 2012).

HM Government, *Securing Britain in an Age of Uncertainty: The Strategic Defence and Security Review* (Cm 7498, 2010).

HM Government, *Europe 2020: UK National Reform Programme 2011* (2011).

HM Government, *Open Public Services White Paper* (Cm 8145, 2011).

HM Revenue & Customs, *Business Plan 2012–2015* (2012) at: <https://www.gov.uk/government/uploads/system/uploads/attachment_data/file/89203/2012-business-plan.pdf>.

HM Revenue & Customs, *Departmental Report 2011–12* (HC 2012–13, 38).

HM Revenue & Customs, *Your Charter* (nd) at: <http://www.hmrc.gov.uk/charter/charter.pdf>.

HM Treasury, *Report of the Committee (Plowden) on the Control of Public Expenditure,* (Cmnd 1432, 1961).

HM Treasury, *A Code for Fiscal Stability* (1998).

HM Treasury, *Stability and Investment for the Long Term: Economic and Fiscal Strategy Report 1998* (Cm 3978, 1998).

HM Treasury, *Public Services for the Future: Modernisation, Reform, Accountability—Comprehensive Spending Review: Public Service Agreements 1999–2002* (Cm 4181, 1998).

HM Treasury *Review of Civil Procurement in Central Government* (1999).

HM Treasury *Financing Britain's Future—Review of the Revenue Departments* (Cm 6164, 2004).

HM Treasury *United Kingdom Debt Management Office: Executive Agency Framework Document*, (2005) at: <http://www.dmo.gov.uk/documentview.aspx?docname= publications/corpgovernance/fwork040405.pdf&page=>.

HM Treasury, *Managing Public Money* (2007), available at: <https://www.gov.uk/ government/uploads/system/uploads/attachment_data/file/179695/mpm_whole. pdf.pdf>.

HM Treasury, *Transforming Government Procurement* (2007).

HM Treasury, *Annual Report and Accounts 2008–09* (HC 2008–09, 611).

HM Treasury, *Alignment (Clear Line of Sight) Project* (Cm 7567, 2009).

HM Treasury, *NS&I Framework Document* (2009) at: <http://www.nsandi.com/ files/asset/pdf/framework_document.pdf>.

HM Treasury, *The Spending Review Framework* (Cm 7872, 2010).

HM Treasury, *A New Approach to Financial Regulation: Judgement, Focus and Stability* (Cm 7874, 2010).

HM Treasury, *Spending Review 2010* (Cm 7942, 2010).

HM Treasury, *Budget 2010* (HC 2010–11, 61).

HM Treasury, *Charter for Budget Responsibility* (2011).

HM Treasury, *GARR Study: Report by Graham Aaronson QC* (2011).

HM Treasury *A New Approach to Financial Regulation: Building a Stronger System* (Cm 8012, 2011).

HM Treasury, *A New Approach to Financial Regulation: The Blueprint for Reform* (Cm 8083, 2011).

HM Treasury, *A New Approach to Public Private Partnerships* (2012).

HM Treasury, *Business Plan 2012–2015* (2012) at: <https://www.gov.uk/govern ment/publications/hm-treasury-business-plan-2012-to-2015>.

HM Treasury, *Improving Spending Control* (2012).

HM Treasury, *Remit for HM Revenue & Customs 2012–13* (2012) at: <http:// webarchive.nationalarchives.gov.uk/+/http://www.hmrc.gov.uk/news/cx-remit-letter. pdf>.

HM Treasury, *Review of HM Treasury's Management Response to the Financial Crisis* (2012).

HM Treasury, *The Funding for Lending Scheme* (2012).

HM Treasury, *Annual Report and Accounts 2012–13* (HC 2012–13, 34).

HM Treasury and Bank of England, *MOU on Financial Crisis Management* (nd) at: <http://www.bankofengland.co.uk/about/Documents/mous/moufincrisis.pdf>.

HM Treasury and HM Revenue & Customs, *Tax Policy Making: a New Approach* (June 2010).

HM Treasury and HM Revenue & Customs, *The Government's Tax Consultation Framework: Summary of Responses and Finalised Framework* (2011).

HM Treasury and the Prime Minister's Office of Public Services Reform, *Better Government Services: Executive Agencies in the 21st Century* (2002).

HM Treasury, the Bank of England, and the Financial Services Authority, *Memorandum of Understanding Between HM Treasury, the Bank of England and the Financial*

Services Authority (2006) at: <http://www.bankofengland.co.uk/financialstability/mou.pdf>.

Home Affairs Committee, *UK Border Controls* (HC 2010–12, 1647).

House of Commons Library, Research Paper 05/92, *The Centre of Government-No 10, the Cabinet Office and HM Treasury* (2005).

Humpherson, E., 'Auditing Regulatory Reform' in D. Oliver, T. Prosser, and R. Rawlings, *The Regulatory State: Constitutional Implications* (Oxford: Oxford University Press, 2010), 267–82.

Independent Budget Review Panel, *Independent Budget Review 2010* (2010).

Independent Commission on Banking, *Final Report Recommendations* (2011).

Institute for Fiscal Studies, *The Mirrlees Review: Reforming the Tax System for the 21st Century* (2011) at: <http://www.ifs.org.uk/mirrleesReview>.

Institute for Fiscal Studies, *The 2015–16 Spending Round* (2013) at: <http://www.ifs.org.uk/projects/418>.

International Accounting Standards Board, *Due Process Handbook* (2008, updated 2013) at: <http://www.ifrs.org/DPOC/Documents/2013/Due-Process-Handbook-February-2013.pdf>.

James, O., 'The UK Executive's Use of Public Service Agreements as a Tool of Governance' (2004) 82 *Public Administration* 397–419.

Joerges, C., 'What is Left of the European Economic Constitution? A Melancholic Euology' (2005) 30 *European Law Review* 461–89.

Joerges, C., and Petersmann, E. (eds), *Constitutionalism, Multilevel Trade Governance and International Economic Law* (Oxford: Hart Publishing, 2011).

Joint Committee on the Draft Financial Services Bill, *Draft Financial Services Bill* (2010–12, HL 236, HC 1447).

Jones, A. and Sufrin, B., *EU Competition Law*, 4th edn (Oxford: Oxford University Press, 2011).

Jowell, J. and Oliver, D. (eds), *The Changing Constitution*, 7th edn (Oxford: Oxford University Press, 2011).

King, J.A., 'The Justiciability of Resource Allocation' (2007) 70(2) *Modern Law Review* 197–224.

Kingsbury, B., Krisch, N., and Stewart, R.B., 'The Emergence of Global Administrative Law' (2005) 68 *Law and Contemporary Problems* 15–61.

Kingston, S., 'A Light in the Darkness: Recent Developments in the ECJ's Direct Tax Jurisprudence' (2007) 44 *Common Market Law Review* 1321–59.

Koutrakos, P., 'The Application of EC Law to Defence Industries—Changing Interpretations of Article 296 EC' in C. Barnard and O. Odudu (eds), *The Outer Limits of European Union Law* (Oxford: Hart Publishing, 2009).

Krajewski, M., 'Public Services and Trade Liberalization: Mapping the Legal Framework' (2003) 6 *Journal of International Economic Law* 341–67.

Krajewski, M., Neergaard, U., and van de Gronden, J. (eds), *The Changing Legal Framework for Services of General Interest in Europe: Between Competition and Solidarity* (The Hague: T.M.C. Asser Press, 2009).

Kroes, N., 'Competition Policy and the Crisis—the Commission's Approach to Banking and Beyond' (2010) 10 *Competition Policy Newsletter* 3–6.

Lavrijessen, S. and Hancher, L., 'Networks on Track: From European Regulatory Networks to European Regulatory "Network" Agencies' (2009) 36 *Legal Issues of European Integration* 23–55.

Leigh, I., 'The Changing Nature of Local and Regional Democracy' in J. Jowell and D. Oliver (eds), *The Changing* Constitution, 7th edn (Oxford: Oxford University Press, 2011), 237–59.

Lenoble, J. and Maesschalck, M., 'Reviewing the Theory of Public Interest: The Quest for a Reflexive and Learning-based Approach to Governance' in O. de Schutter and J. Lenoble (eds), *Reflexive Governance: Redefining the Public Interest in a Pluralistic World* (Oxford: Hart Publishing, 2010), 3–21.

Liaison Committee, *Parliament and Government Finance: Recreating Financial Scrutiny* (HC 2007–08, 426).

Liaison Committee, *Parliament and Government Finance: Recreating Financial Scrutiny: Government and National Audit Office Responses to the Committee's Second Report of Session 2007–08* (HC 2007–08, 1108).

Liaison Committee, *Financial Scrutiny: Parliamentary Control over Government Budgets* (HC 2008–09, 804).

Loughlin, M., *Legality and Locality: The Role of Law in Central-Local Government Relations* (Oxford: Clarendon Press, 1996).

Macneil, I., *The New Social Contract* (New Haven: Yale University Press, 1980).

Maduro, M. Poiares, *We the Court: The European Court of Justice and the European Economic Constitution* (Oxford: Hart Publishing, 1998).

Marsden, P. and Kokkoris, I., 'The Role of Competition and State Aid Policy in Financial and Monetary Law' (2010) 13 *Journal of International Economic Law*, 875–92.

McCrudden, C., *Buying Social Justice: Equality, Government Procurement and Legal Change* (Oxford: Oxford University Press, 2007).

McDermont, M., *Governing, Independence and Expertise: The Business of Housing Associations* (Oxford: Hart Publishing, 2010).

McEldowney, J., 'Public Expenditure and the Control of Public Finance' in J. Jowell and D. Oliver, *The Changing Constitution*, 7th edn (Oxford: Oxford University Press, 2011), 334–64.

McHarg, A., 'Devolution and the Regulatory State: Constraints and Opportunities' in D. Oliver, T. Prosser, and R. Rawlings, *The Regulatory State: Constitutional Implications* (Oxford: Oxford University Press, 2010), 67–91.

Ministry of Defence, Policy Paper 5, *Defence Industrial Policy* (2002).

Ministry of Defence, *Defence Industrial Strategy: Defence White Paper* (Cm 6697, 2005).

Ministry of Defence, *Review of Single Source Pricing Regulations* (2011).

Ministry of Defence, *National Security Through Technology: Technology, Equipment, and Support for UK Defence and Security* (Cm 8278, 2012).

Ministry of Defence, *Better Defence Acquisition* (Cm 8626, 2013).

Moran, M., 'Monetary Policy and the Machinery of Government' (1981) 59 *Public Administration* 47–61.

Moran, M., 'Politics and Law in Financial Regulation' in C. Graham and T. Prosser (eds), *Waiving the Rules: The Constitution Under Thatcherism* (Milton Keynes: Open University Press, 1988), 56–72.

Mullen T. and Prosser, T., 'Financing and Auditing Scottish Government: The Public Finance and Accountability (Scotland) Act 2000' (2001) 7 *European Public Law* 157–64.

National Audit Office, *The Refinancing of the Fazakerley PFI Prison Contract* (HC 1999–2000, 584).

National Audit Office, *Major Projects Report 1999* (HC 1999–2000, 6130).

National Audit Office, *The Re-negotiation of the PFI-type deal for the Royal Armouries Museum in Leeds* (HC 2000–01, 103).

National Audit Office, *Major Projects Report 2003* (HC 2003–04, 195).

National Audit Office, *Improving the PFI Tendering Process* (HC 2006–07, 149).

National Audit Office, *The Shareholder Executive and Public Sector Businesses* (HC 2006–07, 255).

National Audit Office, *The NAO's Work on HM Revenue & Customs: A Short Guide* (National Audit Office, 2010).

National Audit Office, *Progress in Improving Financial Management in Government* (HC 2010–11, 487).

National Audit Office, *Lessons from PFI and Other Projects* (HC 2010–12, 920).

National Audit Office, *The Major Projects Report 2011* (HC 2010–12, 1520).

National Audit Office, *A Summary of the NAO's Work on HM Revenue & Customs* (National Audit Office, 2012).

National Audit Office, *The Regional Growth Fund* (HC 2012–13, 17).

National Audit Office, *The Creation and Sale of Northern Rock plc* (HC 2012–13, 20).

National Audit Office, *The Major Projects Report 2012* (HC 2012–13, 684).

National Audit Office, *HM Revenue & Customs: Customer Service Performance* (HC 2012–13, 795).

National Audit Office, *Improving Government Procurement* (HC 2012–13, 996).

National Audit Office, *Successful Commissioning Toolkit* at: <http://www.nao.org.uk/report/successful-commissioning-toolkit/>.

National Audit Office, *What is a Value for Money Study?* at: <http://www.nao.org.uk/about-us/role-2/what-we-do/value-for-money-programme/what-is-a-value-for-money-study/>.

Nicol, D., *The Constitutional Protection of Capitalism* (Oxford: Hart Publishing, 2010).

Office for Budget Responsibility, *Fiscal Sustainability Report 2012* (2012).

Office for National Statistics, *Public Sector Interventions in the Financial Crisis—Statistical Classification Decisions* (2009).

Office for National Statistics, *Statistical Bulletin: Public Sector Finances* (2013).

Oliver, D., Prosser, T., and Rawlings, R. (eds), *The Regulatory State: Constitutional Implications* (Oxford: Oxford University Press, 2010).

Organisation for Economic Co-operation and Development, *The OECD Report on Regulatory Reform: Synthesis* (Paris: OECD, 1997).
Organisation for Economic Co-operation and Development, *OECD Guiding Principles for Regulatory Quality and Performance* (Paris: OECD, 2005).
Organisation for Economic Co-operation and Development, *Recommendation of the Council on Regulatory Policy and Governance* (Paris: OECD, 2012).
Page, A., 'Regulating the Regulator—A Lawyer's Perspective on Accountability and Control' in E. Ferran and C. Goodhart (eds), *Regulating Financial Services and Markets in the 21st Century* (Oxford: Hart Publishing, 2001), 127–49.
Pallemaerts, M., 'La Constitution Economique Européene et le "Développement Durable de l'Europe"' (2011) XXV *Revue Internationale de Droit Economique* 511–41.
Palmeter, D. and Movroidis, P.C., *Dispute Settlement in the World Trade Organization*, 2nd edn (Cambridge: Cambridge University Press, 2004).
Parker, C. and Braithwaite, J. 'Regulation', in P. Cane and M. Tushnet (eds), *Oxford Handbook of Legal Studies* (Oxford: Oxford University Press, 2003).
Parliamentary and Health Service Ombudsman, *Tax Credits: Putting Things Right* (HC 2005–06, 124).
Parliamentary and Health Service Ombudsman, *A Service for Everyone: Annual Report 2010–11* (HC 2010–12, 1404).
Parliamentary Commission on Banking Standards, *Changing Banking for Good; Summary and Conclusions and Recommendations* (2013–14, HL 27-I, HC 175-I).
Parliamentary Commission on Banking Standards, *Changing Banking for Good* (2013–14, HL 27-II, HC 175-II).
Parliamentary Commission on Banking Standards, *Changing Banking for Good: Oral Evidence* (2013–14, HL 27-III, HC 175-III).
Petersmann, E., 'Multilevel Trade Governance in the WTO Requires Multilevel Constitutionalism' in C. Joerges and E. Petersmann (eds), *Constitutionalism, Multilevel Trade Governance and International Economic Law* (Oxford: Hart Publishing, 2011), 5–57.
Piewitt, M., 'Participatory Governance in the WTO: How Inclusive Is Global Civil Society?' (2010) 44 *Journal of World Trade* 467–88.
Prosser, T., *Nationalised Industries and Public Control* (Oxford: Basil Blackwell, 1986).
Prosser, T., *Law and the Regulators* (Oxford: Oxford University Press, 1997).
Prosser, T., *The Limits of Competition Law: Markets and Public Services* (Oxford: Oxford University Press, 2005).
Prosser, T., 'The Place of Appeals in Regulation: Continuity and Change' in P. Vass (ed.), *Regulatory Review 2004/5* (Centre for the Study of Regulated Industries, 2005), 195–212.
Prosser, T., 'The Powers and Accountability of Agencies and Regulators' in D. Feldman (ed.), *English Public Law*, 2nd edn (Oxford: Oxford University Press, 2009), 241–80.
Prosser, T., 'Conclusion: Ten Lessons' in D. Oliver, T. Prosser, and R. Rawlings (eds), *The Regulatory State: Constitutional Implications* (Oxford: Oxford University Press, 2010), 306–18.

Prosser, T., *The Regulatory Enterprise: Government, Regulation and Legitimacy* (Oxford: Oxford University Press, 2010).

Prosser, T., '"An Opportunity to Take a More Fundamental Look at the Role of Government in Society": The Spending Review as Regulation' [2011] *Public Law* 596–610.

Public Accounts Committee, *Getting Better Value for Money from the Private Finance Initiative* (HC 1998–99, 583).

Public Accounts Committee, *The Shareholder Executive and Public Sector Businesses* (HC 2006–07, 409).

Public Accounts Committee, *HM Treasury: Tendering and Benchmarking in PFI* (HC 2006–07, 754).

Public Accounts Committee, *The Privatisation of QinetiQ* (HC 2007–08, 151).

Public Accounts Committee, *Managing Financial Resources to Deliver Better Public Services* (HC 2007–08, 519).

Public Accounts Committee, *Maintaining Financial Stability Across the UK Banking System* (HC 2009–10, 190).

Public Accounts Committee, *Ministry of Defence: Major Projects Report 2009* (HC 2009–10, 338).

Public Accounts Committee, *The Sale of the Government's Interest in British Energy* (HC 2009–10, 356).

Public Accounts Committee, *Managing the Defence Budget and Estate* (HC 2010–11, 503).

Public Accounts Committee, *PFI in Housing and Hospitals* (HC 2010–11, 631).

Public Accounts Committee, *The Major Projects Report 2010* (HC 2010–11, 687).

Public Accounts Committee, *Management of the Typhoon Project* (HC 2010–12, 860).

Public Accounts Committee, *Lessons from PFI and Other Projects* (HC 2010–12, 1201).

Public Accounts Committee, *HM Revenue & Customs 2010–11 Accounts: Tax Disputes* (HC 2010–12, 1531).

Public Accounts Committee, *Ministry of Defence: The Major Projects Report 2011* (HC 2010–12, 1678).

Public Accounts Committee, *Reducing Costs in the Department for Transport* (HC 2010–12, 1760).

Public Accounts Committee, *Implementing the Transparency Agenda* (HC 2012–13, 102).

Public Accounts Committee, *HM Treasury: Annual Reports and Accounts 2011–12* (HC 2012–13, 659).

Public Accounts Committee, *HM Revenue & Customs: Annual Report and Accounts 2011–12* (HC 2012–13, 716).

Public Accounts Committee, *Carrier Strike: The 2012 Reversion Decision* (HC 2013–14, 113).

Public Administration Committee, *On Target? Government by Measurement*, (HC 2002–03, 62).

Public Administration Committee, *Government and IT—'a Recipe for Rip-offs': Time for a New Approach* (HC 2010–12, 715).

Public Administration Committee, *Strategic Thinking in Government; Without National Strategy, Can Viable Government Strategy Emerge?* (HC 2010–12, 1625).

Public Administration Committee, *Government and IT—'a Recipe for Rip-offs': Time for a New Approach: Further Report with the Government Response* (HC 2010–12, 1724).

Quigley, C., *European State Aid Law and Policy*, 2nd edn (Oxford: Hart Publishing, 2009).

Rawlings, R., 'Changed Conditions, Old Truths: Judicial Review in a Regulatory Laboratory' in D. Oliver, T.Prosser, and R. Rawlings (eds), *The Regulatory State: Constitutional Implications* (Oxford: Oxford University Press, 2010), 283–305.

Reich, A., 'Legislative Comment: the New Text of the Agreement on Government Procurement: an Analysis and Assessment' (2009) 12(4) *Journal of International Economic Law* 989–1022.

Review Board for Government Contracts, *Report on the 2012 Annual Review of the Profit Formula for Non-Competitive Government Contracts* (2012).

Rhodes, R., *Beyond Westminster and Whitehall* (London: Unwin Hyman, 1988).

Rhodes, R., *Understanding Governance: Policy Networks, Governance, Reflexivity and Accountability* (Buckingham: Open University Press, 1997).

Richardson, A.J. and Eberlein, B., 'Legitimating Transnational Standard-Setting: the Case of the International Accounting Standards Board' (2011) 98 *Journal of Business Ethics* 217–45.

Rowland, A.K., 'Is the Revenue Being Fair? Revenue Statements and Judicial Review' [1995] *British Tax Review* 115–21.

Sauter, W., 'The Economic Constitution of the European Union' (1998) 4 *Columbia Journal of European Law* 27–68.

Schammo, P., 'The European Securities and Markets Authority: Lifting the Veil on the Allocation of Powers' (2011) 48 *Common Market Law Review* 1879–914.

Schammo, P., 'EU Day-to-Day Supervision or Intervention-based Supervision: Which Way Forward for the European System of Financial Supervision?' (2012) 4 *Oxford Journal of Legal Studies* 771–97.

Schütze, R., '"Delegated" Legislation in the (New) European Union: A Constitutional Analysis' (2011) 74 *Modern Law Review* 661–93.

Scott, C., 'Accountability in the Regulatory State' (2000) 27 *Journal of Law and Society* 38–60.

Scott, C., 'Private Regulation of the Public Sector: A Neglected Facet of Contemporary Governance' (2002) 29 *Journal of Law and Society* 56–76.

Scott, C., 'Reflexive Governance, Regulation and Meta-Regulation: Control or Learning?' in O. de Schutter and J. Lenoble (eds), *Reflexive Governance: Redefining the Public Interest in a Pluralistic World* (Oxford: Hart Publishing, 2010), 43–63.

Scott, C., Cafaggi, F., and Senden, L., 'The Conceptual and Constitutional Challenge of Transnational Private Regulation' (2011) 38 *Journal of Law and Society* 1–19.

Scott, J. and Trubek, D., 'Mind the Gap: Law and New Approaches to Governance in the European Union' (2002) 8 *European Law Journal* 1–18.

Scottish Enterprise, *Annual Report and Accounts for the Year Ended 31 March 2011* (Scottish Enterprise, 2011).

Scottish Government, *Public Spending in Scotland: Engaging with the People of Scotland* (2010).

Scottish Government, *Scottish Budget; Draft Budget 2013–14* (2012).

Scottish Parliament Economy, Energy and Tourism Committee, *A Fundamental Review of the Purpose of an Enterprise Agency and the Success of Recent Reforms* SP Paper 594 (2011).

Scottish Parliament Finance Committee, *Strategic Budget Scrutiny* SP 283 (2009).

Scottish Parliament Finance Committee, *Report on the Review of the Budget Process* SP 315 (2009).

Scottish Parliament Finance Committee, *Budget Strategy Phase* SP 455 (2010).

Scottish Parliament Finance Committee, *Report on Draft Budget 2013–14*, SP 231 (2012).

Scottish Parliament Information Centre, Research Note RM 00/31 *The Barnett Formula* (2000).

Scottish Parliament Information Centre, *Financial Scrutiny Unit Briefing: Guide to the Scottish Budget—Subject Profile* (2011) at: <http://www.scottish.parliament.uk/S4_FinanceCommittee/General%20Documents/ScottishBudgetGuide.pdf>.

Select Committee on the Barnett Formula, *The Barnett Formula* (HL 2008–09, 139).

Select Committee on the Constitution, *Banking Act 2009: Supplementary Report on Retrospective Legislation*, (HL 2008–09, 97).

Seneviratne, M., *Ombudsmen: Public Services and Administrative Justice* (London: Butterworths, 2002).

Silver, N., *Towards a Royal Bank of Sustainability: Protecting Taxpayers' Interests; Cutting Carbon Risk* (London: Friends of the Earth Scotland, PLATFORM, World Development Movement, 2010).

Simpson, E., 'The *Ramsay* Principle: A Curious Incident of Judicial Reticence?' [2007] *British Tax Review* 358–74.

Snape, J., *The Political Economy of Corporation Tax* (Oxford: Hart Publishing, 2011).

Stewart, R.B. and Ratton Sanchez Badin, M., 'The World Trade Organization and Global Administrative Law' in C. Joerges and E. Petersmann (eds), *Constitutionalism, Multilevel Trade Governance and International Economic Law* (Oxford: Hart Publishing, 2011), 457–93.

Stiglitz, J., *Globalization and its Discontents* (London: Penguin, 2002).

Stoker, G., 'Governance as Theory: Five Propositions' (1998) 50 *International Social Science Journal* 17–28, 17.

Teubner, G., *Law as an Autopoietic System* (Oxford: Blackwell, 1993).

Thain, C., 'Treasury Rules OK? The Further Evolution of a British Institution' (2004) 6 *British Journal of Politics and International Relations* 121–8.

Thain, C., 'A Very Peculiar British Crisis?: Institutions, Ideas and Policy Responses to the Credit Crunch' (2009) 4 *British Politics* 434–49.

Thain, C., and Wright, M., *The Treasury and Whitehall: The Planning and Control of Public Expenditure, 1976–1993* (Oxford: Clarendon Press, 1995).
Tiley, J. and Loutzenhiser, G., *Revenue Law,* 7th edn (Oxford: Hart Publishing, 2012).
Tomkins, A., 'In Defence of the Political Constitution' (2002) 22 *Oxford Journal of Legal Studies* 157–75.
Transport Committee, *Thameslink Rolling Stock Procurement* (HC 2010–12, 1453).
Transport Committee, *Cancellation of the InterCity West Coast Franchise Competition* (HC 2012–13, 537).
Treasury Committee, *Accountability of the Bank of England* (HC 1997–98, 282).
Treasury Committee, *The New Fiscal Framework and the Comprehensive Spending Review* (HC 1997–98, 360).
Treasury Committee, *Bank of England: Operation of Accountability-One Year On* (HC 1997–98, 993).
Treasury Committee, *The Monetary Policy Committee –Two Years On* (HC 1998–99, 505).
Treasury Committee, *The Private Finance Initiative* (HC 1999–2000, 147).
Treasury Committee, *Spending Review 2000* (HC 1999–2000, 485).
Treasury Committee, *The Monetary Policy Committee—An End of Term Report* (HC 2000–01, 42).
Treasury Committee, *HM Treasury* (HC 2000–01, 73).
Treasury Committee, *The Merger of Customs & Excise and the Inland Revenue* (HC 2003–04, 556).
Treasury Committee, *The Monetary Policy Committee of the Bank of England: Appointment Hearings* (HC 2005–06, 525).
Treasury Committee, *Administration and Expenditure of the Chancellor's Departments 2006–2007* (HC 2006–07, 57).
Treasury Committee, *The 2006 Pre-Budget Report* (HC 2006–07, 115).
Treasury Committee, *The 2007 Comprehensive Spending Review: Prospects and Processes* (HC 2006–07, 279).
Treasury Committee, *The Monetary Policy Committee of the Bank of England: Ten Years On* (HC 2006–07, 299).
Treasury Committee, *The 2007 Comprehensive Spending Review* (HC 2007–08, 55).
Treasury Committee, *Banking Crisis: Dealing with the Failure of the UK Banks* (HC 2008–09, 416).
Treasury Committee, *Banking Crisis: Reforming Corporate Governance and Pay in the City* (HC 2008–09, 519).
Treasury Committee, *Banking Crisis: Regulation and Supervision* (HC 2008–09, 767).
Treasury Committee, *Administration and Expenditure of the Chancellor's Departments, 2008–09* (HC 2009–10, 156).
Treasury Committee, *Reporting Contingent Financial Liabilities to Parliament* (HC 2009–10, 181).
Treasury Committee, *Office for Budget Responsibility* (HC 2010–11, 385).

Treasury Committee, *Financial Regulation: a Preliminary Consideration of the Government's Proposals,* (HC 2010–11, 430).
Treasury Committee, *Appointment of Robert Chote as Chair of the Office for Budget Responsibility* (HC 2010–11, 476).
Treasury Committee, *Spending Review 2010* (HC 2010–11, 544).
Treasury Committee, *Principles of Tax Policy* (HC 2010–11, 753).
Treasury Committee, *Accountability of the Bank of England* (HC 2010–12, 874).
Treasury Committee, *Financial Regulation: a Preliminary Consideration of the Government's Proposals: Government Response* (HC 2010–12, 958).
Treasury Committee, *Private Finance Initiative* (HC 2010–12, 1146).
Treasury Committee, *Closing the Tax Gap: HMRC's Record at Ensuring Tax Compliance* (HC 2010–12, 1371).
Treasury Committee, *Financial Conduct Authority* (HC 2010–12, 1574).
Treasury Committee, *Accountability of the Bank of England: Response from the Court of the Bank to the Twenty-first Report from the Committee* (HC 2010–12, 1769).
Treasury Committee, *Financial Services Bill,* (HC 2012–13, 161).
Treasury and Civil Service Committee, *The Role of the Bank of England* (HC 1993–94, 98).
Treasury and Civil Service Committee, *The Role of the Bank of England: The Government's Response* (HC 1993–94, 338).
Treasury and Civil Service Committee, *The Regulation of Financial Services in the UK* (HC 1994–95, 332).
Tuori, K., 'La Constitution Economique Parmi les Constitutions Européenes' (2011) XXV *Revue Internationale de Droit Economique* 559–99.
UK Financial Investments Ltd, *UKFI Investment Mandate* (2010) at: <http://www.ukfi.co.uk/releases/UKFI_IM_180110.pdf>.
UK Financial Investments Ltd, *UKFI Shareholder Relationship Framework Document* (2010) at: <http://www.ukfi.co.uk/releases/UKFI_FD_180110v2.pdf>.
Villiers, C., 'A Global Framework for Management Commentary Disclosure?' (2009) 60 *Northern Ireland Legal Quarterly* 63–84.
Vincent-Jones, P., *The New Public Contracting: Regulation, Responsiveness, Relationality* (Oxford: Oxford University Press, 2006).
Walker, N., 'Beyond Boundary Disputes and Basic Grids: Mapping the Global Disorder of Normative Orders' (2008) 6 *International Journal of Constitutional Law* 373–96.
Weatherill, S., (ed.), *Better Regulation* (Oxford: Hart Publishing, 2007).
White, F. and Hollingsworth, K., *Audit, Accountability and Government* (Oxford: Clarendon Press, 1999).
Wilks, S., 'Competition Policy' in D. Coen and W. Grant (eds), *The Oxford Handbook of Business and Government* (Oxford: Oxford University Press, 2010), 730–56.
Winckler, J.T., 'Law, State and Economy: The Industry Act 1975 in Context' (1975) 2 *British Journal of Law and Society* 103–28.

World Development Movement, *Serving (Up) the Nation* (London: World Development Movement, 2002).

World Trade Organisation, *The Future of the WTO: Report by the Consultative Board to the Director General Supachai Panitchapkdui* (WTO, 2004).

Wymeersch, E., Hopt, K.J., and Ferrarini, G., *Financial Regulation and Supervision: A Post-Crisis Analysis* (Oxford: Oxford University Press, 2012).

Index